J. S. MILL'S POLITICAL THOUGHT

The year 2006 marked the two hundredth anniversary of John Stuart Mill's birth. Although his philosophical reputation has varied greatly in the intervening years, it is now clear that Mill ranks among the most influential modern political thinkers. Yet despite his enduring influence, and perhaps also because of it, the breadth and complexity of Mill's political thought is often underappreciated. Although his writings remain a touchstone for debates over liberty and liberalism, many other important dimensions of his political philosophy have until recently been mostly ignored or neglected. This volume aims, first, to correct such neglect by illustrating the breadth and depth of Mill's political writings. It does so by drawing together a collection of essays whose authors explore underappreciated elements of Mill's political philosophy, including his democratic theory, his writings on international relations and military interventions, and his treatments of socialism and despotism. Second, the volume shows how Mill's thinking remains pertinent to our own political life in three broad areas – democratic institutions and culture, liberalism, and international politics – and offers a critical reassessment of Mill's political philosophy in light of recent political developments and transformations.

Nadia Urbinati is Neil and Herbert M. Singer Associate Professor of Contemporary Civilization at Columbia University in the Department of Political Science. She is the author of *Mill on Democracy: From the Athenian Polis to Representative Government*, which received the David and Elaine Spitz Prize as the best book in liberal and democratic theory published in 2002, and *Representative Democracy: Principles and Genealogy*. Professor Urbinati has edited the works of Carlo Rosselli, *Liberal Socialism* (1994), and Piero Gobetti, *On Liberal Revolution* (2002). Her articles and book reviews have appeared in such journals as *Political Theory, Ethics, Constellations, Philosophical Forum, Dissent, Review of Metaphysics, The European Journal of Political Theory*, and *Perspectives on Politics*.

Alex Zakaras is Assistant Professor of Political Science at the University of Vermont. His research interests include the philosophy of democracy and democratic citizenship, the ideal of autonomy and its place in the liberal tradition, and the political thought of the nineteenth century. He is working on a book that explores the idea of individuality in the writings of Ralph Waldo Emerson and John Stuart Mill. He received his Ph.D. from Princeton University in 2005.

For Amy – with thanks
again for your invaluable
advice. As ever. Dennis

J. S. Mill's Political Thought

A Bicentennial Reassessment

Edited by

NADIA URBINATI
Columbia University

ALEX ZAKARAS
University of Vermont

CAMBRIDGE
UNIVERSITY PRESS

CAMBRIDGE UNIVERSITY PRESS
Cambridge, New York, Melbourne, Madrid, Cape Town, Singapore, São Paulo

Cambridge University Press
32 Avenue of the Americas, New York, NY 10013-2473, USA

www.cambridge.org
Information on this title: www.cambridge.org/9780521860208

First published 2007

Printed in the United States of America

A catalog record for this publication is available from the British Library.

Library of Congress Cataloging in Publication Data

J. S. Mill's political thought : a bicentennial reassessment / edited by Nadia Urbinati,
Alex Zakaras.
p. cm.
Includes bibliographical references and index.
ISBN-13: 978-0-521-86020-8 (hardback)
ISBN-10: 0-521-86020-2 (hardback)
ISBN-13: 978-0-521-67756-1 (pbk.)
ISBN-10: 0-521-67756-4 (pbk.)
1. Mill, John Stuart, 1806–1873. 2. Political science – Philosophy. I. Urbinati, Nadia, 1955–.
II. Zakaras, Alex, 1976– III. Title.
JC223.M66J646 2007
320.092 – dc22   2006025161

ISBN   978-0-521-86020-8 hardback
ISBN   978-0-521-67756-1 paperback

Contents

Method of Citation

All page references to the writings of J.S. Mill are to *The Collected Works of John Stuart Mill* (33 volumes), John M. Robson, General Editor (Toronto: University of Toronto Press, 1963–1991). They are written as follows: CW XVIII: 266, for *Collected Works*, Volume XVIII, page 266.

List of Contributors

Bruce Baum is Assistant Professor of Political Science at the University of British Columbia. He is the author of *Rereading Power and Freedom in J.S. Mill* (2000).

Wendy Donner is Professor of Philosophy at Carleton University, Ottawa. She is the author of *The Liberal Self: John Stuart Mill's Moral and Political Philosophy* (1991).

Stephen Holmes is Walter E. Meyer Professor of Law at New York University. He is the author of *Passions and Constraint: On the Theory of Liberal Democracy* (1995), *The Anatomy of Antiliberalism* (1993), and several other books.

Karuna Mantena is Assistant Professor of Political Science at Yale University. She is currently completing her first book, titled *Alibis of Empire: Social Theory and the Ideologies of Late Imperialism*.

Maria Morales is Associate Professor of Philosophy at Florida State University. She is the author of *Perfect Equality: John Stuart Mill on Well-Constituted Communities* (1996).

Jonathan Riley is Professor of Philosophy at Tulane University and a faculty member of the Murphy Institute of Political Economy, Tulane University. He is the author of *Liberal Utilitarianism* (1988), *Mill on Liberty* (1998), and *Mill's Radical Liberalism* (2006) and the editor of Mill's *Principles of Political Economy and Chapters on Socialism* (1994).

Frederick Rosen is Emeritus Professor of the History of Political Thought at University College, London. He is the author of *Classical Utilitarianism from Hume to Mill* (2003), *Jeremy Bentham and Representative Democracy* (1983), and other titles.

Alan Ryan is Warden of New College, Oxford. His books include *The Philosophy of John Stuart Mill* (1970) and *J. S. Mill* (1974), and he is the editor of *Mill* in the Norton Critical Edition series (1996).

Dennis F. Thompson is Alfred North Whitehead Professor of Political Philosophy at Harvard University. His books include *John Stuart Mill and Representative Government* (1976) and *Restoring Responsibility: Ethics in Government, Business, and Healthcare* (2005).

Nadia Urbinati is Nell and Herbert M. Singer Associate Professor of Contemporary Civilization at Columbia University in the Department of Political Science. She is the author of *Mill on Democracy: From the Athenian Polis to Representative Government* (2002) and *Representative Democracy: Principles and Genealogy* (2006).

Georgios Varouxakis is Senior Lecturer in History at Queen Mary, University of London. He is the author of *Mill on Nationality* (2002) and *Utilitarianism and Empire* (2005).

Jeremy Waldron is University Professor of Law and Philosophy at the New York University. He is the author of numerous books, including *Law and Disagreement* (2001) and *God, Locke, and Equality* (2002).

Michael Walzer is Professor of Social Science at the Institute for Advanced Study at Princeton and co-editor of *Dissent* magazine. He is the author of many books, including *Spheres of Justice* (1983), *Just and Unjust Wars* (1977), and *On Toleration* (1997).

Alex Zakaras is Assistant Professor of Political Science at the University of Vermont. He is currently completing his first book on individuality and democratic citizenship in the writings of J. S. Mill and Ralph Waldo Emerson.

Introduction

Nadia Urbinati and Alex Zakaras

The year 2006 marks the two-hundredth anniversary of John Stuart Mill's birth, and although his philosophical reputation has varied greatly in the intervening years, it is now clear that Mill ranks among the most influential of modern political thinkers. His *On Liberty* alone is one of the handful of books indispensable to the liberal self-understanding. Yet despite his enduring influence, and perhaps also because of it, the breadth and complexity of Mill's political thought is often underappreciated. Although his writings remain a touchstone for debates over liberty and liberalism, many other important dimensions of his political philosophy have until recently been mostly ignored or neglected.

Such was not the case during Mill's lifetime. In the mid- to late nineteenth century, Mill was among the most influential European public critics, and his voice was heard across a wide range of disparate political debates. He wrote and commented not only on British politics but also on French and American politics, on the decline of the Austro-Hungarian Empire, and on civil rights movements and movements for national self-determination throughout the world. He penned important reflections on religion and politics, on international relations and despotism, on military intervention and its limits, on the character of democratic culture, and much more. Nor was Mill strictly a scholar or a political philosopher; he was also an activist and an editorialist well aware of his influence on the public opinion of his day. He denounced slavery in the American South and the exploitation of labor in Britain; he wrote vehemently against family violence inflicted on children and women; he campaigned for birth control and against intolerance suffered by atheists and nonconformists. He signed petitions for and sent money to organizations around the world that agitated for emancipation and antidiscrimination. Intellectuals and politicians throughout Europe sought out his suggestions on a host of issues, from institutional

1

reforms and social legislation to taxation and schooling. In these several capacities, Mill contributed self-consciously to the making of a European public opinion.

The reputation that Mill earned during his lifetime as a "saint of rationalism" and one of Europe's leading public intellectuals survived well after his death. In 1924, Harold Laski wrote that "in the fifty years that have passed since Mill's death, no teacher has arisen whose influence upon the mind of his generation has been so beneficent or so far-reaching" (Laski 1924, xiii). In fact, Mill's salience reaches far beyond his own generation: on almost all of the topics just mentioned – many of which remain focal points for contemporary political debate – his ideas still resound with significance. They are at once points of origin for contemporary perspectives and sources of challenging objections to recent orthodoxies. Their relevance has only grown since the end of the Cold War, with the resurgence of nationalism, the emergence of new forms of imperial power, and a renewed interest in state building and the constitution of democracy in non-Western countries.

This volume therefore has two aims. First, it illustrates the breadth and depth of Mill's political writings by drawing together a collection of essays whose authors explore underappreciated elements of Mill's political philosophy. Second, it shows how Mill's thinking remains pertinent to our own political life and offers a critical reassessment of Mill's political philosophy in light of recent political developments and transformations.

The essays in this volume are divided into three groups. The first five chapters address Mill's writings on liberty and liberalism, issues that receive disproportionate attention in the secondary literature. The first lesson one typically learns about Mill is that he was a liberal philosopher, perhaps *the* exemplary liberal philosopher. The essays collected in this section raise questions about the nature and implications of Mill's liberalism and invite us to see it in a new light. They reach beyond *On Liberty* and approach Mill's liberalism through less familiar texts. In many cases, they use these texts to reinterpret Mill's conception of liberty, which lies at the very center not only of his political philosophy, but also of his political and intellectual legacy.

In the first chapter, Jeremy Waldron discusses Mill's appearance in 1871 before a Royal Commission established to assess the Contagious Diseases Acts, which required public supervision of the health of prostitutes, especially those frequented by soldiers. The acts had provoked intense opposition, especially from an influential group of feminist activists who charged that they licensed unwarranted intrusions into women's privacy while entirely ignoring (and tacitly condoning) the agency of their male clients.

Mill's testimony before the commission and his unequivocal opposition to the acts raise a number of questions about the "Harm Principle" and about his willingness to endorse regulation of "harmful" behavior. Waldron's analysis challenges common readings of the Harm Principle (and hence also the role of liberty in Mill's political thought) and draws attention to Mill's concern about the fair *distribution* of liberty and restraint in society.

Maria Morales, too, raises questions about the conventional readings of Mill's ideal of freedom. Her emphasis rests on Mill's *The Subjection of Women* and the conceptions of freedom and subjection that informed Mill's criticisms of Victorian gender relations. Morales argues that Mill is too often read simply as a liberal feminist, concerned mainly with the achievement of formal equality and equal political rights for women. She maintains that Mill was in fact more focused on the problem of domination – patriarchal domination specifically – that cut cleanly across public and private life. She advances a reading of Mill on freedom that better accommodates the argument of the *Subjection* and that has broad implications for his political work as a whole.

Nadia Urbinati also emphasizes the central role of the idea of subjection, or domination, in Mill's political thought. She approaches this theme through a study of Mill's treatment of despotism – which she takes to be the antithesis, for Mill, of liberty. Despotism manifests itself in two related phenomena: on the one hand, absolute arbitrariness in the decisions of those who command; on the other, the exclusion of those who obey from participation in these decisions. Urbinati shows that Mill applies the category "despotism" to Western and non-Western societies in a way that is both classical and innovative. She argues that he uses "despotism" to understand both public and private relations and to justify reforms in political, economic, and familial life alike. She maintains, furthermore, that Mill developed his concept of freedom through a critical examination of the effects of despotism on social, political, and moral life.

Bruce Baum explores Mill's efforts to reconcile liberalism and socialism and in doing so discusses Mill's applications of the concept of freedom to economic life. He shows how Mill justified egalitarianism through appeal not to distributive justice or fairness, but to what Baum calls "maximal economic freedom." He also argues that Mill understood socialism to be quite continuous with liberalism and suggests therefore that Mill's later *Chapters on Socialism* can help us better understand the nature of his liberal commitments. Baum maintains, furthermore, that Mill's writing on socialism can offer moral resources to contemporary, egalitarian critics of market capitalism as they did to liberal socialists in earlier decades.

Finally, Frederick Rosen clarifies the nature of Mill's liberalism by contrasting it to Bentham's and by studying Mill's early borrowings from Coleridge. Rosen argues that Mill's style of radical liberalism is distinguished by its method of reform. Mill believed that political reforms could be effective only insofar as citizens were prepared to receive and support them, and also that successful reforms would have to understand and incorporate elements of the conservative resistance to them. Rosen points out that Mill is often misread as an ideal theorist (and often criticized because his policy proposals are not radical enough for contemporary tastes). These readings misunderstand Mill's critical ambitions, which were very deliberately adjusted to the social and historical circumstances of Victorian England.

The next five essays in the volume focus on Mill's democratic theory and practice – areas that suffer comparative neglect in the critical literature. All of the essays touch on the recurrent tension between Mill's desire for greater citizen participation on the one hand and for competence or expertise in government on the other. Several of the essays explore the ideals of character and citizenship that Mill associates with well-functioning democracy; others inquire into the relationship between Mill's liberalism and his commitment to democratic procedures. All of them seek to deepen our understanding of Mill's democratic theory by juxtaposing *Considerations on Representative Government* to his other political writings – from *On Liberty* and *The Subjection of Women* to his essays on Periclean Athens, India, and his *System of Logic*.

Alan Ryan's chapter identifies several key questions that Mill's political writing leaves mostly unanswered and outlines the responses that he expects Mill would have given. Ryan inquires into the apparent discrepancies between early essays such as "The Spirit of the Age" and Mill's later political works, especially as concerns the role of authority in modern politics and society. He asks, too, whether Mill ever achieved a stable balance between a utilitarian concern with benevolent management and an "Athenian" concern with the self-assertive, engaged, independent-minded democratic citizen. He uses this question to examine the role of bureaucratic expertise in Mill's democratic theory. Finally, he explores Mill's thoughts on colonial government in India and their bearing on his treatment of British politics.

Dennis Thompson uses Mill's brief career in Parliament as a way of studying the relationship between the theory and practice of representative democracy. His aim is to see what can be learned about the challenges a theorist faces when he enters politics and, more generally, the challenges a theory confronts when one of its leading proponents tries to put it into practice. His inquiry is partly historical: to what extent did Mill modify his principles for political advantage? But it is primarily normative: to what extent *should* Mill have modified his principles? Thompson suggests that the answers to this normative question, suitably generalized, can suggest some criteria for assessing the compromises that principled legislators make in any democratic polity.

Alex Zakaras argues that there exists a tension between Mill's discussion of democratic participation in *Considerations on Representative Government* and passages on the same subject in *On Liberty. Representative Government* presents an optimistic view of the effects of political participation on the intellect and the moral sentiments: Mill here describes the practice of democratic politics as a "school of public spirit" and contrasts it favorably with a private life that he imagines to be dominated by the prerogatives of economic self-interest. In *On Liberty,* by contrast, Mill associates political participation with the tyranny of the majority, with the will to dominate others, and with the crippling effects of a hostile public opinion on the individual psyche. Zakaras argues that Mill's conception of individuality, understood as an ideal of citizenship, can help make sense of this discrepancy.

Jonathan Riley looks closely at Mill's assessment of ancient Athenian democracy and at Athens' influence on Mill's own political theory. Riley argues that Mill drew inspiration not only from Athens' participatory institutions but also from its system of checks and balances, which resulted in a prudent blend of popular participation and competent political leadership. Riley rejects the common argument that Mill's elitism made him an equivocal democrat and argues instead that Mill was firmly committed to *liberal* democracy and admired the specifically liberal aspects (in Mill's own estimation) of the Athenian constitution.

Finally, Wendy Donner reconstructs Mill's views on democratic education, drawing not only on Mill's explicit reflections on the subject in his "Inaugural Address Delivered to the University of St. Andrews" but also on Mill's treatment of the democratic character throughout his political works. Donner discusses the importance of virtue in Mill's ideal of democratic character and explores its relationship to his utilitarianism. She also defends Mill against the charge that his emphasis on character undermines his commitment to pluralism.

The final group of chapters addresses Mill's writing on international politics and ethics, including his discussion of military interventions and his attitudes toward empire, patriotism, moral cosmopolitanism, and national identity. Like the previous two groups of essays, this one draws explicit connections between Mill's politics and our own. Our authors examine Mill's ideas in the context of contemporary political problems and conflicts, including the U.S. military intervention in Iraq, the imperial tendencies within contemporary liberalism, and the ongoing philosophical debates over the merits of cosmopolitanism.

Georgios Varouxakis argues that Mill's views on nationality, patriotism, and cosmopolitanism have been widely misunderstood. Mill's most famous treatment of these topics appears in Chapter XVI of *Considerations on Representative Government,* which critics have sometimes read as an uncritical embrace of nationalism. Varouxakis rejects this reading emphatically and argues that Mill is best understood as embracing a form of cosmopolitan patriotism. Mill believed that patriotism could be used to broaden people's sympathies and, if properly understood, to heighten their concern over the morality of their nation's foreign policy. Mill believed, in other words, that patriotism could be used in service of moral cosmopolitanism.

Karuna Mantena, meanwhile, looks specifically at Mill's writings on India and British colonialism and argues that they reveal an important ambiguity at the heart of nineteenth-century liberalism. She contends that the paternalist attitudes of liberal reformers such as Mill, who hoped to educate and edify "backward" peoples, were very easily transformed, when reforms proved more difficult than expected, into ascriptions of racial inferiority. She maintains that Mill himself managed to avoid this move but that others under his influence did not. She argues that the tendency to ascribe inferiority to colonized or otherwise subordinated groups will always haunt liberal justifications of empire.

Stephen Holmes considers Mill's writing on interventions, with a particular emphasis on democratization. Since the end of the Cold War, "democracy promotion" has been an explicit goal of U.S. foreign policy. Holmes asks what Mill can teach us about the prudence of this ambition. He argues that Mill's views on democratization occupied a middle ground between voluntarism and fatalism. Mill believed that democracy could not be suddenly transplanted from London to New Delhi. Democracy is a machine that must be "worked" by the people themselves. It therefore depends, in Mill's view, essentially on their skills, habits, attitudes, and expectations. And although the latter may be stubborn, they are not unchangeable: Mill rejected determinism in favor of the modest hope that societies could, over the long term, be guided toward democracy.

Michael Walzer also explores Mill's writing on interventions, though he focuses exclusively on Mill's influential 1859 essay, "A Few Words on Non-Intervention." In that essay, Mill argued that states ought to be treated as self-determining communities, whether or not their internal politics are free. His prescriptions could be summed up as follows: *always act so as to recognize and uphold communal autonomy.* Walzer offers a close reading – simultaneously critical and sympathetic – of this short essay. He gives line-by-line commentary with the aim of clarifying which parts of Mill's argument still stand and which parts need revision.

It is our hope that these collected essays will not only help change readers' perceptions of Mill's politics but also suggest further avenues for research. There is more work to be done on all of the themes we have outlined here. Many of Mill's political essays remain relatively unexplored by contemporary critics. This volume fills in some of the lacunae and draws attention to many exciting new developments in the scholarship, but without any pretense to completeness. A number of timely themes are left out – notably, Mill's views on religion and the secular philosophy of progress, both of which were extremely important in his work and which scholars have only recently begun to reconsider. We hope, ultimately, that Mill's bicentennial can occasion not only broader interest in his philosophy but also a clearer understanding of its critical influence in the formation of our contemporary ethical world.

PART ONE

LIBERTY AND ITS LIMITS

1

Mill on Liberty and on the Contagious Diseases Acts

Jeremy Waldron

The Contagious Diseases Acts

The health of the roughly 270,000 members of the British armed forces –
the Royal Army and the Royal Navy – was a matter of great concern in the
middle of the nineteenth century.[1] Most of us know this from accounts of the
work of reformers like Florence Nightingale, during and after the Crimean
War, in setting up a properly administered system of field hospitals and
agitating for general reforms in hygiene and sanitation.[2] A more troubling
set of issues concerned the impact of sexually transmitted diseases on health,
readiness, and morale. Prostitution was rife on army bases and in garrison
towns and ports in these areas; many contemporary and modern accounts
accompany this point with the observation that the army did not permit most
enlisted men to marry[3] and sometimes also with a reminder that homosexual
sodomy was unlawful – from which we are supposed to conclude that the
only sexual outlet available to these men was fraught with the risk of disease.
Whatever the reason, it is said that approximately one-third of the members
of armed forces contracted venereal disease. And this – as the administrators

---

[1] Smith 1971 writes at 122: "Sickness . . . was the primary destroyer in the services. . . . The
men were recruited from the dregs of the population, treated like animals and their health
was the health of neglected animals. Army men in England died at twice the rate of the
civilian population."

[2] See Strachey 1988, 78–89.

[3] Smith 1971, 122: "Regulations allowed only six private soldiers in each company of 100 to
marry and have their wives on barracks."

I am grateful to G. A. Cohen, David Johnston, Glyn Morgan Joseph Raz, Carol Sanger, and
Nadia Urbinati for comments on this chapter and discussions of its themes. Earlier versions
were presented at Columbia Law School, Vanderbilt University, and the American Political
Science Association's 2006 Annual Conference. On each occasion, I received very helpful
comments, for which I am most grateful.

and politicians responsible for modernizing the army and navy came to see – was intolerable.

In the 1860s, three statutes were passed by Parliament, known as the Contagious Diseases Acts.[4] They all involved various measures to supervise the health of prostitutes, and they were all focused specifically on port and garrison cities.[5] The first Act, in 1864, required any allegedly diseased prostitute to undergo an inspection by officially designated doctors. If she was found to be infected, she could be held in a secure hospital, known as a lock hospital, for up to three months. The second Act of 1866 set up a special plainclothes "medical police" force to patrol port areas and garrison towns and to require women whom the officers suspected of being prostitutes to undergo fortnightly genital inspections for up to a year. In 1869, a third measure required prostitutes to carry official registration cards.[6]

There is no doubt that these measures were well intended. They were part of a general progressive movement to improve health and hygiene in British society as well as in the armed forces, allowing the practice of medicine to play a larger role in public policy making.[7] But almost immediately, they ignited furious opposition.

Some repealers put their case as part of general hostility to "overlegislation" and to an activist state's taking centralized responsibility for public health.[8] Mostly and most strikingly, however, opposition to the legislation came from a large corps of influential women. Agitation for the repeal of the Contagious Diseases Acts, which has been called "one of the century's most notable protest movements,"[9] has also been described as "the western world's first feminine revolt of any stature."[10] The most prominent

---

[4] Contagious Diseases Prevention Act, 1864, 27 & 28 Vict., ch. 85; Contagious Diseases Act, 1866, 29 & 30 Vict., ch. 35; Contagious Diseases Act, 1869, 32 & 33 Vict., ch. 96. The Acts were repealed in 1886: Contagious Diseases Repeal Act, 1886, 49 Vict., ch. 10 (Eng.). There are good general accounts in McHugh 1980, Smith 1971, and Walkowitz 1980.

[5] The Acts applied to specified localities in England and Ireland. Bartley 2000, 12: "The CD Acts applied to garrison towns and naval ports such as Portsmouth, Plymouth, Woolwich, Chatham, Sheerness, Aldershot, Colchester and Shorncliffe: at no time did cities without an army or navy base, such as Birmingham, London, and Manchester, come under their jurisdiction." In Scotland, different, more directly repressive measures were used: for example, what became known as the Glasgow System involved repeated arrests and penalties for women suspected of prostitution (Smout 1993, 1049).

[6] This account is taken from http://www.english.uwosh.edu/roth/Prostitution.htm (accessed Sept. 26, 2005).

[7] Smith 1971, 121–7

[8] See Caine 1992, 181. McHugh (1980, 25) makes a connection with the struggle against vaccination.

[9] Bristow 1978, 5, cited by McHugh 1980, 16.

[10] Pearson 1972, 173.

opponents of the Acts were women, most famously Josephine Butler – "beautiful, histrionic, compelling, unstoppable."[11] Their grounds of opposition may be read in part as a reaction against male medical authority,[12] but at the time, the most prominent basis of the feminist opposition to the Acts was moralistic.[13] What was sometimes referred to as the "goody-goody" wing of the repeal movement[14] complained that the legislation abetted and promoted prostitution and embodied an ethic of deference to male sexuality. It was premised on the inevitability of prostitution and recognized the need to police it and establish some regime for its regulation of the kind set up in France and elsewhere in Europe.[15] This, Josephine Butler and her fellow repealers opposed adamantly. They believed in male abstinence as a better basis for public policy,[16] they expressed intense anger at the legal and cultural underwriting of male sexual license,[17] and they complained that the administration of the statutes obstructed the redemption of fallen women.

The feminist opposition also focused on two particular aspects of the administration of the Acts. One had to do with the brutal and degrading treatment of the women forced to undergo examination.[18] The examinations amounted to what the repealers referred to as "instrumental rape." "Typically, the woman's legs were clamped open and her ankles tied down. Surgical instruments – sometimes not cleaned from prior inspections – were inserted so inexpertly that some women miscarried. Others passed out from

---

[11] Smith 1971, 127. For good accounts of Butler's involvement, see Petrie 1971, passim and Walkowitz 1980, 113–18.

[12] See McHugh 1980, 25, and Caine 1992, 141–4.

[13] I follow Judith Walkowitz (1980, 5 et passim) in using the word "feminist" to describe the campaign of Butler and the Ladies National Association against the Contagious Diseases Acts. For an argument – although not with reference to this case – that the word "feminism" should not be used to refer to any campaign or movement before 1910 (when the term was first used in the United States), see Cott 1987, 3–6. For a response, see Caine 1992, 5–6 and 150–4.

[14] Smith 1971,128 and 133

[15] McHugh 1980, 17.

[16] Smith, 1971, 128: "The repealers believed in purity. They asserted that copulation was not...a natural male aggressive impulse that wrought last evil when relieved through prostitution, but rather that continence was an instinctive part of the maintenance of strength in young men. Fortified by faith, men could become as sexually quiescent as women were known to be."

[17] Walkowitz 1980, 255–6 points out that this also became a powerful theme in the early-twentieth-century suffrage movement: "[Christabel] Pankhurst's slogan of 'Votes for Women and Chastity for Men' reechoed the older radical refusal to cater sexually to men so long as women remained subordinates."

[18] The lurid semipublic aspect of the examinations is described in Smith 1971, 126.

the pain or from embarrassment."[19] The other particular complaint concerned the peril and injustice suffered by respectable women under the measures that the Acts laid down. All women were under suspicion.[20] Florence Nightingale said of the 1864 legislative proposal: "Any honest girl might be locked up all night by mistake by it."[21] Josephine Butler expressed the same concern in a lecture she delivered in 1871:

Under the present Acts, a man whose infamous proposals have been rejected by a girl, may inform the police against her, and on his evidence the girl may be subjected to examination and ruined.... A like power would ... be legally vested in the hands of the brothel-keepers. If one of these wretches should mark a young and friendless girl for his victim ... his course would be easy. A secret information could be given to the sanitary officer that the girl had been ruined and was diseased.[22]

Most of all, the repealers were angry that there was no provision for examining men, not even clients of the prostitutes subjected to the Act. The discrimination was patent, with a Royal Commission on the statutes refusing to regard the man's involvement as in any sense the equivalent of the woman's.[23] The legislation proceeded on the assumption that women, not men, were responsible for the spread of venereal diseases "and that while men

---

[19] McElroy 2000. See also Morton 1987, 764: "The reports of treatment of the women in the hands of the medical examinators make unpalatable reading. If the girl accused turned out to be a virgin, sometimes her hymen was ruptured. She would be given 5/- and told to get a hot dinner for herself and be a good girl. A strait jacket was used to control the unwilling woman." Walkowitz 1980, 109 quotes a particularly disturbing account of examinations from contemporary pamphlets. See also Petrie 1971, 106. On the other hand, there was an unpleasant side to the preoccupation with these details (and the display of instruments etc.) at some public repeal meetings; Josephine Butler complained that this preoccupation was "needlessly and grossly indecent," though others said that "it rouses men against the Acts more than anything" (Walkowitz 1980, 141).

[20] Prostitution, not being illegal, did not have a legal definition at the time. Kalsem 2004 observes that the following working definition of "common prostitute" was offered by one of the leading proponents of the Acts: "any woman whom there is fair and reasonable ground to believe is, first of all going to places which are the resorts of prostitutes alone, and at times when immoral persons are usually out. It is more a question of mannerism than anything else." Dr. William Acton, quoted in Murray 1982, 425.

[21] Cited at McHugh 1980, 37.

[22] Petrie 1971, 117–18. In fact there were not numerous reports of respectable women falling under suspicion, although there were one or two causes célèbres: see Smith 1971, 130, and see also discussion of the case of Caroline Wyburgh in Petrie 1971, 105–6.

[23] See the following statement by the Royal Commission on the Contagious Diseases Acts (cited in Walkowitz 1980, 71): "We may at once dispose of [any recommendation] founded on the principle of putting both parties to the sin of fornication on the same footing by the obvious but not less conclusive reply that there is no comparison to be made between prostitutes and the men who consort with them. With the one sex the offence is committed as a matter of gain; with the other it is an irregular indulgence of a natural impulse."

would be degraded if subjected to physical examination, the women who satisfied male sexual urges were already so degraded that further indignities scarcely mattered."[24]

The movement opposing the Contagious Diseases Acts sprang up in the fall of 1869, with a spate of pamphlets, articles, and public meetings.[25] That year saw the formation of the Ladies' National Association for the Repeal of the Contagious Diseases Acts.[26] It really was a remarkable campaign. A public "Protest" against the Acts, signed by 124 women appeared in the *Daily News* on New Years Day 1870. A newspaper, *The Shield,* sprang up as a weekly repeal journal. A petition was presented to Parliament with 600,000 signatures. The Ladies' National Association even intervened successfully in a by-election – a very early example of single-issue impact in electoral politics.[27] Of course there was considerable public rage at middle-class women speaking out on such matters.[28] Often attempts were made to break up meetings or clear women from the public gallery in the House of Commons when the possible repeal of the Acts was discussed.[29] But the opponents were indomitable. After an unconvincing debate on the latest of the repeal bills in 1870, the government announced that it would set up a Royal Commission on the legislation.

The Commission consisted of twenty-three persons, all men, including ten parliamentarians (from both Houses), some clergy, and some eminent scientists (such as T. H. Huxley). The repealers claimed the Commission was rigged to secure a conclusion supporting the Acts, but in fact some members were known repealers, and others were neutral. In the event, no clear consensus emerged in the Commission's findings. An anodyne attempt to represent a consensus in the majority report failed, and there were a number of dissenting statements. Paul McHugh observes that in the outcome, "[t]he regulationists suffered most. For years they had dominated, indeed monopolized the argument.... The creation of a militant opposition in 1869 and 1870 threw them off balance.... Their failure to win over the Royal Commission – their sort of forum – must have been especially galling, but can

---

[24] McHugh 1980, 17.

[25] McHugh 1980, 54–7.

[26] There was also a popular movement in favor of the legislation, indeed in favor of extending it to nonmilitary towns: the Association for the Extension of the Contagious Diseases Acts was formed in 1868 (Smith 1971, 121). This may well have galvanized the repeal movement; see Walkowitz 1980, 79–86.

[27] See the account in Petrie 1971, 98–105.

[28] See Petrie 1971, 89 and 101–4, and Walkowitz 1980, 138, for Josephine Butler's apprehension and experience of violence in this regard.

[29] Smith 1971, 127.

again be ascribed to their incompetence in the face of new opposition."[30] The Acts were finally repealed by Parliament in 1886.

John Stuart Mill as an Opponent of the Acts

The repealers claimed not only that the Royal Commission was biased in its membership but that its list of witnesses was one-sided. The repealers had a barrister in attendance at Commission's sessions, and he persuaded them to redress the balance by calling (among others) the liberal philosopher John Stuart Mill.[31] Mill was one of the most distinguished male participants in the campaign against the Contagious Diseases Acts. He spoke out against the legislation at a public meeting in March 1870, saying that under the Acts, "the wives and daughters of the poor are exposed to insufferable indignities on the suspicion of a police officer," and he expressed doubt whether the legislation would have been enacted if women had had the vote.[32] Mill's book *The Subjection of Women* had been published in 1869. His biographer tells us that when the Royal Commission was set up, "Mill... intimated that he would like to be called in evidence; and, as he was known to have knowledgeable if peculiar views on women, he was called."[33] The evidence he gave was implacably opposed to the Acts. "I do not consider [the legislation] justifiable on principle," he said, "because it appears to me to be opposed to one of the greatest principles of legislation, the security of personal liberty" (CW XXI:351).[34]

The basis of John Stuart Mill's opposition to the Contagious Diseases Acts is the subject of this chapter. It is both intriguing and bewildering; intriguing because it brings together the author of *On Liberty* and the author of *The Subjection of Women* so that both can confront Mill the progressive, who we know believed firmly in government taking the initiative to promote public health and hygiene; and it is bewildering on account of a puzzle about the relation between Mill's writings in *On Liberty* and his opposition to the Acts.

Let me explain the puzzle. We know that Mill was solicitous of the rights of women and the liberty of the individual. But the principle he set up to protect liberty – the famous Harm Principle, the "one very simple principle" that he said was "entitled to govern absolutely the dealings of society with

---

[30] McHugh 1980, 67–8.

[31] McHugh 1980, 61.

[32] Kamm 1977, 182.

[33] Packe 1954, 501–2.

[34] John Stuart Mill's evidence before the Royal Commission, as given in 1871, is cited from volume XXI of Mill's *Collected Works*.

the individual in the way of compulsion and control" (CW XVII: 223)[35] –
seemed to permit rather than oppose state regulation in the case of conduct
which tended to spread disease. The Harm Principle was formulated as
follows:

[T]he sole end for which mankind are warranted, individually or collectively, in
interfering with the liberty of action of any of their number, is self-protection.
[T]he only purpose for which power can be rightfully exercised over any member
of a civilized community, against his will, is to prevent harm to others. . . . The only
part of the conduct of any one, for which he is amenable to society, is that which
concerns others. In the part which merely concerns himself, his independence is,
of right, absolute. Over himself, over his own body and mind, the individual is
sovereign. (CW XVII: 223–4)

Because the conduct of the prostitute evidently is *not* just self-regarding,
because it has definite social effects, because one of those effects is that
it tends to spread venereal disease among the class of her customers, and
among anyone who (knowingly or unknowingly) has subsequent sexual
contact with her customers, because this disease represents a social harm
(particularly to the extent that it undermines the health of those, like soldiers
and sailors, who have important public duties to perform) – for all these
reasons, prostitution seems a perfectly appropriate candidate for the sort of
regulation that the Harm Principle could approve.

Mill, after all, was a liberal not a libertarian. He deployed the Harm
Principle in *both* directions – against regulation and *for* regulation – arguing
in *On Liberty* that "owing to the absence of any recognized general principles,
liberty is often granted where it should be withheld, as well as withheld where
it should be granted" (CW XVII: 301). His first maxim might have been that
"the individual is not accountable to society for his actions, in so far as these
concern the interests of no person but himself," but his second maxim
was "that for such actions as are prejudicial to the interests of others, the
individual is accountable, and may be subjected either to social or to legal
punishments, if society is of opinion that the one or the other is requisite for
its protection" (CW XVII: 293). Mill insisted that his philosophy was not
one of irresponsible individualism: "[T]he fact of living in society renders it
indispensable that each should be bound to observe a certain line of conduct
towards the rest" (CW XVII: 276).

Moreover he held a pretty expansive sense of "actions . . . prejudicial to the
interests of others." Injuring others' interests could be done by neglect,

[35] John Stuart Mill's essay *On Liberty*, originally published in 1859, is cited from volume XVII
of his *Collected Works*.

including neglect of self: "If...a man, through intemperance or extravagance, becomes unable to pay his debts, or, having undertaken the moral responsibility of a family, becomes...incapable of supporting or educating them, he...might be justly punished" (CW XVII: 281). And harm to others' interests could be imputed to someone by virtue of his rendering himself unfit for public duty:

[W]hen a person disables himself, by conduct purely self-regarding, from the performance of some definite duty incumbent on him to the public, he is guilty of a social offence. No person ought to be punished simply for being drunk; but a soldier or a policeman should be punished for being drunk on duty. (CW XVII: 282)

It is not much of a stretch to infer from this that if a soldier's self-inflicted harm is a matter of legitimate social concern on account of his public duty, then society may also legitimately focus on those who are *complicit* in the soldier's rendering himself unfit for public duty.

Certainly, Mill would have had little patience with the objection that the transmission of infection did not count as harm inflicted by the prostitute because the transaction was consented to (by the soldier or sailor in question). He knew that the issue was not just harm to the prostitute's client, as an individual, but harm to the armed forces and perhaps harm by transmission to other unknowing (and therefore unconsenting) parties. Nor could his objection have been that the prostitutes were not *to blame* for the spreading of the disease into the general population. Blame was not the issue. The Acts might have been punitive in their administration, but they were primarily preventive in their intent. Surely that was all the Harm Principle required: the issue was not whether the person subject to the regulation was to blame for the harm, but whether regulating the person could help prevent it.[36]

On the other hand, Mill was not always clear about the extension of the realm of legitimate social interference. For example, he said in Chapter Five of *On Liberty* that "[f]ornication must be tolerated," but he vacillated on the question of whether this meant that brothels and pimps must be tolerated (CW XVII: 296–7).[37] To take another case: he said on the subject

---

[36] For a good account of this distinction, see Lyons 1979.

[37] "The case is one of those which lie on the exact boundary line between two principles, and it is not at once apparent to which of the two it properly belongs.... On the side of toleration it may be said, that the fact of following anything as an occupation, and living or profiting by the practice of it, cannot make that criminal which would otherwise be admissible.... In opposition to this it may be contended, that although the public, or the State, are not warranted in authoritatively deciding, for purposes of repression or punishment, that such or such conduct affecting only the interests of the individual is good or bad, they are fully justified in assuming, if they regard it as bad, that its being so or not is at least a disputable question: That, this being supposed, they cannot be acting

of poisons that their sale could not be prohibited entirely because they may be procured "not only for innocent but for useful purposes, and restrictions cannot be imposed in the one case [murderous uses] without operating in the other" (CW XVII: 294). But he also said that there is no affront to liberty in requiring a warning label or in requiring the dispenser to enter in a register the name and address of the buyer and "to ask the purpose for which it was wanted, and record the answer he received" (CW XVII: 294–5). In general he thought it an open question whether market transactions might be regulated to prevent the adulteration of goods and protect their quality, but he never expressed a firm view on this one way or the other (CW XVII: 293).[38] And he did not believe that the state was required to be indifferent, for example, as to the places in which or the conditions under which liquor was manufactured and sold.[39]

Certainly, one would not expect a person who held these (at best) nuanced and (at worst) equivocal views to simply *condemn out of hand* a legislative scheme like that of the Contagious Diseases Acts. I think the legislators could reasonably have expected Mill to support the Acts because they aimed specifically to prevent harm. Or at worst they could have expected him

wrongly in endeavoring to exclude the influence of solicitations which are not disinterested, of instigators who cannot possibly be impartial – who have a direct personal interest on one side, and that side the one which the State believes to be wrong, and who confessedly promote it for personal objects only.... There is considerable force in these arguments. I will not venture to decide whether they are sufficient to justify the moral anomaly of punishing the accessary, when the principal is (and must be) allowed to go free; of fining or imprisoning the procurer, but not the fornicator" (CW XVII: 296–7). Mill's vacillation continued in his evidence to the Commission: "*[W]ould you prosecute brothel-keepers?* That is an extremely difficult question, and I would rather not give a positive opinion about it, because so many *pros* and *cons* have occurred to me when I have thought about it that I have found it very difficult to make up my mind" (CW XXI: 369).

[38] Mill was quite undoctrinaire about regulation of the marketplace and insisted that *On Liberty* was not to be read as a laissez-faire tract: "As the principle of individual liberty is not involved in the doctrine of Free Trade so neither is it in most of the questions which arise respecting the limits of that doctrine: as for example, what amount of public control is admissible for the prevention of fraud by adulteration; how far sanitary precautions, or arrangements to protect work-people employed in dangerous occupations, should be enforced on employers. Such questions involve considerations of liberty, only in so far as leaving people to themselves is always better, caeteris paribus, than controlling them: but that they may be legitimately controlled for these ends, is in principle undeniable" (CW XVII: 293).

[39] "All places of public resort require the restraint of a police, and places of this kind peculiarly, because offences against society are especially apt to originate there. It is, therefore, fit to confine the power of selling these commodities (at least for consumption on the spot) to persons of known or vouched-for respectability of conduct; to make such regulations respecting hours of opening and closing as may be requisite for public surveillance, and to withdraw the license if breaches of the peace repeatedly take place through the connivance or incapacity of the keeper of the house" (CW XVII: 298).

to vacillate, saying what he said about brothels, or poisons, or the sale of liquor, or adulterated products – that the issue was complex, that there was something to be said on both sides, and that we might try regulating them in various novel or ingenious ways. In fact, Mill did not say any of that. He just dug in his heels and opposed the Acts "on principle." He was asked by the Royal Commission: If people engage in conduct which has the potential to spread disease in the general population, is it wrong for society to try and restrain or regulate that conduct? He was asked: Can there possibly be any objection to such restraint or regulation on grounds of liberty, when the restraint is imposed to avoid the harm of infection (and the debilitation and death that may result from it) to innocent members of the community? And his answer in both cases was "Yes." Yes, he said, it *is* wrong for society to try to regulate conduct that has the potential to spread disease in the general population, at least in the way that Contagious Diseases legislation approached the matter. And yes, there *is* a conclusive objection based on liberty, even though the Contagious Diseases Acts did seem to aim at the prevention of harm.

So what was going on? One possibility is that Mill changed his mind on some of these matters between 1859, when *On Liberty* was published, and 1871, when he gave his evidence to the Royal Commission. Another possibility is that, without any change in his philosophical view, Mill just adopted a political position that was inconsistent with his own (enduring) principles. Political interventions have their own logic, and the connection between theory and practice is not always as tight as it should be among political philosophers, even in the case of a high-minded individual like John Stuart Mill. We cannot rule any of this out.[40]

However, before throwing up our hands in this way, we might want to try another tack. The theory set out in *On Liberty* is not a simple one, and we might consider the possibility of reinterpreting it, in the light of what we know about Mill's deployment of it in this case. But if we do this, we have to do it carefully.

Here is a bad way of doing it. In the academic study of political theory, there is an influential school of thought that holds that we should read the classics of the subject as primarily political interventions, not as philosophical tracts, and we should interpret them in the light of what else we know about their

---

[40] Kamm 1977, 14–193, argues that Mill did in fact worry about whether his commitment to the repeal of the Contagious Diseases Acts might be politically inconsistent with other causes he wanted to pursue. His concern was that the repeal campaign might discredit the broader movement for women's suffrage, and in the 1870s he sought – sometimes quite duplicitously – to ensure that the suffrage movement was, as far as possible, uncontaminated by the repeal campaign.

authors' politics.[41] (I call this the originalist approach, because it is rather like bad originalism in constitutional law – i.e., rather like the approach that says capital punishment cannot be regarded as "cruel" under the Eighth Amendment because the framers of the amendment supported the execution of murderers and other felons.)

So, for example, moving away from Mill for a moment, the originalists would say that if John Locke's argument against slavery in the *Two Treatises of Government* is unclear,[42] we should interpret it in a way that makes it consistent with what we know of Locke's politics and his own personal stake in the slave trade. We know that Locke invested money personally both in plantation enterprises and in an enterprise (the Royal African Company) that had a monopoly in the slave trade. In the late 1660s and the 1670s, he worked as a secretary to the Lords Proprietors of Carolina, and in that capacity he played a role in drafting what came to be known as *The Fundamental Constitutions of Carolina,* which say things like "Every freeman of Carolina shall have absolute power and authority over his negro slaves."[43] According to the originalist approach, we should infer from these personal and political positions that Locke did not believe that slavery in the Americas was morally illegitimate. And we should adjust our interpretation of the *Two Treatises* accordingly.[44] Well, in a similar way, it might be argued, once we discover that Mill was opposed politically to the Contagious Diseases Acts, we should adjust our interpretation of *On Liberty* to make that essay consistent with what we now know about his politics. Thus, if there are ambiguities in his views about when the state is allowed to intervene, we should perhaps interpret them more restrictively – in light of his opposition to the Contagious Diseases Acts – than if we were reading *On Liberty* as a free-standing body of philosophical thought.

I am generally opposed to this sort of originalism – in political theory as well as in constitutional law – and I have criticized it vociferously in the case of Locke, both in general and in regard to his particular views on slavery.[45] It underestimates the possibility of simple mistake or inconsistency. And it

---

[41] See, for example, Peter Laslett's introduction to Locke 1988, 79–92. See also Skinner 1988.
[42] For Locke's argument against slavery, see Locke 1988, 283–5.
[43] Locke 1997, 180.
[44] Cf. Welchman 1995, 75: "The man whose career I've just described to you is not a man likely to construct or defend a theory of political or natural rights incompatible with slavery."
[45] Waldron 2002, 10–11, 50–1, and 203–6. I thought it better, in the case of Locke on slavery, to let the inconsistency between theory and personal practice lie, rather than to assume that the theory must be reinterpreted to bring it in to line with the author's practice in the service of what is perhaps an anachronistic model of personal integrity; see Waldron 2002a, 204–5.

slights the fact that the theory or the constitutional text comes with credentials – philosophical argument in one case and formal enactment or ratification in the other – which the political intervention lacks. In the case of a constitutional provision, the text has the standing it does because of the way it was enacted, not because it matches various views or intentions that some of its framers happen to have had. And in the case of a piece of political philosophy – whether it is Mill *On Liberty* or Locke's *Two Treatise* – we are interested in the author's doctrines only to the extent that he can produce convincing arguments for them.[46] Matching his theory to what we know about his personal or political positions is simply a distraction so far as that interest is concerned.

So what should we do with the intervention of the author of *On Liberty* in the debate about the Contagious Diseases Acts? Well, it is possible that instead of knee-jerk originalism, we might consider whether Mill's testimony before the Royal Commission deepens our understanding of what he is arguing for in *On Liberty*. As I said, we are not interested in what he thought; we are interested in what he can defend or argue for. Yet it may be that we have underestimated the subtlety and complexity of his argument. The history of the reading of this great work has been the history of the progressive replacement of simpleminded understandings of Mill's position by more nuanced and considered views.[47] With this possibility in mind – but, still, with the simple inconsistency thesis as our default position – let us turn now to the detail of Mill's testimony to the Royal Commission in 1871.

Mill's Evidence to the Royal Commission

Mill acknowledged several times in his evidence before the Commission that he had little empirical knowledge of the workings of the Acts, and he conceded that any opinion he expressed about its effects would be based on the general principles of legislation (CW XXI: 351). He professed some skepticism about whether there was reliable empirical knowledge to be had: "I have not examined into the statistics of the question, which I have no doubt are very contradictory, because very opposite results are stated at

---

[46] Cf. Waldron 1987, insisting that "harm" in Mill's Harm Principle, should be defined by the tenor of his arguments, not by the word's meaning in a dictionary.

[47] See, for example, the essays in Radcliff 1966, Dworkin 1997a, Eisenach 1998, and Bromwich and Kateb 2002. See also monographs by Himmelfarb 1974, Ten 1980, and Gray 1981. However, none of this literature – indeed, none of the copious philosophical literature on Mill's essay *On Liberty* – so much as mentions the relation between that essay and his evidence against the Contagious Diseases Acts.

different places, with the effect of creating very great distrust in statistics altogether on that subject" (CW XXI: 363).

Mill also acknowledged that the legislation did appear to aim at combating disease and preventing harm to innocent people – "that I understand to be the object" (CW XXI: 354). And he acknowledged also that of course the government had a responsibility to combat disease. Exposure of innocent people to infection by venereal disease is, he said "[n]o doubt . . . a great public evil," which the state should endeavor to avert "by any means which are not objectionable in a greater degree than the evil itself" (CW XXI: 360).

From this, it is tempting to conclude that for Mill, the issue was not one of ends but of the means that were used to combat this disease. That is almost right, except that Mill also had strong views about how one characterized the end itself:

I think the Government ought, so far as it can, to exert itself in putting down all diseases, but I certainly do see some degree of objection to anything special being done by the Government distinguishing between this and other diseases in that respect. (CW XXI: 358)

One of his objections was that the government was taking specific measures against one kind of disease, distinguishing its fight against that from health policy generally. His complaint against singling out this disease or this class of diseases in particular has to do with (what we would call) the message it sends:

The general impression . . . however contrary to the intention of those who support it, would be that the State patronises the class of practices by which these diseases are engendered, since it considers those who contract these diseases as worthy of more attention, and takes more pains to remedy the consequences, than those who have other diseases equally serious. (CW XXI: 370)

Asked whether the policy of the legislation could not be separated from this (perhaps unintended) defect, Mill observed: "I do not see how that which makes illicit indulgence of that sort safe . . . can be prevented from giving some degree of encouragement to it, though far, I know, from the intention of the Act" (CW XXI: 355). In other words, like the feminist opponents of the Acts, Mill was worried that the legislation tended to support prostitution.[48] The State, he said, seemed to be "going out of its way to provide

---

[48] Rather in the way he imagined a licensing system, of the sort practiced on the Continent, would support the profession of the licensees: "all the objections which exist against the Acts, exist in an extreme degree against licenses, because they have still more the character of toleration of that kind of vicious indulgence" (CW XXI: 356). See also the discussion of Mill's position on licensing in Arkes 1981.

facilities for the practice of that profession, which I do not think the State is called upon, or can without considerable disadvantage undertake, to do" (CW XXI: 354).[49]

However, Mill's position on this was a subtle one. There was a distinction, he said, between *ex ante* and *ex post* interference by the State.

I do not think it is part of the business of the Government to provide securities beforehand against the consequences of immoralities of any kind. That is a totally different thing from remedying the consequences after they occur. That I see no objection to at all. (CW XXI: 353)

Facilitating the vice beforehand, he said, is "a totally different thing...from correcting the evils which are the consequences of vices and faults" (CW XXI: 358). I think though that he was aware that this was a tenuous distinction, and he had no choice but to concede the point that modern theories of moral hazard would make:

Undoubtedly... interfering to remedy evils which we have brought on ourselves has in some degree the same bad consequences, since it does in the same degree diminish the motive we have to guard against bringing evils on ourselves. Still a line must be drawn somewhere. (CW XXI: 358)[50]

He wound up this part of his argument by saying lamely that "[i]f we were never to interfere with the evil consequences which persons have brought upon themselves, or are likely to have brought upon themselves, we should help one another very little" (CW XXI: 358). The contrast between his willingness to waive the moral hazard argument in regard to *ex post* remediation and his strident insistence on the moral hazard argument in relation

---

[49] Mill also speculated that it would increase the number of prostitutes, in two ways. It would do so, first, "by the fact that a considerable number of them are withdrawn from their profession periodically, the vacancy or gap that is thus made, as the demand calls forth a supply, has a natural tendency to be filled up by additional prostitutes being brought into the profession," and second, "in so far as the Acts... afford increased security to the men who frequent these women, it is liable to produce an increased demand for prostitutes, and therefore bring forth in that way an increased supply" (CW XXI: 364).

[50] Mill used an analogy with state interference to correct the operation of market processes: "Relieving people who are in danger of starvation is liable to the same objection.... [A]ll relief... to the indigences or distresses of our fellow creatures are liable to it, since the people themselves are often very much to blame for bringing themselves into a position in which they require relief, and no doubt the relief does in some not inconsiderable degree diminish the prudential motives for abstaining. But still all our experience, and the consideration given to the question by thinkers and legislators, have ended in the recognition of this, that we ought not to abstain from helping one another through the evils of life, provided we do it in such a way as that it shall not provide facilities beforehand, but only deal with the evil when it has been incurred" (CW XXI: 359).

to preventative measures leaves a rather unconvincing impression so far as this part of his argument is concerned.

Thus far, Mill's case against the Contagious Diseases Acts was of a piece with that of the more high-minded moralists who were involved in the campaign.[51] Note that this sort of moralism is actually quite compatible with the central argument of *On Liberty*. Contrary to popular belief, *On Liberty* is not an excoriation of moralism in all its forms. For one thing, Mill insisted throughout that work that the Harm Principle did not disqualify us from expressing concern about others' moral lives,[52] provided we did so in a non-punitive way and provided that the net effect of our doing so in thousands or millions was not to create a socially repressive environment.[53] For another thing, Mill left room, in his account of what the Harm Principle *did* justify, for us to take notice of the demoralizing effects of any attempt to prevent harm. The Harm Principle defined a necessary condition for legal regulation not a sufficient condition: "[I]t must by no means be supposed, because damage, or probability of damage, to the interests of others, can alone justify the interference of society, that therefore it always does justify such interference" (CW XVII: 292). The effect of certain legislation might be "to do harm" (CW XXI: 371) as well as prevent harm, and if so we have to look closely at the harm it might cause. Under this heading, we are entitled to look askance at the perverse moral incentives of legislation, for example, because we are entitled to be concerned generally with the encouragement our conduct (including our legislative conduct) might lend to vice. We might not be entitled to prohibit prostitution, but we should be careful even in our attempts to prevent associate harms that we do not promote or encourage it.

Mill's own distinctive opposition to the Acts emerged when he considered the issue of liberty. Asked whether he thought the legislation was justified in principle, Mill said this: "I do not consider it justifiable on principle, because it appears to me to be opposed to one of the greatest principles of legislation, the security of personal liberty" (CW XXI: 351). He went on

---

[51] But Mill's enthusiasm for this line of argument was qualified: "With regard to those who object to the Contagious Diseases Acts as encouraging vice, I do not undertake to defend all that they say" (Mill 1870b, 290).

[52] "It would be a great misunderstanding of this doctrine [sc. The Harm Principle], to suppose that it is one of selfish indifference, which pretends that human beings have no business with each other's conduct in life, and that they should not concern themselves about the well-doing or well-being of one another, unless their own interest is involved. Instead of any diminution, there is need of a great increase of disinterested exertion to promote the good of others" (CW XVII: 276–7).

[53] See Waldron 2002b.

immediately to identify those whose liberty was affected: "It appears to me that legislation of this sort takes away that security [security of personal liberty], almost entirely from a particular class of women intentionally, but incidentally and unintentionally, one may say, from all women whatever" (CW XXI: 351).

How was their liberty affected? Mill's concerns about liberty in this context were not exactly the romantic ideas of autonomy and individuality apotheosized in Chapter Three of *On Liberty* and in much recent liberal thought: choosing one's own conception of life's meaning, developing one's own individuality in connection with one's own conception of the good and so on.[54] They are much more routine – having to do with the ordinary living of an ordinary life, walking the streets, chatting with friends, and so on.[55] They have to do with the very specific effects on personal liberty of liability to apprehension and incarceration, in the context of the very considerable discretion that the authorities needed to have in relation to the enforcement of these laws. "We ought not to give powers liable to very great abuse, and easily abused, and then presume that those powers will not be abused" (CW XXI: 352). Mill worried too about the implications for the Rule of Law of what was essentially an administrative scheme for coercively regulating the health and behavior of prostitutes. Although from one point of view such regulation might seem beneficent, it nevertheless has the character of a penalty in the eyes of the women affected (particular if there is a question of her being falsely identified as a prostitute) and it should be treated as such for the purposes of Rule-of-Law requirements.[56]

Mill's argument had this in common with the more high-minded account of the autonomous individual in *On Liberty*: he said in his evidence that coercive interference tended to negate or undermine any good that the legislation aimed at, so far as individual character was concerned. No doubt the legislation had some good reformatory effects, but these tended to accrue despite its coercive character, not because of it. Thus, on the effect

---

[54] See CW XVII: 261–7. See also Rosenblum 1987, 125–51; Dworkin 1978, 127; and the famous dictum in *Planned Parenthood v. Casey* 505 U.S. 833 at 851 (1992): "Liberty is the right to define one's own concept of existence, of meaning, of the universe, and of the mystery of human life."

[55] For the importance of these non-grand issues of liberty, see Waldron 1991, 318–21.

[56] "If any penalty is to be imposed, and this must be considered a penalty, for being a common prostitute, she ought to have power to defend herself in the same manner as before any ordinary tribunal, and of being heard by counsel, to prove that she is not a prostitute if she can.... There can be hardly any more serious case to the person concerned than that of being charged with being a prostitute, if she is not really so" (CW XXI: 352).

that the Acts might have in removing young women from the streets, Mill observed:

> I think that what removes them from the streets is the moral effect which is produced in their minds ... by the moral influences that were brought to bear on them during their detention, which are no doubt the real cause of reclaiming them so far as they are reclaimed, and therefore they might be applied more effectually without the machinery of the Acts. (CW XXI: 368)

He thought this effect was likely to be undermined by the Acts' coerciveness: "the chance of producing this effect is likely to be lessened by subjecting them to an offensive and what must be considered a tyrannical operation by the force of law" (CW XXI: 368).[57]

Apprehension, detention, confinement – that was one aspect of the coerciveness of the legislation. The other aspect was the intrusive, brutal, and degrading nature of the assault on the persons of alleged prostitutes, particularly in the genital examinations that the legislation provided for. Mill thought women were much more degraded by the examinations envisaged in the Acts than men would be. "Men are not lowered in their own eyes as much by exposure of their persons, besides which it is not a painful operation in the case of a man, which I believe in the case of a woman it often is, and they very much detest it" (CW XXI: 356). When someone asked him whether it was more degrading than being a prostitute, Mill responded: "Both are degrading, but degradation for degradation, that which is compulsory seems to me always more degrading in its effects on the character than what is done voluntarily" (CW XXI: 368). Maybe, he conceded, there are some prostitutes "to whom nothing is degrading, they are so degraded already." But others – many or most – may have "a considerable quantity

---

[57] On the question of redeeming prostitutes, Mill said: "[I]f any effect of that sort is produced, it is produced by a process, not applicable specially to prostitution, but to the criminal and vicious classes, the dangerous classes altogether, all of whom may have some amount of good done them if attention is paid to them by benevolent persons, or ... persons employed by the Government" (CW XXI: 366). This is a fine example of the sort of tone that was associated in those days with mandarin paternalism. We no doubt find it offensive. Mill, however, was completely ingenuous in its expression. He continued the passage just quoted by saying to the Commission: "It would not be beyond the proper function of the State to take means of making these persons understand that they are not considered as totally unworthy of any kind of regard or consideration by the rest of their fellow-creatures, but that it is the object to reclaim them, and do them as much good as their condition makes them susceptible of. Such measures ... might be applied to the dangerous classes generally, much more than ever has been done yet. I should not see the least objection to applying such measures to prostitutes also, but that would not require Acts of this description" (CW XXI: 366).

of modesty left," and it is the impact on their liberty and person that we should consider (CW XXI: 368).

When we say that a statute has an impact on liberty, we sometimes talk as though liberty were a commodity in society which the law can increase or diminish. But Mill never lost sight of the point liberty is held by or denied to individuals, and he thought it made a huge difference how the impact of a given set of measures upon liberty was distributed among individuals. The crux of his case against the Contagious Diseases Acts was not the impact on liberty in an undifferentiated sense, but *the specific impact on women and the studious avoidance of any impact on the liberty of men*. Legislators, he thought, ought to have realized that the Act had a much greater impact on women's liberty than on men's. And because men were at least as much involved in the evils of venereal disease that the legislation professed to combat, an effort should have been made to distribute the burden more equitably. "I think it is exceedingly degrading to the women subjected to it, not in the same degree to men; therefore there is more reason that if it is applied at all it should be applied to men as well as women, or if not to both, rather to men than to women" (CW XXI: 356).[58]

In other words, Mill insisted that if our concern were *really* to avoid the exposure of innocent people to this disease, then we would focus on prostitutes' (male) customers as well as or instead of on the prostitutes themselves.

[A] woman cannot communicate the disease but to a person who seeks it, and who knowingly places himself in the way of it. . . . [I]t must be the man who communicates it to innocent women and children afterwards. It seems to me, therefore, if the object is to protect those who are not unchaste, the way to do that is to bring motives to bear on the man and not on the woman, who cannot have anything to do directly with the communication of it to persons entirely innocent, whereas the man can and does. (CW XXI: 354)

Asked whether there was any practicable way of focusing on clients rather than prostitutes, Mill argued that the former strategy would be no more onerous than the latter: "the same degree of espionage which is necessary

---

[58] Mill connected the issue of discrimination against women with the issue of suffrage; "The position of those men . . . who, while they refuse women any share in legislation, enact laws which apply to women only . . . appears to me as base as it is illogical, unless, indeed, they are prepared to maintain that women have no other rights than the cattle, respecting whom a kindred Act has been passed" (Mill 1870b, 287). He used his point about suffrage to reply to the claim that an act that applies to women only is no worse than a conscription law that applies to men only: "[T]he laws that represent enlistment are not made by women only . . . and then applied to men who have no voice in making them" (Mill 1870b, 288).

to detect women would detect also the men who go with them" (CW XXI: 354).[59] It would be no more difficult to demand of the men who go to houses of prostitution that they should "be obliged to give an account why they are there" and that they be "compelled to undergo examination for a certain period afterwards" (CW XXI: 354). Indeed these requirements would not particularly diminish the liberty of soldiers and sailors, because their conditions of life were already highly regulated: "I do not see why the State should not subject its own soldiers and sailors to medical examination, and impose penalties on them in case they are found diseased" (CW XXI: 360).[60] Mill added that he was not necessarily *recommending* any such system of surveillance, but he said that women should not be subjected to examination unless men are also, "or even if the women were not subjected the men might be, but if the one is, certainly I should say both" (CW XXI: 363).

It would be fairer, moreover, to impose penalties on men whose conduct caused the spread of disease among the wider population than upon prostitutes, for it was only the men who recklessly communicated it to a party who might not be aware of the risk.[61] There could be "very severe damages in case a man is proved to have communicated this disease to a modest woman, and in the case of his wife, divorce as a matter of right" (CW XXI: 354–5).[62] The knowledge of such penalties, Mill said, "would operate as a considerable

[59] "[F]requently ... women are brought under the operation of these Acts through being watched by the police, and its being ascertained that they frequent certain houses along with men, the police can equally ascertain who the men are who go with them" (CW XXI: 362).

[60] Again Mill brought up the moral hazard point. "[T]he impression on the minds of soldiers and sailors, is that ... Parliament does not entertain any serious disapprobation of immoral conduct of that kind. Now the State might exercise an influence opposite to that, by making the being found diseased a ground for military penalties in the case of soldiers and sailors." I should also mention, however, that Mill sometimes associated his opposition to the Acts with his opposition to a standing army: "[T]o any man who looks upon political institutions and legislation from the point of view of principle, the idea of keeping a large army in idleness and vice, and then keeping a large army of prostitutes to pander to their vices, is too monstrous to admit of a moment's consideration. . . . It is a monstrous artificial cure for a monstrous artificial evil which had far better be swept away at its root, in accordance with democratic principles of government" (Mill 1870a, 238).

[61] "When a woman infects anyone the man must always be a consenting party to running the risk: it is only a man who having been infected himself can communicate infection to an innocent person . . . " (CW XXI: 362).

[62] "*William Nathaniel Massey*: Are you aware that for a man to give his wife a disease of that description would be adjudged cruelly by the Court of Divorce, and would be a ground for a divorce, at all events a mensa? Yes, but not complete dissolution of the matrimonial tie. *Sir John Pakington*: Would you make it so? Yes. *William Nathaniel Massey*: You would make it a vinculo? Yes, a vinculo, accompanied with heavy pecuniary damages for the benefit of the sufferers, the wife or children" (CW XXI: 363).

check on the evil" (CW XXI: 355) and the divorce remedy would be strongly expressive of society's disapprobation.

That was Mill's suggestion. But of course it was not the scheme of the legislation. And so, for as long as the Contagious Diseases Acts had an impact on liberty in a lop-sided and discriminatory way, Mill was adamant that they could not be justified. Incredulous at his dogmatism, the Commissioners tried in vain to budge Mill from this position.

Is it your opinion that these Acts have done any physical good at all? I have really no means of judging. (CW XXI: 371) ... *Do you think that the State had better rather continue to suffer from the evil than to pass such Acts as these for its prevention?* I think the State had better continue to suffer as much of that evil as it cannot prevent in other ways ... (CW XXI: 360). *We have received very strong evidence ... that ... whereas there were previously hundreds of children ... practising habitual prostitution, ... since these Acts have passed that class has almost, if not quite, disappeared; ... assuming that evidence to be correct, would it reconcile your mind to the operation of the Acts producing so blessed an effect as that?* It would not remove the objections by any means (CW XXI: 363) ... *If the existence of such a fact would not reconcile you to the principles of the Acts, would it not at least make you thankful that such a result had ensued?* Of course anybody must be thankful for such a result, from whatever cause (CW XXI: 365). ... *You would leave those women to rot and die under the hedges, rather than pass such Acts as these to save them?* I do not think it is quite fair to put the question exactly in that manner ... (CW XXI: 366–7) ... *You would let them come out and spread disease right and left, rather than do good?* I do not think it is the business of legislation of this kind to take special care either of the women who practise this profession, or of the men who frequent them. (CW XXI: 365)

So his evidence came to an end and the Commissioners dismissed him, most of them puzzled, many no doubt convinced (in the words that his contemporary James Fitzjames Stephen used to condemn Mill's vacillation on the subject of brothels) that "there is a kind of ingenuity which carries its own refutation on its face" (Stephen 1993, 84).

Legislative Purpose and the Distribution of Liberty

Can we make any sense of Mill's position? He did not rule out the possibility that the Contagious Diseases Acts might protect soldiers and sailors and also other clients and their innocent spouses from infection. And he said he was aware that "the policy which dictated this legislation in the first instance, was a desire to maintain the health of soldiers and sailors, whose physical efficiency was reported to be very seriously affected by the disease which they contracted at garrison and seaport towns, those towns ... being the resort ... of common prostitutes." In other words, he did not deny that the

Acts were intended to prevent harm and might succeed in preventing harm, both to individual persons (some of them innocent) and to some important social interests.

But still, he thought the measures were objectionable on grounds of liberty. Now this is really quite odd, because when he articulated the Harm Principle in the essay *On Liberty*, Mill did not at all intend to deny that measures calculated to prevent harm might have an impact on liberty. The whole point was that the impact on liberty might be justified when harm was being prevented, not that harm should never be prevented if there was any cost to liberty. Mill's view, I think, was the same as Bentham's. *Every* law restricts liberty: "It converts into offences acts which would otherwise be permitted and unpunishable" (Bentham 1931, 94). And since every restriction on liberty is painful, then (in Bentham's words),

[t]here is always a reason against every coercive law – a reason which, in default of any opposing reason, will always be sufficient in itself: and that reason is, that such a law is an attack upon liberty. He who proposes a coercive law ought to be ready to prove, not only that there is a specific reason in favour of it, but that this reason is of more weight than the general reason against every such law. (Bentham 1931, p. 94)[63]

The whole point of the Harm Principle was to specify the sort of legitimate reason that could overcome a prima facie objection based on liberty. So the mere fact that liberty was affected should not be an objection, if harm prevention was the aim and if harm was actually prevented.[64]

Is it a question of balance or trade-off, comparing the quantity of harm prevented against the quantity of liberty that is lost? We have already heard Mill saying that legislation may cause harm as well as prevent harm, and talk of balance would be perfectly appropriate there.[65] And there is language in Mill's testimony suggestive of a balancing approach. Mill said at one stage: "[O]f course any increased efficacy furnishes an additional argument for the Acts. But no argument that can be produced of that kind, or I believe ever

---

[63] However, Bentham also observed that some people "pervert language; they refuse to employ the word *liberty* in its common acceptation.... This is the definition they give of liberty: *Liberty consists in the right of doing every thing which is not injurious to another.* When someone is permitted to do harm, they say this is not liberty but licence." But Bentham rejected this usage; and I think Mill would have, too. "Is not the liberty to do evil liberty? ... Do we not say that liberty should be taken away from idiots, and bad men, because they abuse it?" (Bentham 1931, 94–5).

[64] Remember, too, Mill's claim (CW XVII: 223 and 301) that owing to the absence of any general recognition of the Harm Principle, "the interference of government is, with about equal frequency, improperly invoked and improperly condemned."

[65] See *supra* pp. 24.

has been produced, would seem to me to overbear the very strong arguments of other kinds against the operation of such Acts" (CW XXI: 364). He also said: "It seems to me there ought to be a very good prospect of complete extirpation to justify anything of that kind, and I do not understand that such hope is entertained by those who are now most in favour of the Acts" (CW XXI: 356). However, the fact that Mill maintained his libertarian objection to the legislation *dogmatically*, despite an admission that he had no idea how much disease the Acts prevented, indicates that something more than merely balancing the harm of disease against the impact on liberty must have been going on. His objection, he said, was an *in-principle* objection, and that's what we have to get to the bottom of.

I propose we examine two connected ideas, which may help us understand Mill's position. The first is about legislative purpose. Mill said he was aware that the policy behind the legislation was a policy of disease prevention. But is that sufficient to identify the legislative intent, for the purposes of the Harm Principle? Or should legislative intent be ascertained in a way that allows us to check that legislators really *do* intend what they say they intend when they say they are aiming to prevent harm? The second point is about liberty. As I said earlier,[66] liberty is not just a cumulative good that we seek to maximize in society; it is a good whose distribution matters crucially and if it is maldistributed then a simple quantitative assessment of the amount of liberty at stake in society will not be a good guide to the decisions we make about legislation. I want to examine Mill's feminist objection to the Contagious Diseases Acts in this light – that is, his insistence on asking *whose* liberty was affected and his complaint that the liberty of men was not affected in anything like the way in which the liberty of women was affected.

Bringing these two ideas together, a third point emerges: we may read Mill's critique as insisting that legislation must be characterized and judged by the nature of its distributive impact on liberty, and it is this, not just the avowals of its sponsors, that should determine whether we regard it as a legitimate measure calculated to prevent harm

Legislative Intent

Many people think that Mill, in the enunciation of his famous Harm Principle, sought to distinguish among classes of actions (as other-regarding actions and self-regarding actions, and thus as actions liable to or immune

---

[66] *Supra* p. 28.

from regulation). But this is wrong.[67] Mill did not seek to distinguish classes of *actions*; he sought to distinguish classes of *reasons* (for interference or restriction).[68] Listen to his language:

> [T]he sole *end* for which mankind are warranted, individually or collectively in interfering with the liberty of action of any of their number, is self-protection. That the only *purpose* for which power can be rightfully exercised over any member of a civilized community, against his will, is to prevent harm to others. His own good, either physical or moral, is not a sufficient *warrant*. He cannot rightfully be compelled to do or forbear *because* it will be better for him to do so, *because* it will make him happier, because, in the opinions of others, to do so would be wise, or even right. These are good *reasons* for remonstrating with him, or reasoning with him, or persuading him, or entreating him, but not [*reasons*] for compelling him, or visiting him with any evil, in case he do otherwise. (CW XVII: 223–4; my emphasis)

"Ends," "purposes," "reasons," warrants," and the law or society doing things "because" they think something is the case – this is what Mill is attempting to sort. Some reasons (e.g., "to prevent harm to others") are good reasons; other reasons (e.g., "because it will be better for the person subject to the restriction") are bad reasons, and they remain bad reasons even if the action that is being regulated is other-regarding, even if it impinges on other's interests. The Harm Principle is a test of legislative intent.

Now legislative intent is a notoriously difficult thing to pin down – not least when, as in the case of the first Contagious Diseases Act of 1864, the measure was passed "without any debate in the House of Commons, at dinner time when there were only about 50 men in the House." It was "passed in silence" and most members who were aware of its passage thought it was about cattle plague and scab. The same was true of the Act of 1866; it was introduced at 1 A.M. and carried at 2 A.M. virtually without debate, again with very few members having any idea what it was about.[69] Still, as far as we know anything about the intentions of their sponsors,[70] the Acts

---

[67] In some twentieth-century discussions of Mill's Harm Principle, much has been made of the fact that there are virtually no self-regarding actions, no actions that are entirely bereft of consequences for others or for society at large: "[E]very action that occurs within a society and rises at all above the level of triviality is bound to impinge upon other members of that society" (Wollheim 1973, 3). In which case, it seems that Mill's principle does not protect any class of actions from state interference, at least on the superficial interpretation.

[68] For particular emphasis on this point, see Ten 1980, 50–1.

[69] Smith 1971, 119–20. So much for the dignity of legislation!

[70] Walkowitz 1980, 71, makes the point that the sponsors of some legislation are articulate in its defense less at the time of its enactment than later, when opposition emerges and campaigns for its repeal get underway.

seemed to satisfy the Harm Principle. They were intended to do good. And at times in his evidence, Mill conceded this: "The object of the Act is ... to protect the innocent from having these diseases communicated to them; that I understand to be the object" (CW XXI: 354). However, we cannot rest with that. The gist of Mill's objection before the Commission was to suggest that if the aim of the Acts were *really* to protect the innocent against disease, they would provide for the surveillance and inspection of men as well as women. But they do not do this; so that cannot be their real intention. This implies we have to distinguish between the *professed* intent of the Act and its *real* intent, so far as the application of the Harm Principle is concerned.[71]

How are we to ascertain the real intent? In modern legislative jurisprudence, we are accustomed to opposing intentionalism to textualism.[72] The text may say explicitly what the purpose is, or the text may reveal what the purpose is; or perhaps we should just apply the text literally, anyway, and forget about purpose. For Mill's analysis, however, I think we are supposed to be interested in something more than textual language. We are supposed to be interested in the *kind* of measure that we are dealing with. So consider this exchange from Mill's evidence:

Am I right in inferring from the evidence you have been so good as to give us, that you would not consider the fact of a very large proportion of the crews of our men-of-war and the soldiers of our army, being incapacitated for rendering service to the State by this terrible disease, an adequate reason for legislation of this kind? Not for legislation of this kind; but it might be for legislation of other kinds. (CW XXI: 360)

The *kind* of legislation it is, is determined by the sort of measures it embodies. Is it a licensing act, or a prohibitory act, or a regulative act, or what? If it is a licensing act, what sort of conditions does it impose on licenses? If regulatory, what exactly does it to regulate and on what basis and with what machinery? If it is a prohibitory act, then what are the terms of the prohibition and how do they apply to different classes of conduct? As I understand Mill's position, we use objective facts like these as a sort of check on the professed reasons for or intentions behind the legislation. The idea is that legislation does not just *have* a purpose, tacked on at the beginning of the bill. If an alleged purpose really is the purpose *of the act,* then it must be related systematically to all the act's provisions. The framing or design of the provisions must, so to speak,

---

[71] Mill talked also about a distinction between the professed intent of the Acts and way they appear to those who are subject to them: "[T]he impression on the minds of soldiers and sailors, is that [prostitution] is not discouraged, that it is considered by Parliament a necessity which may be regulated, but which must be accepted ... " (CW XXI: 360).

[72] Scalia 1997, 16–37.

track the purpose; they must not admit of any better explanation than that *this purpose* was being pursued in their framing and design.

Now before pursuing this further, I want to pause and consider the other idea I mentioned: the distributive character of Mill's interest in liberty.

The Distribution of Liberty

In the superficial way we sometimes talk about these things, we sometimes treat liberty as though it were a general characteristic of a society: there can be more liberty or less liberty, just as there can be more equality or less equality, or just as the gross national product can rise or fall. Sometimes we accept a trade-off between liberty as a social value and, for example, security as a social value, and when we do so we talk as though this were a sort of exchange between two commodities sitting in society's account.

But plainly this is not right. Liberty is a characteristic of individuals, and liberty as an ideal makes claims about what the situation of individuals ought to be. To talk of the society as having more or less liberty is just to talk of (large numbers of) individuals having more or less. Talk of social liberty involves an implicit appeal to a sort of function over levels of individual liberty (just as talk of social welfare involves an implicit appeal to a sort of social welfare function over levels of individual welfare). In the welfare case, some theorists – these days, mostly economists working in law schools – are comfortable with social functions that are purely additive or maximizing: the social welfare can go up even when some individual's welfare goes down, provided others gain more than that individual loses. In the case of liberty, however, this sort of view is much less common. Liberty as an ideal is associated with some quite firmly established views about what the distribution of liberty ought to be. There are strong principles in the liberal political tradition, for example, about ensuring that each person's liberty is made compatible with an *equal* liberty assigned to everyone else. This systematic equalization of liberty or its maximization subject to an equality constraint – "the most extensive basic liberty for each compatible with a similar liberty for all" (in John Rawls's formula) or its equalization subject to an individual adequacy constraint (in Isaiah Berlin's formula) – has been a powerful theme in liberal political philosophy from Immanuel Kant to Ronald Dworkin.[73] The general position is that it would be quite wrong to try to secure greater liberty for some by restricting the liberty of others. To do that would be to act – absent some special explanation – as though the others were not worthy of respect, did not count in society, so far as the government was concerned. It is

[73] See Berlin 1969, 124; Rawls 1971, 250; Kant 1991, 56; and Dworkin 2000, 128.

certainly never enough to say, for example, that the loss of liberty for these few is made up for by the greater liberty of all other individuals or that liberty, in some abstract sense, is better off on average.

To be concerned about liberty, therefore, as Mill is in the application of the Harm Principle, is to be concerned about how liberty is distributed – who wins and who loses, so far as the liberty-impact of a piece of legislation is concerned.[74] I emphasize this because it is sometimes assumed that a liberty-based objection to disease-prevention measures is separate from a distributive objection. Thus Daniel Markovits writes:

> The appropriate balance between the quarantine power and civil liberties is the subject of a lively ongoing debate, but libertarian concerns do not exhaust the ethics of quarantines. In particular, quarantines also generate an egalitarian anxiety, which addresses the distribution of the burdens that quarantines impose and worries that this pattern of burden and benefit may be in itself unfair. The egalitarian anxiety, moreover, emphasizes genetic features of quarantines – burdens and benefits associated with the patterns of confinement that quarantines inevitably involve – and so casts a wider net than the more common libertarian objection.... This egalitarian concern about quarantines has nevertheless been overlooked in discussions of quarantines, and the ethics of quarantine are in this respect not well understood.[75]

But if what I have just said is right, then this may be a false contrast. Libertarian concerns *are* distributive concerns (although of course there can also be distributive concerns about goods other than liberty).

This point is never explicit in *On Liberty*, but it is there all the same. Mill talks, for example, of "each person's bearing his share (to be fixed on some equitable principle) of the labors and sacrifices incurred for defending the society or its members" (CW XVII: 276).[76] No doubt we can read this as referring in part to distributive issues regarding the *expense* of society's measures, but it can and must (I think) also be read as referring to the burdens and restrictions that society's measures impose – that is, as referring to equity in the distribution of restrictions on liberty. And anyway, the distributive concern is there on almost every page of Mill's testimony to the Royal Commission. It is not just aggregate liberty at stake, but the liberty of some people and not others. At the very beginning, when he announced his liberty-based objection, Mill phrased it in terms of the legislation's taking

---

[74] N.B. – the same is true of "harm," which for Mill is always a matter of an effect on individual interests (even when the effect is distant and diffuse). This means that there are distributive issues on the harm side of the equation as well.

[75] Markovits 2005, 323

[76] See the brief discussion of this in Ten 1980, 64–5.

liberty away from a particular class of people – women (CW XXI: 351). When he offered his own suggestion as to what a tolerable piece of legislation would be like, again it was a matter of the distributive profile of the impact on liberty: it should affect the liberty of men no less than women, or men particularly if the justification of the statutes is genuinely supposed to track the prevention of the spread of disease. "If any preventive measures are to be taken I should say it should be in that shape" (CW XXI: 363).

With this in mind, we can revisit a point made earlier. Every piece of legislation, even legislation justified by the Harm Principle, will involve some impact on liberty. The question for the Harm Principle is whether the particular impact on liberty is warranted by the prevention of the harm. As we have seen, that is understood not just as a matter of quantum – how much liberty is affected and how much harm is prevented? – but as a matter of distribution and discrimination so far as liberty is concerned. Is the prevention of harm sufficient to justify *this pattern of impact* on liberty? Or is the distributive impact on liberty gratuitous and discriminatory so far as the prevention of this harm is concerned? Mere invocation of an intention to prevent harm does not excuse us from answering these questions.

The Identity of a Statute (for Purposes of the Harm Principle)
A little while ago, I asked: How can we tell what the intention of a statute really is, for the purpose of determining whether the statute satisfies Mill's Harm Principle? The conclusion we are heading toward is this: whatever the preamble or the professions of the legislators, any claim about purpose is to be checked against the impact of the legislation on liberty, understood distributively not aggregatively. Something doesn't count as the purpose of *this* statute if pursuing it does not require *this* sort of impact on liberty. The fundamental identity of a legislative measure is given, so to speak, by its footprint on liberty – the depth and distribution of the impact it has on people's freedom. Any claims about its purpose – about its having a legitimate purpose or an illegitimate purpose – must be made relative to this.

If a particular claim as to purpose is discredited in this way, then we may have to come up with a new purpose to attribute to the statute, something that will be at variance with the formulation that the legislators have advertised. Instead of saying that the purpose of the Contagious Diseases Acts is *to reduce or minimize venereal disease among the military (or among innocent members of the population)*, we may venture to claim instead that the aim of the Acts is *to reduce such venereal disease among the military (or among innocent members of the population), as can be affected by controlling women (or women of a certain type or class)*. And then we must ask whether this is a respectable reason for legislating.[77]

Intriguingly, the position we are moving toward is comparable to some aspects of the "strict scrutiny" standard in American constitutional law. If a law comes within the purview of the strict scrutiny test, it will be struck down as unconstitutional unless it is shown to be necessary to achieve a compelling government purpose. And we determine whether it is necessary not by what the legislators say but by considering the statute itself and asking whether its provisions amount to the "least restrictive" alternative for pursuing a purpose of this kind.[78] If the statute is "overbroad" in its impact on liberty, then it will be struck down, because we will have to impute to it a motivation other than the one of doing what is necessary for a compelling governmental purpose. But the two approaches are not quite the same. The main differences between the American strict scrutiny doctrine and Mill's Harm Principle (as we have interpreted it) are: (1) the former applies only when some particularly cherished liberty is at stake, whereas the latter applies to all statutes, and (2) in Mill's account, the prevention of harm is seen as a general legitimate purpose for legislation, rather than a particularly compelling one for particularly problematic cases. Those points apart, the logic is similar.

In this section of the chapter, I have tried to make explicit a point that is muted (although not absent) both in Mill's writing and, I think, in the American doctrine that "least restrictive" should be understood not just in terms of aggregate quantity of restrictions, but with a particular eye to the distribution of restrictions. A statute that heavily burdens the liberty of a

---

[77] Mill offers this sort of rewriting of the purpose of the Acts in regard not only to its discriminatory impact but also to moralistic concerns about the encouragement of vice. The sponsors of the legislation may say that it is not their intention to make prostitution safe for men, but the "general impression . . . , however contrary to the intention of those who support it, would be that the State patronises the class of practices by which these diseases are engendered, since it considers those who contract these diseases as worthy of more attention, and takes more pains to remedy the consequences, than those who have other diseases equally serious" (CW XXI: 370).

[78] See, e.g., *Sable Communications v. FCC*, 492 U.S. 115, 126 (1989): "The Government may . . . regulate the content of constitutionally protected speech in order to promote a compelling interest if it chooses the least restrictive means to further the articulated interest. We have recognized that there is a compelling interest in protecting the physical and psychological well-being of minors. This interest extends to shielding minors from the influence of literature that is not obscene by adult standards. . . . The Government may serve this legitimate interest, but to withstand constitutional scrutiny, 'it must do so by narrowly drawn regulations designed to serve those interests without unnecessarily interfering with First Amendment freedoms.' . . . It is not enough to show that the Government's ends are compelling; the means must be carefully tailored to achieve those ends" (citations omitted).

particular class of persons may be *less* restrictive in aggregate terms than a statute with a broader impact. But if diminishing the liberty of the members of this group in particular is not necessary for the best or most effective pursuit of the legitimate legislative goal, then we assume it is motivated by some other purpose. And we will want to scrutinize that closely and critically. That, I think, is what Mill was doing in his hypercritical assessment of the Contagious Diseases Acts. He did not deny that there was harm there to be prevented and that, if one blurred one's eyes enough when scrutinizing the Acts, one could say that they aimed to prevent that harm. But if one considered what the Acts really did, one would have to ask whether concerns about the harsh impact on liberty that it imposed – on women generally and on the members of a particular class of women in particular – could justified by the harm-prevention rationale. Mill's position was that the discriminatory impact on liberty could not be justified in those terms (although perhaps legislation with a more even-handed impact could be so justified or might have to be opposed on other – e.g., moralistic – grounds). It was not a question of balance; we would only be entitled to begin balancing the harm that the legislation caused against the harm that it prevented if we were sure that the harm-prevention rationale had already passed the threshold defined by the concern about liberty. And that concern was a distributive concern.

We are not required to say, therefore, that John Stuart Mill's intervention in the debate about the Contagious Diseases Acts was inconsistent with his views expressed in *On Liberty* or that he must have changed his mind between 1859 and 1871. But we have not had to resort to a crude originalist rewriting of Mill to reach this conclusion. Instead we have taken the opportunity afforded by what we know of his Contagious Diseases intervention to emphasize something that we should have been emphasizing all along. Citing the prevention of harm is not a way of rebutting concerns about a discriminatory or inequitably distributed restriction on liberty. If the best explanation of a pattern of legislative encroachment on liberty is that the members of one group are being favored over the members of another, then the fact that the general context of such discrimination is the prevention of harm is not enough to save the laws in question from condemnation.

Modern Disease Control

It would be wrong to end without saying something more general about the relevance of all this to issues that we have faced in recent years regarding the AIDS epidemic and may face in the future in regard to other diseases or in regard to other threats to society that are thought to require restrictions on liberty.

Daniel Markovits treats the nineteenth-century debate about the Contagious Diseases Acts as an example of "the connection between quarantines and cruel prejudice."[79] "Infectious diseases," he said, "particularly in epidemic forms, commonly trigger retributive and discriminatory instincts, so that actual quarantines often impose inhumane, stigmatizing, or even penal treatment upon persons who are confined based on caprice or even prejudice."[80] He is right. It is rare that social and legislative responses to disease are entirely isolated from other forms of anger and antipathy that people feel toward each other or toward particular classes of persons in their society. Class and race prejudice is always lurking around campaigns against dirt and squalor; different conditions of life, associated with ethnic or racial differences or with the residue of segregation, can all too easily become the focus of suspect concern when talk of the spread of disease is in the air. Nativist and anti-immigrant antipathies are ready and available to be stirred up in relation to epidemics that come to a given country from abroad. That is disease in general. The issue of sexually transmitted disease heightens the stakes dramatically. Most people are uneasy about sex and sexuality to begin with. They readily distinguish normal sex – governed by norms of chastity, heterosexuality, and monogamy – from sex that they regard as deviant or promiscuous, and they are all too ready to associate the spread of disease with sex and sexuality of the latter kind. There is a huge reservoir of hostility toward gay men and women in most societies. And we know that ignorance and panic in the early years of the AIDS epidemic all too readily associated that antipathy with measures deemed necessary to combat the spread of the disease.[81]

Now, measures taken to control the spread of epidemic disease can readily be defended on the basis of harm prevention. The Harm Principle seems to give the high ground to those who seek to protect themselves, their children, and community at large in this way. Invocation of Mill's principle seems

---

[79] Markovits 2005, 323 n. 1.

[80] Ibid, 323.

[81] In regard to the AIDS epidemic, Morton 1987 writes "There will, doubtless, be suggestions in the coming months that there should be compulsory testing of, say, immigrants, visitors, prisoners, the armed forces, prostitutes after conviction and homosexuals found guilty of acts of indecency. The lessons learned from the ten and more years of campaigning by Josephine Butler against the unfairness, brutalization, and discrimination of the [Contagious Diseases] Acts should be recalled, when, rather than if, future legislation is contemplated."

to answer any complaint based on liberty; it seems to provide a basis for rebutting any criticism that such measures are oppressive or discriminatory.

I hope the discussion in this chapter has shown the·importance of dispelling that impression. We need to emphasize, more strongly than we have, that the Harm Principle does not provide a basis for rebutting claims of discrimination. As Mill himself understood, liberty-based challenges to legal interference should be understood as individual-by-individual challenges. Person A's liberty is affected, and she requires a showing that the effect on her is justified by the need to prevent harm; person B's liberty is affected, and B requires a similar showing so far as the impact on *him* is concerned; and so on. The Harm Principle answers to concerns voiced in behalf of individuals, not in behalf of liberty in the aggregate.[82] And because it is answerable to individual concerns in this way, it is appropriate to test the genuineness of a harm-prevention rationale to see how the impact on liberty is spread among a given array of individuals.

I am not saying that an uneven distributive pattern of impacts on liberty is per se out of the question, as though no law can be justified in the name of harm prevention unless it burdens everyone equally. But if the impact *is* uneven, then it deserves the closest scrutiny. It deserves this, partly as a matter of principle – because the unequal distribution of liberty is always a concern, no matter what its motivation.[83] And it deserves scrutiny partly as a matter of moral pragmatics, because we know that prejudice and social antipathy are lurking in the vicinity of any such campaigns, awaiting the opportunity to ride forth on the back of apparently respectable legislative campaigns.

We are currently learning a lesson just like this in the context of measures taken to promote security against terrorist attacks. In defending measures like the USA PATRIOT Act, we talk of striking a balance between security and liberty, as though we were trading off one commodity (liberty) that we all like against another commodity (security) that we all like. We all give up a little of the one in order to avoid losing more of the other. In fact, the

---

[82] Once again, this is very clear from the language Mill uses to formulate his principle: "[T]he sole end for which mankind are warranted, individually or collectively in interfering with the liberty of action *of any of their number,* is self-protection. That the only purpose for which power can be rightfully exercised *over any member* of a civilized community, against his will, is to prevent harm to others" (CW XVII: 223, emphasis added).

[83] Suppose we say more harm can be reduced by legislation with an unequal impact on liberty than by legislation with an equal impact. Then there is balancing to be done: but what has to be balanced is, on the one hand, the good of preventing the extra harm against, on the other hand, not just the additional impact on someone's liberty, but the prima facie evil of departing from the appropriate principle for distributing liberty.

impact of these measures on most people's liberty is negligible. As Ronald Dworkin has pointed out,

None of the administration's decisions and proposals will affect more than a tiny number of American citizens: almost none of us will be indefinitely detained for minor violations or offenses, or have our houses searched without our knowledge, or find ourselves brought before military tribunals on grave charges carrying the death penalty. Most of us pay almost nothing in personal freedom when such measures are used against those the President suspects of terrorism.[84]

Those who suffer the impact on liberty are those who have something in common – in the way of ethnicity, appearance, religion, or politics – with the perpetrators of the attacks that took place on September 11, 2001. What we know about lurking social prejudices against people with these characteristics should put us on alert. If we find ourselves having to say honestly that it is not a trade-off between liberty and security for everyone, but between *their* liberty and *our* security,[85] it is time to revisit the basis of the legislation and consider the possibility that the ostensible security justification may not be the real justification for measures *just like this*.

[84] Dworkin 2002.
[85] Cf. Cole 2003.

2

Rational Freedom in John Stuart Mill's Feminism

Maria Morales

> All the selfish propensities, the self-worship, the unjust self-preference, which exist among mankind, have their source and root in, and derive their principal nourishment from, the present constitution of the relation between men and women.
> John Stuart Mill, *The Subjection of Women*

John Stuart Mill has rightfully earned a place of distinction in the history of the theory and practice of politics for championing the cause of women's emancipation. During his life, he became the object of ridicule and derision both for his theoretical work and for his political activities to promote women's freedom, although his famous work *The Subjection of Women* (1868) was well-received among several of his progressive colleagues and circulated widely among women's advocacy groups.[1] As the "woman question" made progress in the twentieth century, Mill's reputation as one of its earliest supporters improved. Yet as a rule, throughout a significant portion of the twentieth century, Mill scholars persisted in the belief that one can understand Mill's moral and political thought without having to read, let alone reflect on, his views on the relations between women and men in political, social, and domestic life. This general attitude has lingered despite Mill's unequivocal insistence that women's wide-ranging subjection to men is a deeply problematic "isolated fact" in modern institutional and social life that demands serious theoretical scrutiny (*The Subjection of Women*, CW XXI: 275, 294). Thus, systematic philosophical reflection on Mill's significant body of work on matters concerning women's social condition has come relatively slowly and continues to suffer from considerable gaps.

---

[1] For Mill's contemporaries' responses to *The Subjection of Women*, see Pyle 1994.

I thank Michael Monahan for a conversation that made me think harder about violence and Shay Welch for research assistance. I am also grateful to Alex Zakaras and Nadia Urbinati for insightful comments on an early draft of this chapter.

There is no doubt that Mill was a feminist. The debate among contemporary Mill scholars engaged with his feminism has been over what *kind* of feminist he was, particularly over the scope and appeal of his vision for women's emancipation. Mill himself refused to be understood to have said the last word on this matter. He contended that this judgment always would rest with women and in fact could never be made "until women themselves have told all that they have to tell" (CW XXI: 279). Nonetheless, the nature of his feminist vision deserves critical examination both on its merits and for its relevance to contemporary debates. In what follows I highlight certain aspects of Mill's conception of what is required to bring about and to sustain a social world where women can be truly free that show his vision to be anything but dated. I focus on his evaluation of practices of sexual domination in the "private" sphere as fundamentally inconsistent with women's liberation from the shackles of patriarchal power. Specifically, I underscore the centrality to Mill's account of women's subjection of his condemnation of the patriarchal ideal of "femininity" as embodying a sexualized conception of women's "nature." Given that women still contend with the force of this "ideal" at the dawn of the twenty-first century, from a Millian perspective, the work of feminists is far from complete.

Using Catharine MacKinnon's framework, I want to distinguish, broadly, between two approaches to thinking about the relations between women and men in social and political life and about the requirements for women's liberation (MacKinnon 1987, 32–45; 1989, 215–34). The first approach MacKinnon calls the "difference" model, and the aim of this approach is to achieve *equality* between women and men (MacKinnon 1987, 33–4; 1989, 219–34). The "sameness" branch of this approach presupposes that women are "the same as" men and, hence, should be treated as the same socially and politically. For the purposes of equality, sameness treatment requires that laws and policies be sex-blind and that women be guaranteed access to benefits and opportunities on the same terms as men. The "difference" branch of this approach presupposes that women are "different than" men and that that this difference is relevant to their treatment as equals. Thus, a "special rule" that takes into account relevant differences should govern social and political relations between women and men. For the purposes of equality, differential treatment requires that laws and policies be sensitive to the special needs and claims of the protected class – in this case, women. Benefits and opportunities that ignore such needs and claims fail the sex equality test. On either branch, the goal of the difference approach is to reform the legal sphere in particular, by securing women's equal political rights. Thus, the focus of the difference approach is the structure of the "public" world. Feminists who endorse this approach are considered *liberal* in their outlook and *reformist* in their aspirations. This approach does not require any "revolution" in moral, social, or political life: it can be implemented from within the world as we know it.

The second approach MacKinnon calls the "dominance" model, and the aim of this approach is to eradicate the *power* of men over women in all areas of life (MacKinnon 1987, 40–2). The dominance approach presupposes that we live in a patriarchal world – a world, that is, where women are subordinated to men in most, if not all, areas of life. On this approach, the solution to the various problems associated with patriarchal rule lies in critically exposing "women's social relegation to inferiority as a gender" by centering on "the most sex-differential abuses of women as a gender," notably violence against women (MacKinnon 1987, 40–1). Unlike the difference approach, the dominance approach focuses on the "private" world – that is, the social, domestic, and personal world – where patriarchal domination manifests itself much more insidiously than in the at least officially equal "public" realm. Dominance feminists argue that "public" equality – that is, political enfranchisement and legal personhood, and freedom of educational and employment opportunities – is necessary but far from sufficient for women's true emancipation and that "public" equality is not even fully possible without dramatic changes in the "private" realm. In fact, from this perspective, equality advocacy is misguided: it is only necessary because of male normativity and problematic because it does not transcend it. Feminists who endorse the dominance approach are considered *radical* both in their outlook and in their aspirations. This approach requires dramatic changes in a world within which women have not been, and cannot ever be, entirely free.

Not surprisingly, the notion of freedom constitutes a significant conceptual component of both difference and dominance feminism. It is not surprising because, in a straightforward sense, freedom is the antithesis of subjection. What is at stake is not whether freedom is relevant to feminism, but what *kind* of freedom is relevant or, put differently, freedom *from what*. On this question, difference and dominance feminists disagree. Difference feminists conceive of the relevant freedom as freedom from obstacles in the way of women's full participation in political life. Consequently, the kind of subjection with which difference feminists are chiefly concerned is subjection to unjust laws and policies that limit the degree to which women can be the architects of their "public" destinies. It does not follow, of course, that laws never regulate other aspects of women's lives. Yet the target of the difference reformist agenda is above all the law.

In contrast, for dominance feminists, the relevant freedom is freedom from an oppressive sexual ethic that permeates social, domestic, and personal relations between women and men. On this view, women can be subjected

despite their "public" freedom. The case for this claim, critical in much contemporary feminism, is especially hard to make within the framework of
political liberalism. Traditionally, liberals have resisted the feminist impera-
tive to do away with the sharp differentiation between "public" and "private"
spheres of life and to embrace what Rawls calls a "comprehensive" moral conception (Rawls 1985, 1988, 1993). Mill was the first "liberal"[2] to *criticize* the
public–private dichotomy and to underscore the incompatibility of domination in the "private" realm with equality, justice, and democratic rule in the
"public." As we shall see, he argued that there ought to be a *single* standard
of justice for human life in all of its dimensions. Moreover, he repeatedly
stressed that the public–private dichotomy obscures the *extent* of women's
subjection, which cannot be understood in abstraction from women's "private" lives. Along similar lines, contemporary dominance feminists insist
that the only path to women's *real* freedom is through the marshlands of
their fully situated lives, which involve much more than their (presumed or
real) "public" status.

Now we can reformulate the general question about Mill's feminism as
follows: Was Mill a difference or a dominance feminist? Because the orthodoxy has been to construe Mill's moral and political thought as (more or
less narrowly) liberal, the tendency has been to interpret his feminism as
liberal feminism. Some commentators have construed Mill's concerns with
women's emancipation as an application of his concern with "public" freedom (Himmelfarb 1974; Jaggar 1983; Howes 1986; Tulloch 1989) and as
too "narrowly" liberal to be of use to contemporary feminists (Ring 1985;
MacKinnon 1989; di Stefano 1991; Heckman 1992). Other commentators,
although classifying Mill as a liberal feminist, have underscored the rich
character of Mill's liberalism so as to capture some of the complexity of
his feminism (Okin 1973 and 1979; Donner 1993). A few commentators
have recognized the radical *potential* of his feminism yet judged that, ultimately, it fails to be realized (Annas 1977; Krouse 1982; Eisenstein 1981).
Finally, several commentators have focused on the radical elements of Mill's
feminism (Shanley 1981; Burgess-Jackson 1995) and their consistency with
such other key elements of his practical philosophy as his commitment to
democratic rule (Urbinati 1991, 2002; Morales 1996). Despite this spectrum of interpretations, Mill is all too often still *assumed* to be a liberal
feminist concerned primarily, if not exclusively, with "public" sex equality
and as an advocate at most of timid reforms even in that arena. The recalci-
trant nature of this assumption has at least two sources: first, the enduring

---

[2] For my characterization of Mill's liberalism, see Morales 1996. See also Donner 1991.

power of traditional (and older) conceptions of Mill as a classical liberal and, second, the persisting relative neglect of his *many* feminist writings that, as a whole, cannot be adequately understood from within a difference framework.

I do not wish to argue that Mill was a dominance feminist. Where Mill is concerned, my view is that labels are generally dangerous because counterexamples to one-sided interpretations can always be found in his corpus. Yet the view that I have defended (Morales 1996) and will continue to defend here is that many of Mill's feminist concerns are dominance concerns that cannot be *reduced* to difference concerns. Here I concentrate on Mill's impassioned condemnation of crimes against women's persons, especially the (then as now) widespread incidence of domestic violence, as crimes of *sexual domination* motivated and maintained by an oppressive sexual ethic. In this context, I discuss Mill's insights into how the social construction[3] of women's "nature" as fundamentally sexual constitutes the pivotal obstacle to women's liberation. Mill contended that sexualized conceptions of femininity keep women from lives of "rational freedom" (CW XXI: 336). For Mill, I argue, rational freedom is *freedom from domination* and, specifically for women, it is freedom from *patriarchal* domination. In *The Subjection of Women,* as well as in *Utilitarianism,* Mill linked the notion of freedom understood in this way to the notion of justice. Thus, for Mill, freedom from the patriarchal sexual ethic is a requirement of justice. Rational freedom, then, turns out to be a strong, and specifically feminist, moral value.

The Patriarchal Sexual Ethic

Throughout his feminist writings Mill expressed a profound concern with a sexual ethic that keeps women tied to a traditional and problematic conception of femininity with enormous implications for the possibility of their full emancipation. He vigorously denounced the "command and obedience" ethic as representing all that is wrong with society. I have discussed Mill's conception of this ethic and its harms elsewhere (Morales 1996, 121–6). Here I want to highlight two points in particular: that it is a *patriarchal* ethic and that it is a patriarchal *sexual* ethic. Viewed in this light, Mill's condemnation of the command and obedience ethic is a precursor and an ally of many contemporary radical feminist concerns with sexual domination.

---

[3] For an excellent analysis of the notion of social construction, see Haslanger 1995, 2002b, and 2002c. For a discussion of nineteenth-century constructions of "womanhood," see Russett 1989.

Mill had a conception of patriarchy, although he did not use the term. As he conceived of it, patriarchy is the system of privileges and advantages that places men in an absolute position of superiority over women. The conceptual components of this definition (if it is that) must be analyzed: "system," "privilege," "advantage," and "superiority." First, patriarchy is *systematic*: it is a political, social, and personal hierarchical organization of life. The political aspect of patriarchal domination was evident to Mill given women's complete legal disenfranchisement in nineteenth-century England.[4] Yet he understood that the political apparatus is sustained in place by social practices and attitudes, especially socialization. He contended that men want not only women's "obedience," but also their "sentiments." They want "not a forced slave, but a willing one, not a slave merely, but a favourite" (CW XXI: 271–2). To this end, the whole of education is turned to "enslave their minds."[5] Women are socialized to internalize their subjection, that is, to believe that being a woman involves "yielding to the control of others" and "living for others," and that women fulfill their "nature" by self-abnegation and service to men. (I discuss how far Mill believed this life of "service" extends momentarily.) Moreover, women are taught that they ought "to have no life but in their affections" and then only "those they are allowed to have," notably those that find their expression in marriage and motherhood (CW XXI: 272).

Although Mill often used the language of tyranny to describe the power of men over women, his conception of the phenomenon of despotic rule, which is far more than a characterization of a form of government, better captures the nature of his denunciation of male domination in the "private" sphere. Nadia Urbinati has offered a compelling analysis of Mill's use of the classical notion of despotism, which he approached "from within, via the chemistry of emotions, ideas, and behavior that shape the character of master and subjects alike" (Urbinati 2002, 179). Men want to appear as women's protectors, not their masters, so they mold their minds and

---

[4] For a discussion of women's political (especially legal) subjection in Victorian England, see Holcolme 1983; Stetson 1982; Shanley 1989.

[5] For a detailed discussion of Mill's slavery analogy, see Morales 1996, 150–3, and Shanley 1981. Mill contended that the slavery analogy was used "by way of rhetorical license." He wrote:

When it is wished to describe any portion of the human race as in the lowest state of debasement, and under the most cruel oppression, in which it is possible for human beings to live, they are compared to slaves. When words are sought by which to stigmatize the most odious despotism, exercised in the most odious manner, and all other comparisons are found inadequate, the despots are said to be like slave-masters or slave-drivers. ("The Contest in America," CW XXI: 136)

spirits to transform them into dependent beings by crushing their capacity of self-formation. Urbinati writes:

Despotism – as described in *The Subjection of Women* – is a form of total and absolute power because it operates on the emotions, not just on actions. The despot, unlike the tyrant, strikes with fear and love simultaneously. Subjects of the tyrant long to rebel; under the despot they become affectionate chattel slaves. In the first case of repression, potential freedom is always latent; in the other, a condition of total surrender and pacification defines "complete abnegation." (Urbinati 2002, 175)

The domestic despot wants a "willing" slave and, what is more, a slave who has become unable to view her condition as slavery. Thus, despotism is a much more relentless form of control and insidious form of power than tyranny: it crushes the very possibility of free agency. Worse, because the despot aims at concealing his absolute power, he presents his rule as benevolent guidance for the sake of the subject's good rather than as what it truly is – namely, coercion for the sake of the despot's own purposes. Mill understood that the socialization of women, which distinguishes their lot from that of all other subject classes because of the peculiar nature and extent of the domination involved, is the chief obstacle in the way of women's real freedom. The ideology of "femininity" is the master's tool and, ultimately, what needs to be dismantled.

Coupling the power of this ideology with women's "entire dependence," especially their economic dependence, "it would be a miracle if the object of *being attractive to men* had not become the polar star of feminine education and formation of character" (emphasis added). What the social aspect of patriarchy does is to compel women to internalize a self-conception as dependent sexual beings "by representing to them meekness, submissiveness, and resignation of all individual will into the hands of a man, *as an essential part of sexual attractiveness*" (CW XXI: 272, emphasis added). The message that women receive, whether explicitly or implicitly, is that sexual attractiveness is the means to their fulfillment as women and that independence and assertiveness are not sexually attractive. A (Freudian) ideal of femininity that extols submissiveness and passivity as essential and alluring aspects of women's sexuality constitutes the foundation of the patriarchal conception of women's "nature" (Morales 1996, 122–3). This "ideal" is the core of a social structure of discipline aimed at control – specifically, at molding women into the type of being men want them to be (CW XXI: 276–7, 281).[6] This structure of discipline focuses on *the body*: it overemphasizes

---

[6] The argument that femininity is constituted by a complex disciplinary structure has been excellently developed by Bartky 1990, 63–82.

women's biological constitution consistently with a certain view of their "nature" as essentially sexual. Femininity is the normative way of being a woman superimposed on the sexualized body. The disciplinary character of the normative ideal of femininity becomes apparent in the treatment of "transgressors," who, Mill noted, are called "masculine" and other names conveying censure ("Edinburgh Review," CW I: 312).

Mill forcefully rejected the view that femininity is "natural" and that dependence is a basic constituent of women's "nature." That a complex apparatus of political and social control is maintained in place to prevent women from being and living any other way betrays men's "fear" that women's "nature" is not what they claim it to be (CW XXI: 279–80). The "anxiety of men to interfere on behalf of nature," Mill cleverly noted, reveals that men are simply not ready to give up "the bounties and protective duties" in their favor and to live with women as equals (CW XXI: 280, 299, 322). In this context, the closely related notions of *privilege* and *advantage* are most relevant.[7] The privileged in a system (consciously or unconsciously) view their position in that system as a right that is legitimately withheld from others – because, say, those others are not "naturally" fit. As a necessarily hierarchical notion, privilege carries with it connotations of superiority. In patriarchal systems, the privilege of men is cashed out as male-right, which is ultimately founded on sex-right. Mill noted that privilege as male-right is perpetuated by institutions and social practices that give men "absolute power" over women, both "public" and "private." The ubiquity of male-right (historical, across cultures, and in all areas of life) appears to support the argument that it is "natural." But what form of domination, asked Mill, does not, conveniently, appear "natural" to those with the power to exercise it? (CW XXI: 269). The argument from nature is convenient precisely because it favors men by enabling them to make use of their more favorable position for their own gain. The payoffs of patriarchy, for men, are the "benefits" of domination, notably the unhindered license to live as they see fit, to rule according to their self-seeking interest, and to be supported in their pursuits, "public" and "private," by servants and adorers (CW XXI: 285, 289). Mill viewed these benefits *as harms* and denounced the ethic of command and obedience for fostering the vices of power in the privileged, notably self-worship and selfishness (CW XXI: 293, 324–5; Morales 1996, 121–6).

The notion of advantage also carries with it connotations of superiority and, in Mill's view, men's superiority is not only harmful but groundless (CW XXI: 324–5). *Superiority,* or the condition of being above others

[7] For a detailed account of the notion of privilege, see Bailey 1988 and MacIntosh 1991.

because one is on some criterion, better, is the polar star of male education. It breeds in boys feelings of exaggerated and undeserved self-importance that themselves breed arrogance, overbearingness, and both political and personal insensitivity (CW XXI: 289, 293, 324). In short, the patriarchal socialization of boys trains them to be despots and, worse, to view their despotism as a prerogative of their sex.

For Mill, the systematic character of patriarchy reaches its apex in the power of men over women in the home. Mill's forceful denunciation of patriarchal marriage is relatively familiar (see, for example, Lyndon Shanley 1981, 1998; Eisenstein 1986; Morales 1996; Urbinati 2002). Less familiar is the extent of his indictment of practices condoned by patriarchal right in domestic life: battery, murder, rape, and child abuse. As exercises of male-right, these practices are *problems of sexual domination* and not merely aberrations but *corollaries of patriarchy itself*. With this insight, Mill propelled his feminism well beyond the boundaries of the difference model.

We need some framework for understanding how certain kinds of violence are problems of sexual domination. Briefly, what makes domestic violence sui generis is that it is inextricably tied to patriarchal relations of power–subjection in the "private" sphere. One way to grasp the dynamic at work in domestic violence is to view it as involving a particular attitude on the part of the perpetrator toward the subject: the objectification of the subject of violence. In Martin Buber's (1970) terminology, the subject becomes an "It" rather than a "Thou." An "It" has neither *independent status* nor *intrinsic value*. The "It" has no independent status in the sense that it becomes a kind of extension of the perpetrator's perception of his physical world and, specifically, a portion of this world over which he can have dominion by the exercise of his will (in this case, via physical force). The "It" has no intrinsic value in the sense that it becomes a mere instrument for the fulfillment of whatever aim or desire the perpetrator wishes to satisfy through the act of violence. The objectified subject has the same value as any other physical object – namely, *use-value*. One problem with the objectification of the subject in this context is that use-value is the *only* value of the objectified subject. The personal relationship construed as an *owner-ship* relationship creates in the perpetrator a sense of *entitlement*, and hence of *superiority*, over the objectified subject. Thus, violence in this context becomes fundamentally hierarchical. Moreover, the violence itself reinforces the hierarchy: it is used to "confirm" the perpetrator's sense of his superiority over the objectified subject. Thus, the act of violence is essentially an expression of *power over* the objectified subject. When "successful," the act of violence renders the power tangibly real. Yet the power is no less real when not actively exercised provided the perpetrator can exercise it with relative impunity.

Mill's discussion of domestic violence should be understood within this framework. In a series of newspaper articles published as "joint productions" with Harriet Taylor between 1846 and 1851,[8] Mill decried "the habitual abuse of brute strength" against women and children as "the worse order of crimes of violence."[9] I have discussed these texts elsewhere (Morales 1996, 157–62). Here I want to underscore that, like many contemporary dominance feminists, Mill conceived of domestic violence as inextricably tied to relations of power–subjection within the patriarchal family. At the heart of Mill's analysis of the dynamic involved in domestic violence is his examination of the perspective from which the offender performs his acts of violence, including the way in which he views the subject of violence. Mill wrote:

> It is evident to all who take any pains to read the indications of the feelings of the populace, that they are impressed with the belief of their having a *right* to inflict almost any amount of corporal violence upon *their* wife or *their* children. That anyone should claim to interfere with this supposed right, causes them unaffected surprise. Is it not *their* wife or child? Are they not entitled to do as they will with their own? These phrases are not, to their apprehension, metaphorical. The shoes on their feet, or the cudgel in their hand – the horse or ass that carries their burdens, and that dies a lingering death under their cruelties – their wife and children – all are "theirs," and all in the same sense. They have the same right, in their own opinion, over their human as over their inanimate property.[10]

Men who abuse the power they *can* abuse do not view the women and children over whom they exercise dominion as subjects, but rather as objects or things. They are like "shoes" and "cudgels" (things, strictly speaking) or like "horses" and "asses" (nonhuman animals), all having the same value – namely, use-value. Mill's phrase "human property" is revealing: wives and children are like slaves, exposed to ill treatment "at every hour and every moment of their lives."[11] Moreover, their "slavery" is complete: they have no way out of their subjected lot because, first, they are entirely dependent

---

[8] The first series goes from February to December 1846, and the second series from February 1850 to August 1851. (For a complete listing of these articles, see "Newspaper Writings," CW XXIV: 865.) Two of the seven articles in the first series and seven of the eight articles in the second series address the subjection of women within marriage. The articles in the second series examine the problem of violence against women, except for two, which are devoted to child abuse.

[9] "The Case of Anne Bird," CW XXV: 1145.

[10] "The Law of Assault," CW XXV: 1173. See also "Wife Murder," CW XXV: 1186.

[11] "Wife Murder," CW XXV: 1186.

on their tormentors for economic survival; second, they are typically unable to retaliate (physically or legally), which the offender knows; and finally, the law and public opinion fail to protect victims fully or at all.

Mill was especially appalled by the double standard governing domestic crimes. "It seems almost inconceivable," he wrote, "that the smallest blow from a man to a man should be by law a criminal offence, and yet that it should not be – or should not be known to be – unlawful for a man to strike a woman."[12] The arm of the law should be made to reach "the tyranny of bodily strength in every instance in which it comes to light" and should "distinctly" set forth "that it is *not* lawful for a man to strike his wife any more than to strike his brother or his father." Mill also was dismayed by the practice of reducing the severity of the crime when committed by a man: "[i]t is necessary that it should be, once and for all, understood by juries that to beat a human being to death is not manslaughter, but murder."[13] If a woman is charged with killing a man, "no matter under what circumstances of just exasperation," she would not only be charged with the graver crime but also subjected to the gravest penalty allowed by law. Yet even when wives die from maltreatment, husbands are not sent to trial or, if tried, they are "in a majority of cases, acquitted – sometimes in the face of the clearest evidence. Even if found guilty, it is only of manslaughter, and they get off with a year or two of imprisonment."[14] Thus, Mill concluded, "[t]he vow to protect confers a license to kill."[15]

This state of affairs is, for Mill, directly linked to the power of husbands over "their" wives. If a man kills a wife other than his own, Mill hypothesized, "there can be little doubt" that he would be indicted for murder and dealt the harshest of penalties, and the reason is that, in that case, she is someone else's property. Thus, for Mill, the far from metaphorical male ownership

---

[12] "The Law of Assault," CW XXV: 1175.

[13] "The Case of Susan Moir," CW XXV: 1169.

[14] "The Case of Anne Bird," CW XXV: 1154–5.

[15] "Wife Murder," CW XXV: 1185. In Parliament, Mill addressed the argument that men's power over women in the "private" sphere is justified on the grounds that men may thus "protect" women's interests. He said:

I should like to have a return laid before this House of the number of women who are annually beaten to death, kicked to death, or trampled to death by their male protectors: and, in the opposite column, the amount of the sentences passed, in those cases in which the dastardly criminals did not get off altogether. ("Public and Parliamentary Speeches," CW XXVII: 158–9)

The "identity of interests" argument assumes that men are benevolent, an assumption that is not supported by facts. Mill noted that "we do not live in Arcadia, but, as we were lately reminded, *in faece Romuli.*" For Mill, that there always have been exceptions – benevolent "masters" – can never become an apology for despotism.

relationship in the domestic sphere is the enabling factor in domestic brutality toward women and children. "[W]hen a person, like a thing, is suffered to
be spoken of as their own – as *their* wife, *their* child, or *their* dog – [men] are
allowed to do what they please with it . . . and justified in supposing that the
worst they can do will be accounted for as a case of slight assault." The husband's power and the wife's "degradation" are all the more complete because
husbands, upon discharge, are given back their power and wives dismissed
"with a piece of kind advice to be gentle and submissive."[16] The disciplinary
character of violence against women is obvious. Male violence, whether real
or threatened, ensures that women remain "obedient" and "in their place,"
that is, under the authority of some man. The exercise of male violence is
the most extreme "punishment" patriarchy may impart for women's rule
breaking or defiance.

Mill's concern throughout these writings is not exclusively with the state
of the law on heinous domestic crimes against women and children. The
law in effect renders normative certain *preexisting* social and personal power
asymmetries between women and men and, in so doing, becomes a further
instrument of control. Mill targeted the cruel and unjust rule of the male
head of the patriarchal family by means of the exercise of his arbitrary will.
Mill decried "the tyranny of physical force in its coarsest manifestations,
constantly exhibited as the most familiar facts of [women's and children's]
daily lives."[17] That this tyranny is in effect condoned not only by the law's
weakness but also by the ignorance, silence, or inaction of the general public
is, to Mill, a sign of "superficial civilization."[18] Mill maintained that "domestic tyranny" is "now the only kind of tyranny which, in the more improved
countries of the world, still exists in full vigor."[19] In *The Subjection of Women*,
he claimed that men's "rule of force" over women is an aspect of the rule
of force as a way of life prevalent throughout much of human history (CW
XXI: 264–5). He pointed out that people generally have abandoned the rule
of force as a justification for governmental authority. However, those who
compliment themselves for having dethroned it were apt to forget just how
slowly the notion of equal justice had entered the pantheon of principles of
social morality (CW XXI: 265–6). Mill noted that as concerns the relations
between women and men, the doctrine that might makes right is not generally perceived to clash with modern civilization, and he sternly denounced
his society for ignoring this incongruity (CW XXI: 265). In fact, he called

[16] "The Suicide of Sarah Brown," CW XXIV: 919.
[17] "The Case of Anne Bird," CW XXV: 1157.
[18] "The Case of Mary Ann Parsons," CW XXV: 1151.
[19] "The Case of Anne Bird," CW XXV: 1156.

domestic tyranny "the primitive state of slavery lasting on" (CW XXI: 264) and "a slavery in civilized life, from which the most savage maltreatment, judicially proved, cannot liberate the victim."[20]

Nowhere is the "slavery" of women in domestic life more apparent than in their complete lack of sovereignty over their bodies. Mill forcefully decried the unbound and unquestioned power of husbands to rape their wives. His discussion of marital rape is especially noteworthy because the nineteenth-century law of coverture (or spousal "unity") made it conceptually impossible for there to be rape within marriage.[21] In virtue of the power of the ideology behind coverture, laws protecting women from rape within marriage have appeared historically much later than laws criminalizing rape in the "public" arena.[22] Arguably, there is still more resistance to acknowledging that women can be raped by their husbands than to recognizing the widespread incidence of rape in society at large and even within the family outside of spousal relations (including rape of female children by male relatives, whether or not the relative is the father). Why this resistance?[23] Mill offered the following analysis. Patriarchal marriage confers on the husband the power to "claim from [his wife] and enforce the lowest degradation of a human being, that of being made the instrument of an animal function contrary to her inclinations" (CW XXI: 285). Mill contended that patriarchal marriage "holds" the wife in the "worst description of *slavery* as to her own person" (emphasis added). It is not the "animal function" that worried Mill, but the wife's "slavery": by raping "his" wife, the husband reinforces his status as "owner" and her status as "instrument." The slavery analogy is appropriate in this context: historically, the power of the slave master was not deemed to be complete in the absence of absolute power over the slave's *body* (Morales 1996, 157–8). This power gave the master the "right" to claim "use" of the slave's body for his own purposes, whether as a labor instrument or a sexual one.

The same power, Mill claimed, is given by law to every husband (CW XXI: 268). It is irrelevant whether any husband exercises it. What is relevant is that any husband can "claim" and "enforce" his "right" over his wife's body at *his* discretion and that this right is understood to be a *husband's* right and

[20] "The Law of Assault," CW XXV: 1175.

[21] On coverture, see Holcolme 1983, Stetson 1982, and Shanley 1981.

[22] Laws criminalizing marital rape appeared in the United States in 1976 and in the U.K. in 1994.

[23] I encountered this resistance most recently (spring 2005) in an undergraduate class in contemporary political philosophy in the context of discussing Pateman 1988. Interestingly, I have never had a female student argue that there cannot be rape within marriage, no matter how "traditional" might be her conception of what marriage should be as far as gender roles.

protected in a sui generis way, including, overwhelmingly, by public opinion. Yet only if we view marriage as *patriarchal* will we understand this "right" as constituting a legitimate claim and, hence, as different *in kind* from a sexual "claim" that a nonhusband could make over an unwilling nonwife. Mill understood that there is something deeply wrong with marriage if it is presumed to give the husband sexual control over the wife and is understood to render the wife a mere sexual object at his disposal. Furthermore, not only are women and men differentially situated with respect to their sexual freedom within patriarchal marriage but also the *exercise* of their sexuality is construed quite differently – and hierarchically. For men, it is the exercise of a "right," whereas for women, it is the rendering of a "service." Within the context of patriarchal marriage, the husband has the freedom to exercise or not to exercise his "right," but when he does, the wife is expected to provide her "service" regardless of her wishes. The right/freedom of the husband and the service/subjection of the wife renders women's sexuality within patriarchal marriage anything but consensual.[24]

A chief problem with patriarchal marriage, on this view, is precisely that, in entering into the married relation, the woman is understood to give irrevocable "consent" to sex. But what this amounts to is "consent" to become a sexual object, or, most strongly, a sexual slave. Women's consent to their subjection cannot any more be presumed than it can in the case of slavery in general (CW XXI: 270–1; Morales 1996, 100–1). That women's consent in the area of sexuality is either ignored or presumed is in fact a mark of their sexual subjection. The *presumption* of consent is especially problematic, given that women's voices are dismissed when expressed (CW XXI: 271; Morales 1996, 141–2) or silenced by the reality of their subjugation. Mill contended that women's alleged compliance with their subjection did not prove anything, let alone that they accepted it willingly, because silence is a means of self-preservation for many women.[25] Because the command and obedience ethic reinforces women's silence, effective checks against abuses of power are all the more difficult. Mill insisted that women's "consent" is a sham as long as women

---

[24] For an excellent argument that the notion of consent is essentially hierarchical, see Pateman 1988.

[25] On the issue of silence, MacKinnon writes:

when you are powerless, you don't just speak differently. A lot, you don't speak. Your speech is not just differently articulated, it is silenced. Eliminated, gone. You aren't just deprived of a language with which to articulate your distinctiveness, although you are; you are deprived of a life out of which articulation might come. Not being heard is not just a function of lack of recognition, not just that no one knows how to listen to you, although it is that; it is also silence of the deep kind, the silence of being prevented from having anything to say. (MacKinnon 1987, 39)

themselves "have given but little testimony, and that little, mostly suborned" (CW XXI: 278). Against the background of coercion, whether direct or indirect, we cannot presume to know what "testimony" women would give. Mill maintained that men's power over women in social life is the hardest to eradicate because it has "its yoke tightly riveted on the necks of those who are kept down by it" (CW XXI: 268). Interestingly, MacKinnon uses the same image to make the same point: "Take your foot off our necks, then we will hear in what tongue women speak" (MacKinnon 1987, 45).

Once again, Mill's conception of despotism illuminates his discussion of women's "consent" in civil society. In his view, it is sinister and pervasive forms of coercion and control that explain women's subjected social status. Women do not create their world but rather live in a world generated and maintained by men. What is more, women are ideologically coerced to live in the world that men create and ideologically induced to "consent." Unlike tyranny, despotism requires some form of consent by the subjects, which in effect conceals its deeply problematic character. Mill radically diverged from the traditional understanding of patriarchal rule in civil society as grounded on the consent of women, conceived of as "naturally" prone to subjection and content with men's protection, by criticizing the ideology of consent as a disingenuous sham that obscures the extent of women's lack of freedom. *Rational* freedom, for Mill, is premised on moral subjecthood, which is precisely what is crushed by subjection to the will of others.

Rational Freedom

Toward the end of *The Subjection of Women,* Mill contended that freedom and power are in "eternal antagonism" (CW XXI: 338). He understood that power need not be institutionally bound, that is, need not be tied to specific institutional forms that exclude certain people from political life or limit their choices of ways of life. He appreciated that the various influences on character formation, which begin in the family, are even more critical because they can impair people's capacities for autonomous self-formation and self-determination. Given his lifelong and passionate preoccupation with human freedom, his chief concern, in fact, was with forms of *social* power that, more or less explicitly, "educate" certain people for *un*freedom. If the mind is restricted, the passions deformed, and the spirit trampled, then talk about freedom becomes nothing but "a piece of tiresome cant." Precisely *that* is what freedom is for women under patriarchal conditions. Gender socialization disempowers women from the outset, a disempowerment that is made all the more profound once their "disabilities" elsewhere in social and political life are added to the ledger. Mill's most important and discerning criticism of gender is that its norms shape women into beings incapable of autonomy and relegates them to ways of being and of doing that are marked as socially inferior. For women, gender constitutes the paramount obstacle to real and complete freedom.

We have seen that, on Mill's view, the patriarchal sexual ethic is an intricate and multifaceted force in women's lives. Mill grasped with uncanny insight the great impact of this ethic on women in social life, including the home. This ethic tolerates, and even condones, the use of intimidating, threatening (and fear-inducing), harassing, and violent male behavior to manipulate and control women. The ethic also stands for and behind the sexual objectification[26] of women, thus depriving them of independence and agency. Mill called a life of agency, including sexual agency, "a life of rational freedom" (CW XXI: 336–7). Women will not lead lives of rational freedom until sexual domination in the social and personal arenas is condemned as unjust and, on that ground, eradicated. Mill claimed that men generally condemn as unjust the "wrongful exercise of power over someone" (*Utilitarianism,* CW X: 256) and the deprivation of someone's "moral rights" (CW X: 243, 247). Women's subjection ought to be recognized as unjust on both counts: it involves men's wrongful exercise of power over women, and it deprives women of their moral rights, especially rights in their person. Women's "public" freedom is not sufficient: "the first principles of social justice" ought to apply consistently to all areas of life (CW XXI: 325). Domestic despotism ought to be condemned on the same grounds as political despotism (CW XXI: 286). Only then will the "aristocracy of sex"[27] give way to a democracy of sex, with women leading lives of self-determination and self-rule in all that concerns the integrity of their persons (CW X: 259; Morales 1996, 151–2). Rational freedom as a moral value requires that women become full *subjects.* Because under patriarchy women are presumed to be *and are always viewed as* objects – notably, sexual objects – rational freedom requires that patriarchy be torn down. Thus, for

---

[26] For excellent accounts of the notion of sexual objectification, see Bartky 1990, 22–32; Haslanger 2002a.

[27] Mill wrote:

The entire history of social improvement has been a series of transitions, by which one custom or institution after another, far from being supposed a primary necessity of social existence, has passed into the rank of a universally stigmatized injustice and tyranny. So it has been with the distinctions of slaves and freemen, nobles and serfs, patricians and plebeians; and so it will be, and in part already is, with the aristocracies of colour, race, and sex. (CW X: 259)

Mill, rational freedom is, ultimately, *freedom from patriarchy*. Millian rational freedom is a specifically feminist value.

I have come to believe that the notion of "rational freedom" understood in this way is a better characterization of feminist aspirations than the notions of "gender equality" or "sex equality." The phrase "gender equality" involves something like a category mistake: gender is a necessarily hierarchical notion and cannot be made "equal" other than by its transcendence. Because transcending gender would amount to *ending* gender, we might as well talk about ending gender. The phrase "sex equality" is also problematic: to the extent that gender is gender/sex – that is, to the extent that gender maps onto "biological" sex construed as binary difference – sex equality is not a more reasonable feminist objective than is gender equality. Radical feminists like MacKinnon have criticized difference approaches because they do not transcend male normativity, and, consequently, they fail to appreciate that feminism is not about making women "equal" to men but rather about *freeing women from subjection* to men (MacKinnon 1987, 39; 1989, 220–1). By focusing his analysis precisely on women's *subjection,* Mill placed his feminism squarely within the dominance framework. The overarching goal of his feminism *is* freedom for women, but his conception of freedom in this context is radical indeed.

Relatively recent discussions of freedom as nondomination are in line with Mill's notion of rational freedom. Both within and outside of Mill scholarship, political philosophers have become increasingly more sensitive to, and interested in, the dynamics of subtle forms of coercion and control ("power") as real and substantial impediments to freedom. Within Mill scholarship, Bruce Baum's comprehensive study of the relationship between power and freedom in Mill's thought is especially noteworthy. Baum systematically develops Mill's understanding "of how people's powers of self-determination and self-development are shaped by the power dynamics they encounter in their political, economic, educational, gender, and family relationships" (Baum 2000, 4). How people are socially situated dramatically affects the success of their efforts to achieve self-determination. Freedom is not to be understood in an abstract vacuum but rather is itself "situated" with respect to various relations of power in political and civic life. The more "radical" elements of Mill's theory of freedom, Baum believes, tackle the many and complex ways in which our social situations – where we stand with respect to various matrices of social power – enable or inhibit our freedom. Baum shows how in his political thinking, Mill moved toward concrete understandings of the limits imposed by education (broadly conceived), social practices, and institutions on the possibility of autonomous self-formation. Baum rightly construes Mill's rich ideal of freedom not on the model of noninterference but rather on the model of nondomination, understood as concerned with the many social causes of what Urbinati calls "autonomy deprivation" (Urbinati 2002, 174). In fact, both Baum and Urbinati have demonstrated that Mill deemed the ideal of nondomination as central to the possibility of democracy not only in "public" but also in civic (including domestic) life.

Outside of Mill scholarship, the contemporary revival of the notion of freedom as nondomination can be found, for example, in Philip Pettit's work. Pettit conceives of freedom as inextricably tied to "discursive control," which involves social recognition of oneself as a subject "with a voice and an ear of one's own" (Pettit 2001, 140). Such recognition is undermined "under any conditions where one lives *in potestate domini*, in the power of another," whether or not that power is exercised. Domination comes in many forms, but all of them involve life "at the mercy of others." Pettit writes:

> That person is dominated by those others in the sense that even if the others don't interfere in his or her life, they have an arbitrary power of doing so: there are few restraints or costs to inhibit them. If the dominated person escapes ill treatment, that is by the grace and favour of the powerful. The price of liberty in such a world is not eternal vigilance but eternal discretion. The person lives in the power or under the mastery of others: they occupy the position of a *dominus* in his or her life. And so far as the person is subject to domination of this kind, they are bound to censor or inhibit what they do, so that the net effect on their behaviour will be just as deep as any that active interference might have achieved. (Pettit 2001, 137)

An agent's freedom is compromised by the very exposure to arbitrary power, which in the case of the dominated, leads to self-censorship. Pettit's key claim is that "interference" takes various forms and the more subtle ones, those that depend on one's social and personal standing with respect to others, are just as critical for freedom – if not more – than the relatively transparent ones. A theory of freedom that ignores the dynamics of social power and control is impoverished. Among other things, it cannot account for how domination *damages* the dominated by destabilizing their capacity for self-formation and condemning them to lives of "eternal discretion," which is to say lives where the dominator's norms are the standard for being and doing. The corollary of Pettit's ideal of freedom as nondomination is that a person can lack freedom even if no one directly "interferes." The "success" of (subtle and not so subtle) forms of social control that characterize dominator–dominated relationships depends precisely on the dominated becoming their own monitors, whether for literal or metaphorical survival within those relationships.

The ideal of freedom as nondomination has an illustrious historical pedigree, going back to the Roman tradition of "republican" thought.[28] In the eighteenth century, it was gradually replaced by the ideal of noninterference, which can be explained at least in part by a growing concern with expanding traditionally restrictive categories of political participation. Yet the notion of freedom as nondomination did not altogether vanish at this point in time: Mill and many of his progressive contemporaries themselves revived the concept in an effort to analyze the lot of subject classes, especially women and other economically dependent or dispossessed groups.[29] Those of our contemporaries who, like Pettit, believe that we ought to revitalize this way of understanding freedom must look back to Mill's political thought as a source both of insight and of inspiration. In fact, a conscious reappropriation of Mill's keen understanding of despotism and of the dynamics of domination would lend substance and appeal to contemporary reconceptualizations of freedom. The point of the reappropriation would not be merely to acknowledge an often unacknowledged intellectual debt, although it certainly would do that much. Rather, the point would be to enrich our own thinking about freedom by keeping our attention focused on the social conditions for its possibility.

The Enduring Relevance of Mill's Feminism

It should be evident by now that Mill was far from a timid reformist. Because Mill *was* a social reformer – and an active one throughout his life[30] – he paid special attention to the state of the law and other "public" institutions affecting women's lives. However, he understood well that laws derive their content from, and compel allegiance in virtue of, a broader social ethic. For Mill, this ethic is the real culprit, and, consequently, *it* must be exposed, crushed, and replaced. Even if forthcoming, changes in the law will not by themselves eradicate problems of domination until the social ethic that underlies and sustains them is overhauled. To this day, laws against domestic violence, stranger and intimate partner rape, and child abuse have failed to eliminate the terrifyingly widespread incidence of these practices

---

[28] For a development of this idea, see, for example, Pettit 2001, and also Urbinati 2002, chap. 5.

[29] See, for example, William Thompson and Anna Wheeler's *Appeal of One Half of the Human Race, Women*, with which Mill was familiar (Morales 1996, chap. 1). Arguably, Bentham should be included in the list of progressive thinkers on the centrality of nondomination for a good (utilitarian) society. See, for example, Campos Boralevi 1987.

[30] On Mill as an active social reformer throughout his life, see Shanley 1981 and Morales 1996.

of sexual domination. One hundred and forty-five years after Mill wrote on this topic, domestic violence continues to be endemic. In the United States, for example,[31] it is the leading cause of injury to women. According to the American Institute on Domestic Violence,[32] 85 to 95 percent of all domestic violence victims are female; 4.5 million women are physically assaulted every year; 1,232 women are killed each year by an intimate partner; and more than 500,000 women are stalked yearly by an intimate partner. The National Center for Injury Prevention and Control[33] (NCIPC) offers consistently horrifying statistics: nearly 5.3 million intimate partner victimizations occur each year among U.S. women aged eighteen and older, and this violence results in nearly 2 million injuries and nearly 1,300 deaths. In addition, nearly 25 percent of women have been raped or physically assaulted by an intimate partner at some point in their lives, and more than 40% of the women who experience partner rapes and physical assaults sustain a physical injury. Finally, according to the NCIPC, intimate partner violence accounts for 20 percent of all nonfatal violent crime experienced by women. When fatal, 44 percent of women murdered by their intimate partner had visited an emergency department within two years of the homicide, and 93 percent of those women had at least one prior injury visit. It is revealing that among other contributing factors to the perpetration of intimate partner violence, the NCIPC cites "male dominance in the family," "strong patriarchal relationship or family environment," "belief in strict gender roles," and "desire for power and control in relationships;" it also cites "societal norms that support male superiority and sexual entitlement."[34]

The figures for rape, which is still the least reported of violent crimes, are no less ghastly: the National Violence Against Women Survey[35] estimated that 302,000 women were raped in the twelve months before the survey administration in 2000 and that victims often experienced more than one rape during that period. The same survey found that one in six women in the United States has experienced an attempted or completed rape at some time

---

[31] For UK current statistics, see www.cwasu.org, the Web site of the London Metropolitan University, Child and Women Abuse Studies Unit, which offers up-to-date information on domestic violence, femicide and homicide in the context of domestic violence, rape, and sexual assault. This site also has links to international data. For international data, see also Krug, Dahlberg, Mercy, Zwi, and Lozano, 2004, available at www.who.int/violence_injury_prevention/violence/world_report/wrvh1/en.

[32] See www.aidv-usa.com and Department of Justice 2002.

[33] See www.cdc.gov/ncip.

[34] See www.cdc.gov/ncip, "Sexual Violence Facts."

[35] See Tjaden and Thoennes 2000.

in her life and that in eight of ten cases the victim knows the perpetrator. (A parallel study estimated that between one in four college women experienced an attempted or completed rape during her college years.) In addition, the incidence of wife rape is much higher than that of stranger rape. According to the Wellesley Centers for Women,[36] a recent survey in the United States found that 10 percent of all sexual assaults reported by women involved a husband (or ex-husband). This figure must be considered a low estimate, because many women are still less likely to label nonconsensual sex with a husband as "rape" than nonconsensual sex with a stranger. The practice is still often condoned on the grounds that having sex with a husband (or ex-husband) at least once "implies" the wife's "consent" to future sexual acts. Stereotypes about women and sex – for example, that women say "no" when they really mean "yes," that it is a wife's "duty" to have sex with her husband – continue to be socially reinforced through public opinion and mainstream and pornographic media. These messages encourage men to believe that they can (or should) ignore a woman's protests and mislead women into believing that they must have sent "the wrong signals" or that they are "bad wives" for not being readily available sexually to their husbands even against their own desires. Both national surveys and projects such as the Wellesley Centers find that researchers who have spoken to husband-rapists conclude that they rape "to reinforce their power, dominance or control over their wife, or to express anger." Thus, in this area also, it is recognized that a patriarchal sexual ethic shapes attitudes and practices obviously harmful (to put it mildly) to women.

These "public" statistics paint an abysmal picture. However, the reality of women's lives would be much worse in the absence of laws criminalizing male violence in the domestic sphere. That is the reality that Mill confronted in nineteenth-century England. He was not wrong to think that the existence of laws and other social mechanisms for the protection and aid of victims of domestic and sexual violence would at least ameliorate their lot and lend formal recognition to the appalling reality within which many women's and children's lives are embedded under patriarchy. It is unfair to criticize Mill for having been "overly" concerned with the state of the law, when, at the time of his writing and activism on behalf of women, the law imposed constraints on women's lives that are almost inconceivable from our perspective today. Even in the 1860s, Mill recognized the need to change much more than the law if women's real freedom was ever to become a reality rather than a

---

[36] See www.wellesley.edu/wcw/projects/mrape/html. See also Kilpatrick, Edmunds, and Seymour, 1992.

utopian dream. Moreover, unlike most thinkers in the liberal tradition, past or present, Mill grasped that "women's disabilities" in the "public" realm are "clung to" to maintain their domestic subordination (CW XXI: 299) and that bridging the chasm between "public" and "private" life is vital to *women's* lives. Mill knew that it is unreasonable to suppose that "private" despots will be "public" democrats – hence his insistence that the whole process whereby males are socialized as despots must be changed radically. He also appreciated that the social construction of women's "nature" as sexual would get in the way of their "public" agency – hence his commitment to free women from the patriarchal sexual ethic.

Christine di Stefano has argued that to make room for women in the "public" sphere, Mill had to fashion them as men: "[w]omen must be disembodied, desexed, degendered, and made over into the image of middle-class and upper-class men if they are to benefit from the promises of rational liberalism" (di Stefano 1991, 176). This claim is problematic for at least two reasons. First, Mill did not believe that women should be fashioned into men but rather that they should be free to fashion themselves into *subjects*. Did he assume a male norm for subjecthood? We can answer this question with another: *Why would he?* If under patriarchy men as a norm are as Mill depicted them – arrogant, selfish, narcissistic, self-seeking, overbearing, insensitive, and often brutal – why would he recommend that women become like *them?* Moreover, if in his view these "vices of despotism" impede not only healthy and life-affirming relations between women and men but also the possibility of forming well-constituted social and political communities, why would he recommend that men continue to indulge in them and that women join in? If anything, from a Millian perspective, women ought to be careful *not* to become like patriarchal men and mindful *not* to become despots themselves.

In the second place, di Stefano criticizes the view she attributes to Mill that women's "public" life would require them to become "disembodied, desexed, and degendered." Because this claim is part of what I take her to mean by "becoming like men," the idea is that women must be disembodied, desexed, and degendered *as women*. Although Mill never put it quite in these terms, I think di Stefano is right to attribute this view to him, yet wrong in her interpretation of what it means. I cannot do justice here to this large and important topic. Very generally, my view is that Mill, like many contemporary radical feminists, worried deeply about the identification of women with their bodies and their sex/gender. To the extent that, as I have argued here, he regarded this identification as a critical impediment to women's emancipation, he would have advocated that women become "disembodied" and "de-sex/gendered." Yet this radical transformation would not be so that women can become like *men*, but rather so that women can become free from the constraints that being gendered *woman* imposes. The freedom that Mill sought for women is not the "freedom" that being gendered *man* would entail, but rather the freedom to live *beyond* gender – a freedom that would liberate men as well. Granted, Mill did not know what a world without gender would be like nor what "women" and "men" would be when "de-gendered" – and he recognized this (CW XXI: 277–8, 313). Yet *we* do not know either: although we live in a world where (many) women are dramatically freer than nineteenth-century women ever could have dreamed of becoming, we are not even close to living in a world without gender. Whatever else life without gender would be like for women, it *would* be a life free of their identification with the body *as* sex/gendered *woman*.

The concerns that I take to be central to Mill's feminism – namely, concerns with the patriarchal sexual ethic in social and personal life, show the enduring relevance of his feminist vision. It would probably not have come as a surprise to Mill that the "radical" elements of his vision have been relatively disregarded or their importance and urgency downplayed. Mill's spirited struggle to bring intellectual respectability to feminism and to implement its liberating potential, alas, quite closely mirrors much contemporary feminist theory and practice. As we celebrate the bicentennial of this remarkable philosopher's birth, we should reflect on this reality so that we might come not only to appreciate the lasting value of Mill's feminism but also to scrutinize our own.

3

The Many Heads of the Hydra

J. S. Mill on Despotism

Nadia Urbinati

"But (however it be with pain in general) the abolition of the infliction of pain by the mere will of a human being, the abolition, in short, of despotism, seems to be, in a peculiar degree, the occupation of this age; and it would be difficult to show that any age had undertaken a worthier. Though we cannot extirpate all pain, we can, if we are sufficient determined upon it, abolish all tyranny: one of the greatest victories yet gained over that enemy is slave-emancipation, and all Europe is struggling, with various success, towards further conquest over it."

> J. S. Mill, "The Negro Question," 1850, CW XXI: 95

"The attempt to establish freedom by foreign bayonets is a solecism in terms. A government which requires the support of foreign armies cannot be a free government."

> J. S. Mill, "The Spanish Question" [July 1837] CW XXXI: 374.

Liberty and despotism, an inverse pair, have configured Western civilization since its Mediterranean inception, troubling its major political thinkers from Herodotus and Aristotle to Montesquieu and Tocqueville. Although liberty has won many battles, despotism has never disappeared but has mutated to preserve itself. Such mutations demand analysis. Modern usage has emptied the term "despotism" of its classical meaning by making it synonym for tyranny, autocracy, dictatorship, authoritarianism, and absolutism. In recent decades, totalitarianism has almost replaced it completely.[1] Finally, liberalism's global victory over totalitarianism has rendered the nonliberal regime a temporary condition along the fatal march towards democracy. Like despotism, the term "nonliberal authoritarian regimes" conjures up a homogeneous and vague reality apparently embodied by all non-Western undemocratic states; unlike despotism, however, the term lacks the conceptual

---

[1] Per effect of totalitarianism, "older words like dictatorship, tyranny, and despotism seemed well short of descriptive or conceptual mark" (Katznelson 2003, 24–5).

I thank Alex Zakaras from whose excellent comments I profited greatly.

precision of a working category, its meaning being essentially negative, or what is not. Yet democratic theorists have at least two valid reasons to revisit the concept of despotism. First of all, the term's semantic richness can provide workable guidelines for analyzing regimes that escape the Western model of good government although may not be unstable and illegitimate (like tyranny), absolutely unreformable and criminal (like totalitarianism), or transient exceptions (like dictatorship). Furthermore, the concept of despotism can be used to highlight the presence of areas of subjection within consolidated democracies, such as stubborn old inequalities or new forms of domination incubated by modern society itself. John Stuart Mill's writings offer a seminal contribution on both counts.

The category of despotism played two fundamental roles in Mill's writings, one descriptive and the other normative. As an epistemic tool, it allowed him to explain some specific institutions and decode processes of emotion and identity formation: this made his study of the patriarchal family a masterpiece of social and behavioral analysis. As an evaluative concept, it allowed him to denounce conditions of domination in vivid and powerful rhetoric so as to exhort lawmakers to promote political reforms and citizens to vindicate and support them (which is why *On Liberty* is a political manifesto and *The Subjection of Women* is the blueprint of a social movement and a legislative platform).

Furthermore, Mill used the concept of despotism in a way that was both classical and innovative. It was classical because he associated it with the occurrence of the absolute discretion of the will of those who exercise command and the absolute exclusion of the subjects from participation in both the formulation of decisions and their post factum evaluation.[2] A despotic decision was modeled on a domestic form of authority; its outcome was the dominant "preference" as opposed to the law (*The Subjection of Women*, CW XXI: 269). His approach was innovative because Mill used it to denounce abusive power relations in modern social domains that the ancients had seen as natural (and legitimate) sites of despotism. Mill politicized human relations in areas that were not traditionally subjected to public scrutiny, such as the workplace and the family, and he also uncovered new forms of domination in modern politics and society.

Finally, Mill used despotism as a heuristic concept or an *a contrario* introduction to liberty. This made his theories of liberty and representative

---

[2] On the basis of those very same premises, Kant presented despotism as a private kind of power because it was held directly (will-to-will) whereas political power should be held indirectly (law-to-behavior) (Kant 1991 §§ 47, 49, 51).

government extraordinarily rich and complex in that their goals were liberal but their structures of argumentation were republican and democratic. Mill did not reduce individual freedom to negative liberty alone but enriched it to a state of freedom from subjection. And he considered representative government not just a matter of institutional engineering but as the site of deliberative politics and a school of a constitutional ethos whose cornerstone was the sovereignty of individual judgment.

Mill reveals his theoretical perspective in his use of the Hydra metaphor to describe despotism because he believed despotism could adapt to the environment and change its appearance so as not to be seen or felt as arbitrary. Despotism can disguise itself within social practices that appear to be based on consent while actually denying individual freedom. Depending on the circumstances, it can take the classical form of direct imposition of the will of the master (as in the factory and the patriarchal family) or the modern form of "tyranny not over the body, but over the mind" perpetrated by public opinion in a democratic society (*On Liberty*, CW XVIII: 178). Thus, in *On Liberty*, Mill defined public opinion as despotic (*the despotism of custom*) when it forced people holding minority beliefs or living eccentric lifestyles either to conform to the values and manners of the majority or to hide them to avoid public discredit or stigmatization; despotism consisted, in part, of docile and conformist habits of mind, ubiquitous and common to liberal societies. In *Considerations on Representative Government*, Mill describes a regime as despotic (*pedantocracy*) when bureaucratic structures and regulatory practices do more than administer and regulate, thereby narrowing the domain of political deliberation and depressing public freedom. Finally, in *The Subjection of Women* and his writings on the condition of the working classes, Mill explains how despotic social relations manipulate the perceptions women and men have of their interests, power, identity, and responsibilities, and render them resigned recipients of an authority that acts in its own interests at the expense of the good of its subjects. These differences notwithstanding, the outcome is always the same: weakened self-reliance and the formation of individuals who long for others' approval and recognition to the point of becoming mentally dependent subjects afraid to choose and act independently.

Such criticism also pervades Mill's writings on "paternal despotism" in non-European countries. With regard to colonized peoples, he reworked the concept of Asian despotism along the lines of its eighteenth-century formulation and made paternal despotism into a preparatory stage for national self-determination. Like the *philosophes,* Mill set up an ad hoc connection between despotism and constitutional government by seeing the former as a short-term expedient and latter as a long-term process and goal.[3] Although this aspect of his thought has received little analytical attention, it has been harshly criticized. Apparently there is nothing to add to the fact that whereas he vigorously promoted liberalism at home, he justified despotism abroad in "backward states of society" (CW XVIII: 224).

My intention is neither to exculpate nor to condemn. Rather, I would like to explore the multiple uses Mill made of despotism to illuminate a relevant aspect of his work and retrieve a critical tool of social and political analysis from oblivion. The category of despotism can be used to track the genealogy of his philosophy of freedom, understand its richness, and grasp its political implications and power. Mill's concern with pedantocracy in representative government illuminated his theory of politics as deliberative practice. His abhorrence of individual surrender to shared public morality was an important step toward his ideal of Socratic self-scrutiny as a political virtue modern citizens need to cultivate. His concern about the despotisms of marriage and capitalism provided an impetus for the social reforms he regarded as essential for the establishment and consolidation of modern democracy. Finally, his positive evaluation of paternal despotism in colonized countries contained implicit reflections on the preconditions of democracy and the politics of transition to self-government that are not wholly outdated and are not reducible to the justification of imperialism.

Tyranny and Despotism, Ancient and Modern

To grasp Mill's contribution to the study of despotism, we must draw a brief conceptual profile of this category and its main transformations. The word despotism comes from the Greek *despotes*, "slave master," and means mastership behind domestic walls and absolute rule. Ancient Greeks did not view it as completely negative, although they conceived it in opposition to politics (*oikonomía* was the realm of *despoteía*; *politikè* was the realm of *basilikè*). In cases where a king acted as a despot-like ruler, his undisputed authority led them to believe that either arbitrary rule was exceptional (tyranny) or that it implied a people of servile character (despotism). Indeed, because absolute power entails the use of force, it could hardly endure for long or be imposed

---

[3] For an excellent analysis of the connection between despotism and constitutionalism along temporal lines wherein the former was like a "preliminary to the realization of representative constitution in an enlightened age," see Krieger 1975, 67.

on a large number of people by brute force alone.[4] For longevity, despotism requires emotional and psychological interpersonal relations (hence its domestic nature) that are somehow accepted by its subalterns. This perspective enabled Mill to detect patriarchalism in family relations: men's despotic domination could endure because it made women its allies, treating them as favorites rather than slaves (*The Subjection of Women*, CW XXI: 268–71). But this also explained his hostility toward promoting "native despotism" in colonized countries, as we shall see later.

Because despotism could not exist without some kind of compliance by the ruled, the crucial issue was whether subjected people were naturally predisposed to subjection or were trained to become so – in a word, whether despotism was permanent or temporary, a means to an end or an end in itself. This was where classical and modern theories of despotism parted company, because whereas the former were essentially inegalitarian, the latter were not. According to Aristotle, there were circumstances in which despotism (and slavery) was "natural" (slaves and masters "qualified by nature for those positions") and circumstances in which it was against nature or the outcome of artificial constraints imposed on free people. The former applied only to non-Greek peoples whose docility made them naturally disposed to obey as slaves.[5] The latter, although they could also be found in Greek polities, were arbitrary violations of Greeks' naturally free status: only in this case could despotism be confused with tyranny and result in a thoroughly arbitrary regime. In sum, whereas despotism was or could be "advantageous for a part and for the whole" for non-Greek (read: unfree) peoples, it was totally harmful for naturally free peoples because it served only the good of the ruler.

This distinguishes despotism from tyranny, despite the fact that in both cases the ruler acts with complete discretion. Furthermore, it explains why, as we will see in Mill's analysis of women's subjection, despotism does not manifest itself through brute force and why it cannot be ended quickly. A tyrannical regime does not entail a tyrannical society because opposition from below, although violently crushed and suffocated, never sleeps. Hence tyranny, unlike despotism, can never be stable or enduring. This is why

---

[4] "Now, by physical force alone a man can dominate children, old men, and some women, at the outside two or three adults, but he cannot in this way impose himself for long on a group of able-bodied men, however small it may be." Hence, to succeed, despotic power needs to exploit people's fear of death and transform the entire collectivity into a prison. "For even nowadays, no one criticizes the governing of children or criminals or madmen by force" (Kojève 2000, 144).

[5] "It is manifest therefore that there are cases of people of whom some are freemen and the others slaves by nature, and of these slavery is an institution both expedient and just" (Aristotle 1995, 27).

we have words to designate the murder of the tyrant (tyrannicide) and the absolute monarch (regicide), but no word to denote the killing of the despot.[6] Much more perverse than a tyrant, the despot induces his subjects to transfer to him their freedom to make choices; he will eventually be seen as a source of tutelage rather than coercion, of love rather than terror. As a result, a condition of total or quasi-total surrender and pacification defines a despotic condition as one of "complete abnegation." So whereas tyranny produces a bipolar situation (we tend to disassociate the people from their illegitimate ruler and feel solidarity toward the former against the latter), despotism is more intriguing. So much so that the ancients believed that it could only succeed if a people were somehow fit for it or culturally disposed to accept obedience without formal guarantees of control.

The theory of despotism split apart in the eighteenth century.[7] On one hand, Aristotle's idea that despotic rule could prove "good" in domestic governance was applied to European societies as well and associated with administrative efficiency in new domains such as social planning, infrastructure, market regulation, civil legislation, and demographic policies for vast geopolitical spaces. On the other, despotism was reconceptualized and identified with total and totalizing power. The Physiocrats epitomized the former orientation, Montesquieu the latter. Both of them are crucial for an understanding of the place and character of despotism in Mill's political thought.

The Physiocrats, who developed the concept of *despotisme éclairé*, thought of it as rational "tutelage" ("tutelary authority") in a developing society and a necessary first step to implementing the natural law of wealth and profit and creating a class of skillful bureaucrats. Enlightened despotism was an efficient regime for European society that foreshadowed the time when state authority would diminish (Bluche 1968, 339; Krieger 1975, 63–82; Kurtfirst 1996). Like Aristotle's "natural" and "arbitrary" despotism, "legal" or good despotism was opposed to "arbitrary" or bad despotism.[8] It denoted a "rationalist"

---

[6] Mill expressed his admiration for the killer of the tyrant, "a persecuted patriot, a hero and a martyr" on more than one occasion ("Catilina's Conspiracy," CW XXVI: 343).

[7] According to historians, Louis XIV absolutism was a turning point in the theory of despotism, when the policies of economic expropriation by absolute monarchs made kingship into a total regime incorporating both society and the state, thereby distinguishing it from mere tyranny (Andrews 1967, 179–85). Mill agreed with this interpretation ("Writings of Alfred de Vigny," CW I: 472–3).

[8] Despotism was "legal" or legitimate if and when the king's edicts were like secondary causes or "subjected *without variation* to laws from which they cannot depart," and the king was like the authoritative executive of laws that nature and reason, not he, had made (Koebner 1951; Venturi 1960). The engineer, not a capricious prince, was the model of the good despot as the implementer of the dictates of truth's irresistible force.

philosophy and made politics a matter of "solutions" and "technique." The promotion of the general interest was the main goal of this managerial view of politics, the first consistent expression of utilitarianism applied to government (Parry 1967, 11–12; Bluche 1968, 316–23). Bentham's model of good government, the social planning dreamed of by the Saint-Simonians, and the later variants of state socialism were branches of this eighteenth-century utopia that Tocqueville correctly perceived as a metamorphosis of despotism in an age marked by the passion of equality and economic well-being. As we shall see, *despotisme éclairé* provided the theoretical background that allowed Mill to conceive of "paternal despotism" in premodern Europe and non-European countries as competent and rational "administrative realism" rather than a political government in its own right. But it was also the insight that led him to detect a new form of despotism within Western societies as a result of the increasing power of the executive and the expansion of administrative functions ("Notes on the Newspapers," CW VI: 216; "Catiline's Conspiracy," CW XXVI: 347).

The Spirit of the Laws painted a different picture. For a start, Montesquieu delegitimized all forms of slavery and described slavery as a plague that "makes one man so much the owner of another man that he is the absolute master of his life and of his goods" (Montesquieu, *The Spirit of the Laws*, bk. 15, chap. 1).[9] Furthermore, he turned the traditional theory of the forms of government upside down. Indeed, on one hand, he systematized the category of oriental despotism by exiling political despotism from Christian Europe but not from Europe as a whole. (Like David Hume and Edward Gibbon, Montesquieu located the European origins of military despotism in the late Roman Empire and its transformation in "a military and civil [read: bureaucratic] despotism" under Constantine; Montesquieu, *The Spirit of the Laws*, bk. 6, chap. 15.[10]) On the other hand, Montesquieu improved on Aristotle's definition and depicted despotism as a comprehensive regime, carefully describing its institutional and bureaucratic organization, geographic, and climatic factors. He characterized it as a system based on fear, a depressing passion that paralyzed action and eroded all energy for resistance and rebellion, improvement and development. Despotism perpetuated itself

---

[9] Montesquieu argued in this way against Grotius and Puffendorf who thought the voluntary selling of oneself into slavery was legitimate, and against Locke who justified slavery that was a result of conquest.

[10] Mill made similar references to "Roman despotism" when he argued that it could neutralize internal conflicts and insecurity but could not guarantee to protect subjects against itself, hence the economic impoverishment and eventual deterioration of its populations (*The Principles of Political Economy*, CW II: 114).

by means of apathy, passivity, resignation, and stagnation, which were also its end-products.

Like Aristotle, Montesquieu believed that the people's character was a powerful factor, but unlike Aristotle, he did not regard it as completely natural. Although Montesquieu thought that European countries were endowed with traditions (social pluralism) and mores (sense of honor and virtue) that were natural impediments to despotic domination, he left the door open to the possibility that despotism could arise in the West as a result of the leveling effect instilled by the desire for economic progress and social equality. Despotism, Aristotle had pointed out, is accepted by its subjects. Despotism's acceptance, Montesquieu added, can be created artificially. "Men grow accustomed to anything, even to servitude, provided the master is not harsher than the servitude" (Montesquieu, *The Spirit of the Laws*, bk. 15, chap. 16).

Montesquieu's persuasive and totalizing depiction provided thinkers in the post-Napoleonic age with an invaluable blueprint that enabled them to detect the potential for despotism within modern European societies (Constant [1814] 1988, 114–15).[11] Along these same lines, in a comment on Tocqueville's first volume of *Democracy in America*, Mill wrote that in a Europe then in transition to democracy, the "universal aim, therefore, should be, so to prepare the way for democracy, that when it comes, it may come in this beneficial shape; not only for the sake of the good we have to expect from it, but because it is literally our only refuge from a despotism resembling not the temperate and regulated absolutism of modern times, but the tyranny of the Caesars"; that is, Fascism and the forms of mass despotism that twentieth-century Europe knew all too well ("De Tocqueville on Democracy in America [I]", CW XVIII: 57).

To conclude, the moderns thought that despotism, like its opposite, liberty, could be ubiquitous, as well as shaped and stabilized through a sort of consensus. By the same token, however, it could also be subverted, opposed, and even directed toward a liberal end. The meaning of this universal and artificial (nonnatural) perspective changed even further because

---

[11] Following Ernst Cassiser, Louis Althusser wrote that Montesquieu did not regard totality as the characteristic of despotism alone, but created the universal category of "regime" (the State) as totality (unity of nature-principle) whether in the form of republic-virtue, monarchy-honor or despotism-fear) (Althusser 1972, 41–53). Interpretations of despotism reflect the interpretation of the notion of the norm in Montesquieu's work, as either as an expression of scientific determination of what it is or an expression of moral determination of what should be. The author of *The Spirit of the Laws* can be pulled, as it were, on the side of Marx or of Condorcet-Mill; the interpretations are not unanimous (see for instance Schackleton 1961, 251; Richter 1977, 20; Manent 1994, 55).

pre-Montesquieu despotism was associated with paternal domination in the private sphere, but in the wake of his writings, despotism became politically charged. In any event, despotism was withdrawn from the domain of nature and placed squarely in the realm of politics. Along with the teachings of the Physiocrats, this set the theoretical premise of Mill's conception of despotic rule in non-European societies.

Colonizers and Colonized and the Idea of a Limited Despotism

Eurocentrism and Occidentalism are deeply rooted ideologies in Western political culture, whether in the form of the self-appointed ambition to direct global emancipation or the complacent acceptance of the "backwardness" of the non-Westerns. Bringing Christian salvation or the "rights of the man and the citizen" to people who still live in darkness is the other side of the coin of a worldview that deems non-European cultural heritages an impediment to progress or, alternatively, a justification for either leading "backward" peoples along the road of history or making them the servants of the dominant race in the hope that they learn from their masters how to walk the difficult path of freedom. Distinguished nineteenth-century liberals, democrats, and revolutionaries justified colonialism as a painful but necessary school of modernization or self-government (or both) (Wittfogel 1957; Harris 1964). Mill was no exception.

There is a consensus that Mill added little to the eighteenth-century belief in the utility of enlightened despotism and, moreover, that he believed it applied only to non-European peoples, because Europeans had achieved political self-determination through their own efforts. Moreover, whereas the Physiocrats' thoroughly utilitarian and instrumental view of politics explained their benign acceptance of despotism, Mill's belief in the viability of "paternal despotism" directly contradicted his theory of the "sovereignty of the individual" and seemed to have no reasonable justification other than his racist prejudice concerning the superiority of European (read English) culture (Mazlish 1975, 407; Parekh 1995, 53; Mehta 1999, 15; Pitts 2005, 146–50). Mill has been criticized by liberals and identified as a forerunner of the imperialism of Disraeli and Chamberlain since he transformed the liberal tradition of the British Empire, which was "primarily anti-imperialist," into a liberal defense of English imperialism.[12] It would be anachronistic

---

[12] The expression "paternal despotism" was used by his friend George Grote to describe the regime of the Arcons in ancient Athens, before the democratic revolution of Cleisthenes; it meant "censorship of expression" and dependence of the demos on the judgment of the best few (Grote 1906, VI, 1–48).

to try to salvage Mill from his ideological narrowness. However, it is no less anachronistic and wrong to reduce his philosophy of liberalism to the dualism between oriental stagnation and England's civilizing mission.[13]

When it came to foreign politics, Mill acknowledged the empirical fact that countries ruled by representative institutions exercised domination over colonized peoples that earlier nonrepresentative (read: unfree) regimes had subdued. However, he categorically denied that a country ruled by representative government could legitimately conquer and colonize (CW XIX: 562–3). In chapter 18 of *Considerations on Representative Government,* he distinguished three kinds of relations between a "free country" and its existing colonies: military servitude (like Gibraltar); equal representation or confederation (like Canada and Australia, which were "composed of people of similar civilization to the ruling country"); and paternal despotism (with people who, like the Indians, were "still at a great [cultural] distance" from the "ruling country") (CW XIX: 563–7).[14] Hence, while he blamed colonialism as a "vicious theory" and a policy "once common to all Europe, and not yet completely relinquished," he thought that colonies of non-European "race" were not yet "capable of, and ripe for" representative institutions, and

---

[13] Adam Smith, Jeremy Bentham, and James Mill himself did not believe that colonies benefited English society (Sullivan 1983). James Mill has recently been appreciated as a critic of British colonialism (Pitts, 123–33); however, although he might have thought that colonial domination was not an economic benefit for his country, the elder Mill judged Indian culture much more harshly than his son (and Bentham) and thought it would be better to Anglicize it rather than translate liberal values into "vernacular," to use J. S. Mill's apt expression (CW XVII: 1970, fn. 3). Finally, because James Mill regarded the nation as a prejudice and moreover an irrelevant factor in politics, he deemed the idea that a government was illegitimate or bad because "in the hands of foreigner" a bias (James Mill 1858, II: 342). He believed that the measure of political legitimacy was utility, not self-government. As a result, he thought the issue of Indian emancipation from colonialism was wrongly posed because utilitarian legislation was a liberating force no matter who implemented it (Majeed 1992, 131, 145–7; Zastoupil 1999, 111–48).

[14] The second case comprised those colonies that Bentham thought of as "ripe for self-government;" these colonies (*not* all colonies) were the object of his call for political autonomy. Yet in his address "Emancipate Your Colonies!" to the French National Convention in January 1793, he advised the French to grant emancipation to their colonies in the West Indies but not to give their colonies in India back to the Indians themselves because, once left to their own native princes, they would inevitably be ruled by despots. In contrast to the situation in the well-established Europeanized colonies, it was not in the interest of the Indians if they governed themselves: "whatever applies to the West Indies, applies to the East with double force. The islands present no difficulty: the population there is French: they are ripe for self-government. There remains the continent: you know how things are changed there: – the power of Tippoo is no more. Would the tree of liberty grow there, if planted? Would the declaration of rights translate into Shanscrit? Would *Bramin, Chetree, Bice, Sooder,* and *Hallachore* meet on equal ground? If not, you may find some difficulty in giving them to themselves" (Bentham, Works, IV: 417). See Mill, CW XXX: 201; Majeed 1992, 123–7.

agreed with Bentham that "a lawgiver, who having been bred up with English notions, shall have learnt how to accommodate his laws to the circumstances of Bengal" (Bentham [1793] *Works* I, 172).

Mill identified two forms of political authority: liberal and nonliberal. His approach to the latter was paternalistic; he thought paternalism should be a temporary expedient and be judged in relation to its goal. As I shall explain in the penultimate section, John Locke's parental authority, which emphasized the future autonomy of the subjected, not the rulers' benefit, was Mill's model for despotic power in colonized countries. As with class relations in British society, Mill located paternalism within a teleology of self-dependence (*The Principles of Political Economy,* CW III: 763). In any event, the transition from mere security to an autonomous security was a universal one in terms of individual development. In this sense, Mill's view of paternal despotism in non-European countries was not racist: all humans had the right to become an independent person or independent peoples by virtue of their being human (Donner 1991, 169–72). "Modern nations will have to learn the lesson that the well-being of a people must exist by means of justice and self-government, *dikaiosúne* and *sophrosúne*, of the individual citizen" (CW III: 763).

The relationship he posed between liberal and nonliberal regimes is reminiscent of John Rawls's: both presume an asymmetrical relationship between the two types of regime and assign liberalism a universalistic character. Neither of them raises the problem of whether nonliberal states would accept the principles set up by advanced liberal states. Their concern is "to specify how far liberal peoples are to tolerate non-liberal peoples" and how they should help them to progress toward a liberal state.[15] In both cases, nonliberal peoples are seen as recipients rather than full creators of their liberal destiny insofar as they do not participate in defining the liberal principles, although they are expected to actively contribute to their implementation (Fabre and Miller 2003, 13–14). This explains why Mill approached the problem of the "transition" of non-Western countries to liberal government as a foreign policy issue for Western countries, either because the latter's political order was a model for all peoples or because they were given an active political role in "facilitat[ing] their [non-Western peoples'] transition to a higher stage of improvement" (CW XIX: 567). Liberalism was the norm for both Mill and Rawls (*On Liberty* and *A Theory of Justice*) while "decent non-liberalism" or "paternal despotism" was the contextual variation the norm

---

[15] "This indicates that non-liberal peoples will not be granted the same consideration as liberal peoples in the creation of such a law of peoples" (Butler 2001, 7).

allowed (*Considerations on Representative Government* and *Political Liberalism* and *The Law of Peoples*) beyond which authoritarianism or despotism becomes simply unacceptable. Good and bad despotism imply good and bad colonialism. Mill ascribed two moral duties to the colonizing country, one toward the colonized peoples and one toward its own people: rendering the former "capable of a higher civilization" through "a vigorous despotism" (CW XIX: 567) and freeing the latter of a plague (colonialism) they had inherited from previous nonliberal governments. Bad colonialism was rapacious despotism or "plantocracy," which was how he referred to the "most disrupting European influence in Bengal and Bihar" (Peers 1999, 213).

Despotism could be paternalistic or decent under two conditions: first, that the despotic domination was *not* held by the political government of the colonizing country; second, that the despotic domination was *not* exercised by the natives. In both cases, *political* despotism was banned.

In the spirit of the Aristotelian conception of politics and the Physiocrats' enlightened despotism, Mill confined paternal despotism to managerial rule (I shall explain in the next section why he thought that management was a denial of politics). In contemporary language, we might say that he treated it as governance, not government. Ignoring this crucial point, scholars have rushed to the conclusion that Mill was a theorist of imperialism. Yet he radically opposed direct domination by the government of the colonizing country, a solution that would indeed translate into imperialism. "To govern a country under responsibility to the people of that country, and to govern one country under responsibility to the people of another, are two very different things. What makes the excellence of the first is that freedom is preferable to despotism: but the last is despotism. The only choice the case admits, is a choice of despotism: and it is not certain that the despotism of twenty millions is necessarily better than that of a few, or of one" (CW XIX: 568).

Political despotism or the direct rule of the colony by the political branches of the colonizing country would hinder toleration and local government policy making, both of which were fundamental to the formation of a liberal society and an autonomous political class in the colony. Indeed, on the one hand, it would in all probability interfere with domains of life that demanded respect, if no harm was being committed, in the area of popular traditions and religious beliefs (Mill doubted that the government of a Christian country would be as tolerant of non-Christian subjects as it was of Christian ones).[16] On the other hand, it would centralize its enactments

---

[16] "A free country which attempts to govern a distant dependency, inhabited by a distant people, by means of a branch of its own executive, will almost inevitable fail" and become

and hamper the natives' training in self-government. Political domination by the colonizers would be simply crudely despotic with no beneficial effect on the subjected population since legal and political institutions would be used to exploit the colony for the exclusive good of the rulers rather than as a check on exploitation: "when a country holds another in subjection, the individuals of the ruling people who resort to the foreign country to make their fortunes, are of all others whose who most need to be held under powerful restraint" (CW XIX: 571).[17]

Hence, Mill concluded that to control the colonial administrators and guarantee the rule of law, the political branches should not exercise despotic domination (CW XVII: 1799–80 and 1561). It was thus preferable that only nonpolitical agencies exercised "paternal despotism" and acted as an "intermediary instrument of government." "The only mode which has any chance of tolerable success, is to govern through a delegate body, of a comparatively permanent character; allowing only a right of inspection, and a negative choice, to the changeable Administration of the State" (CW XIX: 573). This is how he justified the East India Company's rule in India as a well-designed governance of "leading-strings" and criticized the Company's termination (CW XIX: 577). The alternative would have been imperialistic domination by the English people through the political branches of their government, the cabinet and the Parliament, whose priority had indeed to be the good of the English people.

This is perhaps Mill's most important argument about the incompatibility between representative government and colonialism. Because the latter was a subspecies of despotism, either it was held by a private (as nondirectly governmental) kind of potentate for a short-term period or could not be legitimately held at all.[18] Even if this argument can be rightly seen as

---

a "tyrant" that forces "English ideas down the throats of the natives; for instance by means of proselytism, or acts intentionally or unintentionally offensive to the religious feelings of the people.... In other respects, its interferences likely to be oftenest exercised where it will be most pertinaciously demanded, and that is, on behalf of some interest of the English settlers" (CW XIX: 570–3).

[17] He agreed with Bentham that direct domination by a free government would be even more oppressive than domination by an absolute monarch: "Greater precautions are requisite to protect the subjects in a conquered country, or under an absolute government, than among the citizens of a free state. On the other hand, a conquering republic is more oppressive to the conquered country than a conquering monarch: a monarch may be rapacious; but he is interested in preventing the exactions of his officers: in a republic, on the other hand – in the Senate of Rome, for example – there existed a tacit collusion among those that possessed authority" (Bentham [1793] 1962b, 176).

[18] "The only one which has any chance of tolerable success, is a government through a delegate body, of a comparative permanent character; allowing only a right of inspection,

instrumental to his defense of the rule of the English East India Company (his lifelong employer), it is interesting to note that, although he might have been unaware of it, Mill was making a rough distinction between *colonialism* as capitalist exploitation and *imperialism* as political domination by the government of a capitalist country. It seems to me that Mill was guilty of the former, not the latter.

To understand the connection he made between despotism and constitutionalism, we need to remember the fundamental distinction between state and government: the legal and institutional system of law enforcement and the criteria of power formation and distribution in the lawmaking processes. Mill insisted that liberty could only be protected if it was dependent on political authority: "By security I mean the completeness of the protection which society affords to its members. This consists of protection *by* the government, and protection *against* the government" whereby the latter presumes public officials or a system of checked power not the absence of power (CW II: 112).[19] Although Mill never realized his ambition to create a science that could measure the correct relationship between national culture and political regime, in a Saint-Simonian vein he tried to perfect a rudimentary temporal theory of institutional evolution toward representative government within which "paternal despotism" played the role of an excusable means to discipline a "people in a state of savage independence," an expression he used to mean anarchical refusal to obey the law as well as insecurity in property rights and individual life and liberty (CW XIX: 394–5). Once the colonized people had learned to obey the law, a different form of government was desirable and necessary, one that would allow the subjects to learn "self-government, and this, in its initial stage, means the capacity to act on general instructions" (CW XIX: 395). This too was the function of "paternal despotism" in the societies of Far East Asia as it had been in Middle Age Europe (CW II: 157). "I need scarcely remark that leading-strings are only admissible as a means of gradually training the people to walk alone . . . [A]ny education which aims at making human beings other than machines, in the long run makes them claim to have the control of their

and a negative voice, to the changeable Administration of the State" (CW XIX: 573). A perceptive way to frame a political, not moralistic criticism of modern imperialism has been advanced by Carl Schmitt, who suggested scholars to pay attention to the "countless new governmental forms" that British imperialism took to conform to economic and technical development and associated them to the extension of democracy "within the motherland" (Schmitt 1988, 10).

[19] On the crucial principle that "rights pit power against power" so that "no legal system can defend people against public officials without defending people by means of public officials" see Holmes and Sunstein 1999, 55–8.

own actions" (CW XIX: 396, 403). This brings us to the second condition of good despotism, namely, that it must not result in "native despotism."

"Native despotism" was just as undesirable as the habit of slavish obedience and the masterly domination it engendered. Adapting one of the leading themes of *On Liberty* and *The Subjection of Women* to British India, Mill, like Kant, believed that foreign knowledge could play the positive function of instilling new ideas and breaking the old "chains of habit" so as to stimulate the natives to reflect critically on their traditions, feel new needs, and foster new tastes and ambitions. This is perhaps his most original use of Montesquieu's category of oriental despotism as identical with stagnation and social immobility: the "despotism of custom" was something colonized societies should try to counter if they were to take advantage of foreign domination.

Despotism of custom is not merely an updated version of oriental despotism. It may very well be the common destiny of all societies and therefore a new category altogether, not geographically specific and anthropological in character. As Alex Zakaras argues in this volume, Mill did not see the phenomenon of conformity as unique to democracy or modernity, although "it assumes an especially dangerous form in modern, commercial democracies." Zakaras maintains that conformity is, for Mill, bound up with the inveterate human desire for control over others, adaptation, and human sociality. Our deference to the "common sense" of our peers starts as an "innocent" fact: "we trust our party or church or sect because it is the only world we know" and becomes gradually a source of orthodoxy and mental inertia (see Zakaras, Chapter 8). Encounters with difference can challenge this condition because although they initially make us tighten our hold on our own orthodoxies as a form of self-defense of "what we are," they have the potential to open our minds gradually to self-critical reflection on what we are, think, and believe. Mill advocated commerce and the circulation of Western ideas in non-Western countries over direct despotism by Western governments so that colonized people could begin to develop the habit of criticism necessary for self-government. The principle of "the sovereignty of individual judgment" and the habit of dissent it cultivated were political virtues needed in both European and non-European countries.

Pedantocracy or the Despotic Threat to Modern Democracy

Mill's distinction between administration and politics in the rule of the Indian colony was consistent with the main guidelines of his theory of politics, which was based on the separation between state and government. It was also consistent with the distinction he formulated in *Considerations on Representative Government* between the "deliberative bodies of the entire people" (which he called "democracy" and made the site of politics and the expression of political liberty) and the "work of government" (administration and justice). The political and the nonpolitical differed in two key respects: the kind of "competence" they required and the procedures they implied. The institutions and offices that performed the "work of government" required "skilled persons" with specialized training, an instrumental and impersonal rationality, an apolitical sense of responsibility that was relative to specific tasks, and a disciplined judgment that could follow direction and abide by hierarchical procedures. Mill did not associate bureaucratic expertise with any particular form of government but, like Hegel, identified the features of a universal class that was the marrow of the state, whose only goal was the successful execution of their official duties. Instrumental knowledge, limited freedom, and functional responsibility were the criteria of an organizational class that was hierarchical and narrowly focused. That class was to administration what political equality and liberty were to governing: "[w]hat can be done better by a body than by any individual, is deliberation," whereas "[n]o body of men, unless organized and under command, is fit for action, in the proper sense" (CW XIX: 424, 393).[20]

Deliberation demands exactly what bureaucracy must avoid: an open exchange of opinions among a group of people willing to discuss, argue, and possibly change their minds. Whereas experts must narrow their options and place "narrow-mindedness" at the service of efficiency and deadlines, deliberation opens up a broad range of possibilities and compels politicians and public officials to provide "a full exposition and justification" of their choices. Mill was elaborating on Aristotle, who acknowledged "some truth" in the democratic claim that the assembly must have a central role in the polis, because whereas single individuals might lack knowledge and competence, "when they all are brought together" they profit from the aggregation of "practical wisdom" (CW XIX: 432).[21] This was the basis of his claim for an inherent affinity between politics and "free government."

---

[20] Mill applied the same criteria to government that he had been developing for political economy in the *Essay on Some Unsettled Questions of Political Economy* (1843), where he introduced the distinction between the laws of production and the laws of distribution, claiming that the former were "natural" in the sense of invariable and that the latter socially variable.

[21] "the people may thus become something like a single person, who, as he has many feet, many hands, and many senses, may also have many qualities of character and intelligence" (Aristotle 1995, 108–9).

Mill uses two criteria to judge government: the *common interest* and the *common culture*. According to the former, good government results when the governing class pursues the general interest of the community. According to the latter, good government is contingent on the character of both leaders and citizens and fosters educational political institutions; human beings are not simply interest seekers but "progressive" beings who develop their mental and moral potentials through practice and social interaction.[22] The cultural criterion set the tone for Mill's political thought as a whole. Any given form of government must be judged in terms of the intellectual and moral attributes government needs for optimal performance. Thus there are two main ways governments can be "bad": they can either produce evil directly or prevent people from acting. Of the two, Mill thought the latter was perhaps more pernicious, because it contradicted his basic assumption that action is the very foundation of the moral sentiments and of intellectual and economic life. As we saw earlier, security – protection by and from the government – was the key to good government. Although a good despot could provide the former, only a representative constitutional government could provide both; this made the former contingently good (short term), whereas the latter was the norm (long term).[23]

Political institutions require "not their [the people's] simple acquiescence, but their active participation; and must be adjusted to the capacities and qualities of such men as are available." A government can be "negatively defective" when it does not "concentrate in the hands of the authorities power sufficient to fulfill the necessary offices of a government" or when it "does not sufficiently develop by exercise the active capacities and social

[22] Both criteria belong to the legacy of historicism and bring us back to Aristotle who, after presenting the rationale for the best constitution, urged politicians to pay attention to the cultural and social conditions of their society in framing a constitution (Aristotle 1995, 134). The criterion of the common interest was a topos among the utilitarians who, however, gave it a merely quantitative meaning: the "greatest interest of the greatest number."

[23] "When a person known to possess anything worth taking away, can expect nothing but to have it torn from him, with every circumstance of tyrannical violence, by the agents of a rapacious government, it is not likely that many will exert themselves to produce much more than necessary. . . . The Roman despotism" was able to put an end to wars and internal conflicts "though the empire" and in this way it relieved the population from insecurity; "but because it left them under the grinding yoke of its own rapacity, they enervated and impoverished, until they were an easy prey to barbarous but free invaders" (CW II: 112, 114). It is not hard to see in this sketch an analogy with India at the time of the British conquest, a territory surrounded and periodically conquered by local potentates with the support of domestic potentates and tribes. This analogy was quite common among British intellectuals in Mill's times. As Thomas Macaulay argued in his speech in the House of Commons in 1833, "At Delhi, as at Ravenna, there was a mock of sovereign, immured in a gorgeous state prison" (Macaulay 1875, 68).

feelings of the individual citizens" (CW XIX: 375–6, 435). The former situation could temporarily excuse elitist and even despotic solutions. Mill did not exclude the possibility that monarchy and aristocracy could be good regimes under certain circumstances. Honor, prudence, and steadiness could indeed shelter political decisions from the influence of "sinister interests" while keeping mental capacity from sinking into passive routine (CW XIX: 438–41).

Rome – where mixed government continued to produce positive effects for a relatively long time – was the counterexample that validated Mill's opinion that aristocracy was simply inadequate during ordinary times because it provided good government only so long as the state pursued a politics of "exceptionality." For the Roman republic to be progressive and to preserve political liberty, it had to pursue a policy of war and aggrandizement. Thus governments of the few gave the best of themselves in exceptional times and could fulfill their greatest potential by making exceptional politics ordinary policy. They belonged to an age when "security by the government" (war and threat from outside enemies or social conflicts) absorbed all human energies. Yet in modern societies that gave priority to commerce or peaceful competition over war and civil war, a government's performance can be evaluated and judged in terms of its ordinary politics. Society's movement from "force" to "politics" – from military to public officials – mirrored its institutional evolution from a government that required the concentrated "vigor" and "energy" of the few to one that requires good administration and good political judgment of the many. Good government in the modern age required new, unheroic passions. "The truth is that great talents are not needed for carrying on, in ordinary times, the government of an already well-ordered society" (CW XIX: 437–9; "On Grote's History of Greece," CW XI: 302–3; CW XVIII: 76).

Mill's insight was that the complexity of modern society itself demanded free government. Sismond de Sismondi and Benjamin Constant had already made this point, and le marquis de Condorcet had previously claimed that the transition from "vigor in the conduct of affairs" to the kind of "political skill and ability" that had to be "other than exceptional" was more than mere change, it was progress. Mill endorsed Condorcet's view and argued that progress entailed a social condition wherein the "dignity and estimation" of the public was to be measured by "the prosperity or happiness of the general body of the citizens" not the state or its "public functionaries" (CW XIX: 438; Condorcet 1970, 58; Urbinati 2002, 54–60). The paradox of the moderns is that the more citizens abandon direct political participation to dedicate themselves to their private interests, the more the state tends to intrude on and regulate their lives. As a consequence, a commercial society does not imply a less pervasive or weaker state. The state becomes pervasive and strong in a different way: it might be less visible and less violent than before, but it still poses a danger to liberty.

The principal despotic threat in a liberal society is the absorption of politics by experts. Whereas a government that places sovereign power in an assembly risks becoming a tyranny (the "tyranny of the majority,") only regimes dominated by the bureaucracy risk becoming despotic. Pedantocracy was Mill's name for the despotism of "aristocracies of public functionaries," the kind of homologation that modern European societies risked. Like oriental despotism, it denoted a comprehensive system rather than simply a degenerate form of government.[24] In *Considerations on Representative Government,* despotism loses many of its violent features and becomes synonymous with stagnation and routinization. It denotes a regime that, much like that of the despot and his viziers in Montesquieu's description, depresses people's moral and intellectual attributes. By replacing politics with the management of policy issues, pedantocracy makes the public realm into an enlarged household. In the final analysis, it makes political government unable to cope with social complexity precisely because it is inherently unable to profit from political deliberation or draw on a broad spectrum of opinions to make enlightened decisions.

The source of the despotic disease that can afflict modern representative government is, therefore, the wholesale displacement of politics. Representative democracy is the best form of government because, although not immune to such degeneration, it contains the antidote within itself: its ruling class is not chosen "merely from social position" but according to the principle of legal and political equality, and its representatives are selected through open competition and are publicly accountable (CW XIX: 421, 439–40). Political deliberation was the most powerful antidote to the threat of despotism, which, however, was never completely neutralized (Mill believed that August Comte epitomized the modern form of "spiritual and temporal despotism," a mix of religious faith in scientism and public conformity) (*Autobiography* CW I: 221). This explains Mill's attention to a wide range of reforms designed to configure the agonistic space of politics, guarantee pluralism, and structure the social institutions in which the moderns spend most of their lives (family and the workplace) according to principles of equal dignity and cooperation. Only thus can these sites become the schools

---

[24] Mill listed under pedantocracy all those countries that Montesquieu had defined as despotic (for instance the Russian and the Chinese governments) along with the Ausburgic Empire, all of them ruled by "a bureaucracy of mandarins."

of social sentiments democratic society requires to avert the risk of new despotism.

Despotism as Dogmatism

We can see what makes decisions despotic by analyzing paternal despotism and pedantocracy. Just because a decision expresses the will of the stronger does not necessarily mean its recipients are either hostile and rebellious or passive victims. Despotic decisions resemble the outcome of a blindly endorsed faith or dogmatic beliefs shared by subjects and their master by force of habit and inertia. This is why despotic domination does not necessarily need to translate into direct repression and may actually face little or no resistance. Despotism designates power relations marked by the absence of autonomously reached consent, not by the absence of any kind of consent. It designates a hegemonic consensus that molds the entire society, rendering people docile. As a matter of fact, Mill objected to Bentham's rationalism, "acquiescence of mankind" to government is based more on people's tendency to go on with their daily life than on their rational evaluation of the utility they receive from their government ("Bentham" CW X: 99–100, 106–12).[25]

This brings us to one of the most striking aspects of despotism and the reason this system is different from other nonliberal or autocratic regimes. Unlike tyrannical regime, for instance, despotism can and most of the time does enjoy a certain amount of support by its subjects, by either tacit consent or habitual perpetuation of a given set of practices. Mill used the category of despotism to grasp the complex nature of political consent and predict that it is the *process* of consent formation and the way consent is gained, articulated, and changed that makes it an indispensable requirement of moral and political legitimacy, not acceptance of authority per se.

As we know, the main purpose of *On Liberty* was to examine the kinds of coercion that the state and society can legitimately exercise over individuals "in the maturity of their faculties." Mill used the consequentialist principle of harm to set limits to coercion and the normative argument of the sovereignty of individual judgment to define the legitimate forms of coercion. Of the

---

[25] Lynn Zastoupil stresses, correctly, the difference between the abstract rationalism of James Mill and, although to a lesser degree, of Bentham and compares it with Mill's attention to the context, as evidence of the latter's awareness of the role of Oriental culture in the process of Indian emancipation (1999, 111–48). Mill was attentive to the formation of a "clergy class" and the role of the "vernacular" to transmit values that were consonant to representative institutions; to use Antonio Gramsci's vocabulary, he was attentive to the issue of how to change obedience from despotic imposition to consensual government (CW XVII: 1970 and fn. 3; Majeed 1992, 173, 147).

two, the latter was fundamental because it allowed him to categorize the forms of government and evaluate human relations in general. In a society in which people are "capable of being improved by free and equal discussion" – that is, a society that is ruled by representative institutions – the form of coercion must be consistent with this feature (CW XVIII: 223–5).

Coercion can be both *direct* (when harm to others is involved) and *indirect* (such as moral disapproval of particular acts or persuasion to desist from particular acts when direct harm to others is not implied). The individual can suffer injustice as the result of a direct offense (security violation) or when "hindered in his freedom of pursuing his own good" (autonomy violation). The most serious cases of injustices (direct harm) are those that violate a person's physical and mental integrity. They are, as he put in *Utilitarianism*, "acts of wrongful aggression, or wrongful exercise of power over some one," which infringe upon a person's actions or her freedom of expression. A person is thus free because she is not subjected to the will of another and enjoys the "indispensable conditions or the flowering of [her] individuality," not simply because no obstacle obstructs her acts (*Utilitarianism*, CW X: 256; CW XVIII: 224; Ten 1980, 84).[26]

The analysis of indirect obstruction or coercion is at the core of *On Liberty*. When state or direct coercion is not required because direct harm is not involved, what kind of coercion – if any – can a free community legitimately enforce? In issues of religious beliefs, lifestyles, and private choice, Mill's free community can adopt only noncoercive methods such as discussion and persuasion to influence peoples' choices. Verbal persuasion does not, however, exclude coercion: "To maintain that talking is better than fighting we must look at how we use speech" (Chambers 1996, 7). Mill perceived the manipulative and coercive potential of discourse and made an important contribution to understanding the art of deliberation and the self-critical habits of the liberal Self.

He detected two coercive potentials in persuasion: blind faith and blind rationalism. Both were features of the same illiberal attitude, which engendered uncritical acceptance of beliefs ("dead dogma") and prevented or blocked the people's tendency to examine and explore ("living truth.") Dogmatism is to the life of the mind what despotism is to the political life of a representative government. In both cases, the suppression of critical deliberative

---

[26] There are controversies about how these two notions of harm fit into Mill's theory of liberty. Some scholars read the notion of harm in a narrow sense, as referring only to the basic interest in individual freedom (Brown 1972, 144–45; Gray 1996, 52–4). Others maintain the thesis I am endorsing here: that harm also entails injury by omission (Donner 1991, 196–7; Lyons 1994, 89–96).

judgment promotes unscrutinized opinions and blind conformity, habits that tend to produce treachery and mendacity because any opinion (including "correct" ones) that achieves consent through passive endorsement renders counterarguments either null or invisible. In the long run, the decline of the habit of criticism produces moral degeneration and promotes intolerance because it makes people deaf to others' reason and stultifies their own.

From his crisis years on, Mill extended his criticism of dogmatism to abstract rationalism, or the inculcation of rational truths in people's minds regardless of their direct efforts in critically acquiring and retaining such truths. He then turned his attention to the process whereby truth is received and concluded that a "collision of ideas" could also be coercive. This was why he criticized the Enlightenment's *esprit critique* and his father's style of argumentation – a style he gradually came to regard as an act of indoctrination rather than a process of emancipation from mental passivity. "I have not any great notion of the advantage of what the 'free discussion' men call the 'collision of opinions,' it being my creed that truth is sown and germinates in the mind itself, and is not to be struck out suddenly like fire from a flint by knocking another body against it: so I accustomed myself to learn by inducing others to deliver their thoughts, and to teach by scattering my own, and I eschewed occasions of controversy (except occasionally with some of my old Utilitarian associates)" (Mill to Thomas Carlyle, 18 May 1833, CW XII: 153).

A certain style of reasoning and speech was implied if persuasion was not to be coercive. The Socratic method of self-inquiry was the protective device Mill envisioned. Like political representation in relation to the way political power was held, this method was characterized by *indirectness* insofar as it implied that the individual would withdraw temporarily from the *agon* for a critical inner recapitulation of opinions brought to his attention as a result of dialogue with others. The purpose of Socratic self-inquiry was to complement the deliberative type of political influence undertaken by individuals "in the maturity of their faculties," or as citizens. Once he had established that a "silent" public realm could not be a model for "government by discussion," Mill felt he had to shelter individual judgment from the despotic threat that could arise in the collision of opinions. In sum, he had to distinguish between discussion merely oriented toward victory – dialectics as polemics – and discussion oriented toward conscious conviction – dialectics as deliberative discourse.[27] He therefore gave deliberation two functions, one

---

[27] This can be the answer to Himmelfarb's theory of "the two Mills" which equates discussion with polemical discussion. Himmelfarb has stressed the contradiction thwarting Mill's

dissenting and one transformative. A representative government needs both an open agora in which partisan groups compete to achieve parliamentary majority and a civil society that is open to different beliefs and lifestyles. This ensures that individuals have the right to question majority opinion, check their leaders, and put a healthy distance between their beliefs and those that circulate in the larger society.

The outcome of Mill's search during the years that followed his rupture with the utilitarians was the conviction that a reformist politics could succeed only if it taught people to recognize their own fallibility and think for themselves. It was useless to bestow emancipation or the truth on a population of passive recipients. This was the lesson he extracted from his refined knowledge of paternal despotism, along with the conviction that the role of the intellectual in a representative democracy should be to help the citizens to achieve autonomous judgment and a "high state of moral and intellectual culture." In his maturity, he applied this logic to class relationships: "free discussion with them as equal, in speech and writings, seems the best instruction that can be given to them"; they are "not to be indoctrinated" but "to be induced and enabled to think for themselves" (to Gustave D'Eichthal, 6 March 1830, CW XII: 46–9; and to Carr, 7 January 1852, CW XIV: 80–1).[28]

In sum, Mill invites us to think of despotism as a practice of power that does much more than repress pluralism and free agency, because its aim is to induce unity in a collective by crippling autonomous individual judgment, not simply by coercing action. If the process of despotic domination begins in the mind, its antidote should also be sought in the mind. On this account, the Socratic command to "know thyself" is the most antithetical answer to the obliteration of the Self suffered under despotic power. How can I know myself if I see myself through my master's eye? How can I judge things and events if there is no distinction between inner and outer, my opinion and that of others? These questions illuminate an aspect that at first glance appears to

---

liberalism between a deliberative and a conservative phase: in the early 1830s, Mill exalted a "sternly authoritarian" view that opposed "dogmatic disputatiousness" and controversy; while in *On Liberty*, he exalted the role of liberty of discussion in opinion formation. In the latter case, Mill based legitimacy on people's understanding and judgment, in the former, he grounded it on rational evidence and the intellectual authority of the wisest regardless of people's consent (Himmelfarb 1974, 37–43). But as I shall argue in what follows, Mill's change was internal to the deliberative perspective: the 1830s were the years in which he passed from a polemical use of dialectics to a critical one.

[28] "In general, those who attempt to correct the errors of the working classes do it as if they were talking to babies" ("Representation of the People [2]," CW XXVIII: 65). Both the distinction between Sophism and Socratism and Mill's egalitarian interpretation of free discussion seem to contrast with Villa's conclusions that Mill shared a "narrow conception of the relevance of negative Socratic thinking," because he framed it "as but one element in the training of the elite" (Villa 2001, 124; Urbinati 2002, chap. 4).

be an oxymoron: in a despotic system a certain degree of negative freedom can subsist with no danger to the stability and longevity of the system. As Isaiah Berlin taught us, freedom as noninterference does not require a democratic government; a nonliberal decent authoritarian government might be enough (Berlin [1958] 1992, 161).

Despotism as Infantilization

Mill's most touching and complete picture of despotism comes from his insightful reflection (from personal experience rather than intellectual inquiry) on the subjection of children and wives in the patriarchal family. "Not a word can be said for despotism in the family which cannot be said for political despotism" (CW XXI: 286). His depiction of marital supremacy and the manipulation of women's personality in the Victorian family remains a powerful study of the process of domination operating from the inside as an active work of character formation that moves from external coercion to hegemonic domination over the life of the mind. Through the dialectics of the negative, he succeeded in grasping the complex nature of liberty: liberty from subjection found its most effective expression in the context of his advocacy for women's equality and the denunciation of its despotic alternative.[29]

Mill depicted domestic despotism as a vicious school of habituation rather than tyranny, a comprehensive reeducation of passions over the course of a kind of molecular change in women's conscience that transforms them from victims of other's "animalism" to individuals who are no longer aware of themselves as victims, and, finally, to beings who are no longer capable of perceiving their condition as one of subjection (CW XXI: 283–5, 288–9). The father-husband-master shrinks his daughter-wife's autonomy – he undermines her mental and spiritual life – to make her dependent on him in her basic liberty: "Men do not want solely the obedience of women, they want their sentiment," because they want to be seen by women as their protectors, not their masters. Thus, the husband-master's power was most apparent in the suppression of his wife's mental and moral autonomy. Social life in its entirety conformed to this goal. Because their ultimate aim is to dominate women's spirits, men are "averse," Mill remarked astutely, "to instructed

---

[29] On these premises, Mill called the arbitrary rule of an elected majority a "tyranny" (*On Liberty*, CW XVIII: 219) and "despotic" the democratic society in which the plurality of voices and opinions was extinguished by the habit of consent and conformism rather than by violent oppression.

women." For them to master women's right to security, they must first deprive them of "their moral right to autonomy" (CW I: 311; XXI: 271).

Precisely because domestic despotism does not consist in a discrete series of violent deeds and brutal acts, it cannot be reduced to interference with women's natural freedom of choice or direct and crude repression. Despotism – as described in *The Subjection of Women* – is a form of total and absolute power because it operates on the emotions, not just on actions. The despot, unlike the tyrant, strikes with fear and love simultaneously. Subjects of the tyrant long to rebel; under the despot they become affectionate chattel slaves. In the first case of repression, potential freedom is always latent; in the other, a condition of total surrender and pacification defines "complete abnegation." Tyranny represses action and violates negative liberty. Despotism violates the individual's very determination to act and robs her of her self-reliance. Much more perverse than tyranny, it induces its subjects to transfer their choice- and decision-making power to their masters, who eventually will be seen as a source of tutelage rather than of coercion. This is why Mill argued that, because women are not merely forced to serve their masters but are trained to desire to serve them like "cattle slaves," the position of women differs from that of all other subjected classes. "All women are brought up from the very earliest years in the belief that their ideal of character" is "not self-will, and government by self-control" like men, but instead "submission, and yielding to the control of others... to live for others; to make complete abnegation of themselves, and to have no life but their affections" (CW XXI: 268, 271–2).

By annihilating liberty as autonomy, despotism annihilates all liberty. Whereas tyranny can clearly be explained in terms of violation of negative liberty, despotism cannot. We need a notion of *liberty as nonsubjection* and a view of individuality as a process of self-dependence. Indeed, the primary purpose of the dominant power is to make free choice (negative liberty) impossible through "real interference" not merely with the subject's action but also with her will to act. "In this sense, servitude implies the consciousness of being vulnerable to other's enterprises, of the impossibility [for the subordinate] to defend [herself] effectively against infringements" (Spitz 1995, 182). So although arbitrary interference indeed undermines autonomy, its actual agenda is the suspension of liberty as security. The moral degradation of the subjected wife provides the excuse for restricting her opportunity to act according to her own decisions. Despotism triumphs when both the sense of resistance and the consciousness of having a right to security are tamed, when its subjects are naturally obedient and domesticated. Thus, insofar as the two "rights," security and autonomy, are concerned, autonomy must be crushed for security to be destroyed. "If adults are treated as children they will come in time to be like children. Deprived of the right to choose for themselves, they will soon lose the power of rational judgment and decision" (Feinberg 1980, 110).

Clearly, there is little room for compromise in a portrait of marriage as a form of despotism. Even legal reforms are insufficient because although the legal guarantees of individual freedom can fence out and limit the absolute power of the despot, they cannot make the despot a cooperative partner or make marriage a mutually respectful and cooperative union. The principle of liberty as noninterference could neither have motivated Mill's critique of the subjection of women nor could it have inspired his view of the ideal marriage (CW XXI: 329, 273–4). Thus, while he was quick to claim that the law should allocate rights and duties among women and men equally and marriage should be consistently turned into a legal contract among equal partners, he did not think that an equal and respectful marital union could be built on the maxims of legal justice alone. His ideal marriage transcended the discourse of rights and liberalism because it entailed a whole ethical life, a personalized unity of formation and reproduction of values and habits that was radically opposite to the despotic form of marital life.

The category of despotism allowed Mill to politicize all facets of women's lives and gave his feminism a radical twist. The cause of women's freedom became a cause of freedom for the entire society, just like the cause of the slaves in American abolitionist writings or of the working class in Karl Marx's theory. This represented a decisive break with the liberal principle of the responsible individual agent that underpins the theory of negative liberty. The marital system, like slavery in America and the capitalist system of production, constituted an objective system of relations that operated independently of the will and the intention of the individual actors. The husband in Mill's theory, like capitalism in Marx's, was driven to act according to the logic of domination.[30] Patriarchal relations shaped and

---

[30] In his later writings, Mill also described capitalism as a form of domination that "enslaves or makes dependent" the large majority not "by force of the law" but "by force of poverty." As in the case of marriage, he used the category of despotism in an innovative way, applying it to a condition of subjection that could not, realistically, be imputed to the will or direct responsibility of anyone in particular. He defined as despotic a social "arrangement" whose effect was to diminish individual responsibility. By accident of birth and social status, workers were "chained to a place, to an occupation, and to conformity with the will of an employer," all conditions that obviated any personal efforts to change their situation. The dominant class was devoid of the principle of individual responsibility for the opposite reason, because its members enjoyed their "mental and moral advantages . . . without exertion and independently of desert." Like Marx, Mill believed that capitalism engendered

determined his identity just as they did his wife's. So just as a "good" capitalist could not change the exploitative nature of capitalism, a few "good"
and humane husbands couldn't change the patriarchal nature of marriage.
By the same token, a husband's respect for his wife's negative freedom could
not in itself guarantee her security or recognition as an equal. Mill used
the same argument to support women's enfranchisement. Once again, he
devised a demonstration *a contrario*: the right to vote is not a guarantee
unless it is universally distributed. In fact, he argued, against his father, that
it could easily become an instrument of arbitrary power. Those who are
"protected" in their persons by a law they did not participate in making and
could not check, are not protected at all: "we know what legal protection
the slaves have, where the laws are made by their masters" (CW XXI: 302).

Mill's analysis of marital despotism illuminates the nature of rights and
shows that only when they are equally distributed do they qualify as instruments for a secure environment and become inherently opposed to privilege.
Furthermore, it reveals the complexity and potential of liberalism, a theory
of liberty that can hardly be reduced to a policy of individual security (negative liberty) and that translates into citizenship and a conceptualization of
rights as an active labor of vindicating reciprocal relations.

Mill believed that autonomy was available to everyone, to those who
are already conscious of their individual independence although they are
deprived of the means to express it (wage workers) as to those whose consciousness has been silenced or crippled (women). Mill did not theorize a
dual notion of liberty – a minimum one (security) for all individuals alike
(children and adults, men and women, Europeans and non-Europeans)
and a maximum one (autonomy) only for few full-fledged, autonomous
adults. Rather, he situated the discourse of liberty within a dynamic vision
of individuality and made it egalitarian in principle.[31] We all are born with
the potential to become self-dependent beings although we become, rather
than are, autonomous persons. The fact that children hold the right to an

a fatal monopoly of opportunity that led to an imbalance of power, thereby violating its
own principles of open competition and personal initiative. Capitalism, said Mill echoing
Marx, tends to reproduce a "new feudality" and a new serfdom (*Chapters on Socialism*,
CW V: 713, 710, 716).

[31] John Gray's identification of the moral right to autonomy with its actual possession by the
few (full-fledged individuals) suggests that Mill viewed autonomy as a status rather than a
process and as a predicament of inequality. Unlike security, Gray argues, "the moral right
to autonomy is possessed, not by all men, but only by those possessing in some minimal
degree the capacities of an autonomous agent" (Gray 1990, 217–4, 224–9). For a dynamic
and potentially egalitarian view of liberty as autonomy see Donner 1991, 181, 169; see also
Ten 1980, 71.

autonomous life "in trust" does not mean that while they are children they do not possess the moral right to autonomy. On the contrary, it means that they need help to become free and autonomous beings. So to disrespect their immediate right to security compromises the possibility of their future enjoyment of their moral right to autonomy.[32] Liberty as security and liberty as autonomy comprise a single liberty that manifests itself in different life circumstances and different uses of politics (as containment and as enhancement). All humans, by virtue of their humanness, have the right to become, and to be, independent persons. It is the actual enjoyment of autonomy that can be deferred, not the right to it. This is the argument that explains Mill's acceptance of *temporary paternalism*.[33]

Paternalism restricts liberty in a way that implies a temporarily unequal distribution of power.[34] As a power relation that is structurally inegalitarian, it is justified in terms of the criteria that regulate it. Mill singled out "two conflicting theories" concerning the "desirable position" of groups or individuals that still do not enjoy an actual autonomy: "one may be called the theory of dependence and protection, the other that of self-dependence."[35] The first, which may be traced to Aristotle, stresses the status of parental authority over children – or inferiors – whereas the theory of paternalism as an aid to self-dependence, which may be traced to Locke, stresses the parental duty to help children become autonomous beings. The former places obligation on those who need protection, and the latter places it on those who give help.

Aristotle saw the parent–child relationship from the perspective of the privileged authority figure and the affectionate dependence of those requiring his protection. Locke, however, viewed that relationship from the perspective of the right of the child and thus transformed the argument for parental power into an argument for emancipation. He overturned the logic shaping Aristotle's hierarchical paternalism by stressing the parents' obligation rather than the child's. "The bonds of this subjection," Locke wrote in the *Second Treatise*, "are like swaddling cloths they are wrapt up in and supported by in the weakness of their [the children's] infancy." Because he analyzed parental power in terms of children's rights (in view of their future

---

[32] "One would violate that right in trust [autonomous locomotion] now, before it can even be exercised, by cutting off the child's legs" (Feinberg 1980, 98–9).

[33] Donner 1991, 169–72.

[34] Thompson has provided three stringent criteria for a "justifiable paternalism": the person to be constrained must be *impaired;* restrictions must be *limited;* and restrictions should aim at preventing a "serious and irreversible *harm*" (Thompson 1987, 154–8).

[35] *Principles of Political Economy,* CW III: 759.

autonomy) rather than the rulers' privilege, Locke made the power of parents *posterius*, not *prius*, to their children's need, rendering it a function of the children's acquisition of autonomy, and thus temporary and not self-referential. "Children, I confess, are not born in this full state of equality, though they are born to it" (Locke 1993, nos. 55, 56, 64–7; Aristotle 1995, 33–5).

Mill took the Lockean view. As I mentioned at the beginning of this chapter, it was *in this sense* that the teleology driving his paternalism was egalitarian and participatory in principle. Mill did not deprive children – or lower-class citizens or "backward" peoples – of their moral status as persons with inherent dignity and the potential to be independent. Their acquisition of an actual condition of autonomy did not mean that they passed from a nonhuman to a human status. The transition, or progress, from mere security to autonomy in security was a movement intrinsic to the individual's life trajectory. This premise allowed him to define dignity as a good all possess equally and to discriminate between forms of despotism in relation to their structural teleology.

The notion of temporary paternalism – short-term reforms in preparation of long-term constitutional guarantees – shapes Mill's overall analysis and denunciation of despotism as an unlimited system of domination for the sake of the ruler's interest, or *indefinite authority*, which would constitute infantilization. Infantilization presumes a racist perspective, the existence of a two-tiered humanity or, in John Gray's words, a society in which "the moral right to autonomy is possessed, not by all men, but only by those possessing in some degree the capacities of an autonomous agent."[36] Mill explicitly rejected this dichotomy. Despotism is such a great evil because it obstructs the path to independence and aims to keep individuals in a status of perennial childhood and under paternal command, rendering them mentally and practically subaltern, mere instruments in the hands of the stronger. Mill was condemning infantilization when he defined marital power as perennial paternalism or when he identified pure exploitation and paternal despotism in colonized countries.[37] In this sense, it is fair to say that his conceptualization of despotism can be used to decode his normative notion of individuality and the democratic perspective of his liberalism. Had Mill envisioned autonomy as a liberty belonging only to the few – had he identified it with a status enjoyed only by actually autonomous individuals – he would have

---

[36] Gray 1996, 55.
[37] Paternalism, writes Gerald Dworkin, has an "important moral limitation" insofar as it aims at a "future-oriented consent" (Dworkin 1972, 74).

been unable to criticize despotic institutions. It is no coincidence that the most virulent critics of his political thought concentrated on his feminism (Stephen 1993, 130–46). Indeed, the call to grant women complete freedom exemplified Mill's egalitarian extension of liberty as autonomy and legitimized the denunciation of all forms of infantilization.

Conclusion

All Mill's reflections on despotism in non-liberal countries and in liberal societies can be summed up in a question: How can despotism be ended? Mill must have asked himself that question when he decided to start his political campaign for women's enfranchisement and the reform of family and marriage law. The complexity of the strategy he adopted reflected his awareness of the complex nature of despotism: the fact that no hasty initiative or reform could be successful because in the case of despotism the goal was not merely to abolish a set of arbitrary rules but to change an entire way of life that people were accustomed to. Aware of the intriguing nature of despotic domination, Mill "insisted that the subjection of women could not be ended by law alone, but only by law and the reformation of education, of opinion, of social inculcation, of habits, and finally of the conduct of family life itself" (Krouse 1982, 39; Shanley 1991, 170).[38] This explains his overall reformist strategy: his choice to be circumspect in launching the campaign for women's suffrage; his proposal for unionization as the first stage in the gradual transition from capitalism to cooperation; and his belief that it was "altogether chimerical to expect that the main portion of the mental cultivation of a people can take place through the medium of a foreign language" (CW XVII: 1970, fn. 3).

Whereas emancipation from tyranny could, and most of the time does, come from resolute and radical action, liberation from despotic domination may require a *longue durée* perspective and synergistic transformations (legal and cultural, social and economic, political and constitutional). It assumes a radically different perspective that transcends a simple change in the rules of the game and resembles a "revolution without a revolution," to paraphrase Antonio Gramsci. I would say that Mill anticipated a kind of "passive revolution" when he sketched the transition from despotism to freedom and, moreover, proposed a revision of the Enlightenment attitude toward politics. This can be illustrated by his criticism of Bentham, who "was not, I

---

[38] "It is necessary on such subject [women's equality] to be as far as possible invulnerable" (CW XVI: 1377; see also CW XIV: 66 and CW I: 265).

am persuaded, aware, how very much of the really wonderful acquiescence
of mankind in any government which they find established, is the effect of
mere habit and imagination, and, therefore, depends upon the preservation
of something like continuity of existence in the institutions, and identity in
their outward forms; cannot transfer itself easily to new institutions, even
though in themselves preferable; and is greatly shaken when there occurs
anything like a break in the line of historical duration – anything which can
be termed the end of the old constitution and the beginning of the new one"
("Remarks on Bentham's Philosophy," CW X: 17).

Mill's revision of the *esprit abstrait* of the eighteenth century finds its most
eloquent expression in the correlation between contextualism and voluntarism. In 1861, criticizing the relativistic implications of German Romanticism, he clarified that he never meant the reference to the context to be an
excuse for worshiping tradition or justifying the status quo. Historical context should be recognized and respected both because it structures human
actions and because it inhibits abstract and top-down plans for political
emancipation. The role of intellectuals and reformist leaders was to provide
critical information about relations of domination while inspiring people
to act for political self-determination. Mill's maxim of political transformation was Aristotelian ("Knowledge of the particular people, and the general
practical judgment and sagacity, must be the guide") but with an important
voluntarist caveat:

A people may be unprepared for good institutions; but to kindle a desire of particular
institution or form of government, and set its advantages in the strongest light, is
one of the modes, often the only mode within reach, of educating the mind of the
nation not only for accepting or claiming, but also for working, the institution. What
means had Italian patriots, during the last and present generation, of preparing the
Italian people for freedom in unity, but by inciting them to demand it?

Contextualism and voluntarism checked one another. This made Mill's theory of political transition and his theory of progress more generally, resemble
the old art of combining fortune and virtue. "People are more easily induced
to do, and do more easily, what they are already used to; but people also learn
to do things new to them. . . . We cannot make the river run backwards; but
we do not therefore say that watermills 'are not made, but grow' " (CW XIX:
379–80).

As a result, an attentive reader of Mill's writings on India may reasonably
surmise that he would have presumably been just as supportive of non-
European democratic movements, had they emerged and grown. His choice
of the principle of popular consent as the primary criterion of political

legitimacy indicates that he would have been just as sympathetic to Gandhi as he was to Giuseppe Mazzini. The problem with Mill's approach to paternal despotism lies elsewhere, in the fact that he never clarified what form the people's will should take for it to qualify as sufficiently mature for self-government or how to distinguish rebellions that signalled to the world that a people was "ripe for" representative institutions from mere rebellions against oppression. Although he understood the complexity of the process of transition to constitutional government, he did not reflect on the political actors and the forms of collective action that comprised that complexity. In sum, he did not make any meaningful distinction between politics within a constitutional context and politics as constitutional creation. Mill's whole reformist strategy was modeled on the political forms of a parliamentary regime. If British social institutions, such as the family, marriage, and the workplace, were to be transformed, reformist political battles needed broad popular discussion, political movements, and the support of the press. The application of this model to the politics of transition from colonial despotism to representative self-government was, however, unsuitable. Although he understood the constitutive link between the will to self-determination and democratic government, Mill did not leave us with any valuable reflections on the revolutionary processes that make a subjected people into a sovereign people. It is doubtful that paternal despotism can promote and oversee this process peacefully, as Mill wished – doubtful that it can be an impartial and disinterested judge of the right time for the subjects to become free and their guardians to relinquish power.

4

J. S. Mill and Liberal Socialism

Bruce Baum

[I]t is not the pursuit of happiness but the enlargement of freedom which is socialism's highest aim.

R. H. S. Crossman[1]

The beginning of the twenty-first century is a tough time for socialists and socialism, so it may seem to be an odd moment to revisit John Stuart Mill's relationship to socialism. Socialism today is hardly a major locus of mass mobilization as it was in the early twentieth century, or as various forms of nationalism, populism, and religious fundamentalism are at present. Of course, socialism also was not a major object of mass mobilization in Mill's time, although it had begun to preoccupy European intellectuals.[2] That said, political theory has rarely been satisfied merely to confirm prevailing notions of what is possible or desirable, and Mill's political theory is a case in point. Mill wrote to Pasquale Villari near the end of his life that his work "lies rather among anticipations of the future than explorations of the past" (Mill, "Letter to Pasquale Villari," 28 February 1872, CW XVII: 1873). One of the remarkable features of his thought is just how much this claim still resonates.

Although socialist politics currently is in retreat, Mill's sympathetic engagement with socialism still speaks powerfully to current political economic challenges, especially to the barriers to equal freedom and democratic self-government embodied in contemporary global capitalism. The experience of the past century indicates strongly, against doctrinaire Marxism,

---

[1] R. H. S. Crossman, quoted in Coser and Howe 1966, 29.

[2] Here I am oversimplifying a rich history. Still, the rise of European socialist parties and the twentieth-century communist revolutions in Russia and China occurred well after his death in 1873. On the history of nineteenth-century socialist thought, see Lichtheim 1975; on the rise of socialist politics in Europe, see Sassoon 1996, 5–59.

that socialism is by no means historically inevitable. If a democratic form of socialism is going to be achieved anywhere, it will likely occur only when a mass of people come to see its moral advantages as a means to combine and maximize freedom, social justice, and equality.[3] In this regard, at a time when many progressive thinkers and activists have abandoned any idea of socialism and come to regard the liberal tradition as marking out the limits of emancipatory political possibilities, much can be learned by reconsidering Mill's liberal engagement with socialism.[4] As I have argued elsewhere, Mill remains a key figure for thinking about the emancipatory potential of modern liberalism (Baum 2000, 2003). Most commentators on Mill and liberalism, however, fail to appreciate the extent to which his liberal commitment to individual freedom led him, as he says in his *Autobiography,* toward socialism as the "ideal of ultimate improvement" (CW I: 239).

In our era of neo-liberalism, many (if not most) people have been taught to regard capitalism, or the "free market" system, as the institutional manifestation of individual economic freedom. Meanwhile, contemporary liberal egalitarianism, as exemplified in the work of John Rawls, offers some support for liberal socialism, but chiefly to achieve distributive justice rather than as a way to maximize freedom (Rawls 1971, 280, and 2001, 138–40).[5] Mill, in contrast, advances a form of liberal democratic socialism for the enlargement of freedom as well as to realize social and distributive justice. He offers

---

[3] This was one of the central threads of Eduard Bernstein's ([1899] 1993) "revisionist" approach to socialism. For a related contemporary approach, see Cohen 2000.

[4] This is not the place to discuss the general abandonment of socialism among progressive thinkers, but a couple of signposts are indicative. In the United States, the left periodical *Dissent,* which was initially devoted in part to democratic socialism when it began in 1954 (Howe 1966, 2), has basically abandoned serious discussion of socialism since the late 1990s. In England, the *New Left Review* spoke to the "task of socialism" at the start of its 1960 inaugural issue (*New Left Review* 1960, 1); in 2000, introducing a "second series" of the *New Left Review,* editor Perry Anderson observed, "Socialism has ceased to be a widespread ideal" and called for "an uncompromising realism" (Anderson 2000, 9, 14).

[5] Ronald Dworkin, in contrast to Rawls, appeals simultaneously to equality, liberty, and justice. Yet he lacks the expansive conception of freedom as realized autonomy and self-determination in different spheres of life that guides Mill's liberalism, as I explain shortly (Dworkin 1996a, 39–57). There are significant links between Mill's liberalism and that of Rawls and Dworkin concerning the relationship between individual liberties, or basic liberties, and property rights. None of these theorists gives rights to the accumulation and employment of private property comparable weight to such liberties as freedom of speech, religious freedom, and freedom to choose one's own employment. Rawls and Dworkin implicitly affirm Mill's view that property rights may be rightfully modified when the change would be "beneficial to the public and conducive to the general improvement" as long as the existing proprietors are justly compensated by the state for the property they are "dispossessed of" (COS, CW V: 753). See Dworkin 1996a; Rawls 2001, 114–15; Nagel 2003, 66–7.

a powerful account of economic injustice and justice that is centered on his understanding of freedom and its conditions.

The idea of going back to Mill to rethink progressive political economic possibilities is hardly unprecedented. Among such efforts, Paul Starr's return to Mill's political economy in *The American Prospect* in the wake of the Eastern European revolutions of 1989 merits special attention because of how Starr appealed to Mill to lay socialism to rest (Starr 1991). Highlighting the reform liberalism evident in Mill's *Principles of Political Economy*, Starr encourages liberals and progressives to look to Mill for guidance about feasible social reform and to give up any lingering hope that liberal democracy can be "reconstructed into a benign and democratic socialism." Yet Starr also acknowledges Mill's interest in socialism: "[F]ar from condemning socialism outright, [Mill] saw merit in socialist ideas and accepted the possibility of a fundamental reconstruction of industry with the ownership of firms belonging to those who provided labor rather than those who provided the capital . . . But Mill could not agree with socialists on some fundamentals. He argued that whatever the ownership of the firm, competition was essential" (Starr 1991, 74–5).

Starr was quite right as far as he went. Nonetheless, his way of framing the choice between liberalism and socialism forecloses serious attention to just the kind of synthesis between these traditions that Mill himself sought. Mill worked toward such a synthesis precisely because of how the ethical commitments of his liberalism – particularly to freedom and distributive justice – led him to adopt a number of socialist proposals along with socialist sympathies. Furthermore, when Starr points out that Mill disagrees with socialists "on some fundamentals," he glosses over some crucial questions. Most important, to what extent does Mill's defense of market competition, his chief difference with then-existing socialists, exclude him from the designation of "socialist"? And does Mill's liberal engagement with socialism offer any lessons for developing a feasible socialism, or a synthesis of liberal democracy, market competition, and socialism that would (to borrow Jürgen Habermas's words) "tame capitalism to some point where it becomes unrecognizable as such"?[6]

My argument, in short, is that Mill's account of the political economy of freedom leads him to sketch a radical liberal political economic program that is feasible and, in significant ways, socialist. Rather than advocating an ideal standard for just distribution of income or wealth, Mill recommends a market economy dominated by decentralized democratic cooperative firms

---

[6] Habermas now calls this ideal "radical democracy." See Habermas and Michnik 1994, 26.

that would achieve social justice by establishing a standard of what I will call *maximal economic freedom.* In what follows, I largely leave aside the now well-worn debate about whether Mill, despite his socialist self-designation, should be counted as a socialist.[7] I suggest that whether Mill's ultimate political economic ideal is indisputably a form of socialism is less important than the extent to which he provides support for the democratic socialist goal of extending democracy and the freedom of self-government beyond the state and into modern economies. Notably, he proposes significant qualifications to private property rights in the means of production and affirms the democratic socialist goal of democratizing industrial society's relations of production. In so doing, he outlines a promising response to the challenges to individual freedom, human well-being, and ecological sustainability presented by modern capitalist development.

In effect, with his emphasis on individual freedom, decentralized power, and industrial democracy within a market economy, Mill pioneered an important ongoing liberal socialist tradition that includes Eduard Bernstein, G. D. H. Cole, John Dewey, Carlo Rosselli, and, more recently, Norberto Bobbio and Chantal Mouffe.[8] Moreover, Mill's liberal socialism differs in fruitful ways from other prominent currents of nineteenth-century socialism – such as Saint Simonianism, Fourierism, and Marxism – as well as from the statist "welfare socialism" that eventually triumphed politically in post–World War II Europe – a democratic socialism that used the centralized state to craft comprehensive welfare states and managed capitalism (see Sassoon 1996, 131–49).[9] Although Mill's engagement with socialism is not without limitations from a contemporary perspective, he provides considerable support for Bernstein's claim that "with respect to liberalism as a historical movement, socialism is its legitimate heir, not only chronologically, but also intellectually.... The aim of all socialist measures ... is the development and the protection of the free personality" (Bernstein 1993, 147). At the same

---

[7] On Mill and socialism, see Robson 1968; Sarvasy 1985; Claeys 1987; Ashcraft 1989 and 1998; Riley 1996a; Stafford 1998a; Ten 1998; Levin 2003; Miller 2003; Medearis 2005.

[8] See Bernstein [1899] 1993; Cole [1920] 1964; Rosselli [1929] 1994; Dewey [1927] 1991; Bobbio 1987; Mouffe 1993; Urbanati 2004. Mouffe notes, for instance, that Bobbio belonged "to an important tradition of Italian liberal thought that, since the nineteenth century, under the influence of John Stuart Mill, has been receptive to socialist ideas" (1993, 91). On Mill and Rosselli, see Urbanati 1994, xxv.

[9] For a representative statement of the latter approach, see Crosland [1956] 1964. Welfare socialism, or social democracy, has roots in Bernstein's Marxist "revisionism" along with important affinities to the economic interventionist "New Liberalism" exemplified by Leonard Hobhouse ([1911] 1980) in England and contemporary liberal egalitarians such as Rawls and Dworkin.

time, Mill gives persuasive grounds to conclude that any desirable socialism must be a democratic and *liberal* socialism.

I

Mill's interest in socialism stems largely from his understanding of the restraints to and possibilities for freedom contained in modern economies. For Mill, freedom is not simply a negative concept, realized merely by the absence of constraints or impediments on people's efforts to satisfy their existing desires, whatever these are (Smith 1984; Baum 2000, 21–31; Urbanati 2002, ch. 5).[10] Crucially, his conception of freedom is distinct from his famous principle of liberty, which he elaborates in *On Liberty*. With the principle of liberty, he prescribes a sphere of "self-regarding" choices and actions regarding which the freedom of individuals ought not be restricted. As G. W. Smith says, the principle of liberty "is a normative rule of liberty invoking a logically distinct and independent concept of freedom" (Smith 1984, 182). The liberty principle, in short, is an institutional device for securing only one of the forms of freedom that concerns Mill: our freedom as independent individuals "of pursuing our own good in our own way, so long as we do not attempt to deprive others of theirs, or impede their efforts to obtain it" (*OL,* CW XVIII: 226).

Moreover, when Mill refers to the freedom "of pursuing our own good in our own way," he means something distinct from merely satisfying unreflective desires. Pursuing our own good in our own way requires what Mill calls "mental freedom" and what is now called *autonomy* – that is, the capacity of persons to reflectively formulate their own goals and objectives. According to Mill, individuals are free with respect to their choices and actions only to the extent that they reflectively cultivate individuality of character and preferences so that their choices and actions are really *their own* (*OL,* CW XVIII: 264–5; CW XXV: 1179). He regards the development of individuality of character and preferences as a necessary condition of freedom.[11]

Overall, Mill's conception of freedom is best understood as the capacity of persons for self-determination (Baum 2000, 21–36). It encompasses not only people's choices and actions as independent individuals but also domains

---

[10] For interpretations of Mill as a proponent of "negative liberty," see Berlin 1969, 139, 198; Ten 1980; Berger 1984; Rees 1985.

[11] See Freidman 1966; Gray 1983; Berger 1984; Smith 1984, 211; Skorupski 1989, 254; Gibbons 1990; Ryan [1970] 1990, chap. 13; Donner 1991; Morales 1996; Baum 2000, chaps. 1 and 4. Mill recognizes degrees of freedom in this regard rather than regarding "being free" in all or nothing terms. See Baum 2000, 31–4.

in which people share with others in practices of mutual self-government with respect to social and political institutions that govern their lives. Thus, in *The Subjection of Women,* he describes "freedom of action" as "the liberty of each to govern his own conduct by his own feelings of duty, and by such laws and social constraints as his conscience can subscribe to," and in terms of people having "sufficient influence in the regulation of their affairs" (CW XXI: 336, 337).[12]

In Mill's view, then, freedom encompasses each of the two distinct kinds of questions that Isaiah Berlin associates with "negative" and "positive" senses of freedom, respectively: "What am I free to do or be?" and "Who governs me?" (Berlin 1969, 130). His emphasis on mutual self-government as an aspect of freedom is basic to his view of political freedom; he also gives it a central place in his conception of economic freedom (Claeys 1987; Baum 2000, chaps. 7 and 8; Urbanati 2002, chap. 5). Whereas Mill's conception of freedom embraces the two aspects of freedom that Berlin called "negative" and "positive," Berlin's understanding of two distinct and separable kinds of freedom does not fit Mill's thinking (Berlin 1969, xliii, 121–72).[13] For Mill, freedom is always freedom of some agent (or agents) from certain obstacles or constraints, to do or be or become something.[14] It always involves the presence of enabling conditions, such as rights, resources, and opportunities for self-government, as well as the absence of burdensome constraints (Baum 2000, 6, 23–44). In this regard, Mill's conception of freedom in the economic domain differs notably from the views of Berlin and Rawls, who distinguish, respectively, between freedom and the "conditions of its exercise" and liberty and the "worth of liberty" (Berlin 1969, liii–liv; Rawls 1971, 204). Mill does not sever freedom from the conditions of its exercise.[15] Furthermore, as I discuss later (in sec. IV), he recognizes potential tensions between practices of individual liberty – the freedom "of pursuing our own good in our own way" – and practices of democratic self-government in economic life as in political life, but he regards both as indispensable.[16]

---

[12] In addition, while highlighting the importance of freedom for happiness, he writes: "What citizen of a free country would listen to any offers of good and skillful administration, in return for the abdication of freedom?'" (CW 21: 337).

[13] Nadia Urbanati (2002, 158–72) develops this point in somewhat different terms.

[14] Here I am adapting Gerald McCallum's (1973) triadic account of freedom.

[15] In this regard, Mill's principle of liberty can be understood as a necessary but not sufficient condition for practices of individual economic freedom. Moreover, Mill tends to use the terms "liberty" and "freedom" in distinct ways that correspond to the difference between his principle of liberty and his underlying conception of freedom (Baum 2000, 23–5).

[16] Mill's understanding of two distinct but interrelated forms of economic freedom parallels his broader effort to balance *political freedom* – that is, the freedom of citizens to share in

Mill's conception of economic freedom is a direct extension of his broader conception of freedom (Baum 2000, chap. 7). Alongside his attention to individualistic practices of economic freedom, such as the freedom of individuals to pursue particular types of work and professions and, as consumers, to purchase desired goods and services (Baum 2000, 207–21), Mill also maintains that the freedom of democratic self-government should be extended to associated workers with respect to governing economic enterprises.[17] As Jonathan Riley says, "A proper distinction between [the] respective doctrines of laissez-faire and of [individual] liberty is crucial for understanding Mill's art of political economy" (Riley 1998b, 317). Mill's distinction between the doctrines of laissez-faire and of individual liberty, however, is just one part of his conception of *economic freedom*.[18] Indeed, despite his qualified support of the laissez-faire principle (CW 3: 944–71), he challenges the now prevailing conception of "economic freedom" in Western capitalist countries. Economic freedom is commonly understood as if it is equivalent to "free markets," "free trade," "free enterprise," and "freedom of contract," as in Friedman's view of "competitive capitalism . . . [as] a system of economic freedom" (Friedman 1962, 4).[19] Therefore, it is misleading to say, as Pedro Schwartz does, that Mill himself regards capitalism as "the system of economic freedom" (Schwartz 1968; 1972, 122–3, 150).[20] On the contrary, Mill employs his conception of freedom to evaluate the merits and failings of different economic systems and to advance a form of cooperative liberal democratic market socialism.

---

determining the laws and public policies governing them – with *individual liberty*. On one hand, he warns that democratic self-government, particularly with regard to laws of the state, could result in the political "tyranny of the majority" as well as tyranny of "those who succeed in making themselves accepted as the majority" (*OL*, CW XVIII: 219). On the other hand, Mill insists that a benevolent and limited monarchy that allowed some of the advantages of "a free government," such as public debate, would realize these advantages only "in a very imperfect degree . . . since how ever great an amount of liberty the citizens might enjoy, they could not forget that they held it on sufferance" (*RG*, CW XIX: 402).

[17] Similarly, Mill seeks to extend the freedom of mutual self-government equally to women and men with respect to governing families. See Baum 2000, 185–91.

[18] For related interpretations, see Arneson 1979; Ryan 1983; Claeys 1987.

[19] Similarly, Michael Oakeshott conceives of economic freedom in terms of the unrestricted opportunities of individuals to accumulate and use of private property: "The institution of property most favorable to liberty is, unquestionably, a right to private property least qualified by arbitrary limits and exclusions" (Oakeshott [1962] 1991), 393–4.

[20] Mill does refer to capitalism, however, as the "voluntary" system and as "the system of individual agency" (*POPE*, CW II: 947, 961, 970). He also uses such phrases as "to set free" capital, "freedom of commercial intercourse," and "free" competition in *Principles*; yet he consistently distinguishes these notions from the economic freedom of individuals (*POPE*, CW II: 82–3, 130, 140).

Mill highlights one aspect of his view of economic freedom in *On Liberty* when he says that "the principle of individual liberty is not involved in the doctrine of free trade" because "trade is a social act." Yet there are some interferences with trade "which are essentially questions of liberty" (CW XVIII, 293).[21] Mill explains:

As the principle of individual liberty is not involved in the doctrine of free trade, so neither is it in most questions which arise respecting the limits of that doctrine, as, for example, what amount of public control is admissible for the prevention of fraud by adulteration; how far sanitary precautions, or arrangements to protect workpeople employed in dangerous occupations, should be enforced on employers. (293)

He adds, "Restrictions on trade, or on production for purposes of trade, are indeed restraints; and all restraint, *quâ* restraint, is an evil; but the restraints in question affect only that part of conduct which society is competent to restrain, and are wrong solely" when they fail to produce the desired results (293).[22] Interference with trade *is* a question of liberty in "all cases . . . where the object of interference is to make it impossible or difficult to obtain a particular commodity." Here the infringement of liberty at issue is not that "of the producer or seller, but on the buyer" (293). For *buyers*, the availability of desired goods may have a direct bearing on their freedom to pursue their preferred way of life, although regulations on trade may protect them from deception, fraud, and harm.[23] The freedom of producers or sellers would not be affected in a comparable way unless either the restricted good is for some reason the only one that they can produce and sell or producing or selling *that particular good* is integral to their plans of life. Such restrictions might be justified, but they would still constitute restrictions of economic freedom.

Mill similarly understands the implications of taxation and property rights for individual economic freedom. Concerning taxation, he starts with the premise that there are no limits *in principle* to the positive activities that a government may undertake insofar as it left individuals "free to use their own means of pursuing any object of general interest" (CW III: 937). He

---

[21] For related discussions of this point, see Hollander 1985, chaps. 11 and 12; Riley 1994, xlii, and 1998b, 317–18.

[22] "Such questions involve considerations of liberty," Mill says, "only insofar as leaving people to themselves is always better, *caeteris paribus,* than controlling them; but that they may be legitimately controlled for these ends is in principle undeniable" (*OL,* CW XVIII: 293).

[23] Thus, a law requiring warning labels on poisonous drugs "may be enforced without violation of liberty: the buyer cannot wish not to know that the thing he possesses has poisonous qualities" (*OL,* CW XVIII: 294).

says, "When a government provides means for fulfilling a certain end, leaving individuals free to avail themselves of different means if in their opinion preferable, there is no infringement of liberty, no irksome or degrading restraint" (938–9). He acknowledges that "[t]here is, however, in almost all forms of government agency, one thing which is compulsory; the provision of the pecuniary means," because it requires compulsory taxation (939). Nonetheless, what is important for Mill is that taxation is sufficiently restrained so that, as Fred Berger says, "it leaves the people free to chart out the course of their own lives as they see fit; it imposes a way of life on no one" (Berger 1984, 180; Baum 2000, 216–19).[24]

Mill's view of property rights is more pivotal to his socialism. He implicitly extends to the regulation of property rights the principle that while the state must respect "the liberty of each individual in what specifically regards himself, [it] is bound to maintain a vigilant control over his exercise of any power which it allows him to possess over others" – a corollary of his principle of liberty (*OL*, CW XVIII: 301). Accordingly, he follows other socialists in treating private ownership of articles of consumption, or personal property, differently from private ownership of the means and instruments of production. Although the former is a necessary condition of the freedom of individuals to pursue their own manner of life, private ownership of the means of production gives some people power over others (*COS*, CW V: 738, 749ff; CW 10: 157–8). Mill summarizes this aspect of his view of property rights in "Coleridge" with special reference to property in land. He says that when the state permits any person to own more land than is necessary for subsistence, "it confers on him power over other human beings – power affecting them in their most vital interests; and that no notion of private property can bar the right which the State inherently possesses, to require that the power which it has so given shall not be abused" (CW 10: 157–8).[25] Overall, Mill rejects the view "that all the rights now regarded as pertaining to property belong to it inherently" (*COS*, CW V: 750). He notes that that

[24] For instance, Mill said that a policy of taxing "stimulants" for the purpose of making them more difficult for people to obtain differed "only in degree" from laws that simply prohibit their sale "and would be justifiable only if [prohibition] were justifiable. Every increase of cost is a prohibition, to those whose means do not come up to the augmented price; and to those who do, it is a penalty laid on them for gratifying a particular taste" (*OL*, CW XVIII: 298).

[25] Elsewhere Mill contends that "the interests of society would in general be better consulted by laws restrictive of the acquisition of too great masses of property, than by attempting to regulate its use." He adds, however, that society has the "same right" to interfere with "capital, and moveable property generally" as it does with property in land (Letter to Charles Eliot Norton, 26 June 1870, CW XVII: 1740).

"idea of property" is not "one thing" but is historically "variable like all other creations of the human mind." Therefore, it may be politically altered to serve the public good in different ways in different societies (CW V: 753).

II

Mill goes to the heart of his case for a liberal socialism when he compares the "restraints" to freedom imposed by existing capitalism with various forms of socialism. He begins by contrasting existing capitalism to the "restraints of Communism." He reserves the term "Communism" for socialist schemes that aim at "absolute equality in the distribution of the physical means of life" and the "entire abolition of private property," and he considers communism a distinctly unpromising form of socialism (*POPE*, CW II: 203; Levin 2003, 70; Miller 2003, 225–7). Nonetheless, he says, "The restraints of Communism would be freedom in comparison with the present condition of the majority of the human race. The generality of labourers in this and most other countries, have as little choice of occupation or freedom of locomotion, are practically dependent on fixed rules and on the will of others, as they could be on any system short of actual slavery" (CW II: 209).

He amplifies this critique of existing capitalist system in *Chapters on Socialism*. Writing in the wake of the English Reform Bill of 1867, Mill echoes the socialist critique of the limitations of working class's attainment of "purely political rights" such as the franchise. "Notwithstanding all that has been done, and all that seems likely to be done," with respect to the extension of franchises,

a few are born to great riches, and the many to a penury, made only more grating by contrast. No longer enslaved or made dependent by force of law, the great majority are so by force of poverty; they are still chained to a place, to an occupation, and to conformity with the will of an employer, and debarred by the accident of birth both from the enjoyments, and from the mental and moral advantages, without which others inherit without exertion and independently of desert. (CW V: 710)

In short, while working people were gradually gaining equal status as free citizens with regard to political rights, such as the rights to vote and to stand for office, the great majority of them remained *economically unfree* within existing capitalism.[26] They were unfree insofar as their poverty and power-lessness prevented them from choosing their occupations and plans of life

---

[26] Mill addresses this issue from a different but related angle when he challenges the "gospel of work" in his 1850 response to Thomas Carlyle's views on "Negro" slavery and wage labor (Mill, "The Negro Question," CW XXI: 91–4).

and because they lacked a voice in determining the rules that governed their work lives. The general prosperity achieved in advanced capitalist societies in the post–World War II era has undoubtedly diminished some of the unfreedom experienced by working people in these societies – notably, the degree to which they are "chained to a place, to an occupation" and "debarred" from enjoying the material comforts produced by these societies. Mill makes clear, however, that some of this unfreedom is intrinsic to capitalism (see sec. IV later in the chapter).

In contrast to the restraints on freedom imposed by the "present system," Mill warns that "Communism" chiefly threatens "mental freedom" and individuality (CW II: 203, 209; CW V: 745–6). What is crucial for a comparative assessment of these two alternatives is "which of the two systems is consistent with the greatest amount of human liberty and spontaneity" (CW II: 208). Any alternative system must meet a difficult test: "whether there would be any asylum left for individuality of character; . . . whether the absolute dependence of each on all, and surveillance of each by all, would not grind all down into a tame uniformity of thoughts, feelings, and actions" (CW II: 209). Mill notes that this kind of "compression" of freedom is already a problem within existing capitalist societies – due to conformist pressures of prevailing opinion – but would be exacerbated under communism (CW II: 209; CW V: 746; CW XVIII: 264–5; CW XXV: 1179).

That said, he contends that not all socialist reform programs, as distinct from "communism," would intensify this problem. "The two [most] elaborate forms of non-communistic Socialism known as St. Simonianism and Fourierism are totally free of the objections usually urged against Communism" (CW II: 210). In Mill's view, there are difficulties with both of these forms of socialism – notably, tendencies toward elitism, state centralism, inflexibility, and undemocratic governance (particularly in St. Simonianism); overestimation of the moral and intellectual preparedness of ordinary people; overemphasis on fixed principles of "just distribution" at the expense of democratic control of production and distribution; and failure to appreciate the benefits of market competition (CW II: 210–14; CW III: 794; CW V: 747–50). Still, as I explain subsequently, Mill does not dismiss socialism per se (CW II: 213–14; CW III: 794; CW V: 746–50).

Moreover, he insists that to secure substantial freedom for the "generality of labourers" would require radical reform of capitalism in a socialist direction. He considers the goal of securing economic freedom for all to be integrally related to "social and distributive justice." In his 1852 preface to *Principles of Political Economy,* Mill describes his political economic ideal as combining "the greatest personal freedom with that just distribution of the fruits of labour, which the present laws of property do not profess to aim at" (CW II: xciii). His ultimate aim is not the greatest *sum* of freedom in a society, which could entail great freedom for some and little for others, but rather substantial freedom for all. He implicitly advances a notion of *maximal economic freedom*, which he summarizes in the *Principles* as follows: "The perfection both of social arrangements and of practical morality would be, to secure to all persons complete independence and freedom of action, subject to no restriction but that of not doing injury to others: and the education which taught or the social institutions which required them to exchange the control of their own actions for any amount of comfort or affluence, or to renounce liberty for the sake of equality, would deprive them of one of the most elevated characteristics of human nature" (CW II: 208–9). According to Mill, *some* ways of achieving greater equality would limit freedom in significant ways – for instance, a command economy that administered equal wages to all workers indiscriminately. Yet maximal economic freedom, in his view, requires considerable equality with respect to educational and occupational opportunities, income and property holdings, and opportunities to share in governing economic enterprises.[27]

Consequently, to secure maximal economic independence and freedom of action would actually entail that no one could have "complete" economic independence and freedom of action. Instead, restrictions of certain economic activities, such as unlimited accumulation of private property and the pursuit of activities otherwise harmful to others, are required to secure substantial individual liberty and opportunities for democratic self-government for all. In this regard, Mill anticipates John Dewey's later observation that "[t]here is no such thing as the liberty or effective power of an individual, group, or class, except in relation to the liberties, the effective power, of *other* individuals, groups or classes" (Dewey [1935] 1958, 112). Mill does not advocate the unrealizable goals of unrestricted economic freedom and absolutely equal freedom for all members of society, or the same freedom for all persons in all societies. Instead, he holds that the scope and character of freedom must be qualified by utilitarian considerations

---

[27] Mill spoke of *equal freedom* most explicitly in "Centralization" (1862), saying that the only "solid security" for the freedom of each person is "the equal freedom of the rest" (CW XIX: 610). Overall, he puts forward a view of democratic equality that includes but goes beyond what Fred Berger calls his "baseline" conception of equality. Mill accepts certain inequalities as just – particularly some inequalities of income and political power – but only conditionally and only insofar as they are based on differences of merit and compatible with respect for the equal moral status of all persons (Berger 1984, 159–60, 199; Baum 2003, 414).

related to claims of justice, expedience, and the existing states of individual and societal development.[28]

III

In his *Autobiography,* Mill links these ideas to the socialist commitment that he shared with Harriet Taylor: "The social problem of the future we considered to be, how to unite the greatest individual liberty of action, with a common ownership in the raw material of the globe, and an equal participation of all in the benefits of combined labour" (CW I: 239). Elsewhere he says that existing capitalism is "obviously unjust" because the distribution of the produce between the rich and poor has so little connection to "merit and demerit, or even with exertion" (CW V: 444). He explains that the usual justification for private property was that it "assure[s] to all persons what they have produced by their labor and accumulated by their abstinence" (CW II: 227). Ideally, then, a system of private property "would be accompanied by none of the initial inequalities and injustices which obstruct the beneficial operation of the principle in old societies. Every full-grown man or woman . . . would be secured in the unfettered use and disposal of his or her bodily and mental faculties; and the instruments of production, the land and tools, would be divided fairly among them, so that all might start, in respect to outward appliances, on equal terms" (CW II: 201). Mill cautions, however, that these conditions have been absent wherever private property has been established and that existing capitalism undermines the private property ideal: "The laws of property have never yet conformed to the principles on which the justification of private property rests. . . . They have not held the balance fairly between human beings, but have heaped impediments upon some, to give advantage to others; they have purposely fostered inequalities, and prevented all from starting fair in the race" (CW II: 207). Given these initial inequities, he maintains that the equilibrium wage for

---

[28] See Robson 1968; Sarvasy 1985; Claeys 1987; Ashcraft 1989, 1998; Donner 1991; Ten 1998; Baum 2000, chap. 2. Given Mill's commitment to the aggregative principle of "utility as the ultimate appeal on all ethical questions," it is important to be clear about just how he relates the goal of equal economic freedom to distributive rules of justice (*OL,* CW XVIII: 224). He appeals to "utility in the largest sense, grounded on the permanent interests of man as a progressive being" (*OL,* CW XVIII: 224). Accordingly, he rests his utilitarian case for maximal freedom on his view that freedom and individuality are among the "permanent interests" of people as "progressive beings." For Mill, then, promoting freedom is intimately connected to achieving the greatest happiness or well-being (*OL,* chap. 3). See Gray 1989; Skorupski 1989.

working people that emerges from market competition under the present system is unjust. One problem from his perspective is that the unequal initial distribution of property is itself established unjustly (Medearis 2005).

These considerations leave room for reforming the "system of private property," or capitalism, so that it *would* conform to "the principles on which the justification of private property rests." Mill also discerns deeper problems with capitalism, however. First, there is the problem of inherited inequalities. He says that the principle of private property encompasses the right of individuals "to what has been produced by others, if obtained by their free consent," but it *does not* entitle anyone without qualification to "the fruits of the labour of others, transmitted to them without any merit of exertion of their own" (CW II: 217, 208; COS, CW V: 750). Because of inherited inequalities "[m]any, indeed, fail with greater efforts than those which others succeed, not from difference of merits, but difference of opportunities" (CW II: 811). In brief, even if everyone started "on equal terms" in one generation, people would start on quite unequal terms in the next. Mill argues, therefore, that although private property inevitably perpetuates some inequality of opportunities, judicious legislation could go a considerable way to foster relatively equal opportunity. In this respect he exemplifies the kind of reform liberalism Paul Starr endorses. Mill's chief reformist liberal proposals to equalize opportunities across generations are a heavy progressive inheritance tax, taxation of unearned land rents, and publicly supported general education (Baum 2000, 209–21).

Mill's more far-reaching response to the political economy of freedom and equality, however, challenges the capitalist form of private ownership and control of the means and instruments of production from a proximate socialist perspective. Maximal freedom and justice for the "generality of labourers" requires not just a more equitable distribution of opportunities and produce, but also, more fundamentally, democratization of major centers of economic power, industrial firms. Mill looks to socialists for what he called the highest standards of distributive justice – particularly the communist principle of equal division of produce and Louis Blanc's still "higher standard" of "apportionment according to need" (*COS*, CW V: 739). He sees greater promise in Fourierist socialism, which "allow[s] differences of remuneration for different kinds or degrees of service to the community" (*COS*, CW V: 739, 747; *POPE*, CW II: 212).[29] Wisely, though, Mill does not dwell

---

[29] As a matter of principle and possibility, he remains open to the potential advantages of a thoroughgoing form of socialism that would achieve a more fully egalitarian standard of

on an ideal standard of distributive justice. This is partly due to his judgment that realizing an ideal distribution would require considerable enhancement of "the intelligence and morality of the individual citizens" (*COS*, CW 5: 745). It is also due to how he conceives the connection between the just distribution of produce and a just distribution of power within economic enterprises.[30]

IV

Mill brings these considerations together in *Principles of Political Economy* when he outlines his view of what "would be the nearest approach to social justice . . . possible . . . to foresee" (CW II: 794). Rather than any fixed principle for the just distribution of produce, the central feature of Mill's political economic ideal is the democratic reorganization of industrial firms, which would give associated workers a voice in determining the distribution of incomes within their firms. Based on the experience of worker-managed cooperatives in France, Mill points out that establishing worker self-managed firms would often conflict with the "highest" standards of just distribution of produce. (The cooperatives generally abandoned the principle of equal wages to apportion remuneration beyond a fixed minimum for all "according to the work done"; CW III: 782.) In contrast to Saint-Simonian and Fourierist forms of socialism, and in contrast to contemporary Rawlsian egalitarian liberalism, Mill places the goal of expanding workers' freedom through industrial democracy before that of any ideal standard of distributive justice (CW II: 210–14; CW III: 766–96).

Mill defends the "co-operative principle," with reference to the cooperative societies of the time, as the best way to achieve maximal freedom within economic enterprises. He distinguishes the democratic cooperative principle from the repressive power dynamics of capitalist enterprises, seeing them as embodying two opposing theories concerning the proper status

---

distribution (*POPE*, CW II: 210, 213–14; *COS*, CW V: 739, 746–8). He cautions, though, that this idea appeals "to a higher standard of justice, and is adapted to a much higher moral condition of human nature" (*POPE*, CW II: 210).

[30] Mill's thinking on this point parallels that of Karl Marx. Marx, in his 1875 "Critique of the Gotha Program," famously affirms for "a higher phase of communist society" the utopian socialist ideal, "From each according to his ability, to each according to his needs!" But then, responding to the German Workers' Party's notion of "fair distribution," Marx adds that "it was in general a mistake to make such a fuss about so-called distribution and put principle stress on it. Any distribution whatever of the means of consumption is only a consequence of the distribution of the means of production themselves." See Marx [1875] 1983, 541.

of manual laborers – one of "dependence and protection" and the other of "self-dependence." According to the former theory,

the lot of the poor, in all things which affect them collectively, should be regulated *for* them, not *by* them. They should not be required or encouraged to think for themselves, or give to their own reflection or forecast an influential voice in the determination of their duty.... The relation between rich and poor, according to this theory (a theory also applied to the relation between men and women) should be only partly authoritative.... The rich should be *in loco parentis* to the poor, guiding and restraining them like children. (*POPE,* CW III: 759)

This theory of dependence is manifest within capitalist firms in the power that the "employing" class exercises over the laboring class, with "the many who do the work being mere servants under the command of the one who supplies the funds" (CW III: 767–9). This arrangement leaves working people substantially unfree within economic enterprises – that is, lacking self-government – and Mill maintains that this "patriarchal or paternal system of government" is becoming increasingly obsolete (CW III: 762–3). "[T]he civilizing and improving influences of association, and the efficiency and economy of production on a large scale, may be attained without dividing the producers into two parties with hostile interests and feelings" (769). "The poor," he says,

have come out of leading strings, and cannot any longer be governed or treated like children.... Modern nations will have to learn the lesson, that the well-being of a people must exist by means of the justice and self-government ... of individual citizens ...

... If the improvement [in human affairs] ... shall continue its course, there can be little doubt that the *status* of hired labourers will gradually tend to confine itself to the description of workpeople whose low moral qualities render them unfit for anything more independent: and the relation of masters and workpeople will be gradually superseded by partnership ...: in some cases, association of the labourers with the capitalist; in others, and perhaps finally in all, association of labourers among themselves. (CW III: 763, 769)

In short, working people now can be governed according to the democratic theory of self-dependence, which would treat adult members of modern societies as self-governing agents.

Mill conceives the cooperative principle, ultimately, as a means to extend democratic self-government, on equal terms, to virtually all working people with respect to the economic enterprises in which they work within the framework of a postcapitalist competitive market economy. The best form of industrial association "is not that which can exist between a capitalist as chief, and workpeople without a voice in the management, but the association of the labourers themselves on terms of equality, collectively owning the capital with which they carry on their operations, and working under managers elected and removable by themselves" (CW III: 775). This form of association

would combine the freedom and independence of the individual, with the moral, intellectual, and economical advantages of aggregate production; and . . . would realize, at least in the industrial department, the best aspirations of the democratic spirit, by putting an end to the division of society into the industrious and the idle, and effacing all social distinctions but those fairly earned by personal services and exertions . . . the existing accumulations of capital might honestly . . . become in the end the joint property of all who participate in their productive employment. (793)

It is this cooperative form of association, moreover, that Mill considers as "the nearest approach to social justice, and the most beneficial ordering of industrial affairs . . . which it is possible at present to foresee . . . assuming of course that both sexes participate equally in the government of the association)" (794). "What is wanted," he says in an 1864 speech on cooperation, "is that the whole of the working classes should partake in the profits of labour" in a cooperative mode once "all have become capable of co-operation" (CW XXVIII: 6–7, 8). "This is the millennium towards which we should strive" (CW XXVIII: 8–9).[31]

Mill's prescient guiding assumption is that relationships of power and interdependence are unavoidable in modern economies. Members of modern societies are typically involved in economic relationships and institutions that make them interdependent, such as the "large industrial enterprises" that tend to dominate agriculture and manufacturing due to economies of scale.[32] Therefore, most people cannot be made free in the economic domain by placing them "in a condition in which they will be able to do without one another." Instead, extending economic freedom fully to all will require establishing practices of democratic self-government whereby people are enabled "to work with or for one another in relations not involving dependence" (*POPE*, CW III: 768).

For Mill, the cooperative principle represents the fullest expression of this idea because it extends the "democratic spirit" to virtually "all who participate in . . . productive employment" (*POPE*, CW III: 793). Cooperatives, like any other form of economic association, must establish certain general rules

---

[31] See Ashcraft 1998, 184; Baum 2000, 221–4.

[32] "Labour is unquestionably more productive," Mill said, "on the system of large industrial enterprises; the produce, if not greater absolutely, is greater in proportion to the labour employed" (*POPE*, CW III: 768).

of organization and discipline. Yet they offer a substantial gain in societal freedom when compared with the present system by giving working people a voice in determining these rules and policies that govern their work lives. Mill observes, for instance, that managers of cooperatives are typically paid more than other members, "but the rule is adhered to, that the exercise of power shall never be an occasion of profit" (CW III: 784). Moreover, the power managers exercise is limited by their democratic accountability to the whole body of associated workers. Decisions regarding the distribution of wages for different jobs, the distribution of profits between new investments and expansion, and the extent of provisions reserved for the sick and disabled become collective concerns (783–4).

As Jonathan Riley points out, Mill does not abandon his usual concern about the dangers of majority tyranny with respect to unconventional ideas and lifestyles in worker self-governed enterprises (Riley 1994, xlii; cf. Arneson 1979; Ten 1998, 393). Mill addresses this issue directly with reference only to "communistic" associations. He warns that "in Communist associations private life would be brought in a most unexampled degree within the dominion of public authority, and there would be less scope for the development of individual character than has hitherto existed" (CW V: 746; CW II: 208–9).[33] He never suggests, however, that rigid work regimes and repression of individuality in thought and action would be a greater danger in cooperative firms than in capitalist ones. Indeed, although majority tyranny is certainly possible within democratic cooperatives, there is little reason to believe that an economy of decentralized cooperatives would pose a greater danger to individuality and freedom of action than an economy dominated by traditional capitalist firms (Arneson 1979, 241). Conversely, given the powers of surveillance and control wielded in capitalist firms by owners and managers who are largely unaccountable to workers, there are good reasons to expect cooperative associations, generally speaking, to be less rigid and tyrannical than capitalist firms.[34] Moreover, all other things

---

[33] In the 1849 edition of *Principles,* Mill states that his aim of securing "to all persons complete independence and freedom of action, subject to no restriction but that of not doing injury to others." Then he adds that the communist scheme "(at least as it is commonly understood) abrogates this freedom entirely, and places every action of every member of the community under [collective] command" (CW III: 978).

[34] Reflecting on French industrial associations, Mill says that, rather than instituting looser rules of discipline than those found in "ordinary workshops," workers established stricter rules. He notes, however, that "being rules self-imposed, for the manifest good of the community, and not for the convenience of an employer regarded as having an opposite interest, they are far more scrupulously obeyed, and the voluntary obedience carries with it a sense of personal worth and dignity" (*POPE,* CW III: 780–1).

being equal, a decentralized cooperative market socialist economy would provide working people with at least as much freedom to choose jobs and careers as does a capitalist system.[35]

Mill is vague about whether such a cooperative system should be regarded as a reformed type of capitalism or as a form of socialism (Riley 1996a), as well as about just how and when such a system would be achieved. Nonetheless, his ideal of a decentralized system of cooperative associations has important implications for how we construe his relationship to the socialist tradition. He rejects communism, or "revolutionary socialism," which envisions centralized state management of all economic activities; yet he admires Fourierism, which emphasized a decentralized economy and worker self-management while permitting different pay for different work (*COS*, CW V: 739–46; *POPE*, CW II: 212–14). He says that "the very idea of conducting the whole industry of a country by direction from a single centre is . . . obviously chimerical" (CW V: 748).[36] More importantly for present purposes, after making his case for co-operative associations, he declares, "I agree, then, with the Socialist writers in their conception of the form which industrial operations tend to assume in the advance of improvement; and I entirely share their opinion that the time is ripe for commencing this trans-formation, and that it should by all just and effectual means be aided and encouraged" (*POPE*, CW III: 794).[37] He disagrees with socialists, however, concerning "their declamations against competition" and insists that market competition among enterprises would remain "indispensable to progress" (794). Thus, aside from his defense of market competition – which is no

---

[35] Insofar as a cooperative system would equalize opportunities for self-development and entrepreneurship, it would provide more equal freedom in this regard than capitalist systems. In effect, the shift to such a socialist system would entail a "redistribution of freedom" (Arneson 1979, 239).

[36] To my knowledge there is no evidence that Mill was aware of Marx's thought and included Marxism in his understanding of "revolutionary socialism" (Lindsay 2000, 665). Nonetheless, Mill anticipates problems entailed by state centralist and antimarket tendencies in Marx and Marxism. See Blackburn 1991, 184.

[37] Mill reiterates this point in an 1868 letter. "It would not be a correct view of my opinions to suppose that I think everything wrong in the doctrines of Socialism; on the contrary I think there are many elements of truth in them, & that much good may be done in that direction, especially by the progress of the Cooperative Movement" (Letter to Peter Deml, 22 April 1868, CW XVI: 1389). In an 1852 letter, he says that he never regarded his objections to the best socialist theories as conclusive, but that "the low moral state of mankind generally and of the labouring classes in particular, renders them at present unfit for any order of things which would presuppose as its necessary condition a certain measure of conscience & intellect" (Letter to Karl D. Heinrich Rau, 20 March 1852, CW XIV: 87). See also Mill, *POPE*, CW III: 763; *COS*, CW V: 746–9.

longer rejected by all socialists – Mill's view of the political economy of freedom has important socialist aspects.

Mill remains indefinite about the precise details of the best political economic system, although not without reason. He suggests that at least for the near term, individual capitalists with profit-sharing policies should continue to compete with cooperatives, partly to keep "the managers of co-operative societies up to the due pitch of activity and vigilance" with regard to adopting improvements (CW III: 793). Simultaneously, he envisions a gradual multiplication of cooperatives so that they would eventually absorb "all work-people, except those who have too little understanding, or too little virtue" to be economically self-governing (793).[38] His ideal thus embraces sweeping change to existing capitalism that would democratically reconfigure the "industrial department" (793–4). He rather wistfully suggests that as this process proceeds, owners of capital would gradually shift from being old-style capitalists to mere lenders of capital to cooperatives at diminishing rates of interest, "and at last, perhaps, even to exchange their capital for terminable annuities." This transition would result in something akin to socialism because existing accumulations of capital would become, "and by a kind of spontaneous process, . . . the joint property of all who participate in their productive employment" (793). In fact, this economic system would constitute a form of socialism in Mill's own terms. He defines socialism as "the joint ownership by all members of the community of the instruments and means of production" (*COS*, CW V: 738).[39]

V

Given Mill's claim that his work "lies rather among anticipations of the future than explorations of the past" (discussed earlier), it is not surprising

---

[38] As I explain elsewhere, Mill's thinking is somewhat exclusionary here – with his mention of some "workpeople whose low moral qualities render them unfit for anything more independent" than "the *status* of hired labourers" (discussed earlier) – in a way that foreshadows exclusionary tendencies common to contemporary liberal states. See Baum 2003.

[39] In *Chapters on Socialism*, Mill says that cooperative stores are "partly grounded on socialistic principles, [but] consistent with the existing constitution of property" (CW V: 733). Mill's cooperative model is more clearly socialist if we accept Alec Nove's recent definition. Nove suggests that we consider a society socialist "[i]f the major part of the means of production of goods and services are not in private hands, but are in some sense socially owned and operated, by state, socialized or cooperative enterprises" (Nove 1987, 389). Likewise, Jon Elster and Karl Ove Moene define "market socialism" as "a system of labour cooperatives" (Elster and Moene 1989, 26). On Mill's view of socialism, see Stafford 1998a; Miller 2003.

that his ideal political economic system is full of hopes and anticipations and that he leaves several key issues unresolved. Still, we can draw some valuable practical lessons from how he frames the choice between capitalism and socialism. First, his analysis indicates that the usual either–or opposition of liberal and socialist political–economic approaches to social reform, often posed by Marxists, oversimplifies the range of possibilities.[40] Mill's liberal commitment to individual freedom leads him to advocate a form of enterprise-based liberal democratic market socialism.[41]

Second, even if Mill's cooperative ideal does not fit some definitions of socialism, he nonetheless gives us a powerful liberal case for transforming capitalism to a point where it would significantly advance the socialist goal of extending democracy into the economy.[42] Moreover, by foregrounding issues of individual freedom and democracy, Mill provides socialists the moral and strategic advantages of approaching socialism on the basis of the widely accepted liberal democratic principle of individual freedom. The flip side of this is that Mill clarifies the promise of a distinctly *liberal* socialism in which the socialist aspect would substantially revise Lockean liberal notions of private property rights in means of production and the liberal aspect would reaffirm the vision of a free society that Mill articulates at the start of *On Liberty*.[43]

In contrast to calls for socialism that prioritize distributive justice, or "fair distribution" – by Louis Blanc, Saint-Simon, Fourier, and the German Workers' Party (in its 1875 Gotha Programme) in the nineteenth century and by John Rawls in the twentieth – Mill advocates socialist reform principally in

---

[40] On this point, see Lindsay 2000, 658, 669–78. Although I agree with the gist of Lindsay's argument – that it is misleading to draw a sharp dichotomy between welfare state capitalism and socialism – I question his claim that there is *no qualitative distinction* to draw between welfare state capitalism and socialism. Although I cannot defend this claim here, Dale Miller is right, in my view, to suggest that Mill's enterprise-based market-socialist vision is qualitatively different from profit sharing forms of capitalism. The former would entail a major change of capitalist relations of production, whereas the latter requires no such change. See Miller 2003, 224. Cf. Ashcraft 1998; Riley 1994: xxix–xxxviii; and Riley 1996a.

[41] Miller calls Mill's ideal "firm-level socialism" and "community-level incentivistic [i.e., market] socialism (Miller 2003: 223–4).

[42] Mouffe, in advocating liberal socialism, conceives socialism "as a process of the democratization of the economy" (1993, 90).

[43] There he enumerates a set of basic civil liberties, including "liberty of conscience, in the most comprehensive sense; liberty of thought and feeling; absolute freedom of opinion and sentiment on all subjects, practical or speculative, scientific, moral, or theological." He adds, "No society in which these liberties are not, on the whole respected, is free" (*OL*, CW XVIII: 226).

the name of enlarging freedom.[44] In so doing, Mill offers a way to shift the current terms of debate concerning capitalism and socialism. Capitalism, Mill demonstrates, promotes certain limited forms of freedom for many people (e.g., consumer choices) and enormous freedom for relatively few people (i.e., those who own and control the means of production and wealthy people more generally). Meanwhile, it leaves many people substantially *unfree*, lacking self-government with respect to the economic institutions that govern their lives and lacking the resources they need to pursue their own good in their own way.[45] Mill also illuminates how statist forms of socialism (or "communism") that prioritize fixed principles of just distribution – such as equal distribution of income or "a still higher standard of justice, that all should work according to their capacity, and receive according to their wants" – tend to stifle individuality and "renounce liberty for the sake of equality" (CW II: 203, 208–9). In contrast, Mill's cooperative market socialist provides a framework for achieving maximal economic freedom – that is, substantial freedom for every person to achieve her (or his) own good in her own way and opportunities for associated workers to share in self-government with respect to the economic firms that govern their lives.

Even if Mill's specific reform proposals are ultimately insufficient or unworkable, he offers a compelling way to comprehend the meaning and conditions of maximal individual economic freedom in modern economies. Still, by seeking distributive justice *indirectly* – through a market economy of worker self-managed cooperatives – Mill's liberal socialism may sacrifice what he himself called the "highest" standards of just distribution – equal division of produce or "apportionment according to need" (discussed earlier). Liberal market socialism of this sort, G. A. Cohen notes, does not address directly the injustice that is produced (from an egalitarian socialist perspective) "in a system that confers high rewards to people who happen to be unusually talented and who form highly productive co-operatives." That is, it "preserves the income injustice caused by the differential ownership of endowments of personal capacity" along with income injustice

---

[44] I have skipped over Marx here because Marx sought communism chiefly as a means to enlarge human freedom rather than as a means to achieve distributive justice. Under communism, Marx and Engels declare, "the free development of each [would be] the condition for the free development of all" (Marx and Engels [1848] 1983, 228).

[45] Considerations of distributive justice are obviously also at stake here, but Mill, like Marx, highlights how the distribution of wealth and income in a given society is dependent in part on the distribution of economic power.

due to people's membership in more and less successful cooperatives (1992, 288, 290).

This trade-off, such as it is, may well be unavoidable, as Cohen acknowledges (1992, 287–9). To prioritize the "highest" standards of just distribution as a matter of policy would seem to require comprehensive, society-wide political–economic planning that would preclude meaningful worker self-management at the level of the firm.[46] There may be a middle ground position between Millian liberal socialism and approaches that prioritize distributive justice. It may be possible to combine economies of worker self-managed cooperatives with significant nation-state and transnational economic regulation and management, including state provision of such public goods as education and health care.[47] Yet this option would have to overcome the challenges that have already undercut European social democracy (Gray 1995; Sassoon 1996, 768–77).

Finally, Mill's liberal socialist theory clearly has some practical limitations with respect to the political task of transforming capitalism. He says in *Chapters on Socialism* that society justifiably could modify property rights when such changes are deemed conducive to the general good; but he remains reluctant to prescribe state action to bring about a new system of property rights and work relationships.[48] This is largely due to his wariness about expansive state power. It is also due, however, to his failure to develop a systemic critique of capitalism that confronts how the power of capital impedes any "spontaneous" transition to cooperativism.

---

[46] It would not in principle preclude democratic economic planning at the level of nation-states. Marx seems to have had something like this in mind when he spoke, in *The Civil War in France*, of "united co-operative societies . . . regulat[ing] national production under a common plan, thus taking it under their control" (Marx [1871] 1983, 518). Marx, however, did not confront the difficulties posed by comprehensive centralized economic planning, however. See Mill, *COS*, CW V: 748; Blackburn 1991; Cohen, 1992, 290.

[47] I am inclined to think that "the nearest approach to social justice . . . which it is possible at present to foresee" (to borrow Mill's words) in political economic terms – assuming the overcoming of economic inequalities due to sex and racialized identity – would involve a synthesis of Millian and Rawlsian approaches: economies structured around worker self-managed cooperatives combined with national and transnational economic management, regulation, and social provision aimed to realize something like Rawls's "difference principle" – that social and economic inequalities must "be to the greatest benefit of the least-advantaged members of society" (Rawls 2001, 42).

[48] Mill's proposed reforms include not only taxes on inheritance and rents but also the more radical proposal that the state buy up land that becomes available on the market from large landowners and then "leasing it, either to small farmers with due security of tenure, or to co-operative associations of labour" ("Leslie on the Land Question," CW V: 683). See also Mill, "Land Tenure Reform," CW V: 687–95.

Moreover, due to his reluctance to advocate state action to bring about a post-capitalist cooperative economy and his thoughts about a "spontaneous" transformation to such an economy, Mill offers little guidance regarding the politics necessary to achieve this goal.[49] Reflecting on the English Reform Act of 1867, he comments that the changing contours of English class politics would eventually empower the working classes to bring about socialist reforms if they so desired. "The great increase of electoral power which the Act places within the reach of the working classes is permanent.... [I]t is as certain as anything in politics can be, that they will before long find the means necessary of making their collective electoral power effectively instrumental to the promotion of their collective interests" (*COS*, CW V: 707). He also supports the efforts of trade unions to fight for better wages in the context of the existing class division between employers and employees even as he envisions an ultimate cooperative overcoming of this division (CW V: 657; "Letter to John Boyd Kinnear," CW XVI: 1103).

For the near term, Mill seeks to prevent any one social class, such as laborers or employers of labor, from using the state to pursue its "class interests" at the expense of the general interest of society (*RG*, CW XIX: 442, 447). Yet he regards many of the claims articulated by the working class and socialist movements – which were overlapping but not identical – as consistent with laborers' "real ultimate interest" and, therefore, with "justice and the general interest" (CW XIX: 443, 447; see n. 37, this chapter). He hopes that working-class education and political mobilization will spur appropriate socialist reforms through deliberative democratic politics (Sarvasy 1984; Ashcraft 1989; Ten 1998; Baum 2000, 240–5). Even so, he underestimates the extent to which concerted political action by organized workers and their political allies would be needed to bring about liberal socialism, particularly if this was to mean anything more than the existence of occasional cooperative firms within capitalist societies.

In addition, Mill likely would have been perplexed and disappointed by the shift in struggles for economic freedom during the twentieth century (in Zygmunt Bauman's words) "away from the area of production and power and into that of consumption" (Bauman 1988, 7). Mill also would have fretted, as Herbert Marcuse did in the 1960s, about the extent to which the vast range of consumer choices now widely available to most people in advanced capitalist societies is a worthy substitute for meaningful freedom

---

[49] Regarding Mill's optimism about a "spontaneous" transformation to a decentralized economy of cooperative associations, Alan Ryan comments, "Mill contrived to get things as wrong as he ever did" (1983, 230).

and power for working people to share in governing their working lives.[50] Mill would grant that, all other things being equal, such choices contribute to our freedom "of pursuing our own good in our own way." But he would agree with Marcuse that the sheer number of consumer choices is not decisive for assessing the extent of human freedom, and he would insist that the proliferation of consumer choices should not be traded in for the freedom of self-government.[51]

Furthermore, Mill generally addresses the issues of democratic account-ability and industrial democracy as basically national questions. Therefore, despite his attention to international trade, he fails to foresee how global labor markets and capital flows and the advent of transnational corpora-tions would complicate the political task of achieving economic democracy. His contribution here is limited by how he embraces socialist ideas at the level of the firm but not at the level of broader national and international economic forces (Kuttner 1992, 11–12). If there remains any hope to achieve something close to Mill's liberal socialist ideal, it likely will depend in part on the development of a transnational labor movement that champions this cause.[52] Mill's enterprise-based and market-oriented ideal also fails to address directly broader socialist commitments to social solidarity and com-munity entitlements. Specifically, he provides no clear answers to political economic issues such as building bonds of solidarity and social justice across firms and communities in the face of economic dislocations and inequalities generated by market competition, regulating relations between cooperative

---

[50] Marcuse says, "The range of choices open to the individual is not the decisive factor in determining the degree of human freedom, but *what* can be chosen and what *is* chosen by the individual" (Marcuse [1964] 1991: 7).

[51] Mill said "Constraints of Communism" (1850) that even many rich people are unfree in the present society not because of "fear of want" but because they fear "other people's opinions": "They do not cultivate and follow opinions, preferences, or tastes of their own, nor live otherwise than in the manner appointed for persons of their class. Their lives are inane and monotonous because (in short) they are not free, because though able to live as pleases themselves, their minds are bent to an external yoke" (CW XXV: 1180, 1179). On self-government, see n. 12 to this chapter.

[52] Although Mill never systematically considers this idea, he does make some relevant points in an 1868 letter concerning his hopes about "the ultimate working of . . . foreign competition" on the efforts of trade unions and "feud between capitalists and labourers": "The operatives are now fully alive to this part of the case, and are beginning to try how far the combination principle among labourers for wages, admits of becoming international, as it has already become national instead of local, and general instead of being confined to each trade without help from other trades. The final experiment is now commenced, the result of which will fix the limit of what the trade union principle can do." See Mill, Letter to J. R. Ware, 13 September 1868, CW XVI: 1439. For a recent view of the role of "international social-movement unionism" in relation to the socialist project, see Moody 1997, 293–310.

firms, and allocating resources in just ways in a cooperative-based national (or transnational) economy (Robbins 1952, 159).

Mill does offer an important *indirect* response to such challenges, however. "[I]n the moral aspect of the question, which is ... more important than the economical, something better should be aimed at as the goal of industrial improvement than to disperse mankind over the earth in single families, ... [with] scarcely any community of interest, or necessity of mental communion, with other human beings." Cooperative associations, he says, would be a "school" of "public spirit, generous sentiments, ... true justice and equality" (*POPE*, CW III: 768). This claim, of course, has hardly been tested, and its testing ground is a far cry from "the trampling, crushing, elbowing, and treading on each other's heels, which form the existing [capitalist] type of social life" (*POPE*, CW II: 754). That said, Mill's hope rests on an assumption that remains crucial to the project of a liberal democratic socialism: that a democratic reordering of relations of production and exchange would foster, at least to some degree, more generous democratic sensibilities within modern democratic societies.

On balance, Mill gives us a compelling account of the political economy of freedom that illuminates how liberal democratic socialism can enlarge human freedom and advance distributive justice. Although he highlights the links between personal freedom and just distribution in economic life, he persuasively challenges socialists and social democrats – from Louis Blanc and Saint-Simon to Rawls and Dworkin – who placed the goal of just distribution before (or in opposition to) that of enlarging human freedom. He also puts forward a prescient case against continual striving for "the mere increase of production and accumulation." For poor countries, he says, "increased production" remains an "important object"; but in the "most advanced" countries "what is economically needed is a better distribution." The constant "struggle for riches" diminishes human life; more than that, it threatens our connections with and appreciation for "the spontaneous activity of nature" (*POPE*, CW III: 755–6). What Millian socialists would champion, then, is a liberal democratic and ecological socialism.

5

The Method of Reform

J. S. Mill's Encounter with Bentham and Coleridge

Frederick Rosen

In the preface to *Considerations on Representative Government* (1861), J. S. Mill addresses his work to those Liberals and Conservatives who, in his view, seem 'to have lost confidence in the political creeds which they nominally profess' in recent debates on parliamentary reform (CW XIX: 373). He notes that although this loss of confidence seems to have taken place, no better creed has presented itself to either side. We thus encounter in the two creeds two opposing views without any obvious means of reconciling them or moving to a better doctrine or doctrines or to parliamentary reform. Nevertheless, Mill holds out for a better doctrine – not a compromise between the two, but another perspective 'which, in virtue of its superior comprehension, might be adopted by either Liberal or Conservative without renouncing anything which he really feels to be valuable in his own creed' (CW XIX: 373).

Mill's starting point of addressing opposing views and looking for ways to reconcile them from a different perspective is not simply a rhetorical flourish. In the *Considerations,* we find echoes of Mill's approach in the famous essays on Bentham (1838) and Coleridge (1840): Mill begins with contrary doctrines forming an opposition that he then overcomes. Although it would be wrong to see these remarks in the *Considerations* as a simple restatement of views taken in these earlier essays, the arguments seem to presuppose the essays as well as the development of his political thought prior to their composition.[1] By examining these earlier works, we shall be able to understand more clearly Mill's approach to government and particularly

---

[1] Ryan 1974, 190, refers to 'Mill's long-drawn-out attempt to make something of both Bentham and Coleridge, to reconcile Liberals and Conservatives'. But he does not go on to discuss method in the *Considerations,* based on these earlier essays. Nor does he consider Mill's method in his earlier discussion of Bentham and Coleridge (see Ryan 1974, 53–8).

to its reform; we shall also understand the continuing significance of the method of reform for ethics and politics generally.

In this chapter, I hope to provide first a brief survey of some aspects of Mill's early political thought, as it develops from the radical philosophy he inherits from Jeremy Bentham and James Mill to his version of philosophic radicalism, which culminates in the essays on Bentham and Coleridge. To understand more fully his attraction to and use of the ideas of Coleridge, I consider Mill's friendship with the Coleridgean John Sterling. I then discuss Mill's moral and social science in book VI of the *System of Logic Ratiocinative and Inductive* (1843) in which he conceives an historical approach within the context of a deductive science. Drawing on these disparate sources – including also Mill's early 'Remarks on Bentham's Philosophy' – I show that Mill's prescriptions for reform do not follow any simple means–ends calculation that one associates with traditional utilitarianism. Rather, Mill's method is based on his theory of social science in the *Logic* and on the approach to reform that he first developed in 'Bentham' and 'Coleridge'. In employing this method, Mill supported gradual change, based on intelligent consensus in society and both guided and initiated by an intellectual class.

I

Although Mill's earliest political writings are now readily available in the *Collected Works,* for this chapter, I concentrate on his reaction to the ideas of Bentham and James Mill for the starting point of the evolution of his political thought. Prior to the 1830s, even if Mill did not always agree with Bentham and his father, most of his interests and arguments followed in the radical tradition in which he was carefully nurtured. This tradition favoured liberty in numerous fields, from freedom from religious persecution to freedom of speech and action, including the freedom to own property and exchange it. In international relations, the radicals hoped that free trade might lead to a more pacific world. In domestic politics, radical thought favoured the accountability of rulers to the ruled through representative government, based on the secret ballot, near universal suffrage, and equal electoral districts. It stressed the importance of public opinion, a free press, and widespread publicity to enhance accountability in government. In education, radical thought favoured the extension of provision to the middle and lower classes, the cultivation of higher pleasures through education, and the replacement of a classical and religious curriculum by one more firmly rooted in the modern secular world.

For several reasons, some psychological and others political, the young Mill came to feel trapped and even stifled either by his inheritance or by those from whom he inherited his views. Mill's creation of philosophic radicalism and his involvement with the *London and Westminster Review* in the 1830s represented attempts to develop a new perspective. In the *Autobiography,* he wrote that he was pursuing two objects:

> One was to free philosophic radicalism from the reproach of sectarian Benthamism. I desired, while retaining the precision of expression, the definiteness of meaning, the contempt of declamatory phrases and vague generalities, which were so honorably characteristic both of Bentham and my father, to give a wider basis and a more free and genial character to Radical speculations; to shew that there was a Radical philosophy, better and more complete than Bentham's, while recognizing and incorporating all of Bentham's which is permanently valuable. In this first object I, to a certain extent, succeeded. (CW I: 221)

The second object was the attempt to re-invigorate radical politics, which, he admitted, was for the most part a failure (CW I: 221–3). In fact, one can argue that Mill's essays on Bentham and Coleridge are the culmination of this attempt to free philosophic radicalism from what he called 'sectarian Benthamism', and, additionally, constitute a recognition of his failure to advance radical politics in this period just after the success of the Reform Bill. The two essays are also closely related to the *Logic,* which Mill was writing at this time, and hence reflect further a turning away from practical politics.

But what was philosophic radicalism?[2] When Mill used the term, he referred to a small group of radicals in Parliament following the passage of the Reform Bill (see CW VI: 191, 212), who did not always succeed in advancing the cause of reform, men such as George Grote, John Arthur Roebuck, Charles Buller, and Sir William Molesworth. Mill sought to support and lead this group through his editorship of the *London and Westminster Review* (see Thomas 1979, 1ff., 199ff.). When he discussed various kinds of radicals, he distinguished four groups that differed from the philosophic radicals. The first were the historic radicals who believed in popular institutions as the inheritance of Englishmen transmitted to modern Britain from 'the Saxons or the barons of Runnymeade'. The second, metaphysical radicals, believed in democracy based on 'unreal' philosophical abstractions such as natural liberty or natural rights. The third, radicals of occasion and circumstance, opposed the government over particular issues and at particular times; and

---

[2] For a fuller discussion of the evolution of Mill's philosophic radicalism from Bentham's radical philosophy, see F. Rosen, 'From Jeremy Bentham's Radical Philosophy to J.S. Mill's Philosophic Radicalism' in the *Cambridge History of Nineteenth Century Political Thought,* ed. G. Stedman Jones and G. Claeys, forthcoming (2007).

the fourth, radicals of position, were radicals simply because they were not lords. The philosophic radicals 'are those who in politics observe the common practice of philosophers – that is, who, when they are discussing means, begin by considering the end, and when they desire to produce effects, think of causes' (CW VI: 353).

What is curious about this depiction of philosophic radicalism is, first, that neither Bentham nor James Mill would find it alien to their approaches to politics, and second, that Mill distinguished philosophic radicalism by its philosophical method and not its particular proposals for institutional reform. There is no reference here to such radical proposals as universal suffrage, the secret ballot, or constitutional reform (abolition of second chamber, monarchy, etc.). It is as if Mill expected radical reformers to be re-invigorated not by particular proposals for reform, but by a new philosophical method for politics, which was derived from and related to the utilitarianism he inherited from his father and Bentham but was also fundamentally different.

II

To understand this difference we might begin with Mill's efforts to distinguish his views from those of Bentham. In 'Remarks on Bentham's Philosophy', published as an appendix to Bulwer's *England and the English* (1833), he made his first substantial attempt to consider both the favourable and unfavourable sides of Bentham's doctrines 'considered as a complete philosophy' (CW I: 207). For Mill, Bentham's achievements could be compared favourably with those of Francis Bacon. But Bentham went beyond Bacon: whereas Bacon prophesised a science, Bentham actually created one. Bentham was the first 'to declare all the secondary and intermediate principles of law, by direct and systematic inference from the one great axiom or principle of general utility'. Mill also praised him for his 'first, and perhaps the grandest achievement' – his discrediting of technical systems widely prevalent in evidence and judicial procedure, and in the common law generally. Law ceased to be a mystery and became a matter of 'practical business, wherein means were to be adapted to ends, as in any of the other arts of life'. 'To have accomplished this', Mill continued, 'supposing him to have done nothing else, is to have equalled the glory of the greatest scientific benefactors of the human race' (CW X: 10).

Mill concentrated on Bentham's contributions to the civil and penal branches of the law and to judicial evidence and procedure. He curiously omitted numerous important fields, such as constitutional law, logic, codification, and writings on liberty, such as *Defence of Usury*, which was much discussed in the 1820s (see Bentham [1787] 1952–4). He mainly criticized Bentham as a moral philosopher. In his view, Bentham neglected character in his ethics, and particularly in the chapters on motives and dispositions in *An Introduction to the Principles of Morals and Legislation* (see Bentham [1789] 1996, 96–142; CW X: 8–9). Bentham and his followers, he believed, emphasised the consequences of actions alone and 'rejected all contemplation of the action in its general bearings upon the entire moral being of the agent' (CW X: 8).

We should note that Mill ignored those aspects of Bentham's philosophy which might have formed a reply, such as, for example, Bentham's account of dispositions as a theory of virtue (see Bentham [1789] 1996, 3, 125ff.). But Mill sought a more earnest and uplifting morality (see Rosen 2003, 29–57). He criticized Bentham for using the language of interests, when such a language tended to be understood as purely self-regarding interest (see CW X: 14). Bentham's philosophy provided no moral message and uplifting theme:

> Upon those who *need* to be strengthened and upheld by a really inspired moralist – such a moralist as Socrates, or Plato, or (speaking humanly and not theologically) as Christ; the effect of such writings as Mr. Bentham's . . . must either be hopeless despondency and gloom, or a reckless giving themselves up to a life of that miserable self-seeking, which they are there taught to regard as inherent in their original and unalterable nature. (CW X: 16)

In addition, Mill continued, 'by the promulgation of such views of human nature, and by a general tone of thought and expression perfectly in harmony with them, I conceive Mr. Bentham's writings to have done and to be doing very serious evil' (CW X: 15).

If Mill sought a new philosophical method to be applied to politics, he also wanted to infuse it with the spirit of the 'inspired moralist', a Socrates, Plato, or Jesus. His criticisms of Bentham's failure to inspire as a moralist remind one of numerous writings in the seventeenth and eighteenth centuries where Epicurean philosophy, also based on self-interest, was criticized by traditional theologians and moralists for similar self-serving tendencies (see Rosen 2003, 15–28). But his depiction of philosophic radicalism, as we have seen, did not carry with it such moralistic overtones, as it simply concentrated on relating means to ends and causes to effects. Nor did his later writings on logic and philosophy, with the notable exception of *Utilitarianism* (1861) in which Mill acknowledged his critics and answered them by showing how utilitarianism could accommodate the inspired moralist (see Hansen 2005). In *Utilitarianism* Mill's approach was not only that of a traditional moralist but also that of a rhetorician who appreciated that utilitarianism could not succeed unless it captured the imagination and moral sensibility of a wider circle of people than would ever be attracted to Bentham's philosophy.

III

Many of the themes first developed in 'Remarks on Bentham's Philosophy' were considered again in 'Bentham' and 'Coleridge'. Although the essay on Bentham was ostensibly a review of the early volumes of the edition of Bentham's *Works*, edited by John Bowring, the two essays were conceived from the outset as being related to each other (CW X: 76, 77–8).

We might wonder why Mill chose in the first place to write on Bentham and Coleridge as 'the two great seminal minds of England in their age' (CW X: 77; see Bain 1882, 56; cf. Colmer 1976, lxxii). When one considers his critique of Bentham in numerous spheres, and the fact that Coleridge was known more as a literary figure than as either a philosopher or a contributor to political ideas (cf. Morrow 1990, 164; Snyder 1929), his choice of these two figures is somewhat puzzling. It is important to emphasise that Mill was confining his attention to England. Even Scotland, whose eighteenth-century philosophers, such as David Hume and Adam Smith, were the greatest of the age, and which also produced, in Mill's own view, important representatives of the so-called German school, such as Thomas Reid, were apparently excluded. Furthermore, both Bentham and Coleridge were introduced as 'closet-students', secluded 'by circumstances, and character from the business and intercourse of the world', and whose ideas were treated by those engaged in public life 'with feelings akin to contempt' (CW X: 77). Such a depiction, with obvious Socratic overtones, was intended to place both Bentham and Coleridge in a very distinct and special category of thinker, created largely by Mill himself, in which ideas combined philosophical depth and originality with an important practical bearing on ethics and politics. Thus, he could refer to them both in vaguely political terms as progressive and conservative thinkers, and, additionally, call them progressive and conservative *philosophers*.

John Robson has commented that 'the roots of Mill's comparison of Bentham and Coleridge in the opening pages of his essay on the latter, probably go back to arguments with Coleridgeans in the London Debating Society' (see CW X: cxxi). One might take this observation further by pointing to the significance of one particular member of the London Debating Society, the Coleridgean John Sterling, and the fact that throughout Mill's surviving correspondence, virtually every reference to Coleridge occurs in letters to or about Sterling.

Sterling (an exact contemporary of Mill) is not well known today, but until his early death in 1844, he had a profound impact on Mill's life (perhaps overshadowed only by his relationships with his father and Harriet Taylor) (see Capaldi 2004, 76–7). Just before Sterling's death, Mill wrote to him: 'I shall never think of you but as one of the noblest, & quite the most loveable of all men I have known or ever look to know' and earlier in the same letter, he wrote: 'the remembrance of your friendship will be a precious possession to me as long as I remain here' (CW XIII: 635). What we know of their friendship comes mainly from Mill. In the *Autobiography*, Mill depicted the arrival of the two Coleridgeans, Sterling and F. D. Maurice, in the London Debating Society as presenting the view of 'a second Liberal and even Radical party, on totally different grounds from Benthamism and vehemently opposed to it' (CW I: 133). They developed within the society the doctrines associated with what Mill called the European reaction of the nineteenth century against the thought that predominated in the eighteenth century. The debates of the society were unusual in being based at the same time on philosophical principles and intense, direct confrontation between the debating parties. The debates clearly meant more to Mill than intellectual victory, as he began to develop his feelings as well as his intellect in these very personal confrontations. Even though Sterling did not possess the intellectual stature of Mill, as we have seen, Mill was strongly attracted by his warmth as a person and his capacity for friendship.

According to Mill, in 1829 Sterling made a 'violent and unfair attack' on Mill's mainly Benthamite political philosophy to which Mill delivered a sharp response leading to Sterling's resignation from the society, and, subsequently, to his own (CW I: 162). Although it is not possible to reconstruct Sterling's attack, we can obtain some hints from Mill's reply (see CW XXVI: 443–53). Sterling seems to have accused Bentham of advocating immorality or, at least, of advancing a doctrine that would have the effect of increasing immorality generally in society, presumably by being concerned with the external consequences of actions rather than with the internal cultivation of virtue. Mill responded by arguing that an emphasis on the internal cultivation of virtue alone would only serve as a cover for the vilest selfishness and a failure to concern oneself with the welfare of others. Mill thought that Sterling had made two errors. First, he failed to see that most philosophers – including Stoics and Epicureans, those who followed Kant, and those who followed Locke – possessed moral virtue 'very considerably above the average of ordinary men' (CW XXVI: 445n). Second, Sterling had changed his position regarding reform. Where previously his view had been compatible with that of Bentham (in pursuing the same ends but for different reasons), he now seemed to oppose reform generally and particularly that connected with the ballot.

After Sterling left the society, Mill successfully attempted to re-establish their friendship. His letter to Sterling, written on 15 April 1829, is surely one of the most remarkable letters Mill wrote (CW XII: 28–30). Sterling's friendship meant more to him than that of any other man, not only because of the affection he felt toward him but also because of the differences between them. For Mill, the friendship 'appears to me peculiarly adapted to the wants of my own mind; since I know no person who possesses more, of what I have not, than yourself, nor is this inconsistent with my believing you to be deficient in some of the very few things which I have' (CW XII: 29). What did Mill believe that Sterling possessed that he lacked? He was probably referring to Sterling's unique position to help remedy his intense feelings of loneliness and isolation by virtue of the fact that Sterling belonged to another progressive political circle besides that inhabited by his father and Bentham (both of whom were still alive at this time).

In the *Autobiography,* Mill wrote:

He and I started from intellectual points almost as wide apart as the poles, but the distance between us was always diminishing: if I made steps towards some of his opinions, he, during his short life, was constantly approximating more and more to several of mine: and if he had lived, and had health and vigour to prosecute his ever assiduous self-culture, there is no knowing how much further this spontaneous assimilation might have proceeded. (CW I: 163)

In addition to Mill's emphasis on his friendship with Sterling starting at opposite poles, a distinctive feature of the essays on 'Bentham' and 'Coleridge' was Mill's employment of the image of polar opposites, and in a letter to Sterling, Mill wrote that the article on Coleridge served 'as a counter-pole to the one on Bentham' (CW XIII: 405). These opposing poles of thought could be moved or overcome in at least two ways. In 1831, he wrote to Sterling:

I once heard Maurice say . . . that almost all differences of opinion when analysed, were differences of method. But if so, he who can throw most light on the subject of method, will do most to forward that alliance among the most advanced intellects & characters of the age, which is the only definite object I ever have in literature or philosophy so far as I have any *general* object at all. *Argal*, I have put down upon paper a great many of my ideas on logic, & shall in time bring forth a treatise. (CW XII: 79)

Thus, one way to overcome these dividing polarities was to explore them philosophically with the emphasis on method, and one might look to Mill's work on logic to see how Benthamite radicals and progressive Coleridgeans might come closer together. The second way of moving or even overcoming these opposing poles lay in seeing the task of intellect or philosophy as exploring 'the pros and cons of every question' – a position Mill ascribed to Wordsworth and which he contrasted with that of the radicals and utilitarians (CW XII: 81). This is a theme emphasized in a number of Mill's ethical and political writings (see O'Rourke 2001, 42ff.).

IV

Let us now turn to Mill's treatment of moral and social theory in the *Logic* to see how he used a philosophical method first to criticize what he called 'the Bentham school' and, second, to extend his view of the logic of social science by incorporating elements derived initially from his reading of Coleridge and interaction with the Coleridgeans.[3] Mill's use of the language of polarities and contraries is of particular interest.

In book VI of the *Logic*, Mill considered the methods of social science and rejected what he called 'the Geometrical, or Abstract method' (CW VIII: 887–94). After dismissing Hobbes's attempts to base the foundation of government solely on the emotion of fear and the use of the doctrine of the original contract falsely by reasoning in a circle, Mill turned to the most remarkable and important example, that of 'the interest-philosophy of the Bentham school'. Mill argued that, like Hobbes, the Bentham school used a single doctrine, in this case, self-interest, as the basis of its theory of government. Hence, because of the emphasis on self-interest, the school focused on the establishment of the accountability of rulers to the ruled through representative government and other means to minimize the corrupting tendency of this aspect of human nature. Mill, however, believed that this view of accountability as the essence of the problem of government was misleading because it was based on the false premise of universal self-interest. In ringing Coleridgean tones, he declared:

But I insist only on what is true of all rulers, viz., that the character and course of their actions is largely influenced (independently of personal calculation) by the

---

[3] On the difficulties of assessing Mill's indebtedness to Coleridge, see Turk 1988, 44ff. See also p. 232, where he writes: 'Coleridge's influence was probably effective, not only in single ideas, but in the formulation of a whole method of truth.' However, Turk fails to consider how Mill utilized Coleridge not only with regard to truth and its expression but also as a method in practical politics.

habitual sentiments and feelings, the general modes of thinking and acting, which prevail throughout the community of which they are members; as well as by the feelings, habits, and modes of thought which characterize the particular class in that community to which they themselves belong. And no one will understand or be able to decipher their system of conduct, who does not take all these things into account. (CW VIII: 891)

Much of this rejection of the self-interest principle can be found in the earlier 'Bentham' and 'Coleridge', as well as in Sterling's critique of Bentham. What is important here is Mill's argument that the Bentham school was mistaken due to its 'unscientific' method in attempting to apply the model of geometry to politics. Although he granted that the theory was important in the political struggle for parliamentary reform in focusing attention on representation, it possessed no claim to truth beyond this historical moment in practical politics.

There are two main difficulties with the use of what Mill called the geometric method in politics. First, as we have seen in the cases of Hobbes and the Bentham school, those who employed it tended to fix on a single cause to explain the whole of politics and political morality. Mill insisted that whatever deductions were set forth to explain events in society, they must proceed not from one or a few causes but 'considering each effect as (what it really is) an aggregate result of many causes, operating sometimes through the same, sometimes through different mental agencies, or laws of human nature' (CW VIII: 894). Rather than attempting to trace out a few causes and effects in the complex worlds of ethics and politics, Mill looked to more complex natural sciences, such as astronomy and mechanics, to provide better models for social science (see Ryan [1970] 1987, 133ff.). Second, Mill seemed to reject a science of society based on universal principles. This does not mean that the psychological theory (and the science of ethology supposedly deduced from it) was not based on universal principles of human nature and the formation of character. But the pattern of causation determining behaviour in society was complex and changed over time. Human agency and morality became part of historical tradition, and politics at one particular moment depended on a different pattern of causation than it would at another moment.

This relativism provides some insight into Mill's choice of Bentham and Coleridge not as the two greatest thinkers ever but as the two who had the greatest impact at a particular time in relation to a particular field of thought. Furthermore, Mill uses them to understand society from a perspective that has no claim to truth beyond the period in which the essays were written. Mill admitted in the *Autobiography* (CW I: 225–7; see CW X: cxxi) that his essay on Coleridge was written to enlarge and improve the thinking of Radicals and Liberals at that time. That is the perspective from which it must be initially understood, even though the essay touched on numerous philosophical and literary problems which transcended this fairly narrow perspective.[4]

Furthermore, Mill must have realized, for example, that, for Bentham, all actions, even those in politics, were not based on self-interest. Bentham's theory could accommodate most of the traditional virtues and, at the level of motivation, sympathy, and benevolence, could be as powerful as more self-serving motives. His idea of self-interest was also more complex than Mill seemed to appreciate. At one level, a healthy self-regard was essential for survival. If Adam's regard was only for Eve and Eve's only care was for Adam, in Bentham's view both (and presumably the human race) would have perished within twelve months (Bentham [1830] 1983, 119). At another level, Bentham regarded the 'constant and arduous task as of every moralist, so of every legislator who deserves to be so' was to 'increase . . . the influence of sympathy at the expense of that of self-regard, and of sympathy for the greater number at the expense of sympathy of the lesser number' (Bentham [1830] 1983, 119). This is achieved by education on the one hand and law on the other. We are educated within the family and society to deepen and extend our fellow feelings and make them habitual so as to increase happiness generally for others and for ourselves. The laws can also guide us towards the same ends in establishing duties, for example, to pay taxes to defend society; to build hospitals, schools, roads and bridges; and to look after the poor and needy.

It is true that Bentham argued that in devising institutions of government, one must assume a person would attempt to advance 'his own private and personal interest . . . at the expense of the public interest' unless prevented from doing so by institutions or morality (Bentham [1830] 1983, 119). But such an assumption has for its object the prevention of corruption and the advancement of happiness and is not simply a theory of self-interest. For Bentham, most rulers *appeared* to act as if they were ruling in the interests of

---

[4] Hence, other scholars have been attracted to Mill's essay on Coleridge, for example, by seeing it serve a wide range of objects. For one, 'Coleridge' is 'the best introduction to Coleridge's writings' (Barrell 1972, p. xxvi) or, as Leavis thought, an important work providing insights into Victorian intellectual history (Leavis [1950] 1980: 12–13). One might note Morrow's belief that Mill's essay led to the liberal political philosophy accompanying the rise of English Idealism in writers such as T. H. Green and J. H. Muirhead (Morrow 1990, 164), or Williams's Marxist interpretation of Mill's essays on Bentham and Coleridge as forming a prologue to much subsequent 'English thinking about society and culture' (Williams 1958, 49).

the ruled, and most of the ruled seemed devoted to their rulers, even to the point of ignoring self-interest, for example, in cheerfully going to war (placing their lives at risk) in support of their rulers' plans and ambitions. But he ascribed such actions to what in modern times we might call 'false consciousness'. A good deal of his political theory was devoted to an explanation of how this false consciousness originated and persisted in societies, affecting politics, religion, language, and even feelings. An understanding of interests, both self- and other-regarding, beneath the façade of ordinary politics is an important part of Bentham's approach and crucial for an understanding of its scientific character.

Another important element in Bentham's political theory, which was not based on self- or other-regarding interest was that of public opinion. At one point, he depicted public opinion as a body of law emanating from the people and on a par with the so-called Common Law. In depicting its role in government, he wrote:

To the pernicious exercise of the power of government it is the only check; to the beneficial, an indispensable supplement. Able rulers lead it; prudent rulers lead or follow it; foolish rulers disregard it. Even at the present stage in the career of civilization, its dictates coincide, on most points, with those of the *greatest happiness principle*; on some, however, it still deviates from them: but, as its deviations have all along been less and less numerous, and less wide, sooner or later they will cease to be discernible; aberration will vanish, coincidence will be complete. (Bentham [1830] 1983, 36)

All members of a given society and, indeed, all of those in the world who take an interest in that society belong to what Bentham called its public opinion tribunal. Its object is to advance human happiness through writings, attendance at public meetings, serving on juries, and even by popular demonstrations and uprisings. Public opinion has a critical function in society, as well as one of gathering and disseminating information. Through the encouragement of obedience and disobedience, the public opinion tribunal also performs an 'executive function' in rewarding and punishing rulers.

Although Bentham was not original in basing government ultimately on public opinion, he was original in making public opinion the engine of reform (see Rosen 1983, 19–40). Mill ignored this important aspect of Bentham's theory, perhaps because he grew increasingly wary of public opinion and feared its potential power in the tyranny of the majority. But to neglect this most important element in Bentham's theory led Mill to present a misleading account of Bentham's political ideas in his writings on Bentham, including book VI of the *Logic*. It is clear that Mill was using Bentham at a particular time and place and for his own purposes.

If Mill's own approach, then, rested partly on Coleridgean foundations, what were those foundations? Consider, for example, Mill's discussion of polarities, particularly in the essays on Bentham and Coleridge. Coleridge, himself, although using a slightly different terminology, employed the idea of opposites to explain a number of his ideas. In expounding the ideas of 'permanence' and 'progressiveness' as opposites, he referred to them as being like the positive and negative poles of a magnet – 'opposite powers are always of the same kind, and tend to union, either by equipoise or by a common product' and they 'suppose and require each other' (Coleridge [1830] 1972, 16n). Elsewhere, he referred to the opposition between 'Property' and 'Nationalty' as opposites: 'correspondent and reciprocally supporting, counterweights, of the commonwealth; the existence of the one being the condition, and the perfecting, of the rightfulness of the other' (Coleridge [1830] 1972, 26). Similarly, in expounding the idea of the Christian church in the context of opposing forces and institutions, Coleridge used the metaphor of opposite banks of the same stream and words like 'counter-balance' and 'contra-position' (Coleridge [1830] 1972, 100).

Mill developed this imagery and mode of argument at the beginning of 'Coleridge', bringing Bentham and Coleridge together as 'completing counterparts'. They were in Mill's terminology 'contraries' – 'the things which are farthest from one another in the same kind'. The two men contributed to awaken the spirit of philosophy, and although they never interacted, together they defined English philosophy at this time (CW X: 120–1). One cannot approximate the truth simply by adding Bentham's and Coleridge's philosophies together, but their combination requires, as Robson suggests, 'careful analysis and comparison, with the aim of revealing limitations of experience and errors of generalization' (Robson 1968, 192).

In the *Logic*, Mill adopted a new approach to understanding society, taken partly from Auguste Comte, which he called the 'Inverse Deductive, or Historical Method'. In explicating this approach, he declared that the object was to discover 'the causes which produce, and the phenomena which characterize, States of Society generally' (CW VIII: 911). By a state of society (also called a state of civilization) he meant:

the degree of knowledge, and of intellectual and moral culture, existing in the community, and in every class of it; the state of industry, of wealth and its distribution; the habitual occupations of the community; their division into classes, and the relations of those classes to one another; the common beliefs which they entertain on all the subjects most important to mankind, and the degree of assurance with which those beliefs are held; their tastes, and the character and degree of their aesthetic development; their form of government, and the more important of their laws and customs. (CW VIII: 911–12)

The state of society at any given time must be understood in terms of what he called 'the progressiveness of the human race'. This idea, he believed, should not be confused with a tendency towards improvement and increased happiness in society. This element of progressiveness provided a 'theorem' of social science on which a predictive science of society might be based. He depicted this theorem as follows:

there is a progressive change both in the character of the human race, and in their outward circumstances so far as moulded by themselves: that in each successive age the principal phenomena of society are different from what they were in the age preceding, and still more different from any previous age: the periods which most distinctly mark these successive changes being intervals of one generation, during which a new set of human beings have been educated, have grown up from childhood, and taken possession of society. (CW VIII: 914)

The theorem of the progressiveness of the human race had led thinkers, particularly those on the continent, to study history to discover the 'law of progress' and thereby predict future events. Mill rejected this approach as never forming a science of society because its laws were simply empirical generalizations, often erroneous ones, and not verified by psychological and ethological laws. But he did not abandon this general approach. He first distinguished, following Comte, between social statics, which investigated stability in society, and social dynamics, which was concerned with progress and succession. In illustrating the nature of social statics, he quoted at length from his own essay on Coleridge (CW VIII: 921–4) to illustrate how one might identify certain requisites in every society, which maintained 'collective existence' (CW VIII: 920). Although these requisites were only empirical laws, some of them 'are found to follow with so much probability from general laws of human nature, that the consilience of the two processes raises the evidence to proof and the generalizations to the rank of scientific truths' (CW VIII: 920). The passage from 'Coleridge' mentioned three requisites for stability: (1) a system of education which established 'a restraining discipline' in society; (2) a feeling of allegiance or loyalty to settled aspects of society or to people or to common gods; and 3) a strong and active principle of cohesion in society – not based on nationalism – but a principle of sympathy which united members of a given society.

Besides the intrinsic value of Mill's discussion, the effect of this material is to use part of the essay on Coleridge to undermine, if not dismiss,

Bentham's approach to government. For Bentham, representative democracy could be shown to be the best form of government and universally applicable to all societies in placing the rulers under the control of the ruled. The only conditions necessary for its success were that the people desired such a government for themselves and developed the habits of obedience to maintain it. For Mill, no form of government could be universally applicable to all societies. Societies must first have developed a number of principles of stability and cohesion, and forms of government depended on the character and continuity of these principles.

Mill's account of social dynamics followed in a similar vein as that of social statics, except that the former, social dynamics, was concerned with the explanation of changes in social conditions. In the history of societies, one found 'general tendencies', and he noted, as examples, that as societies progressed, mental qualities tended to prevail over physical ones and that an industrial spirit tended to prevail over a military spirit. In combining the static with the dynamic view of society, Mill hoped to develop scientific laws concerned with the development of human societies. Yet such a process, even as Mill outlined it, seemed a difficult, if not impossible, task because of the complexity of the data to which such a science must be related and from which it was ultimately derived.

Mill then turned to what he called the 'predominant, and almost paramount' of the agents of social progress, 'intellectual activity' or 'the speculative faculties of mankind' (CW VIII: 926). Although he accepted that only a few individuals gave a major role to intellect in their lives, he nonetheless claimed that 'its influence is the main determining cause of the social progress' (CW VIII: 926). All other changes were dependent on them. He illustrated this view by pointing first to the force for improvement in the conditions of life in the desire for increased material comfort. Such a desire, however, could only be realized by the knowledge that was possessed at a given time. Furthermore, as the strongest propensities in human nature were those of a selfish nature, social existence required discipline, which established a common set of opinions and which upheld the social union. Thus, Mill argued, 'the state of speculative faculties' determined the social and political state of the society in the same way that they determined the physical conditions of life (CW VIII: 926). He then asserted:

Every considerable change historically known to us in the condition of any portion of mankind, when not brought about by physical force, has been preceded by a change, of proportional extent, in the state of their knowledge, or in their prevalent beliefs. (CW VIII: 926–7)

Mill thus believed that every advance in civilization was based on a prior advance in knowledge. He pointed to the way a succession of religions, from polytheism to Judaism to Christianity and to Protestantism, followed by the critical philosophy of the Enlightenment and the positive sciences related to it, had changed society in each successive period. He rejected the view that philosophy and science were changed by developments in the material conditions of life. Thus, speculation, although often confined to a few, determined the development of society as a whole unless conditions were such (e.g., the breakdown of society) that no progress was possible.

Mill's methodology of social science was also related to his accounts of Bentham and Coleridge. In choosing to focus on the two greatest thinkers of the age, Mill implied a rejection of the view that the industrial revolution or productive forces alone determined the character of society. Mill himself thought that progress in social science required the rejection of the geometrical method of Bentham and his father and its replacement by the historical method of Comte, which he also associated with Coleridge. But he did not simply replace one with the other, because the historical school was wholly dependent on the sciences of psychology and ethology, which were ultimately derived from the school of Locke and Bentham, as revised by his father's work in psychology. And the revival of associationist psychology was stimulated by the critique of modern eighteenth-century empiricism by those in the 'Germano-Coleridgean' school. Thus, Mill's approach to social science reflected his attempts to identify these polarities of thought in Bentham and Coleridge and to show how they might be reconciled and used to advance new thinking in this field.

V

What can Mill's encounter with Bentham and Coleridge as well as the development of his ideas in the *Logic* teach us about his method of reform? To answer this question, we might look briefly at the *Considerations* to see how the ideas became part of a more general theory of government. Although Mill did not develop a major category that might be called 'method of reform', he would presumably place the task of political reform under the category of Art (see CW VIII: 943–52). As a utilitarian, Mill might have been expected simply to examine political institutions with an eye to replacing those which produced unhappiness or failed to produce sufficient happiness with those which advanced the greatest happiness of the members of a given society. But Mill did not proceed in this fashion.

He began the *Considerations* with 'two conflicting theories' concerning political institutions (CW XIX: 374). The first saw government as a practical art of adjusting means to ends. Institutions were chosen to realize these ends and the people were stirred to demand the creation of the institutions. Practitioners of the art looked on a constitution, he wrote, 'as they would upon a steam plough, or a threshing machine', as a series of mechanisms for producing good government (CW XIX: 374). The second theory saw the development of institutions as a spontaneous development and not a matter of choice. One simply learned about them and adapted oneself to work with them. Political institutions were then regarded as an 'organic growth' from the people and 'a product of their habits, instincts, and unconscious wants and desires, scarcely at all of their deliberate purposes' (CW XIX: 375).

Mill's starting point for these two conflicting theories should not be assumed to be the same starting point for the essays on Bentham and Coleridge, and the two theories cannot be assumed to be those of Bentham and Coleridge. The two conflicting theories seem closer to the general views Mill ascribed to Liberals and Conservatives in the preface to *Considerations,* and they are prevented by these positions from joining together to adopt an agenda of reform. Mill challenged the Conservative position more than the Liberal one, but in important ways, he challenged both. He sought to show that the views expressed by both of these theories could not lead to or sustain good government, because one excluded the other and without general support from both reform was not possible.

Mill was clearly on the side of reform, and he set forth a view of opposing positions, which were not hostile to reform and which could be reconciled to achieve radical reform. In this first chapter, Mill thus moved deftly from two conflicting theories, which contradicted each other, to two opposed theories, which were merely contraries and which, together could accommodate arguments for the reform of existing institutions. He insisted that political institutions were constructed by human beings and, within limits, were open to choice. But these limits included three conditions: (1) the people must be willing to accept or not to oppose the institutions, (2) they must be willing to maintain the institutions, and (3) they must be willing and able to take steps for the institutions to realize their purposes. Thus, although political institutions were a matter of human artifice, the reformer was constrained by what the people were willing to adopt and sustain. To this extent, the reformer was reconciled with the 'new' conservative who, although accepting the role of human endeavour in building institutions, did not agree that a society was free to accept or reject any institution that one wished and at any time one pleased.

Mill also added a further ingredient in this reconciliation of contrary positions. He rejected the older conservative view that political institutions were determined by social circumstances by insisting on the role of intelligence in their construction and adoption. He employed examples of enlightened reform in the past to support this view of the importance of intelligence. Such a view did not accept that institutions were a matter of free choice but insisted rather that they were a matter of intelligent and rational choice. This element not only assisted in the reconciliation of the two contrary views but also alerted the reader to Mill's position in the *Logic* regarding social science as mainly a matter of the way the ideas of one generation determined the institutions of the next.

We see in this opening chapter Mill's method of reform taking a longer view of the development of institutions than that taken by earlier radicals and drawing in conservatives who were not wholly opposed to intelligent change and reform. Yet the issues he proposed to discuss within this framework were issues of radical reform. Let us see very briefly how he proceeded to combine these various views.

In the next chapter, Mill considered not the best form of government but the objects or functions of government that this best form was designed to achieve. He began with two provisos, which were taken from the *Logic*. First, the functions of government could not be fixed because they differed in different states of society; second, the character of a government could be understood only by looking beyond the sphere of government institutions to take into account the well-being of society as well as the nature of government itself. In the ensuing discussion, Mill critically invoked both Coleridge and Bentham, not to accept or reject aspects of their political thought, but to transform them. He took up Coleridge's famous distinction between permanence and progression in society reflecting the landed and mercantile interests, which, in Coleridge's view, should be balanced. Mill argued that the distinction was a false one because progression was not possible without permanence and that these were therefore not opposites (see CW XIX: 385). Mill also removed order and permanence from the province of particular sections of society and made them part of progression in both its psychological and institutional contexts. When Mill referred to Bentham in this chapter, he adopted Bentham's idea of aptitude and its different components (moral, intellectual, and active), but he then applied it to the people generally, whereas Bentham applied it only to those holding public office (CW XIX: 390). However Mill used Bentham and Coleridge in the *Considerations*, the important point is that he carried forward the distinct legacy of the method of reform he developed fully for the first time in the essays on Bentham and Coleridge.

According to Robson, the influence of Coleridge on Mill was mainly confined to the 1830s, and the essay on Coleridge was 'less a criticism of Coleridge, or a reassessment of Bentham, than a declaration of assured and well-founded independence' (Robson 1968, 76). Robson's comment is partly true, though the influence of the essays on Bentham and Coleridge surely extended throughout his life. Mill's starting point for reform was not the identification of means to established ends, as he found in Bentham, but, as in Coleridge's thought, the initial identification of contradictory views that constituted obstacles to reform, which were then transformed into contraries and reconciled in a distinctive way to advance reform. One might argue that Mill's use of contraries for this purpose was simply part of a rhetoric of politics, employed in drawing in the enemies and encouraging the friends of reform. But the method of reform had deeper foundations and objects. It allowed Mill to emphasize more easily that reform must be adapted to particular times, and the means devised to achieve given ends could not be assumed to apply universally. Thus, a particular reform, like the introduction of the ballot, might have to be secret at some points and open at others in the development of a society. Mill believed that we could not simply assume, as did earlier radicals, that the secret ballot was universally valid as an important means to prevent corruption and establish good government through a system of representation, because such a view did not take into account the new factor in emerging democracies: the tyranny of the majority. But whatever the outcome, Mill's method looked beyond the traditional radical arsenal, which was based on the assumption of a tight means–ends conception of the art of government.

Furthermore, Mill's method of reform started with the preparation of the people to receive and support ongoing reform. It began with the ideas of intelligent elites in one generation (equivalent, perhaps, to those of a clerisy) who then prepared the minds of the people generally to see the merits of reform and progress in particular institutions and practices. Although Bentham's radicalism was intended to lead to gradual reform rather than to revolution, Mill's method itself ensured that successful reform had to be gradual by its very nature in that the ideas, which could establish and support such reform, had first to develop in society. That is to say, the new institutions had to be preceded by the understanding of the institutions and their acceptance by members of society. Otherwise, the politics of reform would become an empty and futile rhetoric meeting determined opposition from those who, rightly or wrongly, felt that they had much to lose from whatever reforms were proposed.

Mill's *Considerations* has always lacked the appeal and popularity of *On Liberty* and even *Utilitarianism*. To some, it seems eccentric in its advocacy of such proposals as plural voting, the open rather than the secret ballot, and the scheme of proportional representation originally devised by Thomas Hare. To others, it seems remarkably conservative in relation to the earlier radicalism of Bentham and many of his followers.[5] It is no wonder that Bentham's star as a *reformer* has outshone that of Mill, except perhaps in the sphere of liberty. But this examination of Mill's radicalism reveals a different method of reform than is commonly found by commentators, one based initially on his personal encounter with the Coleridgeans in the London Debating Society in the 1820s, developed in the essays on Bentham and Coleridge and refined in book VI of the *Logic*.

When Dennis Thompson discusses Mill's theory of government, with its two principles of participation and competence, he fails to embed this discussion into Mill's method of reform (see Thompson 1976; see also Ten 1998, 374ff.). This failure leads him to write of Mill's theory of democracy as if competence and participation are important aspects of Mill's conception of the end of government and are combined to advance this end. But Mill himself rejects the idea of an ideal form of government that can stand apart from society. This aspect of his approach sees him turn away from traditional discussions of forms of government to emphasize the method of reform through the transforming power of intellect in society. Thompson deals with some aspects of this problem under the heading of a theory of development, which draws on the *Logic*, but not on Mill's essays 'Bentham' and 'Coleridge' (see Thompson 1976, 136ff.).

One consequence of Thompson's approach is that he dismisses earlier views suggesting that Mill was never a democrat (see Thompson 1976, 4). He does so partly because his theory requires that democracy serves as the overarching end. The opposing thesis, as, for example, developed by J. H. Burns, concludes that although Mill's political thought was consistent throughout his life, he never adopted 'the viewpoint of a democrat' (Burns [1957] 1969, 328; cf. Robson 1968, 224). In my opinion, Burns, rather than Thompson, has a better understanding of Mill's position, insofar as Mill's attitude towards democracy is much less enthusiastic than Bentham's was a generation earlier. But even Burns's conclusion needs qualification. What makes Mill consistent in his political thought from the 1830s to the *Considerations* is his commitment to a method of reform, derived from the early

---

[5] For a discussion of Mill's institutional proposals in relation to earlier radicalism, see Rosen 1983, 183–99.

philosophic radicalism, which matures into the doctrine of the *Consider-*
ations. Although Burns is correct in stating that Mill never adopted the
viewpoint of a democrat, he might have added that there is nothing in Mill's
method of reform that prevented him from doing so and, at another point,
rejecting it.

What makes democracy an end to be sought through reform is the willingness of the people to accept and support a particular version. This version
must be adapted to that society so as not to destroy numerous other constituents of happiness to which that society aspires and will support and
are within its capacities at a given time. In other words, as Mill works out
clearly in the *Logic,* the theory of government is subordinate to social science generally. This is not to deny, as Mill states in the *Autobiography,* that
the *Considerations* consists of an exposition of 'the best form of a popular
constitution' and that this requires a 'general theory of government' (CW
I: 265). But Mill's discussion would be seriously deficient if his method of
reform is not recognized as an essential ingredient of such an exposition
and, particularly, of the theory itself. To focus simply on the pros and cons
of particular institutions as the best means to increase happiness would be
somewhat similar to taking Marx's comments on a future communist state
as a fully developed theory of government. For Mill, one needs to understand
how society works at a given time and then use the method of reconciling
opposing views to see what reforms are possible. Reform then becomes a
process of adapting means to ends by human effort and artifice and persuading other members of society to see the matter in this fashion. Without
such a method, it is arguable that Mill's theory of government becomes idle
speculation, at best a form of utopian thought, and without much relevance
to practical politics. The method of reform, as worked out in the *Considera-*
tions and as explored in 'Bentham', 'Coleridge', and book VI of the *Logic* can
still raise the major questions of any given age, even if the practical solutions
might have to await a later stage in the evolution of particular societies.

PART TWO

DEMOCRACY AND THE INDIVIDUAL

6

Bureaucracy, Democracy, Liberty

Some Unanswered Questions in Mill's Politics

Alan Ryan

Mill's *Autobiography* was intended to provide the reader with the authorized version of Mill's life. It was the life of the John Stuart Mill who had been born the son of James Mill, author of *The History of British India,* and nobody whose interest lay in anything other than the education he had received first from his father and then from Mrs. Taylor was encouraged to read it. At the outset, Mill says: "The reader whom these things do not interest, has only himself to blame if he reads farther, and I do not desire any other indulgence from him than that of bearing in mind that for him these pages were not written" (CW I: 5). There are many reasons for lamenting Mill's preoccupation with paying his debts to his father and Harriet Taylor. On this occasion, my regret is that Mill was reluctant to unbutton himself about issues about which he might have changed his mind between his precocious youth and the years of retirement during which he published *On Liberty, Considerations on Representative Government,* and *The Subjection of Women* along with *Utilitarianism, Auguste Comte and Positivism,* and *An Examination of Sir William Hamilton's Philosophy.*

When writing about Mill's contribution to the development of utilitarian ethics, we might wish that he had said much more about the way his essays 'Bentham,' and 'Whewell's Moral Philosophy' together with the final chapter of *A System of Logic,* underlay or did not underlie *Utilitarianism.* For my purposes in this chapter, it would have been interesting to know more about what Mill thought about the bearing of the way India was governed on the way the United Kingdom should be governed; about the extent to which he had grown out of the anxiety about moral authority that permeated his youthful essays on 'The Spirit of the Age'; and about the extent to which he felt that he had achieved a stable balance between a utilitarian concern with benevolent management and an "Athenian" concern with the self-assertive, self-critical, engaged, public-spirited but independent-minded citizen (Urbinati 2002).

In the absence of Mill's answers to my questions, I offer speculative answers on his behalf. But the best I can say is what Thucydides said of the speeches he put into the mouths of Greek statesmen and generals in his history of the Peloponnesian War on those occasions when he had neither been present nor obtained firsthand reports: "in the way I thought each would have said what was especially required in the given situation, I have stated accordingly, with the closest possible fidelity on my part to the overall sense of what was actually said" (Thucydides 1991, 13 or bk 1, § 21).

India and Empire

India illuminates, sometimes in alarming ways, Mill's views on many subjects: peasant proprietors, the nature of progress, the governance of dependent states, the ethics of coercive intervention in the affairs of other societies for liberal reasons, and the limits of the doctrine that we may not coerce other people for their own good. I here discuss only Mill's views on the government of India and their implications for his views about empire, progress, and pluralism. Then I move on to the issue of authority and the difficulty of knowing quite what Mill's final assessment was of the condition of modern society: whether we suffer from a deficit of authority, a surfeit, or, more plausibly, from a deficit of the right kind of authority and a surfeit of the wrong kind. I end by doing what I can to balance Mill's deep conviction that man for man, the Athenian was a better citizen than the Victorian Englishman with his equally deep conviction that the making of law and the administration of public business were best left to experts.

First, India. Mill's account of his time in the East India Company (EIC) is not dismissive, but it is brief and not suggestive of any great passion for the work. If it was not a faute de mieux, it was certainly not the centre of his interests; its merit was that it gave him a reasonable income for work that was a great deal better than drudgery and not too onerous. He had initially been destined for a career at the Bar, which would have given him a much larger income and no more work than the EIC. But his father was appointed to the senior permanent position in the company's London offices in 1819 and appointed his son to a clerkship in the company in 1823, when John Mill was sixteen. He remained there for thirty-five years, retiring when the company was wound up in the aftermath of the India Mutiny of 1857. He disapproved of the dissolution of the company and refused to serve on the successor council, but his loyalty to the company does not appear to have been very great. He says in the *Autobiography*, "I do not know of any one of the occupations by which a subsistence can now be gained, more suitable than such as this to anyone who, not being in independent circumstances, desires to devote a part of the twenty-four hours to private intellectual pursuits" (CW I: 83–7). His position at India House was highly suitable to his requirements; he worked from ten to four, and during much of that time he was free to write essays and portions of his books, rather than drafts of the instructions that were to go to officials in India. He goes on to say that he had "through life found office duties an actual rest from the other mental occupations which I have carried on simultaneously with them. They were sufficiently intellectual not to be distasteful drudgery, without being such as to cause any strain on the mental powers of a person used to abstract thought, or to the labour of careful literary composition" (ibid).

Mill's position was in the office of the examiner of India correspondence, a somewhat odd title for the man who ensured that the East India Company was able to manage the affairs of the subcontinent effectively. By the time J. S. Mill joined it, the East India Company was operating a "contracted-out" form of government on behalf of the government of the United Kingdom. It lost its last commercial functions in the 1833 charter renewal. Earlier, the company had had a chequered history; it had never made money, but its individual employees – the company's servants – had made a great deal. Until the late eighteenth century, individuals could trade on their own account; the profits this allowed, together with the "presents" or bribes they received from Indians hoping for favours, enabled young men to accumulate quantities of wealth that astonished and outraged their compatriots: having grown up on the history of the subversion of the Roman Republic by men who had grown rich on the plunder of the East, their critics feared – or said that they feared – that the "Nabobs" would return from India, buy seats in Parliament, and exercise a corrupt influence on British politics.

In Mill's day, it was still possible to make a great deal of money in India, but this was not because company employees traded on their own accounts, or took bribes. It was rather because the hazards of working in an unhealthy climate were such that in addition to the already substantial income that a lawyer, for example, might make in England, there was a substantial risk premium for working in India. Otherwise, anyone wanting to make a great deal of money had to do it by working for someone other than the company, whose civil and military servants benefitted from the cheapness of life in India more than from the size of their incomes. What Mill worked for was a curiosity, but it was in essence an arm's-length administrative mechanism of the British government, the virtues of which Mill defended at the time of the 1853 renewal of the charter, in the last year of the company's existence when he was fighting to prevent its extinction, and in *Considerations on*

Representative Government, when he was contemplating the best way of governing colonies (CW XIX, 562–77, esp. 577).

Mill's views on empires and the British Empire have been much discussed in recent years.[1] They aroused little interest until recently, and there is much to be said for this neglect. Mill was not a very interesting theorist of the imperial project and does not show to advantage in his casual comments on the subject. The centre of his attention was mid-Victorian England, and when it was not, it was the France of Guizot and Tocqueville, Louis Blanc, and Auguste Comte, of philosophers such as Victor Cousin and adventurers such as Napoleon III. He could not but take some interest in imperial adventures both French and British, partly because of his detestation of the foreign policies of Lord Palmerston and Thiers in the late 1830s and early 1840s and perhaps more because once he had absorbed Coleridge's ideas about nationality in the mid-1830s, he was forced to pay attention to issues of national identity. Mill acknowledged that nations were held together by sentiment and that one of the most powerful of these sentiments was the fellow-feeling created by a common political history; and one element in fellow-feeling might well be pride in our forebears' achievements. Among those achievements was the acquisition of an empire, and Mill writes as though it is incontestable that the possession of an empire adds to Britain's prestige in the world, although he does so in an arm's-length fashion (e.g., CW XIX: 564–6).

Recent readers have been more startled than they should that Mill was unembarrassed that Britain possessed an empire and that many Britons were pleased by this. Mill's unembarrassment, however, was not the same thing as enthusiasm for, or deep interest in, Britain's imperial possessions. He was interested in colonization in the context of the English settlement of New Zealand and Australia, but as a contribution to resolving the population problem in Britain and Ireland not as a contribution to national self-esteem. Territorial expansion for its own sake was not something in which he saw merit, and it is worth remembering that until late in the nineteenth century, the conventional British view was that a trading nation such as Britain needed bases for refitting its naval vessels and revictualling its crews, not the encumbrance of unprofitable territories. It was a characteristic trope in Mill that he allowed the French more latitude in expressions of national pride in their empire than he allowed the British. The British had evicted the French from North America and India and ought neither to be surprised that the

---

[1] See, for instance, Jennifer Pitts 2005, chap. 5.

French felt aggrieved nor dismayed that the French wished to acquire a new empire. But Mill's tone of voice was that of someone who acknowledged a forgivable human failing, not that of someone who himself *felt* surges of national pride at the contemplation of imperial glory. It was the same tone of voice in which Mill's godson Bertrand Russell criticised the foreign policy of the British government in 1914. Germany was playing 'catch-up' and might be forgiven a degree of obstreperousness and self-assertion impermissible in the British.

Contrasting Mill's attitude to India with Tocqueville's attitude to Algeria is instructive, although less so than it would have been if they had corresponded on the subject. Tocqueville was not merely less squeamish than Mill about the violence of the conquest but almost exultant about it; as Mill did not, Tocqueville came from a family that were *noblesse de l'épée*, and he lamented as Mill would not have known how the fact that he was too frail to take up a military career. Tocqueville's two brothers served in the military, as did his distant cousin and close friend Louis de Kergolay, with whom he corresponded about Algeria. Mill was concerned with good government, not national glory. His discussion of the government of dependent territories in *Representative Government* is a concise defence of the proposition that it is possible to achieve *good despotism*, but that such a government is likely to be achieved only when the despotic government is drawn from somewhere other than the country over which it is exercised. "Under a native despotism, a good despot is a rare and transitory accident: but when the dominion they are under is that of a more civilized people, that people ought to be able to supply it constantly" (CW XIX: 567).

The argument is simple. Ordinarily Mill thinks benevolent despotism is a contradiction in terms; and in a country capable of self-government, despotism is intolerable. Benevolent despotism in that context is even worse than non-benevolent despotism on the principle of "damn braces, bless relaxes" – for a government to nanny its citizens when they are capable of governing themselves is worse than simple oppression leading to rebellion. The argument for despotism applies where an alien power governs under conditions where the governed *cannot* provide good government for themselves. The puzzle is how an unaccountable government is to be kept honest. Unaccountable governments habitually descend into something like kleptocracy. There was no question of relying on British settlers to observe the decencies. Like most nineteenth-century British liberal writers, Mill was concerned about the tendency of settlers to become savage and exploitative; if English settlers in India are not to treat Indians with contempt and exploit them mercilessly, they must be held in check by government. This sharpens the puzzle; if settler governments are unashamedly exploitative, how is an alien government to be made to behave better?

Mill's argument, whether in *Representative Government* or in explaining the virtues of the EIC in the *Morning Chronicle* in July 1853, or before that when giving evidence to the House of Lords Committee on the renewal of the company's charter, was always the same.[2] The government *on the ground* must be carried on by persons trained to the job but answerable to an authority in Britain. For the sake of fostering self-government, Mill envisaged more and more of the senior posts within the Indian administration inside India being occupied by Indians over a period of years; and for the sake of fostering simple efficiency, he was pleased that by the time he retired, the mixed system of patronage and examination that had prevailed since 1805 was giving way to a more purely competitive system – it was no accident that Sir Charles Trevelyan, the joint author of the Northcote-Trevelyan Report of 1854 that launched the modern British civil service, cut his administrative teeth in India. It is often observed that Mill never saw India, with the implication that he can have known nothing about the country whose affairs he was helping to direct; but Mill's role was that of drafting questions and advice for the directors to send to the people who knew India and were working there. Nor was Mill drafting for people who did not know the country at firsthand. The rules governing the composition of the board of directors required a steadily increasing number of its members to have served at least ten years in the administration of India in India itself. It was not news to the London office that it was inevitably at the mercy of its in-country staff in the short term; but the directives that were sent were agreed to by experienced people, were frequently broad-brush statements of policy and principle, and often took the form of retrospective approval or disapproval of acts taken by local officials.

One may think Mill's view of the ease of achieving good government for dependent territories were Pollyannaish; he may have been readier to believe that good intentions would translate into good practice than he should have been. However, Mill knew that good intentions allied to ignorance would cause trouble. He was, for instance, adamantly hostile to letting missionaries get their hands on the Indian educational system. This was not because he was hostile to Christianity or because he had a deep respect for the native culture of the subcontinent, but because he thought it was politically

---

[2] For example, Letter to the *Morning Chronicle,* 5 July 1853 (CW XXV: 1193–4).

dangerous. *We* might think religious freedom was enhanced by allowing any religion whatever to set up schools. Indians would believe that the schools were part of a plot to overthrow Hinduism and establish Christianity in its place. After the Mutiny, the last thing any rational person wanted was to excite that fear. Mill may have been overoptimistic about the virtues of the East India Company, but he was not gullible (CW XIX: 570).

Progress

Mill's argument for the right way to govern an empire was simple. Governments that are unaccountable to their subjects were despotisms; that was true by definition. Colonial governments were unaccountable to their subjects and were therefore despotisms. The question that could not be settled by definition was whether the British government could secure that India was governed by a good despotism. The answer was that the government could, but not by allowing a lot of ignorant members of Parliament or vote-seeking ministers to occupy the role of despot. Governing through a 'double government' in which people with an interest in the local welfare could filter ministerial views and ministers could ensure that those people were of reasonable probity and intelligence was the way to achieve good despotic government.

The justification of despotism for the short run was progress over the long run, and that meant inter alia progress towards rendering despotism obsolete. Mill's readiness to announce that a good stout despotism was sometimes the best route to achieve progress strikes different readers differently. Some like the abrasiveness of the approach; others flinch and fear that Mill overlooked the obvious fact that it is easier to install good stout despots than to ensure that they remain good and produce progress. Mill offered a short and highly selective list of candidates for the title of good despot, not all of whom provide persuasive evidence. Peter the Great, Elizabeth I, and Charlemagne are in different places offered as having a better understanding of their people's needs than the people themselves had. This may be true enough; it is likely to be true under many sorts of regime that the rulers of a society have a better understanding of affairs than do their subjects; but it is not obvious that the *despotic* qualities of Mill's heroes were essential to whatever good they did their people. In the case of Peter the Great, it is all too plausible that it was the despotic and absolutist aspects of his government that ensured that social and political progress were not sustained. Conversely, it is not obvious that Elizabeth exercised a truly despotic authority. She declared herself 'an absolute princess', but she frequently had to persuade a sceptical Parliament to grant her the resources to govern with at all.

Mill's argument is one from the occasional necessity for violent and irregular methods, for it was not only despotism that Mill advocated as an intrinsically undesirable but sometimes inescapable means of progress. In an interesting letter on the Polish insurrection of 1863 addressed to the editor of *Penny Newsman* – his old friend Edwin Chadwick – Mill argued that almost any country in eastern Europe would benefit from revolution. He admitted that the Emancipation Decree of 1861 by which the tsarist government had emancipated the serfs had been a step forward; he went on to point out that it had secured the serfs' personal liberty without doing anything for their access to the land to which they had once been enserfed. The French Revolution had secured the ownership of the land they worked for French peasant proprietors, and a Polish revolution would be wholly justified if it did the same for Polish peasants. Mill was not impressed by military glory, and he had no taste for violence for its own sake, but he found it easy to sympathise with violent insurrection from below.[3] The point is worth making only because his views on despotism have attracted attention in a way in which his views on revolution have not, and it is easy to think that the point at issue is Mill's 'elitism.' It is not; the point is rather one about the permissibility of violent shortcuts when more deliberative methods are unavailable.

Mill's conception of progress needs more discussion than it will receive here. For our immediate purposes, the discussion here serves only to raise the familiar question whether progress for Mill is convergent or divergent. The answer is that it is both; but it is not both for all sorts of progress. More important, there are several forms of progress that need to be disentangled but also to be re-entangled in due course. In the case of India, which in this respect is very like the case of Ireland, there is a sub-stratum of practical advancement that is the precondition of other sorts of progress although once a virtuous circle is established, they become the means of practical advancement as well. When Mill set out to defend the EIC against dissolution, he produced a memorandum of the improvements in the condition of India that the Company had made over the previous three decades. Many of the improvements were infrastructural: docks, roads, and railways. Others were legal and institutional. Inducing Thugs to become tent makers might be thought to have been both infrastructural and psychological ("Memorandum of Improvements," CW XXX: 91ff.) The point, viewed in the long

---

[3] Letter to *Penny Newsman*, 15 March 1863 (CW XXV: 1201–4).

term, was to create a country in which there was an adequate infrastructure and a citizenry well-adapted to use it to make themselves prosperous.

Down that track lay Indian self-government and the extinction of the EIC. Did that imply cultural convergence and the extinction of a distinctively Indian culture? Mill was neither an Orientalist in the sense of having a great sympathy for, and understanding of, Asian cultures at large and Indian, or Mogul, or Hindu, culture in particular, nor a Westerniser in the sense of thinking that the sooner Indian superstitions were stamped out, the better for everyone. The remarks at the beginning of *Representative Government* provide most of what evidence there is about his views. The *machinery* of administration could be assessed against settled and uncontroversial standards of efficiency. Room for discussion about the quality of administration was limited to means–end issues; where there are specific problems, there are solutions on which rational people will converge. *Culture* comes into the equation only because there are many cultural influences on our willingness to seek the most efficient solution and our promptness in adopting it. Mill retained enough of his father's suspicion of 'sinister interests' to know that some social groups had rational – if corrupt – reasons to oppose efficiency; but in the context of the broader theory of progress, it was rather the aptness of a whole culture for improvement that he focused on. The chequered history of well-meaning efforts in the field of economic development attests to the importance of the subject. That chequered history does not undermine our belief that there are standards of efficiency of a cross-cultural kind. A sense of the complexity of social change may make us more generous towards cultures that sacrifice efficiency to other goals, but that is a separate issue.

Modes of government allow more room for divergence, because there is more room to suit ourselves. Even then, Mill hardly looks at possibilities other than some form of what we call liberal democracy and he more fastidiously called representative government. He contemplates the possibility of a modernized Venetian form of government incorporating aristocratic and bureaucratic elements, but he mentions it very much in passing. Representative government was not 'democracy' because it played down the role of simple majority voting, both where the election of representatives was at issue and in the operations of Parliament. Mill perhaps ought to have opened the field rather wider because one could imagine many possibilities opening up for people who had become the fully fledged responsible, self-disciplined, imaginative, and cooperative persons that Mill hoped that we might eventually become. Jefferson's preferred system of 'ward republics', which is to say a federation of small direct democracies handling most of their needs for themselves and delegating upwards only those powers it was essential for a larger government to possess, is not representative government in Mill's sense, but it would be attractive to citizens of the kind he hoped for. Whether it could work only in an agrarian economy is another matter; Jefferson thought farmers were the only reliable republicans, but the obvious retort is that he was simply wrong. Mill's ideal system of economic self-government founded on worker cooperatives would be a natural counterpart to a system of ward republics and would not be constrained by technology ("Chapters on Socialism," CW V: 703ff.).

Seeking a divergent view of progress in Mill, however, involves stepping outside *Representative Government* and digging into the ambiguities of *On Liberty*. This is not the place to do more than note the familiar tension. Mill offers two justifications for freedom, one in terms that would readily fall under the rubric of a natural right to do as we please so long as we do not interfere with the exercise of that right by others except in self-defense, the other in terms of the need to encourage experiments in living, which is to say in terms of progress. Then the question arises of whether those experiments lead to one answer to the question of what is the good life for man. It is plain that they do not lead to one answer in any literal sense, because Mill takes it for granted that human beings are so varied that the good for one of us is not in all respects – or is only at a very high level of generality – the good for others of us. What experiments tell us is what our own individual nature is, and therefore what the good for us individually is. The sense in which that yields one answer is that it supposes that there is a single, determinate answer to the question, 'what is the best life for me?'

Progress is – on this view – a matter of becoming increasingly clear about the good for each of us and being increasingly able to realize it. This is not a process that we should expect to be very rapid; Mill observes wryly that since what Comte, following Saint-Simon, had described as the 'critical' phase of European cultural and social history had lasted for eight centuries, the return to a 'natural' or 'organic' state in which there were universally agreed standards of judgment was not to be expected in the near future – *pace* Comte's belief that he had inaugurated it (*Auguste Comte and Positivism*, CW X: 263ff.). It is not surprising that Mill's essay *Auguste Comte and Positivism* is the other face of *On Liberty*. The question before us, however, is whether Mill's view of moral progress, in the sense of progress towards a more complete understanding of our own and, therefore, the general good, is a convergent or a divergent conception. The answer is quite unclear to me; Mill seems never to have posed the question to himself in that form and therefore seems to have seen no need to answer that question precisely.

We can press answers on him, but we cannot know whether he would have assented to them. One possibility is that because Mill had an objective conception of good, there is a genuine fact of the matter about what the good for each of us consists in; the fact is different for different people because what is good for one of us may not be so for another, but for each of us there is a fact of the matter. The other is that Mill's emphasis on creativity and imagination means that *at some point* facts of the matter give out; as in painting, there are objective or near-objective standards such that any informed observer could distinguish a mere daub from a genuine painting, but where invention takes over, there is a diversity of routes leading in different, non-competing directions, not all of which can be pursued, but along any of which there is something that practitioners and observers agree is progress – or the arrival at a dead end. Talk of the competent observer brings us to the issue that lies beneath the surface of *On Liberty* and *Representative Government*. This is the question of authority.

Authority: The Anxieties of "The Spirit of the Age"

Because there has been a long tradition of complaining about the way Mill tended to revise his work by qualifying bold initial statements into statements hedged about with 'may be', I am reluctant to wish that he had concentrated on turning "The Spirit of the Age" and the essays on Bentham and Coleridge into a full-length work on the culture of modern society. We know that he regretted that he had not been able to make headway with the unformed science of 'ethology', and it is clear that progress with it would have been both a condition and a result of pursuing the anxieties and intimations of the essays of his late twenties and early thirties. But there is a freshness and an unguardedness – visible also in his *Essays on Some Unsettled Questions in Political Economy* – that to a considerable extent disappeared from the later works in which Mill attempts to provide a settled view. Too often, what he gained by making his views less vulnerable to criticism was lost by making them less thought provoking.

"The Spirit of the Age" was an unfinished series of articles written for the *Examiner* in 1830–1. It was a time of upheaval in Mill's life, as well as in British and French politics. He had fallen in love with Harriet Taylor, had been vastly excited by the French Revolution of 1830, had encountered the Saint-Simonian missionaries, and was in the full tide of rebellion against the narrower kind of Benthamism. So the idea that this was an age of unsettled opinions, contestable standards, and deep uncertainty about what the future might hold was something he did not merely believe but something he deeply felt. This is so, even though Mill's politics were astonishingly untouched by the years of Sturm und Drang. He retained his father's contempt for the political competence of the English landed aristocracy and wrote as though it was obvious that their political ascendancy was over. Only in reviewing the second volume of *Democracy in America* did Mill concede anything to the legitimacy of a landed class, but even then it was more nearly a matter of conceding the Hegelian claim for an agrarian culture than urging the political merits of a landed aristocracy (CW XVIII: 153ff.). We are so accustomed to thinking of Mill as an 'aristocratic liberal' that we sometimes take our eye off the fact that as the child of an archetypal aspirant middle-class striver, he grew up as the protégé of aristocrats whose aim was to take the government of Great Britain out of the hands of Tory landowners and put it into the hands of virtuous public servants from the middle ranks of society. James Mill's *Essay on Government* was as hostile to neglectful mill owners and industrialists as to landed aristocrats, but the only heroes of the essay were the virtuous middle ranks (Mill 1978, 53–98).

What strikes all readers of "The Spirit of the Age," however, is Mill's anxieties about the absence of intellectual authority in the modern world. Some of these anxieties are to all appearances a straightforward reiteration of Saint-Simonian themes: we live in a critical age and suffer from the loss of the security that characterizes organic or natural periods. There is an interesting undercurrent of a more private kind. Having fed himself the medicine of Wordsworth, Shelley, and Goethe as a prophylactic against the depression of his mental crisis, Mill needed a coherent account of the moral or psychological authority of the poet. Mill avoided the trap of treating poetry as merely an expression of emotion, and settled on the view that poets intuited truths that philosophers could subsequently elaborate; the social philosophy that was needed by the modern age was "poetic intuition plus logic." How this was to work in practice was never quite explained, but it survives as an aspect of *Utilitarianism* and in the insistence on the role of the individuals who perceive new human possibilities in *On Liberty*.

Because Mill was inclined to see himself as the importer of Parisian intellectual insights for the benefit of the excessively practical English, it is difficult to get a concrete sense of what he hoped a more organic condition of English society might yield. The general answer is obvious enough: there would be a consensus on the (nature of the) answer to questions about the good life, and by extension on the (nature of the) answer to questions about the duty of individuals to society; this would sustain a hierarchy of intellectual authority, because a consensus on the nature of the answers we sought would – as in the sciences – sustain a ranking of not only suggested answers but also of the capacity of different individuals to provide them. Just as, in the sciences, a neophyte can understand *why* a given answer is the right answer, even when he would have been quite incapable of reaching it for himself, so in these conditions, a cultural, moral, and political neophyte could understand why a given answer was right, even if he was incapable of reaching it for himself. Just as in the sciences, too, the proper attitude of the neophyte would be to embark on a process of understanding in greater and greater depth the answers he was given, initially with no idea of overturning them, but regarding their exploration as an apprenticeship in self-understanding and social understanding.

The disanalogies between moral and political judgment and scientific inquiry need no emphasis here; what needs emphasis is the fact that all his life Mill wrote as though there were no such disanalogies but fought for causes that presupposed that there were many. It is this that links Mill's concerns to Isaiah Berlin's criticisms of the Enlightenment faith in the sciences of man, but also makes it hard to say anything illuminating about what Mill and Berlin had in common. Berlin always insisted that the kind of consensus at which science aims is not to be looked for in cultural and ethical matters, but Mill was ambivalent. "The Spirit of the Age" is sufficiently unfinished to look very different to different readers; some have thought it authoritarian, others have thought it intelligently nuanced and to be preferred to *On Liberty* (Himmelfarb 1963, vii–xx).

The difficulty is knowing about what, if anything, Mill may have changed his mind between the one work and the other. Mill could have written these very different essays without changing his mind on fundamentals. He might have believed first and last that mankind was fated eventually to be of one mind about the good life and the ends of human existence. As we have said, they would not believe there was only *one version* of the good life, because one thing they would understand would be the open-ended diversity of individual natures. Still, they would be of one mind about how to think about the good life, their beliefs about the good life would be well founded, and some among them would be better judges of the worth of different lives than would others, and we would happily defer to their judgment. It remains entirely possible that at the outset Mill thought it more urgent to reach that terminus and believed in addition that it was not far distant, whereas later he thought it less urgent to reach it and that it was very far distant indeed (CW X: 263ff).

Authority and *On Liberty*

That indeed is what I think the truth is. There is one further element in the case. Another thing about which we might feel that we would like to know a lot more is what changes occurred in Mill's understanding of the role of 'the mass' – or public opinion, the majority, 'society', or however we describe the starting point for a rational discussion of the way in which large numbers of others have an impact on the individual in virtue of their numerousness. Mill's exploitation of his French resources was not only a matter of borrowing extensively from the Saint-Simonian view of history as a process driven by ideas and involving the decay and recreation of orthodoxies; he also borrowed a French understanding of the conflict between mass and individual. Tocqueville's understanding of *individualisme* in *Democracy* was not borrowed from Mill, but it is not dissimilar to the condition that Mill described in "The Spirit of the Age" in which individuals who are at a loss to know what to do with themselves and seek in vain for a settled doctrine about how to live turn in on themselves and lead self-centered but unsatisfactory lives (CW XXII: 227ff.).

Conversely, the Saint-Simonians not only taught Mill about the need for association, as Tocqueville also did, but persuaded him that history was increasingly being driven by mass phenomena, the famous tendency for masses to predominate over individuals that he announced in "Civilization" (CW XVIII: 117ff.). We now have the ingredients for the argument that it is possible in a mass society for there to be, at the same time, too much and too little authority. Public opinion exerts a pressure on individuals by way of the unofficial social sanctions of ostracism, disapproval, and the more official sanctions associated with the law and with differential enforcement of and access to the law; an individual who does not take the rule of thinking like everyone else will find himself under acute psychological pressure. Mill was emphatic that the tyranny to be feared was not the tyranny of proletarian insurrection but that of a form of mutual psychic policing that came all too easily to the Victorian English middle classes. At the same time, mere pressure does not supply genuine authority; it can supply an alarming simulacrum of it, because a person who internalizes these sanctions acquires an inner censor that dictates his behavior. An inner censor is what real authority supplies as well; so the crucial abilities we need are the ability to distinguish the real from the fraudulent and the ability to distinguish rational acquiescence from simple fear. That mass society makes these abilities impossible to acquire is the chilling thought behind *On Liberty,* and the fear that unites Tocqueville, Mill, and Nietzsche. Authority, the real thing, allows us to follow someone else's lead with our eyes wide open and our brains fully engaged. Merely being frightened to think for ourselves is not an acknowledgment of authority but simple submission to the tyranny of opinion.

Because Mill's sociology was an eclectic construction from a variety of different sources, he rarely provide a detailed account of how these deplorable processes operated. This poses a problem, not of supplying the missing account of these pressures and their operation, for that is easy enough, but of providing a persuasive account of how these pressures can be resisted and on what basis real authority can be erected. The aspect of Mill that some readers admired as a kind of Stoic bleakness – the icy, aristocratic aspect that Charles Kingsley saw and admired while he flinched from it – is an argumentative and theoretical weakness. It appears that individuals have only their own resources to rely on, and society's tyrannical pressures can be held back only by the force of arguments that, if Mill himself is to be believed, society is not likely to heed. It is easy to see how attractive he and Harriet Taylor must have found the image of lonely defiance that *On Liberty* exudes, as well as the thought that they might be among the few individuals who are the origin of all great advances. The emotional attraction of the position does nothing to hide its weaknesses. What Mill required was a sociological theory of the open society, so that he could explain what sorts of association encouraged boldness and imagination and would sustain their members against a conformist wider society. As it is, he leaves too much on the individual's shoulders.

The Englishman's *Agora*

Mill's need for a sociology of the progressive society is obvious in light of his hopes and fears for modern liberal democracy – representative government. Mill was convinced that, man for man, the citizens of Athens were more politically competent than his contemporaries. Given all the many things one might say against Athenian politics – its vulnerability to superstitious terrors, the domination of politics by family feuds, the incapacity of the Athenians to create the stable federal system that would have saved them from subjection to the Kingdom of Macedon and its Hellenistic and Roman successors, the skittishness of the Athenian populace as described by Thucydides, and its taste for exploitative imperialist adventures – this was a contestable judgment, but it was not a foolish one. The Athenian citizen faced responsibilities greater than those of the modern citizen; he voted for war or peace, and when he voted for war, he put his own life directly at risk. The judicial murder of Socrates and the frivolous expulsion of Aristides were not the only ways in which Athenian opinion expressed itself; they were remembered because they were the exception. Ordinarily, the need to persuade the *ecclesia* of the validity of what one was saying was an exercise in taking public responsibility of a kind that the modern world provides little of for anyone other than a handful of professional politicians. In the sophists, it may have given rise to a breed of spin doctors who would teach people appearing in the courts to make a bad case look better and to make an opponent's case look worse, but the energies that democratic politics liberated in Athens were astonishing to contemporaries and remain astonishing still.

But by the time Mill wrote, all the commonplaces were well established. From Polybius onwards, the inferiority of Athenian democracy to the Roman mixed constitution was taken for granted; from Montesquieu onwards, the thought that democracy could only be practiced in very small units was widely accepted, only disturbed by the cleverness of Madisonian federalism and the utopianism of Jeffersonian ward republics. And after Constant's essay on the contrast between ancient and modern liberty, enthusiasts for the *juste milieux* could comfort themselves for the dreariness of parliamentary politics with the thought that it was the price we had to pay for avoiding the more alarming features of ancient, more participatory republicanism. Constant himself, of course, was not anxious to go down that track; like Mill he thought that a committed liberal should want both the liberty of the ancients and that of the moderns.

Mill was acutely aware of the benefits of rational administration. However, this was not to put himself wholly at odds with classical Athens, where activities such as the building and equipping of the fleet were confided to the hands of professionals whose judgment was very widely accepted. Whether to go to war was for the people at large to decide; whom to employ and where to find the best timber was a job for those who knew what they were doing. The greater breach was not so much at the level of orderly management as in the sphere of legislation. Mill was horrified at the way Parliament drafted legislation on the floor of the house; his own ideal was in effect that Parliament should assent to the principle of legislation: trained lawyers draft legislation to give effect to the principle, and then Parliament considers the results and agrees or not (CW XIX: esp. 428ff.). Given that the members of Parliament imagined by Mill had already been filtered by a voting system that awarded extra votes on the basis of education and had survived the rigours of a single transferable vote electoral mechanism, one would have thought that they were about as competent a body of representatives as any legislative assembly has ever possessed. To give them the power to say no more than yea or nay to what was proposed by expert draftsmen was to tilt the mechanism of representation a very long way from direct democracy of the Athenian kind. The practicality of Mill's proposals is not the point; the British legislative mechanism at presents places on parliamentary draftsmen the burden of trying to give effect to what they frequently, although privately, regard as the incoherent and half-formed views of cabinet ministers and of assisting ministers in patching up the larger errors of phrasing or the most disliked elements of legislation as a bill winds its way through committee.

The difficulty with assimilating Mill's wish to give the task of drafting legislation to experts to the present system in Britain is that the British system works as it does because British governments are elective dictatorships, a one-party government which can get its own way except in very odd circumstances and can therefore resist all amendments to a bill. Mill disliked parties, even though he voted almost straight down the liberal party line in his three years in Parliament. Mill's ideal version of parliamentary government is hard to visualize, but it seems that a chamber elected for its personal merits on Mill's elaborate franchise would form something more like a deliberative jury than a body in which government and opposition benches faced each other in the familiar way. Policy would be put to it, although it is not absolutely clear by whom, and upon it being agreed that a given policy was to be pursued, legislation to give it effect would be devised, brought back, and voted up or down. Although it is very different from the British parliamentary system as it has evolved, it is not difficult to see how such a system could work. With a little imagination, it is the Athenian or Florentine system: one could have a directing committee, elected (or chosen by lot) from the body itself or separately; its task would be to produce policy and present it; such a committee could have members specializing in different tasks – a secretary for the navy, foreign affairs, or whatever – and would certainly need a chair. It would be more like the U.S. system of government than the British, save that legislation would be introduced by the cabinet and civil service rather than by members of Congress.

Balance or Incoherence

If that catches some of Mill's intentions, we can defend Mill against the charge of incoherence. Mill's support for ways of engaging individuals in the direct governance of their own neighborhoods suggests that a jury model of citizen engagement might be a plausible implementation of liberal democracy. We do not volunteer to serve on a jury but perform – more or less willingly – the social duty that we are required to perform when we are picked out by lot.

It would be easy to run city planning committees in the same fashion; they would – as Mill knew – need efficient permanent officials to present options and implement the policies on which they decided. Indeed, almost all of local politics could operate on such a basis; there are few technical issues that require much education to grasp; all the interesting questions occur at the margins where it is a matter of coordinating one locality's decisions with another's. That is where Mill's dictum – following Bentham – of "centralize knowledge localize power" will not quite do what we want. There is, after all, no point in building efficient sewers in my locality if yours – your locality and yours sewers – won't cooperate.

Coordination is why we need representative government. When Mill describes his version of market socialism, he does not raise these difficulties, because he does not imagine government playing a substantial role in the management of an economy. So far as the economy goes, the market provides all the coordination that is needed. The market can govern the interplay between productive and distributive enterprises, once government has set some guidelines and the framework of appropriate property rights. That, however, leaves untouched the question of coordinating government action. The market is not in general an effective mechanism either within or between different localized governments, because so much of government is a matter of attending to public goods that the market will not provide or of coping with market failures, such as by ensuring that the cost of negative externalities falls on those who cause them and that the creation of positive externalities brings some reward to those who create them. Mill shows a considerable non-technical understanding of these issues in book V of the *Principles* but does not tie the discussion into his account of the cooperative future.

We can imagine Mill subscribing to be a great variety of alternative political arrangements, and he did not spell out which of them he wanted above all others. What he wrote in his later years was quite closely matched to the interests of his readers and to immediate issues confronting British politics, so we should not complain that we cannot find fully described accounts of utopia. There was inevitably a good deal of tension between Mill's wish to see his countrymen and women acquire the self-reliance and public spirit of the Athenians and the unpropitious conditions in which they were going to have to do it. There was also a less inevitable but an evidently unresolved tension in Mill's mind between self-government for its own sake, which may include a great deal of trial and error, and rational public administration, where the elimination of error is an important objective. There is also a tension, which has not been explored at all here, between the intentions of schemes such as Thomas Hare's system of proportional representation and those of systems of choice by lot that marked older sorts of democracy. The one place where there is no tension at all is between Mill's admiration for the life of the *agora* and his admiration for the virtues of the East India Company. Individuals have it in them to be both passionate and efficient, and a political system should find room for both passion and efficiency. How it is to do it is as much a question for us as for Mill.

7

Mill in Parliament

When Should a Philosopher Compromise?

Dennis F. Thompson

The parliamentary career of John Stuart Mill offers a unique opportunity to observe the tension between theory and practice in the public life of a philosopher-politician.[1] Mill is one of the few political philosophers in modern times to have held national political office, and the only one to have won a legislative seat after publishing theoretical works that proposed practical reforms.[2] The aim of this chapter is to see what can be learned from

[1] The literature on Mill's theory tends to ignore his political career, and the literature on Mill's life does not analyze the tension between his theory and practice from a normative perspective. In the entire recent four-volume collection of essays on Mill's theory, there are remarkably few references to his parliamentary career, and no substantial discussion of it at all (see Smith 1998). In the most important biography of Mill, the section of describing his years in Parliament scarcely refers to Mill's theory (see St. John-Packe 1954). The only sustained treatment of his parliamentary career is Bruce L. Kinzer, Ann P. Robson, and John M. Robson, *A Moralist In and Out of Parliament: John Stuart Mill at Westminster, 1865–1868* (cited as Kinzer et al. 1992). But this valuable work is mainly historical; its "judgments" focus on the "initial question" of why Mill was "defeated in the 1868 election, having been returned in 1865" (see Kinzer et al. 1992, 269). The authors pay less attention to the relation of his theory to his conduct and do not address at all the normative question of whether Mill should have made the compromises he did. Nevertheless, I have benefited greatly from this work of Kinzer and his colleagues, as well as from the indispensable edition of the Collected Works, of which John Robson is the general editor.

[2] Among other important theorists, Alexis de Tocqueville and Edmund Burke pursued political careers that are most comparable to Mill's. Tocqueville served in the Chamber of Deputies from 1839 to 1851 (after publication of *Democracy in America*) but is arguably more a social theorist than a political philosopher. More significantly, Tocqueville, according to one of his biographers, was "not one of those politicians who found their career on a programme, who identify themselves exclusively with a particular set of measures.... Rather he seems to have hoped for a career ... where principles and programmes

I benefited from excellent research assistance by Minh Ly, who also gave me substantive suggestions on several points of interpretation. For comments on an earlier version of this article I am grateful to Amy Gutmann, Russell Muirhead, Nancy Rosenblum, and Nadia Urbinati.

that career about the challenges a philosopher who goes into politics faces, and more generally about the challenges a politician of principle confronts in turning theoretical commitment into legislative action. The inquiry is partly interpretive: to what extent did Mill modify his principles for political benefit? It is also normative: to what extent should Mill have modified his principles? The answers to the normative question, suitably generalized, suggest some criteria for assessing the compromises that principled legislators make in any democratic polity.

Mill is an apt subject for such an inquiry not only because he was a major theorist, but also because he was known as, and took pride in being known as, an independent thinker who promoted progressive reform. He espoused unpopular positions – some far ahead of his time, such as women's suffrage, and some opposed even by his own allies, such as the recognition of land claims of Irish tenants. He did not aspire to be a politician and won his seat in Parliament without conducting a conventional campaign. Although he ran as a Liberal, he did not toe the party line once in office. His defeat in 1868 after only three years in Parliament is sometimes attributed to these radical enthusiasms and political reluctances. If any politician of his time could claim to have stood above politics, Mill would surely qualify.

But a closer look shows that he was more of a politician than is often assumed. He regularly worked with his party, not only to advance specific legislation he favored but also to support the party leadership. He was more than willing to make compromises to achieve political aims, even short-term and relatively minor legislative victories. Before he won his seat, he was contemptuous of the moderate Reform efforts the Liberals were

could evolve from the statesmanlike handling of concrete problems" (Brogran 1973). See also Jardin 1988, 301 and 387. Burke served nearly thirty years in Parliament (from 1765 to 1794) but under very different circumstances from those Mill faced a century later. Except for his brief term as a member from Bristol (which ended after his famous speech defending the independence of representatives), he won election in "pocket boroughs" or otherwise through the favor of wealthy patrons. His major political works were written during or after his service in Parliament and deliberately did not present systematic or general theories of politics (see Lock 1998, 477, 481; Harris 2004). In the less philosophical context of American political thought, James Madison would count as a politician who also wrote important political theory, but unlike Mill he was not a philosopher who briefly entered politics but rather a politician who briefly devoted himself to philosophy. Mill himself regarded the *Federalist Papers* as important contributions to political theory and – perhaps more surprisingly – the *Discourse on the Constitution and Government of the United States*, which John C. Calhoun, the South's most eloquent defender in the Senate, finished just before his death in 1850. Mill shared Calhoun's fear of the tyranny of the majority (although not the affection for the southern minority Calhoun defended). Calhoun "display[s] powers of a speculative thinker superior to any who has appeared in American politics since the authors of *The Federalist* (*CR*, CW XIX: 558).

proposing: "no Reform Bill which we are likely to see for some time to come will be worth moving hand or foot for" (*Later Letters,* CW XVI: 997). After a short time in Parliament, he began to see value in moving forward gradually, even if the reforms fell short of what he had proposed in his own writings and were seen by some of his Radical friends as worse than no reform at all.

Mill's political career is an instructive case study because it shows that even one of the most independent and principled politicians we are likely to see in any democratic polity was prepared to compromise. Even a maverick, it seems, must be a politico. Mill of course did not become a complete politico. The limits he set for himself and other reformers were more strict than those that most politicians would be prepared to accept. But by examining compromises that Mill made or refused to make, we can begin to develop criteria to assess whether a politician of principle is acting too politically or not politically enough.[3]

The Independent-Minded Philosopher

When Mill agreed to run for Parliament, he had already written his most important political works and was widely known and generally respected both as a political philosopher and as a public intellectual. He had been reluctant to enter politics (to exchange his "tranquil and retired existence as a writer of books" for the "less congenial occupation of a member of the House of Commons" [*Autobiography,* CW I: 72]). But he believed that it was his duty to consent to the request of citizens if they would accept his strict and unconventional conditions (which were "at defiance of all ordinary notions of electioneering" [*Autobiography,* CW I: 274]). He would not raise or spend any money on the campaign and would not canvas the electors. He warned that, if elected, he not would provide what we would call constituency service: he would "not undertake to give any of my time and labor to . . . local interests" (*Autobiography,* CW I: 274). His campaign platform, presented in a letter to a local political committee, stated these

---

[3] For this purpose, I adopt a neutral conception of compromise to avoid both the tendency to treat all compromises as suspect, and the opposite tendency to regard only justifiable agreements as true compromises. The concept of compromise should be broad enough include any agreement in which politicians accept a measure that gives less than their initial principles imply (where "less" may mean fewer elements of the preferred measure, less desirable means of implementation, adoption on a smaller scale, or combination with other irrelevant or less desirable elements). I focus on compromises in which principles are at stake because those are the type to which Mill's conditions were chiefly intended to apply. For a useful discussion that presents a somewhat different analysis of the concept, see Kuflick 1979, 39–41.

conditions in uncompromising terms and declared his intention to speak forthrightly on controversial issues.[4] He refused to negotiate with the other Liberal candidate in the constituency to form a coalition against the Conservative opponent (although he allowed his supporters to do so [*Later Letters*, CW XVI: 1073–4]). During most of the campaign, he stayed in France, spoke at only a few meetings in the week before the election, and generally observed his own strict conditions. Nevertheless, he and his fellow Liberal won decisively. The constituency was relatively liberal in outlook and the Conservative political organization was weak. But Mill's reputation as an independent thinker probably helped. He was "too distinguished a candidate to be rejected."[5]

Once in Parliament, Mill continued to see himself as an independent, committed to promoting the principles and programs he had presented in his writings, even while recognizing that many people regarded his proposals as crotchets.[6] In his own account of his parliamentary career, written after his defeat, he commented: "I ... in general reserved myself for work which no others were likely to do," and that therefore "a great proportion of my appearances were on points on which the bulk of the Liberal party, even the advanced portion of it, either were of a different opinion from mine, or were comparatively indifferent" (*Autobiography*, CW I: 275). Most biographers and commentators have largely accepted this description of his role.[7] Many of his interventions in Commons certainly

---

[4] *Later Letters*, CW XVI: 1005–7. In this campaign and also in his reelection campaign, Mill did refuse to answer one kind of question – about his personal religious beliefs (*Autobiography*, CW I: 274; *Later Letters*, CW XVI: 1483–4). Because those beliefs were likely to be unpopular with voters, we might be tempted to count his refusal to answer as a questionable political compromise. His own stepdaughter criticized him for being less than "open and truthful" on this question. She was commenting on a letter (written to his committee and published in a newspaper) in which Mill made a point of denying that he was an atheist (Mill-Taylor Collection British Library of Political and Economic Science, London School of Economics, vol. LIII: 53 [12 November 1868], cited by Kinzer et al. 1992, 120; and St.-John Packe 1954, 474). But Mill's claim that he acted on principle is plausible given his consistent affirmation of the view that a politician's religious beliefs are irrelevant to his ability to serve. He held to this view, to his disadvantage during his reelection campaign, in a controversy about his support for an atheist candidate (*Autobiography*, CW I: 289).

[5] Lord John Russell, Amberly Papers, vol. I, quoted by Kinzer et al. 1992, 294.

[6] "I have been accustomed to see that the crotchet of today, the crochet of one generation, becomes the truth of the next and the truism of the one after" ("The Westminster Election of 1865 [1]," CW XXVIII:16–17).

[7] See, e.g., St. John-Packe 1954, 446–75. Mill's "acts were in harmony with his professions" (Berlin 1969, 173–206). While offering a more nuanced interpretation, Kinzer et al. confirm that from the nineteenth century to the present most biographers have followed Mill's own

fit the description. He opposed the secret ballot, a key reform favored by his Radical colleagues, and defended capital punishment, a practice condemned by many Liberals (Kinzer 1978, 19–38; "The Ballot," CW XXV: 1218; "Capital Punishment," CW XXVIII: 266–72). His speech in favor of women's suffrage – widely admired but regarded by many as promoting one of his crotchets – followed the spirit if not the details of the "advanced" position he took in *The Subjection of Women* ("Admission of Women to the Electoral Franchise," CW XXVIII: 151–62; *The Subjection of Women*, CW: XXI). Although knowing that defeat was inevitable, he insisted on a vote on his amendment to substitute "person" for "man" in the Conservatives' Reform Bill of 1867 ("Admission of Women...," 162). His motion to adopt the system of proportional representation he had advocated in *Representative Government* had even less chance of success.[8] He introduced it in Parliament, but made no effort to build political support for it. He spoke as an "eminent philosophical sponsor of a plan that...possessed moral and political significance that entirely transcended party loyalties" (Kinzer et al. 1992, 106).

Although his defeat in 1868 was overdetermined, the perception that he had been too extreme and too independent may have been a factor.[9] The honorary secretary of the Grosvernor-Mill Committee (who today would be called the campaign chair) believed that one important cause was that Mill's constituents failed to appreciate the "rigid independence which led him...to act and write precisely as he would have done had he not been a candidate."[10] The political press and the general public objected to what

description (Kinzer et al. 1992, 8–9). Capaldi, author of *John Stuart Mill: A Biography*, finds "some truth" in Mill's assessment (Capaldi 2004, 324). Capaldi also writes: "Mill's campaign and conduct after the election reflect precisely what one would have expected of the author of *Considerations on Representative Government*" (Capaldi 2004, 321).

[8] "Personal Representation," CW XXVIII: 176–87. On his discussion of this voting scheme, which he attributed to Thomas Hare, see Thompson 1976, 102–11.

[9] Kinzer et al. 1992, 218–68, cite this factor as one, though probably not the most important, cause of his defeat. Mill himself mentions, as one of several causes, what might be considered his refusal to compromise with Conservatives as much as they expected: "As I had shown in my political writings that I was aware of the weak points in democratic opinions, some Conservatives, it seems, had not been without hopes of finding me an opponent of democracy, as I was able to see the Conservative side of the question, they presumed that, like them, I could not see any other side. Yet if they had really read my writings, they would have known that after giving full weight to all that appeared to me well grounded in the arguments against democracy, I unhesitatingly decided in its favour" (*Autobiography*, CW I: 288–9).

[10] William Malleson, *The Times*, 21 December 1868, p. 5, cited by Kinzer et al. 1992, 275.

they saw as his "extremism ... his unwillingness to compromise, his single vision."[11]

The Value of Compromise

Gladstone, the Liberal leader, called Mill the "Saint of Rationalism" (Courtney 1889, 141–2). The epithet stuck – all too well. For many later commentators, it sums up what they regard as Mill's idealistic and apolitical attitude in Parliament.[12] But Gladstone's assessment is actually more nuanced: "though [Mill] was a philosopher, he was not, I think, a man of crotchets ... together with the high independent thought of a recluse, he had, I think, the good sense and practical tact of politics."[13] Despite this reputation for "high independent thought," the adamant positions he sometimes took, and the self-appraisal offered in the *Autobiography*, Mill was not only willing to accept compromise in particular cases but was also prepared to defend compromise in general. He sometimes deployed his "good sense and practical tact" to trim and deal like a seasoned politician. His motives were not those of an ambitious politician, but neither were they always those of a nonpartisan statesman. His compromises were more numerous than the conventional portrait of him would allow, and less faithful to his political goals than a strict application of his theory would require.

Yet the compromises Mill made were for the most part consistent with his views about compromise itself. Those views do not yet amount to a theory of compromise, but they are more substantial than has been appreciated. They were largely formed before, and guided him after, he entered politics.[14] From his years in the East India Company, he became "practically conversant with the difficulties of moving bodies of men, the necessities of compromise, the art of sacrificing the non essential to preserve the essential" (*Autobiography*, CW I: 87). As early as 1839 in a discussion of the reform party, Mill first expressed a favorable attitude toward compromise: "Men may combine in supporting a good thing which is to be had now, and continue to do all they can by speech and writing for something they think better, which the

---

[11] Kinzer et al. 1992, 295. But other factors may have been more important: see Kinzer et al. 1992, 218–68; and nn. 46 and 47 to this chapter.

[12] St. John-Packe uses the phrase as the title of the "book" devoted mainly to Mill's years in Parliament (St. John Packe 1954, 446–75).

[13] Courtney 1889, 141–2. I have reversed the order of the last two clauses for emphasis.

[14] I thank Minh Ly for collecting the textual evidence that confirms that Mill's favorable views of compromise were formed in large part before he entered politics.

time is not yet come for putting into a practical shape and carrying through Parliament" ("The Reorganization of the Reform Party," CW VI: 480–1). The justification is practical, but it is not merely a concession to political necessity. It expresses a recognition that some reforms need a "period of incubation" (*Autobiography,* CW I: 276). Some desirable reforms, even if they could be legislated now, may need time to develop, and would not realize their promise if adopted under current circumstances. If a reform is adopted before its time, it may never come to fruition.

Mill's other justifications were based not on practical considerations of this kind (ripeness of the reform in question) but were derived from his theories of liberty and government. One such justification holds that a compromise may produce a better law than either of the more extreme proposals favored by adversaries on either side of a controversy. In *On Liberty,* Mill suggested a conception of politics in which fundamental differences are not only tolerated but welcomed. He argued that "a party of order or stability, and a party of progress or reform, are both necessary elements of a healthy state of political life. . . . Each of these modes of thinking derives its utility from the deficiencies of the other, but it is in great measure the opposition of the other that keeps each within the limits of reason and sanity."[15] Although he was referring mainly to the value of hearing the views of each of the parties, the implication is that some parts of those views should be incorporated in, or at least allowed to influence, the measure finally adopted by Parliament.

Later, encountering the Conservatives in Parliament, he may have had less enthusiasm for the idea of a party of order. But he continued to recognize the value of accommodating the Conservatives' views on some issues. Sometimes that value seemed to be mostly strategic. He did not hesitate to use Conservative principles to promote Liberal reforms. In his speech in favor of Gladstone's reform bill, which would have given the vote to some members of the working class, Mill argued that the bill is "not a democratic measure . . . but follows from the class theory, which we all know is the

[15] CW XVIII: 253. A related but distinct rationale for compromise could be drawn from Mill's fallibility argument (*On Liberty,* CW XVIII: 253). He argues there that we should not suppress an opinion even if we believe it to be wrong, because our grounds for believing it wrong depend on its not being suppressed. Although Mill did not extend this argument to compromise, it suggests that we should accommodate (rather than simply not suppress) some opinions we believe to be wrong or do not yet have good grounds for believing to be wrong. John Rawls's idea of the "burdens of judgment" – which show why much disagreement in democratic societies is reasonable and should be accommodated – provides a similar but more general rationale (Rawls 2001, 35–6).

Conservative view of the constitution" ("Representation of the People [2]," CW XXVIII: 61). The working class deserves representation, not as individuals but as a class, and that class is now without adequate representation. Although this argument was not his preferred justification – and the bill itself was not his preferred measure – Mill believed that the Conservative notion of class expressed an important truth, which properly interpreted could support measures that both Liberals and Conservatives should endorse. That many Conservatives did not recognize the implication of their own principle did not cause Mill to doubt that his interpretation of the principle was correct.

A third justification does not depend on any assumption that the measures the politician opposes contain truth. Even when politicians believe that their opponents' position is without merit, they should still be prepared to make compromises for the sake of the effective functioning of democratic institutions. An "indispensable requisite in the practical conduct of politics . . . is the readiness to compromise, a willingness to concede something to opponents and to shape good measures so as to be as little offensive as possible to persons of the opposite view" (*CRG*, CW XIX: 514). The "mutual give and take" is so important that democratic institutions should be designed to encourage it. The democracies of England and America benefit more than the Continental governments from "a compromising temper, the lack of which is a cause of failure of liberal institutions." Such a temper is not due to "northern blood" but to the "complicated and balanced character of institutions" ("Recent Writers on Reform," CW XIX: 345–6). The value of compromise, on this rationale, is to be found in the process itself. In a culture of "mutual give and take," the democratic process not only runs more smoothly but respects citizens and their representatives more ethically. Presumably, Mill also hoped that such a process would produce better legislation (promote general utility), but the process itself has value, even if in some cases it produces less than optimal outcomes.

Still another reason Mill could approve of compromise is that he believed history was on his side. If the dominant social trends are creating conditions that favor progressive measures, then reformers can afford to move gradually, making concessions to their opponents and realizing the other values that compromise promotes. The most significant tendency in modern history, which may be expected to continue, is the trend toward equality in all spheres of social and political life. As people read the same publications, attend similar schools, gain the same political rights, differences among individuals and social classes, Mill believed, will narrow. This trend toward equality poses some dangers – mass conformity and tyranny of the majority, which

Mill famously criticized. It also brings some political benefits, which Mill emphasized less but were no less important in his theory: a more enlightened citizenry, greater mutual respect, and fewer economic barriers to political participation (Thompson 1976, 158–64). These benefits create conditions that are increasingly favorable for progressive reform.

Mill did not think that these improvements were inevitable. Contrary to some interpreters, Mill did not subscribe to a "romantic... eighteenth-century Enlightenment" view of progress (Harris 1956, 171). Mill's view is more appropriately called a theory of development – imbued with his own brand of Manicheanism (Thompson 1976, 136–73). In his *Logic*, while expressing a tentative belief in genuine progress, he emphasizes that the belief is unsubstantiated.[16] In *Representative Government*, he explains his view more fully – and more darkly:

> there is an incessant and ever flowing current of human affairs towards the worse... which is only controlled... by the exertions which some persons... put forward in the direction of good and worthy objects.... A very small diminution of those exertions would not only put a stop to improvement but would turn the general tendency of things towards deterioration. (*CRG*, CW XIX: 388)

Thus, reformers have reason to expect that history will be their ally, but only if they keep up their "exertions." They should not expect to move too fast; the "current towards the worse" is constantly resisting their progressive efforts and jeopardizing their prior gains. They will have to make compromises, but if they are diligent, they can turn the compromises to their advantage. In the meantime, some compromises can help promote the other values Mill identified.

One more reason that Mill looked with favor on compromise should be noted. Mill did not wish to see some reforms move too fast. He was willing to accept the compromises that incremental change requires because he favored political experimentation – what today might be called pilot projects – as one of the most effective modes of political improvement.[17] In effect, he sought to bring his experimental method to politics. Theory and practice both should be based on experience, not a priori principles. "English politicians, better aware than their Continental brethren, that great and permanent changes... are not to be accomplished by a coup de main... hold

---

[16] Mill uses "progress" or "progressive change" as equivalent to "cumulative change," which does not necessarily imply improvement or progress in the ordinary sense (*A System of Logic*, CW VIII: 913–14).

[17] I credit Minh Ly with pointing out the connection between Mill's experimental method and his attitude toward compromise.

back all extreme theories until there has been experience of the operation of the same principles on a partial scale" (*Chapters on Socialism,* CW V: 709). Most of the reforms he recommended in *Representative Government,* though intended to have radical consequences in the future, did not require any sharp break with social structures, values, and beliefs in the present. As enthusiastic as he was about instituting Thomas Hare's scheme of proportional representation in the whole nation, he saw value in a small-scale trial. Implementing the scheme in a county or metropolitan district would test the "practicality of the machinery" and build public "confidence" in it ("Proportional Representation and Redistribution," CW XXVIII: 242).

The Conditions of Compromise

Mill's inclination to compromise when he entered politics was therefore firmly grounded in his own political theory. His theory provided substantial reasons to seek accommodation with opponents even for politicians who consider themselves independents and whose legislative aims are radical. The five rationales for compromise I have described support a general disposition to compromise and go some way toward suggesting what kinds of compromises are acceptable. For example, a politician would be justified in making concessions to protect progress already made against the "current towards the worse." It would also be acceptable to agree to a small-scale experiment instead of a general program of reform, especially if the proposal in question is novel. But none of the rationales is sufficiently specific to serve as criteria for assessing many of the compromises that legislators are called on to make, or even those that Mill himself made.

For many ordinary political compromises, Mill would have advised politicians simply to use his principle of utility: a compromise is justifiable if it is likely to produce more net utility than the available alternatives. Assessing a compromise between two public works projects, for example, usually does not require any more than a straightforward calculation of the utilities at stake. Such a compromise – like many political bargains – does not usually call for singling out any particular claim for special treatment. But the compromises about which Mill was most concerned were those in which the commitment to moral improvement had to be partially abandoned. The value of that commitment does not seem adequately represented by treating it in the same way as most other utilities. Claims based on "utility in the largest sense, grounded on the permanent interests of man as a progressive being," should receive greater weight (*On Liberty,* CW XVIII: 224). As Mill recognized, even a utilitarian needs qualitative criteria that give some utilities priority over others. The principle of utility, although the foundation of all moral judgments in politics, is too general to serve by itself as a standard for judging compromises in which principles expressing these permanent interests are at stake.

When confronted with proposals for parliamentary reform that fell short of what he favored but in which he saw some merit, Mill was moved to formulate a test for acceptable compromise – what he called the elements of a "good half measure" ("Thoughts on Parliamentary Reform," CW XIX: 315, 321). A "measure of compromise" that does not satisfy "those who think the present system radically defective" should still be supported if it satisfies two conditions. Both turn out to be more complex than they seem at first and need interpretation and further specification.

First, an acceptable compromise must be directed at the "worst features of the existing system" ("Thoughts on Parliamentary Reform," CW XIX: 315, 321). "Worst" here refers not only to how bad the feature is but also how pressing the need is to correct it. The compromise should apply where it is "most urgently needed." How do we decide what is most urgently needed? Some theorists might be tempted to declare that what is most urgent is what their theory regards as most important. But that is not Mill's response. His theory implies that the worst features of the electoral system are the exclusion of so many citizens from voting and the arbitrary variation from district to district in the qualifications for the franchise (*CRG*, CW XIX: 399–412, 467–70). Yet when he assesses specific reform proposals, he writes that the "most serious mischief is not that only a fraction of the community have the right to vote, but that the majority of the House is returned by a very small fraction of that fraction" (*CRG*, CW XIX: 315). In the current circumstances, the worst element is the small number of boroughs – many of which are under the control of "some great family in the neighborhood" and the rest the "prize of the highest bidder." A reform that would correct this situation – combining several small towns into boroughs or breaking down the barrier between the boroughs and the counties – has the highest priority because it would have the greatest immediate effect on the composition and conduct of Parliament. The test thus directs attention more to institutional effects than to individual rights.

The condition, as Mill applies it, has other qualifications that make it more complex than his explicit statement of it suggests. It is not enough that a compromise correct the worst feature of the institution in question. It must do so without creating another equally objectionable problem either in that institution or elsewhere in the political system. Lord Aberdeen's bill would have reduced or eliminated representation of some of the smaller boroughs, which would have solved what Mill considered the most urgent defect in the system – but at an unacceptable cost. It would have arbitrarily disenfranchised some citizens and extended the franchise much less than a feasible alternative ("combining towns into boroughs" [*CRG*, CW XIX: 318]).

Another qualification of the condition is that the class of "worst feature" may include more than one member. There can be several equally bad features that require urgent attention. This qualification is suggested by Mill's discussion of campaign finance. No less a vice than the multitude of small constituencies is the practice of candidates' paying their own election expenses. This practice conveys the demoralizing message that a public servant should pay for permission to serve and gives citizens reason to suspect that their representatives are elected "not as the best man, but as the best rich man, who can be had" (*CRG*, CW XIX: 320–1). Any acceptable reform bill must include some provisions to deal with this problem.[18]

To summarize the first condition, we may say that an acceptable compromise must deal with at least one of the problems that is the source of the most pressing serious harm to the institution in question and bring about an improvement without creating other equally bad or worse problems in that same institution.

The second condition that Mill imposes to justify a compromise is that the measure in question should "recognize and embody the principles, which if no hindrance existed, would form the best foundation of a complete measure" (*CRG*, CW XIX: 315, 321). Mill writes that the compromise should be a "step in the direction" toward the reformer's goal, but he does not mean that it must actually move the institution in that direction, or even accelerate the movement. With respect to short-term effects, the condition is not very demanding. It directs attention to a long-term consequence: the principle expressed by the compromise should serve as an effective precedent for future legislators who would carry out the full measure of the reform, or at least it should not serve as an impediment to the full measure. Because the principle is so important, a politician should state it clearly and forcefully,

---

[18] One of Mill's solutions – that a candidate's supporters pay election expenses – would not solve the problem of corruption on which modern campaign finance law focuses, but his suggestion that the municipalities and the state pay for general expenses that fall equally on all candidates comes closer to modern proposals for public financing of elections. Mill's suggestion falls short of modern proposals because candidates' supporters would still have to cover expenses specific to the candidate. Because campaign expenses were still remarkably modest by today's standards, it was not entirely unrealistic to hope, as Mill did, that most of the candidates' personal campaign could be run on "gratuitous zeal" (*CRG*, CW XIX: 320).

without qualification. If faced with a matter of principle, "not to go the whole length of it is to sacrifice it."[19] To his fellow reformers, Mill declared: "disclaim nothing which is a legitimate consequence of [your] principles."[20]

This commitment to principle, however, does not mean that the politician may not use other arguments in order to secure agreement, even those based on an opponent's principles. The opponent's principles that he uses still must be consistent with his own. Mill's appeal to the Conservative idea of class to defend the extension of suffrage, mentioned above, is an instance of his using principles other than his own to promote policies of his own. His approach – to show that people with different and even opposing political theories can come to agree on a policy – is not unlike John Rawls's more recent idea of an overlapping consensus.[21]

A fundamental principle in Mill's theory of representation is that voting is not a right but a duty. As a power over others, it should be exercised, and may be regulated, in the public interest.[22] The implication for reform is double-edged: each citizen should have a vote, but only insofar as he (or she) is qualified to exercise it. The ultimate goal is universal suffrage in which every adult citizen would have a vote, but not necessarily an equal vote. Those who are better educated – the more competent – might be entitled to extra votes. Here Mill proposed his notorious scheme of plural voting.[23] But he did not insist on it. He was willing to support any extension of the franchise that respected the principle of competence – for example, by requiring voters simply to certify that they could read, write, and calculate ("Thoughts on Parliamentary Reform," CW XIX: 328). A reform that extends the suffrage,

---

[19] *Later Letters,* CW XVI: 998. Going the "whole length" refers to the principle at issue: Mill was objecting to reformers who declared their principle to be manhood suffrage rather than universal suffrage.

[20] Reformers may ask for "less than their principles would justify" if they do not disavow their principles and if they reasonably believe that "they are doing more good by uniting their efforts with those of others to attain a nearer object, and one more immediately practicable" ("The Reform Debate," CW XXV: 1103–4). See also "The Westminster Election of 1865 [2]," CW XXVIII: 23. In his praise of Gladstone's approach to compromise, Mill later makes a similar distinction: "make no compromise of opinions, except by avoiding any ill-timed declaration of them, but . . . negotiate the most advantageous compromises possible in actual measure" (*Newspaper Writings,* CW XIII: 598–99).

[21] An overlapping consensus is one "in which the same political conception is endorsed by the opposing reasonable comprehensive doctrines that gain a significant body of adherents and endure from one generation to the next" (Rawls 2001, 184; see also 32–8). Rawls's idea applies to conceptions of justice, however, not to particular policies.

[22] "Thoughts on Parliamentary Reform," CW XIX:322; and CRG, CW XIX: 488–90. Also see Thompson 1976, 96; Urbanati 2002, 111–12.

[23] Later, Mill essentially abandoned the scheme because it would have the effect of favoring property rather than recognizing intelligence (Thompson 1976, 99–101).

however minor, with an educational qualification, however minimal, preserves the essential principle of representation.

Two other implications of this fundamental principle should be mentioned because in Parliament Mill did not follow either as far as his theory would imply. One is what he called the "representation of minorities," which tempers majority rule by adopting one of several possible forms of proportional representation.[24] The other is his opposition to the secret ballot, which his fellow Radicals favored. No compromise should include this provision, he maintained, because the ballot expresses the principle that voters are accountable only to themselves not to the public ("Thoughts on Parliamentary Reform," CW XIX: 331–38).

To satisfy the second condition of compromise, then, an agreement must express the general principle that would best support the long-term goal the politician seeks. The agreement should not include any provisions that contradict the principle. The principle may be expressed in the provisions of the agreement itself or (more commonly) in the justifications given for it. In defending the compromise, the politician should draw attention to the ultimate implications of the principle, whether or not they are likely to be realized.

It might seem that if the second condition is satisfied, the first condition is unnecessary. If the compromise is principled and produces some marginal improvement, why not accept it? Why does it also have to address the most urgent problem? The purpose of the further requirement of urgency is to ensure that the compromise brings a significant immediate benefit, a conspicuous gain that expresses a commitment to the principle now. The second condition focuses on the long-term commitment to the principle: it guarantees only that the compromise will promote or not impede the adoption of the full measure when (and if) its time comes. The first condition is needed to protect the principle in the short term. By requiring that the compromise address the most urgent problem, the condition in effect sets a limit on how far the principle can be sacrificed at the time it is made.

To see to what extent Mill's decisions in Parliament were consistent with his conditions of compromise, and to what extent they might guide the decisions of any principled politician in deciding when to compromise, I examine some of the compromises that Mill accepted and some he rejected.

---

[24] "Thoughts on Parliamentary Reform," CW XIX: 328–30. In this pamphlet, Mill suggests several methods of cumulative voting, but later, after hearing about Thomas Hare's scheme of the single transferable vote, which in *Considerations* and later in Parliament Mill advocates as the best system (Thompson 1976, 102–11).

The conditions, it turns out, are definite enough in many cases to distinguish justifiable from unjustifiable compromises. Indeed, they are definite enough that Mill himself can be shown to have not always observed them. But the conditions require further elaboration, and in some respects modification, to meet the challenges of the politics not only of our time but also of Mill's. I focus on the compromises that confronted Mill in several of the episodes that he regarded as important enough to recount in his *Autobiography.*

Urgent Needs: Hyde Park and Ireland

Mill's first condition can be further developed by examining his reactions to two quite different crises – political demonstrations in Hyde Park and English policy on Irish land reform. Both led Mill to support measures that could be seen as "urgently needed," but in the first case Mill accepted, and in the second rejected, compromise. His different reactions were not the result of his applying this condition inconsistently. What was "urgently needed" in each case was different.

In July 1866, the Reform League (a generally peaceable organization agitating for radical electoral reform) had tried to hold a demonstration in Hyde Park. When the police prevented the demonstrators from entering the Park, they turned and began marching to Trafalgar Square. The sudden shift created confusion. A riot ensued, lasting nearly three days. Many people were injured, and much property was damaged. When Parliament took up the matter (while the disturbance was continuing), Mill criticized the government for creating disorder that could have been avoided. He fervently affirmed the "right of the people to meet in Hyde Park" ("The Reform Meeting in Hyde Park [2]," CW XXVIII: 98–100). Under the circumstances, the affirmation was courageous, but it offered no less than what readers of *On Liberty* would have expected.

Yet when the league announced a few days later that it would reclaim its right of free assembly by trying to hold another meeting in Hyde Park, Mill opposed the plan. He persuaded the leaders to cancel the demonstration, in return for his participation in a public meeting at Agricultural Hall. This compromise represented a double concession on Mill's part. On the one side, he was temporarily abandoning his defense of the right of free assembly. On the other, he was associating himself with an organization he had never wanted to join. Mill was strongly opposed to two of the most important aims of the Reform League's program – the secret ballot and manhood (as distinct from universal) suffrage. Furthermore, by agreeing to speak he also risked (and received) severe condemnation not only from virtually all Conservatives but also some members of his own party and most of the press.[25] In the speech itself, Mill attempted to defend the right of free assembly, but the crowd was so agitated that he could not finish ("The Reform Meeting in Hyde Park [4]," CW XXVIII: 102–5). The compromise was an attempt – not entirely successful – to preserve an important principle (as the second condition requires) by publicly reaffirming it in a dramatic way.[26] Also, the compromise could be seen as the "most urgently needed" measure for addressing the crisis. The government had called out the military, and many of the demonstrators intended to come to the meeting armed (*Autobiography*, CW I: 278). The compromise would prevent even more serious violence, which Mill believed might start a revolution, and in any case would set back the cause of reform.[27]

The threat of violence also played a role in Mill's attitude toward Irish land reform.[28] But this time it led him to reject compromise. His first speech on Ireland, given soon after he entered Parliament, criticized the British government more severely than the Fenians, a dissident group of Irishmen fighting for independence from England who were the target of the bill under consideration. To many in the House, Mill seemed to be defending the Fenians, whose violent tactics no one in Parliament (including Mill) wished to condone. The speech was "so unfavorably received" that his friends advised him not to speak at all for while (*Autobiography*, CW I: 276). When he intervened again on the Irish question, he spoke in favor of a very moderate bill – and in very moderate language. Although in his writings he had argued for granting Irish tenants "fixity of tenure," he was now content to support what

---

[25] In his *Autobiography*, Mill defends himself against this criticism: "I do not know what they expected from me; but they had reason to be thankful to me if they knew from what I had, in all probability, preserved them" (*Autobiography*, CW I: 279).

[26] Mill later compensated for his failure here by successfully filibustering a Tory bill that would have prevented public meetings in the Parks: "I not only spoke strongly in opposition to it, but formed one of a number of advanced Liberals, who, aided by the very late period of the Session, succeeded in defeating the Bill by what is called talking it out. It has not since been renewed" (*Autobiography*, CW I: 278).

[27] Mill would not have regarded the government's prohibition on the demonstration as a restriction on speech justified by the exception he described in *On Liberty*: "even opinions lose their immunity, when the circumstances in which they are expressed are such as to constitute their expression a positive instigation to some mischievous act" (CW XVIII: 261). Mill believed (and said so in his speeches) that the government, not the demonstrators, were responsible for any instigation that occurred in this case.

[28] Mill was not opposed to violence under all circumstances and was prepared to defend it if the cause were right and important and if the chances of success were great; see Williams 1989, 102–11.

was by his own account an "extremely mild measure."[29] It would merely give Irish tenants a legal claim to compensation for any improvements they had made on the land, and even then only if, in the contract that all had to make with landlords, they had not waived the claim. Mill spoke "in a manner calculated less to stimulate friends, than to conciliate and convince opponents" (*Autobiography*, CW I: 279). "Do I . . . ask you to establish customary rents and fixity of tenure . . . in Ireland? . . . Certainly not. It is perhaps a sufficient reason that I know you will not do it" ("Chicester Fortescue's Land Bill," CW XXVIII: 75–83). This answer might seem only a concession to political reality. But Mill went on to give a substantive reason for concluding that these proposals were not desirable at the time: they are more likely to succeed if they develop by custom than if they are imposed by law (ibid.). This measure, mild though it was, failed, and for nearly a year and half Mill did not make any further efforts to promote the Irish cause in Parliament.

Then in early 1868, he published a powerful and unequivocal case for the reform of Irish land laws. Justice has always been on the side of reform, he argued, but now the national interest requires it. England can no longer avoid the stark choice between giving the peasantry "permanent possession of the land" or dissolving the union (*England and Ireland*, CW VI: 518). Mill knew that his proposal would be regarded as extreme, but he believed that "to propose something which would be called extreme [is] the true way not to impede but to facilitate a more moderate experiment" (*Autobiography*, CW I: 280). When Parliament took up the question shortly after Mill's pamphlet appeared, Mill used to occasion to defend his proposal ("The State of Ireland," CW XXVIII: 247–61). He made some concessions to the audience. He concentrated less on the moral principles and more on the practical details of the proposal. He spent much of his time correcting misunderstandings and answering objections that had been raised against it. He even suggested some specific modifications (such as limiting the proposal to only arable land), which could serve as the basis for a compromise (ibid). But he did not himself support any compromise and continued to defend his original proposal in its "extreme" form. He concluded with a ringing affirmation of the principle that the "rights of property, subject to just compensation, must give way to the public interest" (ibid, 261).

---

[29] *Autobiography*, CW I: 279; "Chicester Fortescue's Land Bill," CW XXVIII: 75–83. His view on this question presented in the various editions of *Principles of Political Economy* (beginning in 1848) was somewhat more qualified than the claims in his 1868 pamphlet. See *Principles of Political Economy*, CW II: 328–30; *England and Ireland*, CW VI: 505–32.

What had changed to cause Mill to resist compromise now on this issue when earlier he had earlier seemed to welcome it? The Conservatives were back in power, and Mill may have felt less hesitancy in criticizing the government.[30] But this does not seem a complete explanation or even the most important factor. Mill's proposal was probably even more controversial and less likely to be adopted now than earlier. The most important change was the dramatic rise in violence and the growing possibility that the resistance in Ireland might now turn into a full-scale rebellion. Mill truly believed that the union was at risk, and its dissolution would harm not only England but also the Irish. (One of his aims may have been to preserve this part of the empire, but another at least as important was also to respond to flagrant injustice without causing still more harm.[31]) The threat of revolution had raised the stakes and changed the calculus of what was "urgently needed."

Earlier, defending the "mild measure," he could plausibly argue that it addressed the "worst evil" that could be feasibly corrected under the circumstances. Tenants could be given compensation without disrupting the whole system of land law, and fixity of tenure might not work well if it were imposed at this time. In that sense, compensation was the "most urgently needed" reform. But as the costs of ignoring Irish demands rose, the locus of urgency shifted. The future of the union was at stake, and what most urgently needed attention had become the larger problem of the union, which could be saved only by radical reform. Any compromise that fell short of that reform could not be justified.

What counts as "urgently needed" thus depends on the political circumstances, specifically on a calculation of certain risks and benefits that a compromise might bring. But although this interpretation of the condition may seem to be simply an application of Mill's principle of utility, it is not quite the same. The condition is not best understood as calling for a general utilitarian calculation in which all risks and benefits are included. To show that a compromise deals with the most urgent problem, we do

---

[30] Kinzer tends to attribute Mill's shift on this and several other issues largely to his loyalty to the "advanced Liberal party under Gladstone's leadership" (in Smith 1998 205–6). However, in a later work, Kinzer and his colleagues cite additional causes: "the uprising in Ireland and the Fenian incidents at Manchester and Clerkenwell" (Kinzer et al. 1992, 169). Any all-purpose explanation such as party loyalty is not helpful in identifying the differences in Mill's responses that are relevant to interpreting his conditions of compromise.

[31] Mill regarded English policies in Ireland as a failure but still hoped that they might be changed so that Ireland would remain in the empire. His imperial sympathies influenced his views on this question, but reading his speeches and writings one cannot doubt that he was at least equally moved by the injustices that resulted from English policy. See Sullivan 1983, 599–617; Kinzer et al. 1992, 179–80.

not consider all the problems in the political system. Rather we should focus in the first instance on the particular measure or decision and bring in other considerations only if they involve serious harm to the political system as a whole. Only a high risk of the dissolution of the union or a plausible threat of revolutionary violence would warrant broadening the utilitarian calculus. Whether Mill was right in his assessment of the risks (he probably exaggerated them in both cases), his willingness to compromise on the Hyde Park demonstrations and his refusal to compromise on the Irish land question were consistent with this first condition as I have interpreted it.

Dilemmas of Parliamentary Reform

When Gladstone introduced his Reform Bill in 1866, Mill faced a dilemma. The Bill dealt with only the franchise (reducing the property qualification and granting more working class citizens the vote). It did not address the distribution of seats (eliminating small boroughs and correcting the imbalance in representation). Mill of course favored extension of the franchise but objected to the absence of the educational qualification that his theory of representation required. Equally troubling was the complete neglect of redistribution, which he believed to be the more urgent problem. A few months earlier writing to Hare, he worried that enacting a bill limited only to the franchise would doom the scheme of personal representation and generally undermine any effort to deal with the problem of the distribution of seats in the future. Once Parliament has adopted the limited bill, he wrote, "the whole subject of changes in the representation will be tabooed for years to come" (*Later Letters,* CW XVI: 1138–9). Gladstone's bill thus was not a compromise that Mill's criteria would seem to permit. It did not clearly express the principle of representation Mill most favored, and it did not address the problem of representation Mill saw as most urgent. Yet Mill accepted it, and even spoke in favor it.

Can this apparent departure from his own conditions for acceptable compromise be justified? The political circumstances provide part of a justification. His fellow Liberal from Westminster, Lord Grosvenor, and a Conservative member whom Mill respected, Lord Stanley, had proposed a bipartisan motion to postpone any further action on the Reform Bill until the House could address the problem of the distribution of seats. Such a course of action would seem to be exactly what Mill should have supported, given the priority he had earlier assigned to the problem of distribution. But it was well known that Grosvenor and Stanley were part of a coalition (the so-called Adullamites) intent on preventing any reform at all. In this context, supporting them would carry a different meaning than the content of their motion explicitly expressed. The implicit message was the opposite of the position Mill wished to defend. Its antireform implications offended his fundamental principles of representation. It was more important to remain faithful to these principles than to try to address the most urgent problem under these circumstances. The extension of the franchise is "the greatest improvement... which we at present have in our power to make" ("Representation of the People [2]," CW XXVIII: 68). Furthermore, given the political situation, tying the franchise reform to redistribution or other reforms would not bring those reforms "a day sooner" (ibid).

We can say, then, that when the two conditions conflict, Mill's second condition (preserve the principle) takes priority over his first condition (address the most urgent problem). But how could this bill be said to preserve Mill's essential principle that the right to vote depends on the competence to vote? The bill did not contain any educational requirement; it simply lowered the property qualification. The bill can be made consistent with the principle by emphasizing two points. First, the bill did not express the pure democratic principle to which Mill most strenuously objected – equal representation. That was what an educational qualification was most needed to counter. The bill enfranchised only a small part of the working class and gave them only minority representation.[32] An educational qualification was less necessary, and perhaps even less justifiable, when so many citizens were without representation. Second, the principle that the bill did express – one of the justifications Mill gave for it – could be interpreted as supporting a functional substitute for the educational qualification. Working-class voters and their representatives bring knowledge to Parliament that other members do not have (especially on such issues as strikes, trade unions, and hours of labor). This knowledge is important not only for protecting the working classes but for making good laws ("Representation of the People [2]," CW XXVIII: 65–8).

Although it is possible in this way to interpret the bill to make it consistent with Mill's principles, the interpretation does not capture what was probably the most significant reason that Mill accepted this compromise. Mill was willing to stretch his conditions because he wanted to support Gladstone

---

[32] The limited effect of the bill gave Mill the opening for his argument, mentioned earlier, that the bill rested in part on a conservative principle – that classes not individuals should be represented. Mill of course also believed that it expressed a liberal principle because it would lead eventually to universal suffrage.

and his party. The importance of Mill's resolve to support Gladstone can be seen even more clearly by considering his response to a very similar compromise that came before the House about a year later. After the Conservatives had formed a government, Disraeli brought forward his own reform bill, providing for an increase in the franchise that was in principle not so different from Gladstone's abortive bill. Disraeli's bill even gave graduates an extra vote, which should have pleased Mill. But Mill now joined Gladstone in opposing the bill.[33] In his only speech on the bill itself, Mill directed his criticism mainly against his fellow radicals, who were about to ignore Gladstone's pleas and throw their support to Disraeli's bill. They evidently believed that if they compromised with Disraeli they would achieve more reform than Gladstone could deliver. Although they had little basis for that belief, they turned out to be right when several days later Disraeli, to the surprise of nearly everyone (including the Radicals), abandoned the provision that Gladstone and Mill had opposed and endorsed a bill that went even further in expanding the franchise than Gladstone's original bill had dared to go. In a speech a week later, Mill conceded that the bill was a significant advance but refused to give Disraeli credit: "every good thing we have to in this bill, even that which seems to be more than Mr. Gladstone was prepared to give, has only been given for the purpose of out-bidding Mr. Gladstone" ("The Reform of Parliament," CW XXVIII: 171).

The most plausible interpretation of Mill's reasons for his conduct throughout this episode is not to be found in the difference in the bills – the nature of the principle they explicitly embody or the urgency of the problem they directly address. The differences were not great, even before Disraeli's surprising turnaround. The principle that Mill most consistently followed in these debates on the various reform bills and their amendments is better understood in terms of a certain kind of support for the Liberal party leader. Gladstone "appeared to Mill as the great hope to lead a movement and to complete England's transition into the brighter future that history promised."[34] In deciding which compromises to accept (the Liberal bill) and which to reject (the original Tory bill), Mill gave considerable weight to the

---

[33] The specific issue was the section of the bill stipulating that only householders paying rates directly to the parish rather than to the landlord (by means of "compounding") would qualify for the franchise. The issue now seems rather technical but Disraeli made it a matter of principle and question of confidence (even though he reversed himself within a week to win passage of the final bill). See "The Reform Bill [3]," CW XXVIII: 146–9. Also see "The Reform Bill [4]," CW XXVIII: 150–1; "The Reform of Parliament," CW XXVIII:167–74.

[34] Kinzer et al. 1992, 13, 91–2. Several of Mill's contemporaries regarded him as "a thoroughly party man," a description he challenged later in his *Autobiography*. See Stephen 1900, 64; Vincent 1966, 158–60; *Autobiography*, CW I: 275–6.

effect on the capacity of Gladstone to promote future parliamentary reform. Also out of concern for Gladstone, he resisted his urge to add personal representation and women's suffrage to the Liberal bill, even though he regarded these as two of his most important proposals for reform. Although neither had any chance of winning approval, he believed that it was important and urgent to give both greater public attention and an early prominent place on the political agenda. When Disraeli's bill was before the House, he no longer felt any need for restraint. He then gave two of his most radical speeches ("Admission of Women...," CW XXI: 151–62; "Personal Representation," CW XXVIII: 176–87).

During the debates on reform, the independent philosopher might seem to have become a party loyalist. Such a transformation would be puzzling because Mill's theory is pointedly critical of political parties and party systems. Party loyalty is not likely to have been one of the principles that Mill had in mind in specifying his second condition for acceptable compromise. Mill disliked party government because he believed that it limits the range of opinions in the legislature (which should represent "all the feelings of the people, not merely their party feelings"), allows a small group of politicians to choose the candidates (who are usually selected for their personal wealth or partisan dependability rather than their political competence), and weakens the influence of independent members of the legislature (on whom Mill relied to tip the balance toward the public interest.)[35] Also, the scheme of personal representation that Mill favored would have substantially weakened the influence of the major parties – a consequence that he saw as one of its advantages (*CRG*, CW XIX: 463–4).

The tension between Mill's theoretical antipathy toward political parties and his practical allegiance to the Liberal party can be reduced, as one commentator suggests, by arguing that the antipathy was directed not against the "principle of party but against the existing party system."[36] Mill's theory, as I indicated earlier, actually requires something like a party system – an institutionalized "healthy antagonism" between a party of order and a party of progress. But at the time he wrote *Representative Government*, the work

[35] "Personal Representation," CW XXVIII: 178–9, 181–2; *CRG*, CW XIX: 455–6, 446–7. Also see Thompson 1976, 118–21, 125–6; for Mill's earlier disillusionment with parties, see Hamburger 1965, 242–72.

[36] Kinzer 1998, 198. Kinzer's interpretation is a useful corrective to the view that Mill's theory rejects any important role for political parties, but the interpretation depends on attributing to Mill a conception of party that almost no actual political party is likely to satisfy – party as a "a moral ideal" more than an "economic, social, or institutional" organization (see Kinzer 1998, 209–10). Furthermore, if Mill's ideal party were ever to be realized, the role for any opposition party of order would lose much of its point.

in which he was most critical of parties, neither the Conservatives nor the Liberals came close to satisfying his standards for what a party should be. In the preface he complained that "both Conservatives and Liberals . . . have lost confidence in the political creeds which they nominally profess" (*CRG*, CW XIX: 373).

Recognizing that the right kind of party has an important role in his theory, however, does not entirely account for Mill's willingness to soft pedal his own principles to support Gladstone's agenda. Liberals certainly did not constitute anything like the party of progress he favored. Looking back later on the debate on an electoral corruption bill, Mill is bitter: "the Liberal party in the House was greatly dishonoured by the conduct of many of its members in giving no help whatever to this attempt to secure the necessary conditions of an honest representation of the people" (*Autobiography*, CW I: 283–4). Yet although Mill had little faith in his own party in its current state, he had great confidence in his party leader. He regarded Gladstone as "the one politician of national stature capable of placing principle at the center of political discussion" (Kinzer 1998, 206). Under Gladstone's leadership, the Liberal Party had the potential to become a party that stood for principles – and, more to the point, for Mill's principles.

Given Mill's view of the importance of Gladstone's leadership, we can see how he could have regarded his rejection of the Tory bill and support for the Liberal bill as consistent with his conditions of compromise. Unlike the compromise that the Tory bill would have required, the compromise he made to help Gladstone could be seen as embodying a principle that would serve future efforts toward parliamentary reform. The principle affirms not party loyalty but progressive reform.

To make this justification consistent with his conditions of compromise, however, we have to interpret the principles to which the second condition refers more broadly than Mill's original statement might suggest. We have to allow that a principle may be embodied not only in a particular measure but also in a cause that a leader stands for and exemplifies in his actions. The leader must be at least as committed to the principle as the reformer is. To prevent the condition from becoming so broad that it would allow any compromise needed to support a reform-minded leader, we should further require that the principle refer to the specific cause at stake in the measure in question. The specific cause in this case was parliamentary reform, rather than the goals of any of the other measures in the Liberal agenda. Mill himself sometimes carried his loyalty to Gladstone further than this modified condition would warrant. On occasion, Mill seemed willing to accept some compromises simply to protect Gladstone's political prospects. But the condition itself must be limited, more closely tied to the measure in question, if it is to serve as a distinctive test for determining whether to accept or reject a particular legislative compromise.

Putting Women's Suffrage on the Agenda

Mill considered his speech introducing the motion to replace "man" with "person" in the Reform Bill of 1867 his "most important public service" (*Autobiography,* CW I: 285). Certainly the speech that he gave on behalf of the motion – a carefully prepared and occasionally stirring thirty-minute oration – was his finest moment in Commons. The motion, although defeated as expected, won more support than anyone had anticipated (73 of the 269 recorded votes went in its favor). The immediate reaction in Parliament and in the country, even among many of those who were deeply opposed to giving women the vote, was remarkably favorable.[37] The quality of the speech and the dignity with which Mill presented it gained a respectful hearing for the cause and ensured that Mill's intervention would stand as a significant milestone in the movement for women's suffrage. In the spirit of his principles presented in *The Subjection of Women,* Mill had put the question of women's suffrage on the national agenda.

It should not detract from Mill's achievement to recognize that he did not press his principles to the fullest extent his theory implied. Even while promoting one of the causes he cared most about, he was prepared to compromise. He generally avoided mentioning the issue in his election campaign. During the debate on his own party's reform bill, he declined to introduce any amendment on the subject at all.[38] His first motion on the subject was modest: a simple request that the House be given data to indicate how many women who met the property qualification were denied the vote. His speech for the motion was equally modest. He argued that Parliament should give some attention to the issue of women's suffrage not because it is right that women should have the vote but simply because many respectable women in the country have signed a petition declaring their desire to have it ("Electoral Franchise for Women," CW XXVIII: 91–3). Most significantly, Mill kept his appeal well within the established framework of property qualifications. It is often forgotten that in this, his finest moment, the bill about which he was speaking would have granted the vote not to all women in households that

---

[37] For the reaction, see Kinzer et al. 1992, 147–8.
[38] According to his own account in a letter to a colleague in Commons, he was trying to avoid "increasing the accusation of obstructiveness" (*Later Letters,* CW XVI: 1175).

met the property qualification but only to widows and spinsters ("Admission of Women ... ," CW XXI: 161–2). (Married women were generally not entitled to own property.) Mill's acceptance of this compromise on a matter of principle borders on violating his own second condition, which implies that "not to go the whole length of [a principle] is to sacrifice it."

We can bring Mill's actions during this episode into harmony with his conditions of compromise if we further refine those conditions. First, we should keep in mind that one of the first purposes of compromise is to avoid bringing an issue to decision or attention prematurely. If the time is not ripe, raising the issue can be counterproductive.[39] Mill proceeded cautiously because the issue of women's suffrage was not only controversial but also easily ridiculed. Later historians generally confirm his assessment of the risks he faced in simply raising this issue (Kinzer et al. 1992, 88, 123–4, 129, 146). (According to one account, he risked "the smirks becoming laughter" [Kinzer et al. 1992, 126].) Second, Mill's insistence that the compromising politician should not weaken his principles does not rule out the rhetorical strategy (also mentioned earlier) of using the least controversial claim to build support for one's position. Mill himself advised reformers (at least those who wish to persuade English people) to place the "expediency of the particular measure upon the narrowest grounds upon which it can rest; and endeavour to let out no more of general truth, than exactly as much as is absolutely indispensable to make out our particular conclusion."[40] His own actions in this episode and his considered view actually go further than this advice implies. He used minimal claims to get the issue on the agenda and appealed to the principles of his opponents to try to win their support, but then in arguing for the measure he also made sure that he emphasized his own fundamental principles.

Finally, it is important to attend to the distinction between the principle that the measure itself embodies and the principle invoked to justify it. Although the measure he supported did not itself go as far as his principle would require (and violated a basic principle of justice by unfairly discriminating within the class of women), his speech clearly stated a more general

---

[39] In the letter to his colleague cited above, Mill invoked a version of the ripeness justification: "What we are now doing [presenting a petition from the public rather than requesting a discussion or making a motion] will lay the foundation of a further movement when advisable, and will prepare for that movement a much greater amount of support in the country than we should have if we attempted it at present" (*Later Letters*, CW XVI:1175).

[40] "Comparison of the Tendencies of French and English Intellect," CW XIII:446. For a similar but broader conception, see the discussion of the "principle of economy of moral disagreement" in Gutmann & Thompson 1996, 84–94.

principle, one that could be, and later was, used to argue for granting all women the right to vote. None of the essential arguments in the speech depended on accepting a property qualification, and nothing in the speech provided support for the denial of the franchise to married women. Mill alluded to this feature of the bill only in his brief concluding remark (made after other speakers had responded to his main speech). At that point he says only that the question of married women is not before the House, and he will therefore not comment on it, except to say that if in the "progress of experience" it should become "the general opinion" that married women ought to have the vote, "they will have it" ("Admission of Women," CW XXI: 162). Everyone who heard this remark, knew that, unlike some politicians who decline to comment on a question, Mill was not trying to conceal his view. They were in no doubt that what might become "general opinion" was already Mill's.

An Absolute Limit to Compromise: Justice in Jamaica

Mill's stand against the British government's response to the uprising in Jamaica in the fall of 1865 reveals another important dimension of his view of compromise. It shows that there are some matters – notably criminal justice – on which compromise is not appropriate at all. Criminal justice should not be decided by deploying the two conditions or by engaging in any political calculations. Here the question of compromise should not even arise. Generally, the judgment of courts on serious crimes should not involve any compromise. Specifically, when the question is whether a public official is guilty of murder, it should be decided by the courts according to strict standards of the criminal law.

No issue agitated Mill more (or occasioned more antipathy toward him) than the controversy over the conduct of Edward John Eyre, the British Governor of Jamaica. The central question was whether Eyre should be brought to trial for his conduct in suppressing the uprising in Jamaica.[41] After a large group of black residents took over the courthouse and killed the unpopular magistrate and several of his colleagues, Eyre declared martial law. The troops under his authority quickly suppressed the incipient rebellion, but in the process killed more than 400 Jamaicans, flogged many more, and

---

[41] Two contemporary accounts of the episode are "Report of the Jamaica Royal Commission," CW XXX: 518–28, and the statement of the Jamaica Committee (a nongovernmental body that Mill chaired) reprinted in the appendix of *Essays on England, Ireland, and the Empire,* CW VI: 422–7. See also Mill's version in *Autobiography,* CW I: 280–82.

destroyed a thousand homes. The most popular politician on the island (who had been a persistent critic of Eyre) was arrested and executed, even though (as a subsequent inquiry established) the evidence on which he was convicted was dubious ("Report of the Jamaica Royal Commission," CW XXX: 518–28). A Royal Commission issued an evenhanded conclusion: the uprising was a serious threat, but the military reaction was excessive. Eyre was recalled but was hailed as a hero by many in the British establishment; he kept his pension, received legal expenses from the government, and never stood trial.

After some initial hesitation, Mill took the lead in the campaign to bring Eyre to trial. He became almost a "zealot" on this issue (Kinzer et al. 1992, 213). He refused to accept not only the government's disposition of the case, which essentially followed the Royal Commission report, but also Charles Buxton's motions, which many Liberals and other critics of the government regarded a reasonable compromise. Buxton's motions actually tilted very much in favor of the Jamaicans. They called for condemnation of the conduct of Eyre and his military associates, punishment of any officials who had committed "great offences," compensation to Jamaicans who had lost family and property, and amnesty for Jamaicans serving sentences for their participation in the disturbances.[42] Yet the motions pointedly did not demand punishment or even prosecution of Eyre. That was precisely the issue that had earlier divided Buxton and Mill and had led to Buxton's resignation (and Mill's selection) as chairman of the committee. In that dispute, Buxton had argued that bringing criminal charges against Eyre would do no good and potentially much harm to the cause. No jury would be likely to convict Eyre on the evidence, and if he happened to be convicted, the government would probably pardon him. The "result would be to give a triumph to Mr. Eyre and his advocates."[43]

When Mill rose to speak to these motions, he did not specifically address Buxton's argument. Buxton had concentrated on condemning Eyre, the military authorities, and the government's response. So Mill, respectfully, said only that Buxton had expressed a "milder view" than his. Mill continued the attack on the government and, in what he regarded as the finest speech of

---

[42] For the motions, see the headnote to "The Disturbances in Jamaica [2]," CW XXVIII: 105. "Great offences" presumably referred to specific violations of regulations under martial law, not to failure of command responsibility. The first motion passed, and the others were withdrawn after the government made some significant concessions.

[43] Kinzer et al. 1992, 192. Buxton's prediction of the behavior of juries was close to the mark. Later, after a high court judge decided the legal issue against Eyre, an Old Bailey grand jury threw out the bill against him (*Autobiography,* CW I: 282).

his career, gave a fervent defense of the "principle of government by law."[44] To protect the "security of human life," officers of government "must answer for their acts to the same laws and before the same tribunals as any private citizen." Although Mill was explicitly calling only for prosecution, he made no great effort to conceal his belief that Eyre was guilty and that justice would be done only if he were convicted.

Buxton's argument seems on its face a perfectly good utilitarian argument, one that the author of *Utilitarianism* might have been expected to embrace. The motions likewise seemed to be a compromise not so different in form than others Mill had accepted. If anything, they were more favorable to Mill's own views than most other compromises he had agreed to. In that sense, it seemed that the motions could be justified by his conditions of compromise. But Mill considered Buxton's argument to be based on expediency rather than justice (*Autobiography*, CW I: 281). He absolutely ruled out compromise on this issue. In his speech, he hardly appealed to consequences at all; he concentrated on the injustice of Eyre's actions, and the further injustice that would be done if he were not brought to trial for his actions. At several points, Mill began to sound more like a Kantian than like the utilitarian he claimed to be. His outrage seemed to outrun his principles.

Nevertheless, while almost absolutely ruling out compromise on this "principle of government by law," his position is more nearly consistent with his utilitarianism than it might appear. Justice and the rights it protects are based on utility, but it is an "extraordinarily important and impressive kind of utility" (*Utilitarianism*, CW X: 250–1). It protects the "most vital of all interests" – security. This utilitarian justice can even justify a "thirst for retaliation" under some circumstances. "Wrongful exercise of power over someone" – an understated version of the charge that Mill would bring against Eyre – must be for the utilitarian one of the "most marked cases injustice." Such an injustice is even worse when committed by a public official because it undermines the rule of law and the basis of constitutional government. The "worst tyranny of all" is the "emancipation of Government

---

[44] "Disturbances in Jamaica [2]," CW XXVIII: 107. As in his attack on British policy in Ireland, Mill may have been motivated partly by his imperial ideals. "The moral legitimacy of imperial rule" for Mill depended on "the dominant country's providing a government better ... than the subject people could provide for themselves ... the conduct of Eyre and his subordinates ... threatened to subvert this ideal" (Kinzer et al. 1992, 215–16). But Mill's passion in this case seem overwhelmingly driven by his sense of the injustice of Eyre's actions and his avoidance of prosecution. Mill's major speech and all of his public statements on the controversy emphasize the general considerations of justice and the principle of government by law.

officers from responsibility to the courts of justice" ("Centralization," CW XIX: 586).

Reflecting on the episode later in his *Autobiography,* Mill concluded with a justification that is more directly utilitarian. Although Eyre was never brought to trial (and justice was not done), the effort to prosecute him, Mill believed, was still worthwhile. The highest court settled the legal question "in favor of liberty," and an "emphatic warning" had been given to persons in authority to "stop short of such extremities in future" (*Autobiography,* CW I: 282). Mill was stretching here to find a deterrent effect. The deterrent was, after all, not the threat of actual punishment but only the fear of "being put to some trouble and expense in order to avoid" prosecution.

Whether Mill's justification for this campaign to bring Eyre to justice is convincingly utilitarian, his position that this kind of question should not be the subject of compromise is consistently principled. His adamant stance on the question was a factor in his defeat in the election of 1868 (Kinzer et al. 1992, 291–2). Judgments about the conduct of public officials who take innocent lives should be made in a judicial not a political forum and determined by legal rules applied strictly, not political considerations applied flexibly. The compromises that his conditions allow stop at the door of the courthouse.

Conclusion

Mill's parliamentary career offers moments of drama and displays of courage. But we are not likely ever to see a "Mr. Mill goes to Westminster." His career does not provide the material for a Victorian version of the Jimmy Stewart film. Mill cannot be cast as an idealist who naively enters politics, refuses to compromise, and single-handedly defeats the forces of corruption. He could not even play the part that some contemporaries and some commentators wish to assign him: the high-minded philosopher who has no appreciation of low-down politicking. Mill understood the political world quite well before he entered Parliament. He was not surprised by what he found there. He had already written about the value, not merely the necessity, of compromise. He had set conditions that permitted more concessions than a philosopher might be expected to favor. He saw the need to cooperate with his colleagues for short- as well as long-term advantage. Even his self-portrait in the *Autobiography,* with its emphasis on "work which no others were likely to do," suggests a more independent member, a philosopher more above the partisan fray, than the part Mill actually played.

Yet if Mill was a politician, he was even in Parliament also a philosopher. He had more principles than most politicians – or rather, he had worked out and written about his principles more than had any other politician. The principles were also more "advanced" than those of most of his colleagues. Even as he accommodated his opponents, he was, to a remarkable degree, faithful to his principles, at least to his conditions of compromise. His own view of compromise – and the conditions he set for its limits – enabled him most of the time to keep his concessions from undermining his principles. This suggests that these conditions, suitably generalized and brought up to date, could guide modern politicians – at least those who would be principled. If even Mill (fervently attached to his own theory) could act politically without sacrificing his principles, then perhaps ordinary politicians (less encumbered with theory) should be able to do the same.

The conditions of compromise that Mill suggested in his writings, I have shown, need to be further developed and to some extent modified in light of his own parliamentary conduct. For the most part, I have developed and modified the conditions by looking at some of the actual compromises Mill accepted and some he rejected. From that conduct, I have drawn some implications that he never made explicit, and some that he might not have welcomed. The resulting set of conditions can be summarized in terms that are general enough to apply to modern democratic politics. Although Mill initially presented the conditions as a guide for progressive reformers, he did not exclude the possibility that they could serve as a standard for judging the compromises of anyone who claims to be a principled politician, even those whose principles he rejected. Even the Tory who makes compromises can be praised for sticking to his principles or criticized for sacrificing them.

A general summary of the conditions can be presented as a series of judgments that any principled politician should make when deciding whether to accept or reject a proposed compromise. First, before testing a proposal against the conditions, the politician should determine that the issue is appropriate for a compromise: it should not involve a matter that should be decided judicially. Next the politician should make sure that some value of compromise can be realized under the circumstances. The chief considerations that bear on this determination are: the time is ripe for the alternative the politician prefers, the opponents' position contains some truth, the agreement could facilitate future cooperation, and the concessions would not set back progress already made. Then, to evaluate what kind or how much of a specific concession is justified, the politician directly applies the two conditions. First, a compromise is acceptable only if it deals with the most urgent problem in the institution under consideration. If, as is often the case, many problems within one institution are urgent and none is obviously more urgent than others, the politician is warranted in addressing any single problem that is reasonably regarded as urgent. In deciding what is urgent, the focus should normally be not on the system as a whole but on particular elements of an institution and, among those elements, not on individual rights but on the institutional effects. Political circumstances can change this focus: if the effects involve a serious threat to the viability of the political system, the calculus should take the broader consequences into account.

Even if a compromise deals with the most urgent problem, it is not acceptable unless it also expresses ("recognizes and embodies") a principle that supports the more comprehensive goal that the politician seeks ultimately to realize. The measure itself does not have to realize the principle, but at least some of the reasons – preferably the most salient ones – that are presented to defend the measure should call attention to the principle. The principle usually refers directly to the subject of the measure in question. (The right of all citizens to have a voice in government is implicated by a bill to increase the size of the electorate.) But in some circumstances, the principle can refer more generally to the value of supporting parties or persons who are committed to advancing the specific cause the principle expresses. (The cause of progressive reform is implicated by the support of a party leader who exemplifies it.)

This pair of conditions (together with the questions that are to be addressed before the conditions are applied) provides a richer and more nuanced conception of compromise than is found in most recent discussions. A typical approach draws a sharp distinction between conflicts of interest (which may be compromised) and conflicts of principle (which may not) (Benditt 1979, 26–37). Apart from the fact that the distinction is not usually so sharp in practice, politicians sometimes have to accept compromises that conflict with their principles, as Mill himself did. They need criteria to help distinguish among conflicts of principle. Other writers provide lists of what can be compromised (certain kinds of interests or needs) but no guidance about when they may be compromised (Kuflick 1979, 51–2). Still other writers invoke the popular notion of compromise – splitting the difference. But that approach gives too much attention to the distance between the initial positions of adversaries and too little to the moral content of the compromise.[45]

---

[45] Benjamin 1990, 32–45. Despite the title, Benjamin's criteria for an "integrity-preserving compromise" emphasize the attitude of the parties toward the compromise (their commitment to mutual tolerance) and the reasonableness of the positions in dispute (the uncertainty due to moral complexity).

Despite their virtues, Mill's conditions are not entirely adequate as a guide for the modern politician. They are incomplete because any set of conditions of this kind inevitably leave much to judgment and circumstance. But they are also inadequate because Mill did not anticipate, and in certain respects deliberately ignored, some practices of modern legislative politics that are relevant to the question of compromise. Perhaps the most striking is log rolling. In its most familiar form, it involves giving your support to colleagues on a measure that serves their particular interests in return for their support for an otherwise completely separate measure that serves your particular interest. Regardless of whether one or both of the particular interests also serve the general interest, Mill's conditions as I have developed them do not directly address the justifiably of bargains of this kind. Neither did Mill, because he generally disapproved of them. The closest he came to engaging in log rolling was a speech in support of John Bright's opposition to the Cattle Disease's Bill.[46] Mill had little interest in the problem and would have preferred to take no position on the bill. But he needed Bright's support for his own campaign for parliamentary reform. (He may have also thought he could use the debate about the bill to show the aristocratic bias of the House and thereby strengthen the case for its reform.) Log rolling in some modern legislatures has a bad reputation – often deservedly so. But it is also sometimes desirable, and Mill's conditions do not help us to decide when it is and when it is not.

Mill's conception of compromise must be modified in another way if it is to be relevant to modern politics. Although Mill recognized the value of supporting a party leader who is the best hope for furthering an important cause, he did not have any use for party discipline. In his time it was only beginning to develop, but in any case he valued the independent judgment of legislators too much to welcome the practice of giving significant power to party whips. Yet modern legislatures depend on the willingness of at least some members, in the interest of party unity, to put their own causes on hold and even accept some causes they find objectionable. We do not have to believe in absolute party loyalty – "my party right or wrong" – to acknowledge the value of this kind of partisanship. Democratic legislatures would not function well or at all if most legislators, when asked to compromise, gave no more allegiance to their party than Mill was willing to grant.

Mill was not a professional politician. He did not expect to stay in Parliament for long (although he expected to serve more than three years). How a compromise might affect his own political career was never part of his

---

[46] For Mill's role in this dispute, see Kinzer 1984, 2–12.

calculations. To be sure, it is not likely that his principled stands in Parliament were the main cause of his defeat in 1868. He did not think so.[47] The authors of the most careful analysis of his defeat conclude that the Conservative candidate would probably have won a seat "no matter what Mill had done in the intervening years and during the campaign."[48] But the same authors also argue that a more moderate politician than Mill, someone who more consistently took a "middle Liberal line," might have won the second of the three seats in the constituency (Kinzer et al. 1992, 295). Mill's character, and perhaps even his conditions of compromise, militated against that course of action.

Although we rightly criticize politicians who seem to care more about their political career than the public interest, we should not want all politicians to care nothing about their career. Democratic accountability relies on the engine of political ambition. If most politicians did not care about election or reelection, they might possibly less often defer to the unjustified demands of their constituents, but they would certainly less often respond to the justified ones. We may wish there were more politicians like Mill in modern legislatures: we may agree with Gladstone's lament that they are too "rare" (Courtney 1889, 142). But we should acknowledge that Mill's conduct and his conditions of compromise are more immediately attractive to mavericks and independents than to party leaders and party supporters.[49] The conditions can offer sound advice to any politicians, but they would serve more politicians better if they made room for considerations of political ambition.

---

[47] Mill believed that three factors alone were sufficient to cause his defeat: the superior organization of the Conservatives, the vast amount of money they spent, and the opposition of local leaders who were angered by his advocacy of municipal reform (Kinzer et al. 1992, 276). In *Autobiography*, he mentions other causes including his failure to be a reliable "organ" of Liberal opinion, his contribution to the campaign of an atheist, his crusade against Governor Eyre, and his advocacy of municipal reform may have hurt his prospects (*Autobiography*, CW I: 288–90).

[48] Kinzer et al. 1992, 295. These authors attribute the victory of the Conservative candidate to the superior "money and organization" and the "tendency towards the right in Westminster."

[49] For a study of the role of independent-minded members of Congress in a comparable period in American politics, see Shields 1985. Shields distinguishes "conformists" (the typical members, who valued party loyalty and followed their constituents' wishes) from "mavericks" (the members who like Mill favored debate about principles, more often refused to follow their party's line, and valued "individuality and independence of thought" (Shields 1985, 61, 77). Shields is more sympathetic to the conformists, who more consistently recognized the "need for subordinating moral and philosophical issues to the important goal of controlling the government" (Shields 1985, 63).

Mill's conditions could be further modified to take into account these features of modern politics. But even as presented here, they provide a framework that identifies some of the most important considerations that principled politicians should have in mind in deciding whether to accept a compromise and that conscientious citizens should take into account in judging those decisions. If politicians and citizens take such a framework seriously, the "readiness to compromise" that Mill regarded as so essential for liberal institutions will be more securely grounded and more properly practiced in democratic politics (*CRG,* CW XIX: 514; "Recent Writers on Reform," *CW* XIX: 345–6).

8

John Stuart Mill, Individuality, and Participatory Democracy

Alex Zakaras

Two hundred years after his birth, John Stuart Mill's interpreters still disagree about the extent of his commitment to democracy. Many maintain that he was a reluctant democrat, working subtly to insulate government from the vicissitudes of public opinion.[1] These critics usually hold that Mill was above all a liberal who believed that personal liberties would always be too important to entrust fully to the *demos*. Others disagree sharply, insisting that Mill was a radical democrat, even by twenty-first-century standards, and that his ambition to justify broad new avenues for public participation was restrained only by his belief that the British public was not yet completely prepared (but would eventually be) for the fullest self-government.[2]

Recent scholarship has strengthened this latter reading by clarifying the breadth of Mill's participatory ideal: Mill wanted citizens to participate not only in national elections, not only in regular "conferences" between elected representatives and their constituents, but also in local government and adjudication, in volunteer militias and worker-owned cooperatives.[3] Those who defend this view of Mill emphasize his belief, influenced by Alexis de Tocqueville, that participation was part of what made citizens capable of conscientious self-government. Like Tocqueville, Mill describes the practice of democratic politics as a "school of public spirit" and contrasts it favorably with a private life that he imagines dominated by the prerogatives economic self-interest (CW XIX: 412). The transformative effects of public

---

[1] See, for instance, Arneson 1982; Duncan 1973.
[2] See Baum 2003.
[3] See Urbinati 2004; Miller 2000.

Many thanks to Nadia Urbinati, Dennis Thompson, and Jennifer Pitts for their generous comments on earlier drafts of this article.

participation form, on this reading of Mill's philosophy, the very heart of his democratic theory.

Those who resist this view of Mill argue that his enthusiasm for participation was noticeably dampened by his commitment to *competent* governance, which he took to require the sober guidance of educated elites. Dennis Thompson's influential reading of Mill's democratic theory, for instance, sets up the "principle of competence" as one of its two guiding political norms, second only to the "principle of participation."[4] In its most innocuous version, the principle of competence expresses the need for professional bureaucrats, whose technical expertise is required to help run any complex modern government. In its more controversial form, the principle of competence functions as moral check on the excesses of popular politics, a means of counteracting the influence of "sinister" factional interests. In this latter form, it attributes to the elite not only a technical but also a *moral* competence – a capacity for principled moral impartiality – of which less enlightened citizens are incapable. It is this second version of the principle of competence that seems, in the eyes of many of his critics, to cast doubt on Mill's "democratic credentials" (Duncan 1973, 263–4).

In this chapter, I raise questions about both of these common readings of Mill, and I suggest an alternative. I argue, first, that Mill was often skeptical about the benefits of public participation. He worried, specifically, that democracy would encourage mass conformity and intolerance, and I argue that this concern reveals Mill's ambivalence about political participation itself. I turn to the passages in *On Liberty* in which political participation, far from edifying citizens, seems to inflame factional rivalries and to become a vehicle for tyranny. I then ask how such passages can be reconciled with the parts of *Considerations on Representative Government* that seem to celebrate participation as a panacea for democratic ills; indeed, I maintain that these two works reflect strikingly different attitudes toward public participation. I do not, however, use Mill's anxieties about participatory democracy to question his democratic credentials. Mill, like Tocqueville, felt that it would do disservice to democracy to overlook or underemphasize its characteristic dangers. What is more, his answer to these dangers was not exhausted by the principle of elite competence. Instead, I argue that Mill's conception of individuality, understood as an ideal of democratic citizenship, suggests another, more egalitarian means of averting democratic failure.

---

[4] See Thompson 1976.

Conformist Democracy

On Liberty begins with dystopia. Within a few pages of the essay's opening, Mill introduces the specter of a tyranny of the majority, enforced not only through the coercive power of the state, but also by the more diffuse power of "society" (CW XVIII: 219–20). Most of all, Mill laments the "tendency of society to impose . . . its own ideas and practices as rules of conduct on those who dissent from them; to fetter the development, and, if possible, prevent the formation, of any individuality not in harmony with its ways" (CW XVIII: 220). Elsewhere he calls this tendency the "yoke of conformity" (CW XXV: 1180).

The phenomenon of conformity is not, of course, particular to democracy or to the modern world; yet Mill believes that it assumes an especially dangerous form in modern, commercial democracies. As the middle and laboring classes gain political and economic power, Mill maintains that they also win unprecedented social power with which to enforce their norms on the minds and "souls" of other citizens. They achieve this power mainly by controlling public opinion and by ostracizing or otherwise punishing those who deviate from its settled norms. Unlike the clerical or aristocratic power of earlier periods, the strength of these new classes is amplified, not only by the emergent technologies of mass communication but also by the homogeneity of democratic society: because democracies are not divided into social castes that insulate some citizens from popular mores, Mill worries that "there ceases to be any social support for nonconformity" (CW XVIII: 275).

It should be clear that Mill's "conformity" does not simply mean passive acquiescence to group norms; it also connotes an active desire to suppress dissent and difference.[5] This much is evident in Mill's use of the words "tyranny" and "despotism" to describe the condition of mass conformity. Time and again, he emphasizes the *effort* that society expends to compel people to adhere to its customs. In Mill's view, conformity is thus bound up with the inveterate human desire for control over others, which he describes as follows:

The disposition of mankind, whether as rulers or as fellow-citizens, to impose their own opinions and inclinations as a rule of conduct on others, is so energetically supported by some of the best and by some of the worst feelings incident to human nature, that it is hardly ever kept under restraint by anything but want of power. (CW XVIII: 227)

---

[5] Isaiah Berlin discusses Mill's emphasis on the fact that "men *want* to curtail the liberty of other men" [emphasis added] (Berlin 1997, 263).

These lines define an important piece of Mill's project in *On Liberty*, for he believed that the power to impose conformity was growing and that the newly empowered citizens of modern democracies would therefore have to be persuaded not to wield it. They would have to be shown that such impositions advance no one's interests. The argument of *On Liberty* thus begins with an exhortation for self-restraint, alongside a concern that citizens will misuse democratic power.

Mill's account of the psychological affinity between conformity and tyranny is worth exploring in some detail, for it gets to the heart of his occasional pessimism about democracy. It begins with the simple fact of human sociality: "In proportion to a man's want of confidence in his own solitary judgment, does he usually repose, with implicit trust, on the infallibility of 'the world' in general" (CW XVIII: 230). Mill goes on to explain that "the world, to each individual, means the part of it with which he comes in contact; his party, his sect, his church, his class of society" (CW XVIII: 230). Human beings are social creatures; we correct our sense of individual vulnerability by drawing confidence from our social world. We find comfort, especially, in shared beliefs and values, which lend structure and meaning to our lives.[6] We are, as Dana Villa puts it, "encumbered selves" (Villa 2001, 80).

At first, our deference to the "common sense" of our peers is innocent: we trust our party or church or sect because it is the only world we know. What worries Mill is that such deference often outlasts its innocent beginnings:

Nor is his faith in this collective authority at all shaken by his being aware that other ages, countries, sects, churches, classes, and parties have thought, and even now think, the exact reverse... it never troubles him that mere accident had decided which of these numerous worlds is the object of his reliance. (CW XVIII: 230)

Here is where the trouble begins. Mill believes that inhabitants of the modern world – people who know something of the diversity of human beliefs and values – ought to acknowledge the contingency of their inherited commitments. He observes, however, that encounters with difference often tighten our hold on our own orthodoxies. The prospect of unsettling our way of life, premised as it is on shared ethical norms, makes us uneasy: "people feel sure, not so much that their opinions are true, as that they should not know what to do without them" (CW XVIII: 233). We cleave to our group's values not mainly because of their epistemic merits but because they are the

---

[6] Mill elsewhere praises the human desire to feel "unity" with others as the very foundation of the morality. In the passages I am quoting here, however, this very desire seems to find expression in the troubling tendency to defer uncritically to one's fellows.

guarantors of a social world without which we would feel disoriented and vulnerable.[7]

For the most part, Mill thinks that this need for solidarity operates unconsciously. We do not consciously affirm beliefs that we think false or dubious. Our commitments are, for the most part, "perfectly sincere" (CW XVIII: 285). The problem lies instead with the tacit mystification of customary belief. Mill is astonished at how quickly a culture or civilization's beliefs become idols, impervious to criticism. He calls it the "magical influence of custom," that it can so easily disguise itself as nature. Customs present themselves, gradually, as "self-evident and self-justifying" – their relative contingency is thus thoroughly obscured – and Mill thinks that we are often tacitly receptive to this obfuscation (CW XVIII: 220).[8] The transformation of custom into "nature" – which I am describing as a form of mystification – is of decisive importance to Mill, for once it is complete, dissent itself comes to seem like an impious assault on the natural order of things. Here, then, enters the human will to control and dominate others: people will go to great lengths to promote a way of life they have come to think natural or divinely ordained.

The mystification of custom is not strictly a defensive move, an attempt to insulate ourselves from uncertainty and disruption. Mill also sees it as an instrument of aggression, a means by which the powerful secure the consent of those they dominate. Mill is not usually recognized as a theorist of ideology,[9] but *On Liberty* and *The Subjection of Women* show otherwise: "wherever there is an ascendant class," he argues, "a large portion of the morality of the country emanates from its class interests, and its feelings of class superiority" (CW XVIII: 221). *Subjection* is Mill's clearest illustration of this tendency. Men's domination of women, which originates simply in the "law of superior strength," has gradually been clothed in the language of natural right. Patriarchal ideology has become a powerful tool in perpetuating domination, partly by preventing women from understanding the moral

---

[7] Dana Villa captures this strain of Mill's thought nicely in his *Socratic Citizenship:* "As moral beings, we are inevitably 'encumbered selves,' creatures of habit rather than reason. Mill's point is that we don't merely accept this condition, we will it with our hearts and souls. Our acceptance of what is 'unquestionable' for our class, culture, or age provides us with the orientation and support we yearn for in an otherwise contingent (and disturbingly pluralistic) world.... To own up to the conditioned or accidental quality of our most fundamental judgments is to risk a kind of moral/existential vertigo or paralysis" (Villa 2001, 80).

[8] Mill thought philosophical intuitionism a manifestation of precisely this tendency.

[9] By "ideology," I mean specifically a system of beliefs that rationalizes the ascendance of a particular group or class to a position of unequal power, usually by describing inequality as natural or unavoidable.

arbitrariness of their subjection. Again, Mill thinks that ideology develops unconsciously, even for those who benefit most. He acknowledges that men have come to believe sincerely that their unequal power justly reflects their natural superiority. What was once contingent and arbitrary has, over time, been accepted as both natural and just.

In Mill's view, this transformation illustrates the unconscious influence of very deeply felt human desires on the formation of belief. In *On Liberty*, he emphasizes the need for settled solidarity; in *Subjection*, the desire for power and sex. All are among the psychological fixtures that conspire to make ideologies attractive to us. It comes as no surprise to Mill, therefore, that ideology should be closely linked to intolerance, directed especially at those who threaten to thwart these desires. The mystification of custom and desire creates what Mill calls the "illusion of infallibility," which affects our treatment of others: "it is not the feeling sure of a doctrine (be it what it may) which I call an assumption of infallibility. It is the undertaking to decide that question *for others*, without allowing them to hear what can be said on the contrary side" (CW XVIII: 234). This illusion makes it virtually impossible to be receptive to dissenting opinions. It results in the common charges of heresy or immorality brought against iconoclastic individuals and dissenting minorities. The impression of infallibility, manifest as group or class ideology, yields "the feeling in each person's mind that everyone should be required to act as he, and those with whom he sympathizes, would like them to act" (CW XVIII: 221). The result is, once more, the will to dominate others when they deviate from our expectations of them; the will to bring them in line with our own orthodoxies.

A number of twentieth-century critics explored the important role of class and ideology in Mill's political theory, and my purpose is not to examine it in any great detail.[10] What I want to emphasize here is ideology's relationship to "conformity" and its corrosive effect on the discourse and public life of democracy. When group ideology and antagonism take hold of the democratic public, they collapse the public space in which power can be guided by reasons and open public deliberation. They transform political discourse instead into a sectarian, ideological struggle, orchestrated by rival groups and usually dominated by the most numerous of them. The second chapter of *On Liberty* ("Of the Liberty of Thought and Discussion") describes this corruption of democratic discourse, and the ensuing harms that it inflicts on individuals, in great detail. The chapter aims not only to justify free discussion but also to show how easily it can be destroyed by a culture of conformity. In one of its climactic passages, Mill describes

---

[10] See for instance Duncan 1973, chaps. 6 and 8.

Socrates' death at the hands of the Athenian people who, fearful for their own orthodoxies, grew intolerant of his "impiety" (CW XVIII: 235). Mill worries that such intolerance is one of the inveterate tendencies of modern, as of ancient, democracies.

It is worth emphasizing that mass participation is, in these sections of *On Liberty,* an important part of the story of democracy's corruption. By "participation," I mean the whole range of ways in which citizens exert influence over public affairs: holding office, voting, speaking in public, organizing, or simply belonging to and supporting political parties and associations. *On Liberty* is full of examples of citizens – be they Muslims, Catholics, slave-holders, or agitators for temperance – who organize as groups and impose their preferences on others through political means. It is also full of examples of groups who control the tenor of public discourse in such a way as to exclude and intimidate dissenters, or simply to deny them effective channels of communication. In all of these cases, the suppression of dissent results from the political *activity* of powerful groups, the "most numerous or the most active part of the people" (CW XVIII: 219). In all of these passages, participation as such does nothing to inspire altruism or rationality; if anything, it exacerbates the desire for domination. Again, Mill holds up the Athenian jurors who condemned Socrates as examples of participatory democracy gone wrong.

It is significant that these are all instances of *collective* or "class" action: when considering the political agency of groups (including the majority or the "mass"), Mill typically assumes sinister motives; when assessing the political participation of individuals, he is much more sanguine.[11] This difference is pertinent to the two contrasting readings of Mill – as a reluctant democrat on the one hand, and a radical democrat on the other – that I summarized earlier. In the passages that most clearly illustrate Mill's reluctance, the agents of democratic politics are groups – specifically conformist groups, and often religious groups or economic classes. In Mill's more optimistic moments (to which I turn in the next two sections), the agents are individuals acting alongside, and in dialogue with, other free and equal citizens. For the sake of clarity, I call the darker view, in which citizens are subsumed into competing groups, each of which aims to advance its interests at the expense of others, *conformist democracy.* Its antithesis, which I discuss at length later, is a politics in which citizens exchange reasons with the aim of reaching agreement or reasoned compromise; I call this *discursive*

---

[11] Graeme Duncan has observed: "For Mill, classes or groups smaller than the society itself, characteristically revealed sinister interest" (Duncan 1973, 219).

democracy. Mill himself draws no sharp empirical distinction between these two forms of democracy; rather, both identify tendencies that exist in all democratic polities.

I should end this section with a brief caveat. I have been describing Mill's conformist dystopia as "democratic." I should now qualify this claim somewhat. Mass conformity is, for Mill, facilitated by democratic political conditions. It is brought about by a complex of social and economic changes, which together elevate the "commercial class" to a position of strength and gradually erode the privilege of the aristocracy (CW XVIII: 191–2, 200). Yet at the same time it represents, in Mill's view, a perversion of democracy. Mill maintains that "true" democracy "is synonymous with the equality of all citizens," and therefore with the majority's willingness to restrain itself. As I argue later, Mill conceives of the activity of deliberation – the public exchange of arguments and reasons – and the protection of individual rights, as constitutive of democratic equality, properly understood. The use of public opinion as a form of coercion, and its closure to dissenting argument, therefore turns democracy against its own "root and foundation" (CW XIX: 449). In transforming speech into ideology, it collapses democratic politics into a struggle for power, which then threatens to devolve into the tyranny of the stronger. So the dystopia I've been examining, although democratic in form, undermines the egalitarian "principle of democracy."

Discursive Democracy

If conformist democracy is Mill's dystopia, an atavism of the "law of superior strength," discursive democracy embodies Mill's hopes that political power can be responsive to reasons. Mill's description of the representative assembly captures the nature of this hope:

Every person in the country may count upon finding somebody who speaks his mind, as well or better than he could speak it himself – not to friends and partisans exclusively, but in the face of opponents, to be tested by adverse controversy; where those whose opinion is overruled, feel satisfied that it is heard, and set aside not by a mere act of will, but for what are thought superior reasons. (CW XIX: 432)

These lines express Mill's view of the normative force of discursive democracy. Democratic power should ideally belong to those who, in open public debate among equals, are able to persuade others (without manipulation or bad faith) that theirs are "superior reasons," not to those who are able to overpower others by strength of numbers. Democracy in this idealized form happens when people come together in a good-faith attempt to work out reasoned solutions to public problems. Its archetype, for Mill, is the more intimate deliberative setting of the classical Athenian polis.

Nadia Urbinati has shown that Mill, like other democrats of his generation, aspired to transpose the Athenian *agora* into a form suitable for the government of modern Britain. For Mill, this transposition had several elements. First, it had institutional aspects: well-functioning modern democracies must create new institutional spaces for public debate – among elected officials in representative bodies, between representatives and their electors, and among citizens. They must also ensure that minorities are well represented in public bodies, and that various measures are taken to prevent the unchecked ascendancy of any particular interest group. Second, the modernization of the *agora* had human aspects: it required a "civic virtue of the moderns," to borrow Urbinati's phrase (Urbinati 2002, 154). It required that citizens be virtuous enough to use representative institutions to sustain a discursive politics. I focus, first, on the institutional aspects of Mill's democratic theory and ask what role they play in sustaining a discursive democracy. I look especially at Mill's defense of *participatory* institutions before turning, in the chapter's final section, to Mill's conception of civic virtue.

Mill defends participatory institutions at many levels of government. In his ideal polity, citizens would have the opportunity to partake vigorously in public debates around the campaigns for parliamentary election and also in "free and public conferences" with their elected representatives (CW XIX: 501). Each representative's actions would be "discussed, and judged by his constituents" who would keep informed through the newspapers, which he thought an extension of the democratic *agora* (CW XIX: 502; CW XVIII: 165). Citizens would also hold offices in local governments, which would be invested with substantial power over regional and municipal affairs. He shared Tocqueville's conviction that active participation in local politics would make citizens capable of handling democratic responsibility on a larger scale. He went further than Tocqueville, however, in urging that industry be reorganized into competitive collectives owned, run, and overseen democratically by workers themselves.[12] As Dennis Thompson has argued, Mill had little doubt that citizens would participate in these institutions if given the opportunity. He never worried that citizens would

---

[12] Mill's writing on worker-owned, competitive corporations might be understood as Mill's answer to Tocqueville's concern, in the final volume of *Democracy in America,* about the emergence of a modern industrial aristocracy.

prove too apathetic to make use of the participatory institutions at their disposal. Mill's defense of participation, as it appears in *Representative Government* and in his essays on Tocqueville, is thus mainly a defense of participatory institutions.

This defense has several elements. Thompson distinguishes usefully between the "protective" and the "educative" functions of participation. First, citizen participation ensures that everyone's interests are protected: "each [citizen] is the only safe guardian of his own rights and interests" (CW XIX: 404). Mill does not trust those in power to care about the interests of the disenfranchised, nor does he trust them to know how to protect those interests even if they did care. He notes that personal interests are usually "seen with very different eyes" by those whose interests they are, even when others have made nominal efforts to understand (CW XIX: 405). Whether politics unfolds as a contest of interests *or* as reasoned discourse, the interests of those who are not present – either in person or by proxy – are therefore likely to be misrepresented. This is perhaps Mill's strongest and least controversial defense of participation.

In *Representative Government,* Mill goes on to suggest that participation also *changes* citizens for the better. It has several salutary effects: first, as Thompson argues, it gives citizens a "sense of political efficacy," a sense of control over their own lives (Thompson 1976, 39). It makes them less inclined to resign themselves to a fate dictated by others – it makes them active in this sense, rather than fatalistic. This activity makes citizens less likely to devote all of their energies to the "amusement and ornamentation, of private life" (CW XIX: 401). It broadens their interests and intellectual horizons to include the affairs of the polity. Furthermore, it makes them better informed. Active participation counteracts the frightening political ignorance of the voting public and makes voters more skillful participants in the arts of politics. (One might call these the nonmoral or instrumental educative effects of participation.)

The final aspect of participation's educative effect is more Tocquevillean and more controversial. Mill argues that participation ennobles the sentiments and inspires disinterested concern for the common good. In an often-quoted passage of *Representative Government,* he argues that the active citizen

Is called upon... to weigh interests not his own; to be guided, in case of conflicting claims, by another rule than his private partialities; to apply, at every turn, principles and maxims which have for their reason of existence the common good.... He is made to feel himself one of the public, and whatever is for their benefit to be for his benefit. (CW XIX: 412)

In passages such as this one, participation appears to transform citizens into utilitarian moralists and to inspire sympathy for others ("unselfish . . . identification with the public"; CW XIX: 412). The publicity of the citizen's role here exerts a salutary influence on his character: in part because of the example set by other public-spirited citizens, politics becomes a "school of public spirit," a way for every citizen to transcend selfishness and group interest (CW XIX: 412). In such passages, readers find public life abruptly transformed into a loftily consensual exercise, where the harsh conflict of interest and ideology is temporarily banished from view.

What is most puzzling about this argument, especially when set alongside Mill's concerns about conformity and public opinion, is its apparent suggestion that simply assigning public duties to ordinary citizens is enough to begin making them virtuous. "Give him something to do for the public," writes Mill in a review on Tocqueville's *Democracy in America*, "whether as a vestryman, a juryman, or an elector," and he will begin to identify with the common good (CW XVIII: 169). It is difficult to reconcile this view with Mill's acknowledgment that politics often unfolds as an antagonism of competing group interests, in which speech is used to push ideology, not to seek reasoned consensus. Mill knew, as Urbinati puts it, that there were "different types of speech performance," some much more honest and reasonable than others, even in the context of well-designed institutions (such as the Athenian *ecclesia*) (Urbinati 2002, 135). More basically, Mill knew that power corrupts, and therefore that many of those who were assigned public duties would use their power for personal gain.

This inconsistency is explained, in part, by the subtle shift in Mill's emphasis that occurs between *On Liberty* and *Representative Government*. The selfishness he laments in the above passage of *Representative Government* arises out of economic hardship and necessity, out of a life confined by the strictures of the modern industrial economy to the factory or the shop floor. He describes people who have done "nothing in their lives but drive a quill, or sell goods over a counter" (CW XIX: 412). He describes their private lives as places of routine, instrumentality, and self-interest. Against this background, participatory politics emerges as a haven for lofty ideas and noble sentiments. It gives private citizens a means of escape from the monotony of economic life – a means that they are denied under other types of regimes, notably benevolent despotisms. The selfishness he has in mind here is, needless to say, quite different from the aggressive desire to impose one's own group norms on others. For it is selfishness born in part of ignorance of the interests of others, rather than a lasting antipathy

toward them.[13] This difference allows Mill to be more sanguine, in *Representative Government,* about the effects of public responsibility on individual
character.

Later in *Representative Government,* in the context of his discussion of
the open ballot, Mill gives still another defense of participation – and this
one stands in still sharper tension with the argument of *On Liberty.* Mill
argues that voting should be considered a public duty that, like all public
duties, "should be performed under the eye and criticism of the public;
every one of whom has not only an interest in its performance, but a good
title to consider himself wronged if it is performed otherwise than honestly
and carefully" (CW XIX: 490). Mill here treats the "eye" of the public as a
way of holding individuals responsible for their decisions. Throughout the
chapter, it is public exposure to the opinions of others, rather than the mere
assumption of public responsibility, that edifies private citizens. Far from
bullying them into conformity, the public exacts reasons and helps maintain
a disinterested point of view.

The problem that Mill is addressing here is "the selfishness, or the selfish
partialities, of the voter himself" (CW XIX: 491). Left alone in the privacy
of a ballot box, Mill expected the voter to succumb to his own bias and
vote either his own interest or the interest of his class. This bias is no longer
simply the unreflective residuum of a life of labor; Mill now admits the
possibility that the voter will put group interest above the common good, or
be driven by "some mean feeling in his own mind" (CW XIX: 491). Politics
threatens, when conducted in secret, to devolve once more into a power
struggle between antagonistic groups. Mill therefore came to believe that
the secret ballot would be poisonous to democracy and that publicity could
be a means of overcoming the partialities of the electors.

Mill makes note of the objection that public balloting would expose citizens to hostile pressure and make it difficult to express dissent. Mill's own
earlier defenses of the secret ballot had acquainted him intimately with such
concerns.[14] In an 1865 article, he concedes that the open ballot should sometimes be rejected on precisely these grounds: if "voters are in such a state of
helpless dependence – each of them, so to speak, has a tyrant with eyes so
fiercely glaring on him," then none would dare vote their own conscience
(CW XXV: 1213). In this passage, the eye of the public gives way to the

---

[13] Mill believed, like Tocqueville, that individual interests were not fundamentally antagonistic to one another, and therefore that an enlightened self-interest would yield social
cooperation.

[14] The secret ballot was one of the Reform Party's central policy objectives throughout the
1830s.

eyes of the tyrant, which become instruments of intimidating power. Mill concedes that publicity can only undermine democracy so long as citizens are exposed to such severe inequalities of power.

In *Representative Government,* however, Mill rejects this description of the British voter. He argues that the newfound economic self-sufficiency of tenants and tradesmen has made them more independent: "at every election the votes are more and more the voters' own" (CW XIX: 492). And he maintains that publicity will therefore induce rationality rather than conformity. "To be under the eyes of others – to have to defend oneself to others – " he writes, "is never more important than to those who act in opposition to the opinion of others, for it obliges them to have a sure ground of their own" (CW XIX: 493). Exposure to public scrutiny undergoes a striking transformation; rather than inducing servility and fear, it provokes discussion and introspection. Citizens come to feel not only that they must defend themselves, but also that they must have opinions worth defending ("a sure ground of their own" CW XIX: 493). Mill then seems to settle on the slightly weaker claim that publicity compels citizens to give *some* justification for their actions and thus to forgo actions that "can by no possibility be plausibly defended"(CW XIX: 493).

This weaker position is more consistent with the spirit of *On Liberty,* but it still needs reconciling with Mill's argument that confrontation with a hostile public opinion can have crippling effects on the individual, so much so that the prospect alone is usually enough to frighten would-be dissenters into conformity. "To be under the eyes of others," to be exposed constantly to the censorious judgment of public opinion, is a condition Mill deplores throughout *On Liberty,* where public opinion functions as an ideological force inimical to individuality and self-expression, driven by the "demand that all other people shall resemble ourselves" (CW XVIII: 275). Public opinion, as Mill imagines it in *On Liberty,* is the very antithesis of open, deliberative discourse. One of the most striking features of *Representative Government* is that it leaves these concerns aside. Mill replaces hostile public opinion with an agonistic publicity, the aim of which is rational consensus about the public interest. In so doing, he leaves aside the possibility – so prominent in *On Liberty* – that the public itself can have the eyes of a tyrant. He suggests that the only precondition for communicative politics, alongside properly designed institutions, is the relative economic self-sufficiency of the electors.

This view runs afoul of some of *On Liberty*'s most astute observations about the nature of public debate. Mill acknowledges, for instance, "that the tendency of all opinions to become sectarian is not cured by the freest discussion, but is often heightened and exacerbated thereby" (CW XVIII: 257). Even in the absence of domination, argument can devolve quickly into stubborn antagonism, with partisans on each side rejecting opinions "all the more violently because proclaimed by persons regarded as opponents" (CW XVIII: 257). Mill goes on to argue that the benefits of such polarized arguments, if any, accrue only to disinterested bystanders willing to piece together the disparate fragments of truth. These passages anticipate some of the results of contemporary empirical studies of deliberation: as an empirical matter, argument does not necessarily yield mutual understanding, let alone noble altruism.[15] In fact, having to defend ourselves to others can easily make us more, rather than less, stridently ideological.

In the midst of Mill's justification of the open ballot, he volunteers the following peculiar argument: "It is a very superficial view of the utility of public opinion to suppose that it does good only when it succeeds in enforcing a servile conformity to itself" (CW XIX: 493). Mill's rhetorical shiftiness is on full display here: he is claiming that publicity has salutary effects even when the public is not "qualified to form a sound judgment," because even so it forces its opponents to defend themselves rationally (CW XIX: 493). The argument recalls his defense of free expression in *On Liberty*, where he maintains that even erroneous views can contribute to the advancement of human knowledge, for they compel an active defense of the truth. But there is an important difference: in *On Liberty*, the public opinion of the uninformed is precisely what threatens to foreclose free discussion.[16] In *Representative Government*, it seems to inspire rational debate.

This tension is further complicated by the fact that *Representative Government* itself, considered as a whole, is ambiguous about the power of participation to transform human character. Mill spends much of the book trying to engineer a balance of power between the two great British classes, with the assumption that each will dominate the other if it has the opportunity. He makes it clear that institutions should never be designed with the expectation of public altruism. The powerful – be they aristocrats or popular majorities – will find themselves perpetually inclined to advance their own interests under the guise of the public weal. What is needful, then, is some means of preventing any class from exercising "a preponderant influence in

---

[15] See for instance, Tali Mendelberg, "The Deliberative Citizen: Theory and Evidence," in *Political Decision Making, Deliberation, and Participation: Research in Micropolitics*, Vol. 6, eds. Michael X. Delli Carpini, Leonie Huddy, and Robert Y. Shapiro. Greenwich, CT: JAI Press, 2002.

[16] In *On Liberty*, Mill describes the "public" as "that miscellaneous collection of a few wise and many foolish individuals" (CW XVIII: 232).

the government" (CW XIX: 446). These more sober passages reflect Mill's acknowledgment that politics, in the world as we know it, very rarely consists simply in a mutually edifying exchange of public reasons.

In one intriguing passage, Mill argues that a balance of power in Parliament will, at best, allow a minority of its members – those "who are governed by higher considerations" – to tip the balance, in each successive conflict, toward the group whose interests align more closely with the common good (CW XIX: 447). Here, the transformative aspects of public deliberations seem chastened: at most, these few noble souls can persuade a handful of class partisans to defect. If Mill manages to remain optimistic about the outcome of such conflicts, it is not because he expects voters or representatives to become virtuous through political participation but rather because he expects that some of the interests will align "on the side of what is right" and will need the support of only an enlightened few to carry the majority (CW XIX: 447). Regardless of the merits of this hopeful view, it expresses a very different vision of democratic deliberation than the more Tocquevillean passages I quoted earlier. Public spirit, if it exists at all, is here confined to a small minority of elite representatives. What is more, virtue is not kindled by political participation or responsibility; it is rather sustained *despite* the encroaching pressures of political conflict.

One way to solve this puzzle is to allow that *Representative Government* is inconsistent. It slips back and forth between conformist and discursive democracy, between democracy as it is and democracy as Mill wants it to be. In its more Madisonian passages, Mill is finding ways of blunting the ill effects of group antagonism by engineering a balance of power between rival classes. In its more Tocquevillean moments, he is imagining the effects of an ideal public discourse on individual character. Where discussion is conducted in good faith, where it is open and reciprocal, where every new participant is in the company of "minds more familiarized than his own . . . whose study it will be to supply reasons to his understanding, and stimulation to his feelings for the general interest," then participation might work transformative effects on individual character (CW XIX: 412). Athens looms large in Mill's conception of this deliberative ideal, as does his conception of Socratic *elenchus*.

The disparity between conformist and discursive democracy illuminates another important feature of Mill's democratic theory: its *developmental* aspect. In virtually all of his political writings, Mill is alternately defending an ideal of democratic government and suggesting provisional policies that will help move his own, as yet immature, democracy toward perfection. The elitism of some of Mill's proposals in *Considerations,* as well as some of Mill's anxiety over conformity in *On Liberty*, must be understood in this light. Mill believed that social and economic conditions in Britain, and importantly also ethical conditions (to which I turn in the next section), were not yet suitable for the fullest democracy. Democracy in its early, transitional stages would face different obstacles than mature democracy. And conformity would be an especially acute malady in democracy's nonage, when public opinion was still poorly educated.

These temporal complexities do not explain away all of Mill's inconsistency. As I argued earlier, I also think that *Representative Government* shifts its attention away from some of the problems that animate *On Liberty* and in this way avoids some of the challenges it raises. The shift can be explained partly as a matter of emphasis: in *On Liberty*, Mill directs his ire mainly at the intrusive effects of public opinion on *private* belief and conduct; in *Representative Government*, he treats public opinion as a means of constraining *public* speech and action. But this explanation, too, is unsatisfactory. It reduces the scope of *On Liberty* too much. In the chapter's final section, I argue that we should make the opposite move and read *On Liberty* in part as a commentary on democratic citizenship. In doing so, I argue that we can uncover the missing piece in Mill's treatment of political participation.

Let me first restate the problem: Mill's later defenses of participation do not adequately acknowledge the fragility of discursive democracy. It is not enough to put equals, or representatives of relatively equal groups, in a room together to talk, for even then people are not always disposed – as Mill well knew – to hold open, tolerant arguments. Discursive politics requires, among other things, that citizens be willing to examine and revise the grounds of their own opinions, to experiment with alternative points of view, and to express skepticism about received truths; it requires also a willingness to listen to and empathize with interlocutors but also to assume responsibility for the rejection and exposure of arguments offered in bad faith. These are, not coincidentally, many of the virtues that Mill associates with individuality, augmented and constrained by the moral sentiment of sympathy.

Democratic Individuality

Mill was, of course, very explicit in his belief that participatory democracy would fail unless citizens were adequately prepared for it. A people without adequate self-discipline and orderliness, or a public of inveterate egoists, or a public without a modicum of (broadly diffused) intellectual cultivation, or simply a people accustomed to submission, would make it almost impossible for democracy to succeed. Interestingly, Mill also lists "the desire to exercise power over others" as a tendency that renders people, in general, "unfit for representative government" (CW XIX: 420). In his view, democracy presupposes an adequate degree of civilization, as well as cultural characteristics conducive to an "active" yet also tolerant temperament. It also presupposes a sufficiently educated populace (see Wendy Donner's chapter in this volume).

Mill often makes such arguments as a social scientist – an aspiring "ethologist" – from whose perspective individual character seems a product of cultural and institutional forces. *Representative Government* was written almost entirely from this perspective: democracy's success or failure seems to turn almost entirely on its institutions and culture. To his credit, however, Mill was also an ethicist, and as such he believed that individuals could be held responsible for their own lives and politics. His discussion of individuality – and indeed much of *On Liberty* – reflects this ethical point of view, from which the difference between a conformist and a discursive public seems partly a matter of individual choice and will. Mill believed that individuals could exert meaningful control over the formation of their own characters – that is, over their own education – and that democracy's success would depend in part on how they used this power.

"Individuality" means self-authorship: we achieve it when we fashion lives of our own, lives that reflect values and aspirations culled from our own experience and reflection. Its most important element is the "active mind," by which Mill means the will and capacity to form reflective, independent judgments. As I explained earlier, Mill believed that individuals have an obligation, qua citizens, to refrain from voting their (personal or class) interest and to form considered judgments about the common good. The second chapter of *On Liberty* helps explain how this obligation should be approached. "In the case of any person whose judgment is really deserving of confidence," Mill asks, "how has it become so?" He answers:

> Because he has kept his mind open to criticism on his opinions and conduct. Because it has been his practice to listen to all that could be said against him; to profit by as much of it as was just, and expound to himself, and upon occasion to others, the fallacy of what was fallacious. Because he has felt, that the only way in which a human being can make some approach to knowing the whole of a subject, is by hearing what can be said about it by persons of every variety of opinion, and studying all modes in which it can be looked at by every character of mind. (CW XVIII: 232)

Although these lines illustrate the benefits of free discussion – and thus presumably of political participation – they also speak to the importance of certain intellectual virtues, without which such discussion is useless. These virtues include, among others, humility, imagination, and skepticism, each of which helps *prepare* citizens to hold open, receptive discussions with their fellows (I discuss each of these virtues briefly in the next few pages). Individuality encompasses these virtues and others and therefore functions as an ethical complement to democratic deliberation.

Individuality is often read as celebration of individual eccentricity and self-assertion, but this is only part of the story. Individuality is also a project of reflective self-disruption. It requires that individuals fashion a "plan of life" for themselves rather than acquiescing to the one that comes easiest. It therefore requires that they strive to unsettle the ethical assumptions that they inherit, to make room for deliberate self-creation. Mill surveys the many ways of unsettling oneself – through experiments in living, through the patient acquisition of new forms of competence, but also through conversation and identification with others who live and value differently. He never imagines that we can simply take leave of our inherited commitments through abstract or philosophical reasoning; rather, he maintains that these provisional leave-takings happen through particular, receptive engagements with others and with the world. When we succeed in the difficult work of understanding new and unfamiliar perspectives, we can begin to look back on ourselves as though from a distance, and this momentary alienation facilitates reflective self-understanding and self-direction.[17]

Mill's individuality therefore requires an attitude of receptivity to the world and to others, which is itself sustained by particular virtues – virtues such as humility. Humility is Mill's counterpart to the illusion of infallibility. It means allowing that new evidence may lead us to change (and improve) our ethical convictions. Humility is among the virtues that Mill attributes to the empiricist who repeatedly tests his beliefs against the evidence, who is constantly searching for better, fuller explanations. Its corollary is that there are always new discoveries to be made – discoveries that may shed new light even on things we know intimately. Isaiah Berlin describes Mill's conviction "that there are no final truths not corrigible by experience, at any rate in what is not called the ideological sphere – that of value judgments and of general outlook and attitude to life" (Berlin 1997, 267). Humility does not demand suspension of belief but rather a cultivated openness to new observations and argument and a deliberate refusal of the self-protective deference to authority that Mill laments in *On Liberty*.

---

[17] Mill's own transformative encounters were with Wordsworth, Carlyle, Coleridge, Comte, and other luminaries of his day. Mill's *Autobiography* illustrates the way in which these encounters made room for his own reflective self-direction.

Humility finds its complement in imagination, which Mill defines as "the faculty by which one mind understands a mind different from itself, and throws itself into the feelings of that other mind" (CW X: 91). Imagination lends breadth to each person's ethical and epistemic experiments. It allows us to feel the force of ethical commitments very different from our own, and thus to discover living ethical alternatives. In an essay on his mentor, Jeremy Bentham, Mill argues that Bentham lacked imagination and therefore remained ignorant of "many of the most natural and strongest feelings of human nature." With this observation, he illustrates the connection I have just drawn between receptivity and individuality: in misrecognizing the aspirations of others – in reducing them all to the pursuit of pleasure and avoidance of pain – Bentham failed to understand the range of goods that he might have instantiated in his own life and also took too narrow a view of the aims of politics. Mill believes that the activity of reflective self-creation, like the activity of reflective citizenship, requires acquaintance with a range of human goods, and that such acquaintance is available only through imaginative engagement with others. The conformist, to whom difference seems threatening and heretical, fails to exercise this cardinal democratic virtue.

Skepticism, finally, pulls in the opposite direction, for it is skepticism *of* the ethical pronouncements of others, especially those who lay claim to ethical authority. In Mill's eyes, Bentham exemplified this virtue: "he alone was found with sufficient moral sensibility and self-reliance to say in his heart that these [conventions], however profitable, were frauds" (CW X: 81). Bentham suspected that the "sacramental expressions" of religious and political authorities were nothing but rhetorical maneuvers designed to conceal or rationalize the interests of the powerful. Mill would later argue – in *On Liberty* and *The Subjection of Women* – that citizens of democracy are not conscious enough of the influence of ideology on their minds and lives and are far too vulnerable to the mystification of custom and class interest. Skepticism was, for Mill, a means of counteracting these chronic vulnerabilities. He argues that Bentham's skepticism revealed his confidence that any moral or political orthodoxy worth trusting should be explicable to him, should not require that he accept it simply out of faith. Bentham, like Socrates, was self-reliant in precisely this sense.

Together, these virtues encourage certain kinds of reflection. They create, on the one hand, a restless desire for explanation, a curiosity about the world that constantly wants satiation. They militate against the "lazy dereliction of the duty and privilege of thought" that Mill condemns in an early essay he titled "On Genius" (CW I: 338–9). They motivate *activity* of the mind, and openness to honest discussion. Skepticism, furthermore, gives some specific direction to this activity. It motivates careful attention to the relationship between power and ideology, but it also harnesses this attention – in Bentham's case, as in Socrates' – to moral ends. Bentham's skepticism was inseparably linked to his "moral sensibility," by which Mill simply means concern for the welfare of others considered as moral equals. Bentham was especially sensitive to the ways in which "falsehood and absurdity" were used to justify the infliction of suffering on ordinary citizens. Bentham's was not therefore a global skepticism but rather a honed suspicion of certain kinds of rationalization and mystification, grounded in moral sympathy for others.

If these readings are correct, then the ideal of individuality serves a specific function in Mill's democratic theory. It encourages individuals to withdraw themselves from mass conformity, to refrain from perpetuating conformist democracy, and to approach difference with empathy and interest. It pushes citizens not only to form reflective judgments of their own but also to hold others accountable to the discursive standards of democratic debate, properly conceived. So understood, individuality helps explain and qualify Mill's confidence in political participation: if politics is ever edifying, it becomes so not only because of the shape of its institutions but also because of the effort citizens have invested in making it so. Citizens must themselves preserve the integrity of public speech not only by confronting speakers who perpetuate uncritical ideologies but also by exemplifying certain public virtues in their own speech and behavior.

None of this discredits the view that participation can make citizens virtuous. We learn the virtues associated with democratic discourse from others who exemplify them; in this sense our own participation *can* be transformative, if we are fortunate to be exposed to virtuous exemplars. The ideal of individuality – and indeed the ethical dimensions of Mill's political theory – serves as a reminder, however, that participation is not an impersonal, causal process that injects virtue into democratic life. Its benefits are sustained by so many individual practitioners, who are constantly striving to preserve the integrity of democratic speech against the many vices – dishonesty, manipulation, ideology – that threaten to corrupt it. Part of the lesson of *On Liberty* and *The Subjection of Women* is that democracy's success depends heavily on the agency of ordinary citizens. With both of these texts, Mill aspired to exemplify such agency and, in doing so, to inspire others to become more reflective participants in (and critics of) democratic politics.

Mill's ideal of individuality has often been read as the centerpiece of a perfectionist liberalism. On this view, individuality, considered as a conception of human flourishing, is thought to *justify* liberal democracy.

John Rawls is among the philosophers who reads Mill this way, as arguing that political liberty is justified because of its tendency to "arouse strong and vigorous natures," which Rawls understands as an end in itself (Rawls 1999, 184). Although I do not dispute this reading altogether, I have here emphasized a different strain of Mill's political thought, and indeed an alternative reading of individuality. I have suggested that individuality also functions as a conception of citizenship and a part of Mill's democratic theory. I have suggested, specifically, that it helps explain a tension in his writing between two conceptions – conformist and discursive – of the democratic public. On the view I am defending, democracy *needs* individuality if it is to succeed by its own normative standards.

Where, then, do Mill's "democratic credentials" stand, after all of this? Some argue that individuality itself is an elitist ideal, because most people either will not or cannot achieve it. I believe that Mill took a different view. He believed that individuality was something that everyone, not just philosophers or leisured elites, could aspire to. More important, Mill believed that democracy itself *entailed* the extension of the highest ideals of human character to everyone equally. In embracing this extension, he understood himself to be rejecting the elitism of aristocratic doctrines that made human excellence the province of the leisured few.

9

Mill's Neo-Athenian Model
of Liberal Democracy

Jonathan Riley

Mill and the Spirit of Athenian Democracy

John Stuart Mill, like his friend and fellow utilitarian radical George Grote, expresses deep admiration for the Athenian democracy of the fifth and fourth centuries B.C. (CW X, XI, XVIII, and XIX). They both argue that the ancient Athenian political system (as they understand it in light of the limited sources of information) provides valuable lessons for the citizens of modern representative democracies. Mill in particular tries to show what a representative democracy would look like if its system of institutions was designed in accord with the spirit of Athens, and he claims that such a well-constructed representative democracy would be the best form of government for any civilized society, that is, any society whose citizens typically are "capable of rational persuasion" through free discussion and debate.

Despite his explicit commitment to representative democracy, scholars have often viewed Mill as a proponent of oligarchy, more specifically, a trained elite with authority to force the popular majority to accept elitist legislation in the pursuit of some putative utilitarian social utopia. Yet he explicitly denies that such a "bureaucratic oligarchy" is the best form of government for any civilized people, and he goes so far as to argue that even a skilled bureaucracy always tends to decay into the routine incompetence and corruption of a "pedantocracy" unless it is subjected to popular criticism and control (CW XIX: 437–40; see also CW XVIII: 305–10). He is also evidently aware that by defending a well-constructed representative

---

I wish to thank Nadia Urbinati and Alex Zakaras in particular for their detailed critical comments on earlier versions of the paper. Responsibility for the views expressed remains mine alone.

democracy as best even for promoting a competent administration (let alone for improving the intellectual, moral and active capacities of ordinary citizens), he is opposing a received view that the most skillful governments are "bureaucratic oligarchies" such as the aristocratic republics of Venice and Rome.

Even those scholars who have recognized his commitment to democracy have tended to give misleading impressions of his position. His assertions that the average Athenian citizen's intelligence and patriotism were raised to an unrivaled degree by "the practice of the dicastery [popular court] and the ecclesia [popular assembly]" have been highlighted by Moses Finley, for instance, with the implication that Mill is calling for "new forms of popular participation" to bring traditional forms of representative democracy closer to the Athenian model (Finley 1985, 31–2, 36; quoting Mill CW XIX: 411–12). Yet Finley never discussed the system of institutions that Mill recommends in *Considerations on Representative Government* and thus seems never to have considered how Mill proposes to balance the value of popular participation against other valuable considerations to achieve a representative democracy in the Athenian spirit. Rather, Finley leaves the false impression that Mill is advocating a more or less radical participatory democracy, taking for granted that extensive participation by ordinary citizens in public decision making is what is needed for a legitimate and effective representative democracy.[1]

Thompson (1976) and Urbinati (2002) are exceptional insofar as they have carefully analyzed Mill's institutional recommendations, and Urbinati in particular has rightly stressed the influence of the ancient Athenian example. But even they tend to paint him as a reluctant and equivocal democrat, one whose commitment to democracy is ultimately ambiguous if not contaminated by undemocratic elements. If they are correct, his ideal system of institutions has serious drawbacks as a system of popular government. If it promotes the power of an educated elite, perhaps the system is better classified as a form of oligarchy after all. In any case, they imply, whatever admiration he may have expressed for democratic Athens, Mill's preferred system of government surely departs from the Athenian spirit in crucial respects and thus cannot properly be seen as a neo-Athenian form of representative democracy.

---

[1] Since Finley wrote, there has been an outpouring of scholarly works on various aspects of ancient Athenian democracy but leading classical scholars such as Hansen (1996, 1999) and Ober (1989, 1996, 1998) have not been concerned to explore Mill's neo-Athenian theory of representative democracy.

By contrast, my view is that Mill, like Grote, understands Athens as a model of *liberal* democracy, that is, a democracy that includes important antimajoritarian institutions designed to promote competent public decision making, discourage the abuse of power, and encourage individual liberty. His most notorious antimajoritarian proposal, plural voting based on education, has been rejected as undemocratic. But it and his other institutional recommendations are better seen as liberal constitutional elements derived from his understanding of the Athenian system itself. His ideal form of representative democracy is Athenian in spirit insofar as its system of institutions reflects the liberal spirit of the Athenian system as he understands it.

Before attempting to clarify his neo-Athenian model of liberal representative democracy, I should make clear that genuine democracy as Mill conceives it includes any form of government in which the popular majority has ultimate control over lawmaking, either directly or indirectly through representatives elected in proportion to the majority's numbers.[2] Democracy includes crude majoritarian governments, for instance, in which the popular majority has unrestrained power to pass whatever laws it wants, either directly or by means of instructions to its elected lawmakers. But ultimate control need not mean that majorities must always be able to trample over any opposition, however enlightened and justified the opposition may be. Rather, the majority retains ultimate control as long as it or its representatives can block any minority, including an educated elite, from enacting laws. Provided this veto power is retained by the majority or its elected legislators, democracy also includes various sorts of limited and qualified majoritarian governments, in which the majority moderates its demands and accepts that at least some antimajoritarian institutions can serve as prudent checks against incompetence and the abuse of power by the majority or its elected legislators.

Mill's ideal representative democracy is a liberal form of qualified majoritarian government in which the popular majority relies on a well-constructed system of antimajoritarian institutional devices to foster competence, discourage abuse of power, and promote individual freedom. At

---

[2] Democracy is not genuine, of course, if a popular minority has ultimate control over lawmaking. In the case of representative government, Mill emphasizes the possibility of "false democracy" in which the popular majority is able to elect virtually all (rather than a proportionate number) of the representatives to the assembly, so that majority decisions within the assembly itself are at best representative of only a popular minority, that is, a majority of a majority of the voters. To prevent this type of oligarchy from hiding under the "false show of democracy," Mill argues that genuine representative democracy requires a system of proportional representation, more specifically, Thomas Hare's system of "single transferable vote" (CW XIX: 448–66).

this preliminary stage, it is enough to say that he imagines the possibility of a liberal representative democracy that is so well-constructed that a highly educated minority can, by means of plural votes based on education, elect the same number of representatives as the popular majority can, so that neither the mass nor the elite can get its way unless the representatives of the one prove persuasive to some degree to the representatives of the other. In such a democracy, popular sovereignty would not manifest itself in legislative activity unless there was agreement to some extent between the representatives of the mass and those of the elite: disagreement would result in legislative stalemate, which could not be removed until a majority of the assembly was persuaded that the laws under consideration were in the common interests of both the highly educated and the less educated segments of the people.

Evidently, the educated elite has disproportionate power in this ideal representative democracy, although not so much power that its representatives can push through legislation over the opposition of the rest of the assembly. Mill apparently justifies this disproportionate power on the grounds that the more educated are more competent at identifying the common interests of all members of society, which he calls "the permanent interests of man as a progressive being" (CW XVIII: 224). I shall say more in due course (see the third section of the chapter) about these permanent ingredients of the common good, which include, among other things, "individuality" and "security" for certain vital personal concerns that ought to be considered as rights. Mill also seems to believe that the more educated are better able to identify laws (including the fundamental liberal constitution itself) which can effectively promote the common good thus understood.

No doubt this elitist aspect is a very controversial aspect of Mill's prescribed form of representative democracy. In his *Autobiography,* even he remarks that his proposal of plural voting "has found favour with nobody" because democratic reformers favored equal voting whereas conservatives favored plural voting based on "property" and not on "intelligence or knowledge" (CW I: 261). Yet he does not cease to advocate it as a valuable check against ill-considered popular legislation. Rather, he argues that "a systematic National Education" is required to "overcome the strong feeling which exists against it" (CW I: 261–2). Indeed, a national education system, including a national curriculum and national examinations with equal opportunities for all, is the only means "by which the various grades of politically valuable acquirement may be accurately defined and authenticated." Until such an educational system is established, he admits, any attempt to implement plural voting based on education faces "strong, possibly conclusive, objections" (CW I: 262). In particular, there is no very accurate way to identify the educated elite. Even so, Mill favors plural voting once a universal franchise has been achieved, and he hopes that the popular majority can be persuaded to accept it as a national education system is established.

It is important to keep in mind that when he outlines his ideal form of representative democracy, Mill takes for granted that there really is an intellectual and moral elite composed of those citizens who are in fact more competent than others are to perform political tasks that require expertise, including such tasks as deliberating about justice and framing general laws. But he does not deny that there are serious practical difficulties in finding such an elite within any observed society, and that any minority selected to serve the purpose may only approximate the genuine elite to a very imperfect degree. A fortiori, he does not presuppose that any minority selected as "highly educated" under the tests devised by society to facilitate the selection, can simply be presumed to be virtuous and entrusted with absolute power. Rather, he takes for granted that power corrupts and subjects the selected minority to checks and balances designed to prevent them and their representatives from abusing the permanent interests of the popular majority. Despite these problems, though, he insists that competence is of indispensable value, that it is unequally distributed, and that it is right in principle to try to find those who possess it and give them disproportionate influence within representative democracy, so long as the majority and its representatives retain a suitable veto power.[3]

I turn now to major objections pressed by Thompson and Urbinati against Mill's theory of representative democracy.

Mill's Democratic Critics

Thompson depicts Mill's theory as a mixture analogous to Aristotle's theory of a *politeia*: "As Aristotle mixes the competing claims of oligarchy and democracy [in each major institution of the *politeia*], so Mill combines

---

[3] Mill goes so far as to say that once a system of national education is established, plural voting "would perhaps not be needed" (CW I: 262). This does raise the issue of how firmly committed he is to plural voting, at least once everyone has more or less equal access to some threshold level of national education. Nevertheless, I assume that he sticks to the principles he lays down in *Representative Government* and that he defends plural voting as right in principle until virtually all citizens have developed their intellectual, moral, and active capacities to an equally high degree, in which case plural voting would reduce to equal voting. He never explicitly repudiates plural voting or its underlying principle, namely, that "the opinion, the judgment, of the higher moral or intellectual being, is worth more than that of the inferior" (CW XIX: 473). In any case, even an advanced society like the United States today is a long way from establishing a national system of education as Mill conceives it.

the conflicting principles of competence and participation [in each institution of a representative democracy]" (1976, 95). Just as Aristotle leaves it a mystery how a *politeia*, which he regards as a good form of regime, can be compounded out of two forms he regards as bad, Mill leaves it a mystery why his preferred form of representative democracy should be viewed as a best or even acceptable form because he provides no criteria for resolving conflicts between the basic values of citizen participation and competent leadership and merely holds out the hope that the conflicts will eventually disappear after a gradual process of social development that results in an ideal society of equally competent citizens (1976, 158–84, 197–201).

Thompson argues that the institutions prescribed by Mill are not as impressive as they might be for promoting either participation or competence (1976, 89–90, 178–80). But he fails to outline any system that he thinks would be better than Mill's for these purposes. In fact, he generally praises Mill's system as far as it goes, although he does suggest that some of its elements are in tension with each other, for example, plural voting based on education may be inconsistent with the "equal representation" rationale of Hare's scheme of proportional representation (1976, 106–8). His main complaint seems to be that Mill demands too much by seeking to design a system that achieves a precise utilitarian balance of participation and competence. Much of what Mill says is defensible, it appears, but he needs to face up to a kind of ethical pluralism in which intractable conflicts can sometimes arise between incommensurable basic values such as participation and competence.

Actually, Mill could largely accept this objection from ethical pluralism because his utilitarianism is tempered by an assumption of human fallibility such that reasonable people can never be certain as to which particular system of institutions is best; they must be willing to discuss and compare critically the appeal of different institutions in light of the available evidence of their respective social effects; and they must at times admit that the evidence does not allow them to make a reasonable choice among competing alternatives. In light of this, he can admit that the particular system which is best is rationally indeterminate to some extent, with the caveat that the indeterminacy may gradually disappear if social development occurs as he hopes. If this is right, the issue boils down to whether Mill's system can be shown to be defective in comparison to others for promoting participation and competence, taking for granted that both of these ingredients are essential to representative democracy and that some mixtures of them are better than others by any reasonable standard.

Despite what Thompson says, the case against Mill's ideal system remains unproven. Alleged inconsistencies such as that between plural voting and Hare's election method do not really exist. Moreover, it is important to dispel any impression that Mill leans toward oligarchy to the extent that he prescribes antimajoritarian institutions, including plural voting and Hare's scheme, that facilitate competent leadership. Unlike Aristotle, who was apparently indifferent as to whether a *politeia* is called a democracy or an oligarchy, Mill rejects all types of oligarchy and defends popular government. In his view, not even an educated elite, let alone a rich minority, should have authority to force the popular majority or its elected representatives to accept legislation. Competence is not maximized under a well-constructed oligarchy, he insists, but only under a well-constructed liberal democracy in which the popular majority retains ultimate control.

Urbinati's analysis is similar in many respects to Thompson's, although there are also some important differences. Mill shows "resistance to full-fledged democracy," she says, apparently because "[h]is main goal was to replace oligarchy with a natural aristocracy." As she sees it, he seeks an elected assembly of "virtuous, wise, and well-informed orators" to "express whatever is best in and for the community," and he is prepared even to introduce plural voting to achieve this, despite the fact that plural voting contradicts the familiar idea of "democracy as an open competition" in which citizens cast equal votes to "select the best" candidates after broad freedom of discussion and debate (2002, 68–9, 99). Following Thompson (1976, 55–6, 79), she maintains that Mill distinguishes between "skilled competence," a kind of technical ability possessed only by a select few who ought to be appointed to perform the administrative work that demands their technical expertise, and "political competence," a kind of moral and intellectual ability to deliberate over, and ascertain, what is just and good (2002, 43–54). But unlike Thompson, who recognizes that, for Mill, both kinds of competence must be learned on the basis of experience, she adds the twist that political competence is possessed equally by adults and comprises the individual's "inborn 'sense of dignity' " (2002, 145–6, 177). Because he assumes that citizens are equally competent to deliberate, she concludes, Mill's device of plural voting is not only at odds with his own commitment to democracy but also offensive to human dignity: "It is Mill's own premise of an equal competence in deliberation (*téchne politiké*) that makes plural voting unjustifiable and offensive" (2002, 99).

Urbinati's charge that Mill remains a grudging and confused democrat deserves serious consideration, especially because she has made an exceptional attempt to show the strong influence of the ancient Athenian example on his democratic thought. But there is good reason to doubt her charge. Mill seems to reject the premise that adults possess an equal political competence or inherent sense of dignity.[4] He confines the full "sense of dignity" as he understands it to higher natures, with the implication that it is only acquired in the course of developing a noble character (CW X: 212; see also Thompson 1976, 56). Moreover, even if all humans share the potential to develop a noble character that includes high intellectual capacities and firm moral dispositions to frame and comply with a code of equal justice, that does not mean that all will fulfil the potential, let alone do so automatically as soon as they turn eighteen or twenty-one. Such noble characters are evidently uncommon even within advanced commercial societies, many of whose members are observed to be ill-informed and to act at times from narrowly selfish and base dispositions. In short, except perhaps in some ideal "society of equals," there exists an unequal distribution of the higher intellectual and moral abilities needed to deliberate competently over what is just and good, and this is why it is essential to establish institutions that encourage the masses to develop their capacities.

Actually, the notion that citizens possess an equal political competence or sense of dignity seems to involve at least two separate claims, only one of which Mill endorses. The claim he accepts is what Dahl calls the "moral judgment... that all human beings are of equal intrinsic worth" or "the assumption of intrinsic equality" (2001, 131). This moral axiom means that every person's good is entitled to equal consideration, Dahl (1989, 84–87) explains, and (as he indicates) there is no doubt that Mill endorsed it. Yet this axiom, by itself, is "perfectly consistent" with elite rule rather than democracy "if a superior group of guardians could best ensure equal consideration" (1989, 88). Because he rejects elite rule, Dahl argues that a second claim, the so-called presumption of personal autonomy, is also needed to derive the "strong principle of equality," which he associates with genuine democracy. According to the autonomy presumption, "each adult... should be assumed to be the best judge of his or her own good or interests" for decision making purposes, unless "a very compelling showing of incompetence" can be made (1989, 100). Together with the intrinsic equality assumption, this autonomy presumption implies the strong equality principle, namely, that "*every adult member* of an association is sufficiently well qualified, taken all around, to participate in making binding collective decisions that affect his or her good or interests, that is, to be a *full citizen*

---

[4] Kateb (2003) agrees with Urbinati that Mill assumes all citizens possess an inborn sense of dignity associated with equal justice.

of the demos" (1989, 105, emphasis original). As Dahl goes on to make clear, the strong equality principle justifies a democratic process in which every citizen has a right to an equal vote "at the decisive stage of collective decisions" (1989, 109–11).

But Mill evidently rejects the autonomy presumption in the form stated by Dahl and thereby rejects the strong equality principle (including the right to an equal vote) as essential to a democratic process.[5] The autonomy presumption is problematic because national affairs are not matters of purely self-regarding concern, in which each individual rightfully has an equal voice so that he can defend his own separate interest, but rather matters of joint concern, in which each individual properly has a duty to give equal consideration to other persons' interests (especially those interests that ought to be treated as rights) that are inseparable from his own:

> In an affair which concerns only one of two persons, that one is entitled to follow his own opinion, however much wiser the other may be than himself. But we are speaking of things which equally concern them both; where, if the more ignorant does not yield his share of the matter to the guidance of the wiser man, the wiser man must resign his to that of the more ignorant. Which of these modes of getting over the difficulty is most for the interest of both . . . ? If it be deemed unjust that either should have to give way, which injustice is greatest? that the better judgment should give way to the worse, or the worse to the better? (CW XIX: 473–4)

In matters of joint concern, justice requires that "the opinion, the judgment, of the higher moral or intellectual being, is worth more than that of the inferior" (CW XIX: 473). Mill emphasizes that "national affairs are exactly such a joint concern, with the difference, that no one needs ever be called upon for a complete sacrifice of his own opinion" (CW XIX: 474). The opinion of every person concerned can be counted without giving each of the opinions equal weight. Rather, the opinions of the wiser people should be given greater weight than the opinions of the more ignorant. Mill is quite prepared to condemn a country's institutions if they "virtually assert" that these opinions are "of the same value" (CW XIX: 473). He is highly critical of American institutions, for instance, on the grounds that they strongly encourage the "false creed . . . that one man . . . is as good as any other" when it comes to assessing national affairs: "It is not a small mischief that the constitution of any country should sanction this creed; for the belief in it,

---

[5] Dahl argues to the contrary that Mill accepted some "principle that is essentially equivalent to the presumption of personal autonomy" (1989, 103–4). But Dahl strongly downplays Mill's commitment to the value of competence and simply ignores his support for plural voting. Contrary to what Dahl says, Mill endorses everyone having a voice in the political process, but not an equal voice.

whether express or tacit, is almost as detrimental to moral and intellectual excellence, as any effect which most forms of government can produce" (CW XIX: 478).

As long as political competence like technical competence is distributed unequally and possessed in anything like full measure only by a minority, Mill cannot reasonably expect that an assembly of virtuous and wise orators will be associated with "democracy as an open competition." In fact, unless he is prepared to withhold the franchise from adults until they develop the cognitive, sympathetic, and conative abilities that comprise what it means to be fully competent to deliberate about justice and to select the candidates most likely to pursue it, he must expect that more or less selfish and ill-informed voters will elect representatives much like themselves. Because he insists on a universal franchise and proportional representation, he clearly does expect the assembly to consist of a proportionate number of such representatives in the absence of plural voting. Plural voting as he conceives it is a device that enhances the numbers of unusually competent representatives without giving an educated elite any power to impose legislation.

Urbinati goes on to argue that Mill defends plural voting as a device that preserves an open electoral competition in the face of attempts by mass media and political parties to manipulate public opinion and the selection of candidates (2002, 99–103). Yet this seems to assume that he would endorse an open competition in which all citizens have equal votes, if only the mass media and political parties did not intervene. I see no reason for that assumption, given that he does not suppose an equal distribution of political competence. Rather, Mill seems to reject the idea that the most competent candidates would be selected in such an open competition, even if all manipulation of voters by intermediary agencies could be removed. He fears that ignorant voters are unable to recognize the most competent candidates and also unwilling to select candidates much different from themselves. As a result, plural voting is needed to improve the electoral chances of the more competent candidates.

In any case, Urbinati subsequently downplays the argument that plural voting could preserve open competition, and she even suggests that Mill grasps the argument's fundamental incoherence. Plural voting actually "shrinks competition" by giving highly educated candidates an electoral advantage over less educated candidates, she says, and it encourages the more educated representatives to "rest on their laurels and become equally mediocre" as the others (2002, 103). Again, this merely assumes that the most competent candidates would be selected in an open competition without plural voting, an assumption that I have already suggested that Mill rejects.

Ultimately, Urbinati claims that plural voting is mainly justified as a device to counter the emergence of a homogenous society in which middle-class values stifle virtually all opposition to a commercial way of life: "In that it was supposed to preserve social and cultural pluralism, he hoped that plural voting would revitalize political agonism. . . . Mill saw plural voting as a tool that *artificially* promoted the social and political agonism that ancient societies [such as Athens] generated spontaneously" (2002, 103–4, emphasis original). Yet this is not a convincing argument for awarding plural votes to the highly educated, if the educated elite is no more politically competent than the rest of society. Any political conflict thereby generated would not yield more competent public decisions. Why would Mill endorse plural voting merely to promote diversity and conflict, given Urbinati's assumption that deliberative competence is equally distributed across all individuals and groups? It makes more sense to see plural voting as a tool that promotes a greater number of highly competent representatives than would be elected in an open competition with equal voting.

It is also worth reminding ourselves that Athenian democracy did not rely on equal voting for the election of lawmakers. The Athenians had no elected assembly, and they used the lot to select from an eligible pool the citizens who served on the occasional boards of nomothetai that shared legislative authority with the ecclesia.[6] True, Athenian democracy involved equal votes for the making of decisions within the ecclesia, dicastery, and board of nomothetai. Yet equal voting is also employed for decisions taken within the assembly, court, and legislative commission of Mill's prescribed form of representative democracy.

The real question to ask is this: does representative democracy differ from direct democracy in such a way that, to preserve the spirit of Athenian institutions, an unconventional election system of the sort Mill envisages must be introduced? An obvious difference is that the private citizen's opportunities to participate personally in the making of public decisions are by necessity relatively limited in any representative democracy, however well constructed. In this regard, Thompson voices a familiar complaint that Mill's prescribed institutions for enriching participation are disappointingly "modest." The "chief instruments . . . are local government, jury duty, and free discussion," but these do not go very far to enhance citizen involvement and the associated benefits of "civic education" (1976, 178–9). It is

---

[6] The Athenians often used the lot as well to select the citizens who served as magistrates or as jurors on popular courts. But they did elect some senior executive officials, such as the ten generals, by majority voting, each citizen having an equal vote under secret ballot.

not entirely clear what else Mill might have advocated, although Thompson mentions various measures favored by Rousseau for promoting an active citizenry, including "games, festivals, patriotic festivals, didactic theater, and military parades [that] unceasingly occupy citizens in public activity" (1976, 45). Those measures do not involve the citizens in political decision making, however. Also, there is a danger that, if funded by the state, they will encourage blind political loyalty rather than enlightened support for equal justice.

Although he seems to recognize the drawbacks of Rousseau's measures, Thompson complains that Mill fails to see that the civic education to be derived from political participation is quite distinct from intellectual education: "Rousseau ... is not obviously wrong in thinking that a perfectly respectable citizenry may flourish with relatively meager intellectual attainments, and that political activity itself will teach little more than political skills, knowledge, and loyalty" (1976, 49–50). But Mill does not expect political participation alone to produce brilliant intellects or skilled professionals. Other measures, especially the equal right to self-regarding liberty, are essential for that to happen. Rather, he expects citizens to develop to some degree an impartial concern for equal justice and the good of the community as a result of participating, "if even rarely," in political procedures that involve the application of "principles and maxims which have for their reason of existence the common good" (CW XIX: 412). Moreover, he is properly reluctant to permit political leaders to use taxpayer money to finance public celebrations and events that promote uncritical support of the government and its policies. For the most part, private citizens and organizations (including the press) should be left free to celebrate in accord with their own judgment and inclinations, and no doubt they will spontaneously choose to celebrate to the extent that their government is perceived by them to promote equal justice and the common good.

Citizen participation in political decision making cannot help but be significantly curtailed in every representative democracy compared with a direct democracy such as Athens. By implication, the typical citizen of a representative democracy cannot be expected to possess capacities for political deliberation as highly developed as those of the average Athenian citizen, given that the latter's capacities could only be acquired by participating more or less as frequently as he did in public decision making. A case can be made that instruments such as plural voting and Hare's method of proportional representation are needed to facilitate the election of highly educated citizens to the representative assembly, to improve deliberations there so that political decisions about justice and the good of the community might approach the high standard of competence that Mill and Grote both insist was generally (although not invariably) characteristic of the Athenian citizens in their assembly. Competent minorities might then be able to persuade less competent majorities within the representative assembly, without either group having the power to impose its decisions on the other.

In my view, even Thompson and Urbinati misconstrue Mill's firm commitment to a well-constructed representative democracy in the Athenian spirit. As he conceives it, such an ideal representative democracy differs in important respects from conventional representative democracies. The conventional idea of "first-past-the-post" elections from single-member districts is rejected in favor of Hare's proportional representation scheme, for instance, as both Thompson and Urbinati recognize. Also rejected, however, is the conventional idea of an equal right to an equal vote in the election of representatives. Whereas Thompson, Urbinati, Dahl, and a host of others apparently regard equal voting as essential to representative democracy, Mill disagrees and, in so doing, challenges us to reconsider our conventional attitudes about what a well-constructed representative democracy should look like.

In what follows, I try to clarify the main elements of Mill's conception of an ideal representative democracy and explain why the ideal system of institutions may properly be said to reflect the spirit of ancient Athenian democracy. I do not intend to discuss in detail his utilitarian argument that such an ideal representative democracy would be better than any other form of government for helping the people of a large modern society to achieve their permanent interests. But some brief remarks relating to his utilitarian argument are needed for my conceptual purposes.

Democracy and Utility

Mill insists that general utility is the ultimate "test" of a good form of government for any particular society (CW XIX: 383). But it must be "utility in the largest sense, based on the permanent interests of man as a progressive being" (CW XVIII: 224). These permanent interests include security and individuality, although what this involves is not generally well understood in the literature.

A person's sense of security is the expectation that his or her vital concerns are safe and will be protected from grievous injury at the hands of other people. As Mill makes clear in *Utilitarianism*, general security, or the aggregate amount of security experienced by the members of a community, is a variable that is maximized by establishing and enforcing a uniform code of equal justice that distributes equal rights and correlative duties to every citizen. Political and educational institutions must be kept continuously in active play to protect the equal rights of all. Because this activity repeatedly reminds the individual of the importance of protecting each person's vital concerns, the idea of security of equal rights "gathers feelings around it" so intense that it is seen as more valuable than any competing interests: it "assumes that character of absoluteness, that apparent infinity, and incommensurability with all other considerations" (CW X: 251). In short, security of equal rights becomes a permanent interest or higher kind of utility for the individual, of indefinitely more value than "any of the more common cases of utility," and equal justice takes on its familiar importance despite its incorporation within an unfamiliar utilitarian scheme of ethics.[7]

For Mill, then, a well-constructed democracy must be duly organized to secure each individual's basic rights: "Security of person and property, and equal justice between individuals, are the first needs of society, and the primary ends of government" (CW XIX: 541). But the democracy must also be organized to promote each person's individuality. A person's individuality can be understood as the portion of one's character that is genuinely his or her own insofar as the person has fashioned it by freely making choices in accord with his or her own judgment and inclinations. In contrast, the person does not display individuality, does not really have a character of his or her own, to the extent that his or her habits of acting have been formed by blindly imitating the practices of other people, including long-dead ancestors.

As Mill argues in *On Liberty*, general individuality, or the aggregate amount of individuality displayed by the members of a community, is a variable that can be maximized only by distributing equal rights to complete liberty of "purely self-regarding" conduct, where liberty means doing whatever seems best in terms of one's own judgment and desires (or aversions) without any sort of coercive interference from others. A person's self-regarding conduct includes any act or omission that does not "directly, and in the first instance" cause any type of "perceptible damage" to others, or, if it does, only with their genuine consent (CW XVIII: 225–6). Thus, a well-constructed democracy must recognize in its code of equal justice the right of self-regarding liberty, and thereby secure the freedom of the individual to develop his or her own character in his or her own way.[8]

---

[7] For further discussion of my interpretation of Mill's approach to justice and utility, see Riley (2006b).

[8] For further discussion of Mill's doctrine of self-regarding liberty as I understand it, see Riley 1998a, 2006a.

Mill's defense of the right of self-regarding liberty should not be conflated with his defense of democracy. His argument for the individual's right to choose with complete freedom among self-regarding acts and omissions does not depend on any form of government. An oligarchy can recognize such a basic right, for example, even if an oligarchy is less likely than a democracy to do so. Furthermore, a democratic government may not recognize such a claim, even if the popular majority is more likely than a ruling elite to do so. Mill evidently fears that popular majorities, far from protecting self-regarding liberty, will stigmatize minority opinions and lifestyles and perhaps even encourage elected lawmakers to outlaw them.

On the other hand, the right to self-regarding liberty is not the only institution that Mill prescribes for the maximization of individuality. He also prescribes institutions that permit the individual to have liberty to a limited extent with respect to "social" (or other-regarding) conduct that, in contrast to self-regarding conduct, poses a risk of perceptible injury to others without their consent. In particular, he prescribes a democratic system in which the ordinary citizen has opportunities to participate with his fellows, "however rarely," in political decision-making procedures. These procedures involve rules (including rules for creating and changing rules) with which any participating individual must comply – he cannot freely choose to deviate from the rules as seems best to his own judgment and inclinations. By limiting liberty, these rules guide individuals to develop the "social" side of their individuality in some directions but not others, whereas they have complete freedom to develop the "self-regarding" aspect of their character in any direction they like. More specifically, the individual, by freely participating within the rules, develops the capacities needed to cooperate peaceably with fellow citizens for the common good. Ideally, the individual learns how to frame and comply with a code of equal justice that impartially regulates every person's "social" conduct by distributing equal duties to respect equal rights, including the right to "self-regarding" liberty.[9]

In addition to democratic institutions, Mill also prescribes various other institutions to help promote individuality with respect to "social" conduct. These institutions include competitive economic enterprises, for example, of which the individual members have opportunities to participate in decisions relating to the production and marketing of goods and services for a

---

[9] Strictly speaking, freedom of speech is not part of self-regarding liberty because speaking is "social" conduct. Speech is properly regulated to some extent. Nevertheless, freedom to hear, watch, and consider opinions is self-regarding if the opinions can be consumed without causing perceptible injury to third parties without their consent. This places a strict limit on the legitimate scope of regulation of speech. See Riley, 2005a.

reward in competitive markets. Mill does not decide whether some form of market capitalism, market socialism, or a hybrid system would be best for this purpose. In any case, whatever form the best economic system takes, individuals' participation in economic decision making encourages them to develop "social" habits of acquiring material gain at the expense of competitors, given that enterprises must struggle for revenues to survive. Unless abundance someday renders such competition unnecessary, economic participation cannot be expected to foster an impartial concern for the common good in the same way that political participation can.[10]

Mill thus recommends various instruments for promoting both the social and self-regarding aspects of any person's individuality or self-development. But it is crucial to distinguish between the case of an ideal "society of equals," in which these instruments are being worked by highly developed individuals of noble character who freely choose to cooperate in drafting, enacting, and complying with a code of equal justice, and nonideal cases, in which these same instruments are worked by many more or less incompetent and selfish individuals who sometimes barely grasp what is required or resist complying with the rules. A person's individuality can vary not only in scope, narrowing as he thoughtlessly imitates others, but also in content. A "noble" individuality is displayed only if individuals habitually choose to comply with rules of equal justice that they have had a voice in framing and also assert themselves as they please in their self-regarding concerns. In contrast, a "miserable" individuality is displayed if individuals seldom do anything but blindly follow others, or, although they choose in accord with their own judgment and inclinations, they engage in self-degrading conduct or ignore their social duties. Evidently, miserable individuality is a long way from anything like Kantian moral autonomy. But even noble individuality, which is similar to the Kantian ideal insofar as both involve acting in obedience to self-imposed rules of justice, has a non-Kantian element, to wit, acting as one pleases, unconstrained by social rules, with respect to one's self-regarding concerns.[11]

Coercion of any sort is unnecessary in an ideal society of equals. In nonideal societies such as modern Britain and the United States, however, legal

[10] Mill's views on capitalism and socialism are discussed in more detail in Riley 1996a. Private associations and clubs, in which members choose to coordinate their self-regarding activities and thus do not harm third parties, must be distinguished from competitive enterprises, capitalistic or socialistic, that pose a risk of harm to their competitors by driving them into bankruptcy without their consent.

[11] This noble kind of individuality is depicted as a "Periclean" character-ideal by Riley 1996b, and 1998a, 82–90, 169, 175.

penalties and social stigma are properly employed against individuals of "miserable" character solely to prevent them from damaging others' vital concerns that ought to be recognized as rights. Mill suggests that majority opinion in such societies is likely to do a pretty good job of recognizing the vital concerns that deserve protection, with one notable exception – namely, the vital concern in self-regarding liberty. The masses see no harm in expecting everyone to share similar personal tastes and pursuits, he claims, and they take offense at eccentric opinions and lifestyles that are harmless to others. Even a well-constructed democracy is likely to have trouble preventing the majority from oppressing minority opinions and lifestyles, he implies, unless the people can be persuaded to see the great value of self-regarding liberty. This liberal task can be performed only by an educated elite, whose influence in democratic procedures ought to be suitably enhanced to facilitate the creation of a code of justice that includes the right to self-regarding liberty.

The importance Mill assigns to self-regarding liberty is typically downplayed by scholars, including his democratic critics. Thompson mentions the liberty doctrine only in passing, for example, and finds "very little in the way of means to give competence its due" (1976, 78). But complete liberty to hear what can be said for and against any moral and political opinion is the only means that fallible humans who are capable of rational persuasion have available to develop their deliberative capacities and thereby acquire competence to decide which opinions, including opinions about justice, are warranted. Similarly, complete liberty to engage in self-regarding "experiments of living" is the only means individuals and voluntary associations have to learn which lifestyles and professions may be more enjoyable for them than the conventional ones. Those who habitually make use of such liberty to develop their capacities may not succeed in persuading the rest of us either to exercise our liberty or defer to their broader knowledge. But at least democratic procedures should be tailored to enhance the influence of such persons as much as possible without forcing the popular majority to cede ultimate control.

Urbinati recognizes the importance of the argument of *On Liberty* for Mill's democratic theory, and she rightly stresses that political competence is associated with a never-ending process of free discussion encompassing citizens and their representatives. Yet even she argues that "Mill did not believe there was any such thing as a perfect self-regarding action" (2002, 169). Ultimately, she revises his doctrine of complete self-regarding liberty to mean "liberty from subjection," that is, freedom from arbitrary interference by others (2002, 155–202). But this leaves open the possibility that society might have good reasons to regulate any conduct, including conduct that causes no perceptible injury to others without their consent, and that such "reasonable" (nonarbitrary) interference is not really coercive. The idea of a self-regarding sphere within which the individual is rightfully free from all social constraints is lost, replaced by a "quasi-Kantian" idea that individuals are sovereign if and only if they are willing to obey impartial rules that any reasonable person imposes on oneself, if only temporarily, subject to further discussion (2002, 145f).

In any case, Mill praises the ancient Athenians not merely for their democratic institutions but also for their celebration of individual liberty and diversity in a sphere of life which they traditionally viewed as private, even though he acknowledges that the Athenian notion of the private sphere does not match exactly his own notion of the self-regarding sphere.

Athenian Democracy as Liberal Democracy

Mill certainly admires the way extensive participation in political decision making raised the average Athenian citizen's capacities for political deliberation to an unusually high standard. But it would be a mistake to conclude that he admires only the participatory aspect of Athenian democracy or that he would agree with Finley that "new forms of popular participation" are what is needed to achieve a well-constructed representative democracy in the Athenian spirit. Mill's conception of a representative democracy in the Athenian spirit cannot be understood without reference to the other aspects of Athenian democracy he praises.

He praises the Athenian people for their general habit of deferring to individuals whom most regarded as highly competent to perform public functions requiring special skills and training. These skilled public functions include leading the assembly's deliberations. The Athenians relied on skilled orators (*rhetores*) to propose competing policies and lead debate, and the majority of the assembly seems typically to have voted for policies that they were persuaded (not necessarily rightly) were best for their city as a whole. A crucial function of the *rhetores* was to provide a point of opposition to ill-considered majority opinion: Demosthenes in his public orations repeatedly emphasizes the value of this function in the course of warning the people against shameless flatterers like Aeschines who were allegedly attempting to manipulate popular opinion for their own private gain.

The Athenians also repeatedly reelected individuals such as Pericles and Eubulus, of whose unusual skill they were persuaded, to conduct the military and financial business that required technical competence. Indeed, they often relied on citizens who were wealthy and from old aristocratic families, even when such citizens were known to have leanings toward oligarchy: "The Athenians did not confide responsible public functions to Cleon or Hyperbolus..., but Nicias, and Theramenes, and Alcibiades, were in constant employment both at home and abroad, though known to sympathize more with oligarchy than with democracy" (CW XIX: 460). This is not to say that the people were infallible judges of character, whether of orators, generals, or budget directors. If anything, they seem to have been far too willing to entrust leadership to citizens who were aristocrats by birth or fortune, and also too willing to forgive those who showed themselves to be enemies of democracy. The crucial check on the oligarchical party, as Mill and Grote both emphasize, seems to have been supplied by some of the most vilified demagogues, the skilled orators such as Cleon and Demosthenes who were essentially "opposition speakers."

In addition, Mill (CW XIX: 423) praises the sophisticated system of auxiliary checks and balances established by the Athenians against the abuse of power.[12] True, these controls on power may not have been introduced to secure individual rights to be left alone because the Athenians, like other ancient Greeks, do not seem to have conceived of such a right. As Mill puts it: "The ancient commonwealths thought themselves entitled to practise... the regulation of every part of private conduct by public authority" (CW XVIII: 226). Nevertheless, it seems clear that the controls were introduced to ensure that public authority would be exercised in accord with certain definite procedures, and this entails some degree of protection for each citizen's vital concerns. Thus, citizens were apparently entitled to equal votes and equal freedom to speak in the assembly, for example, as well as to due process in the various sorts of prosecutions brought before the popular courts and the board of nomothetai. In short, it remains an open question whether the Athenians properly can be seen as conceiving justice in terms of individual claims, privileges, powers, and immunities (as well as their correlates), even if they did not recognize any individual right to be left alone with respect to some part of life regarded as private.

Mill (CW XI: 317–21) also agrees with Grote (1846–56, V, 64–74) that the Athenians, even if they had no concept of an individual right to be left alone, do seem to have tolerated considerable individual liberty and diversity in a portion of life traditionally seen as private. In fact, the picture of ordinary personal life at Athens drawn by Grote in his gloss on Pericles' famous funeral

---

[12] For discussion of the myriad checks and how they evolved during the fifth and fourth centuries, see, especially, Roberts 1982; Hansen 1999.

oration, seems to have inspired Mill's defense in *On Liberty* of the rights of individuality. Like Pericles, Demosthenes in some of his orations also speaks of the Athenians' respect for privacy and of their "casual" and "easy-going" style in personal life, in marked contrast to the situation at Sparta and other oligarchies. This is not to say that the Athenians were never oppressive or that their customary notion of private life matched exactly Mill's idea of the self-regarding sphere where complete individual liberty is "appropriate" (CW XVIII: 225–6). He and Grote both point out, for example, that the Athenians did not view religious beliefs and practices as private matters that each citizen should be free to decide for himself. Rather, an Athenian citizen had social duties to express faith in Athena and the other gods of the city: he was expected to participate in various public festivals celebrating the gods, for example, and also occasionally to bear the costs of certain related public activities such as financing new plays for the theater or new warships for the navy, if sufficiently wealthy to do so. In terms of Mill's doctrine of individual liberty, the Athenian society must be considered illiberal, and its citizens unfree in their personal lives, to that extent. This conclusion cannot be avoided merely by claiming with Biagini (1996, 33–6) that the Athenians did not view the individual's religious opinions and practices as self-regarding conduct. Mill is explicit that no society is entirely free, whatever its form of government, until it protects complete freedom of self-regarding conduct as he defines it, including religious opinion and ceremony.

With due caveats relating to slavery, the scope of the franchise, and religion, I claim that Mill admired ancient Athens as a genuine liberal democracy and not merely as a participatory democracy of the sort Finley suggests. The term "liberal," although freighted with confusing popular associations, seems apt for summarizing the concern shown in this form of democracy for education and skill, for checks and balances against abuse of power, and for broad toleration of individual choice and diversity with respect to a sphere of life recognized as personal or private. At the same time, in a genuine democracy, Mill insists, the popular majority must have ultimate control over lawmaking, and the average citizen must participate, "if even rarely," in public functions. Some form of liberal democracy in this sense is, he argues, the best of all possible forms of government for any civilized people.

A Liberal Representative Democracy

A well-constructed representative democracy in the Athenian spirit, Mill makes clear, must be similarly liberal in spirit: the system of representative institutions must facilitate competent leadership, embody suitable checks and balances against the abuse of power, and recognize the individual's right to complete self-regarding liberty. Nevertheless, a representative democracy is not a direct democracy. For one thing, popular sovereignty is exercised by voting for representatives, not by voting directly for laws. In a genuine representative democracy, Mill insists, every voter must have a "personal representative" in the assembly so that a majority vote in the assembly can reasonably be assumed to represent the popular majority. By a "personal representative," he means a representative for whom the voter has actually cast a vote. This requirement leads him to endorse Hare's scheme of proportional representation.

Second, Mill realizes that the typical citizen of a representative democracy cannot hope to match the political competence acquired by his Athenian counterpart through frequent participation in the ecclesia and dicastery. To compensate for this deficiency, steps will need to be taken to enhance deliberative competence within the representative assembly. Although Hare's election method can help to some extent on this score as well, plural voting based on education is required in principle, with the caveat that it cannot be carried so far as to transform the democracy into an oligarchy of the educated.

I now discuss some of the main elements of the representative system prescribed by Mill, with a view to illustrating the system's Athenian spirit. In doing so, I take for granted that he is entitled to assume the existence of an educated elite akin to that at Athens and that the teachers, philosophers, orators, artists, professionals, and others comprising this elite largely developed their unusual competencies independently of political participation, via courses of personal study that each chose and fashioned for himself in accord with his own judgment and inclinations. Moreover, nothing I say should be taken to imply that Mill is an uncritical admirer of Athenian democracy. I am concerned merely to show how the Athenian example shapes the design of his preferred form of representative democracy.

Neo-Athenian Institutions

Mill proposes at least four major institutional devices for promoting competent decision making within a liberal representative democracy. Two of them, a partial separation of legislative and executive powers and, within the executive, an agency of experts to draft and codify legislation, largely promote technical competence. The germs of both are found in Athenian practices. The other two, Hare's election scheme and plural voting, promote within the elected assembly competent deliberation about achieving the "permanent interests" of the people. No such electoral devices were required at Athens.

Both are needed in a representative democracy to close the gap in deliberative competence that results from the ordinary citizen's comparatively fewer opportunities to participate in its decision-making processes.

Separation of Powers

As Thompson (1976, 121–6) and Urbinati (2002, 54–64) discuss, Mill distinguishes between "controlling the business of government, and actually doing it" (CW XIX: 423). Control is the job of the assembly and, in the last resort, the people, whereas actually doing the "skilled business" is the function of the trained elite in the bureaucracy. The assembly's functions include "talking" about issues in light of the different shades of opinion expressed by the citizens, ordering bills to be drafted by the experts, and then deliberating over them with reference to the "permanent interests" of the people, enacting (but not amending) legislation by majority vote and monitoring the bureaucracy. In contrast, the bureaucracy is charged with drafting and amending bills, administering and enforcing the laws, and judging cases and controversies as they arise under the laws. Ordinary citizens are confined to voting, freely voicing their opinions, and performing aspects of the administrative and judicial business that anyone capable of rational persuasion can perform, such as serving on juries and local agencies.

The assembly appoints a chief executive, who need not be a member of the assembly, to head the bureaucracy, and checks his abuse of power by means of impeachment or nonconfidence motions. Otherwise, the assembly has no authority to appoint or remove the administrators, lawyers, judges, scientists, and other experts who comprise the bureaucracy. Rather, the experts should be selected on the basis of competitive examinations designed to test merit and should also hold tenure during good behavior. Authority to proceed with appointments or removals under these procedures rests with the chief executive and his chosen advisors. The assembly does not even have authority to nominate candidates for positions within the bureaucracy. The chief executive can also discourage the lawmakers from usurping the privileges of his office, by threatening to dissolve the assembly and call for new elections.

This separation of legislative and executive powers is partial insofar as the assembly and the chief executive retain powers to interfere with each other's abusive activities. It promotes technical competence by making the chief executive responsible for the appointment of qualified bureaucrats and by subjecting bureaucratic activities to legislative oversight and popular criticism, thereby helping to prevent the emergence of a pedantocracy in which technical judgment is supplanted by dead routine. A representative democracy whose bureaucracy is required to struggle against elected law-makers will outperform a "bureaucratic oligarchy" even with respect to the skilled business of government, Mill argues, just as the Roman Republic outperformed other oligarchies in this respect because its bureaucracy in the Senate experienced repeated conflicts with the popular assemblies (CW XIX: 437–40).

But by promoting technical competence in the bureaucracy, the separation of powers also promotes deliberative competence in the assembly. In particular, the experts who skillfully draft bills help to focus deliberation on the most effective laws and policies for dealing with the issues under consideration, provided there are suitably competent speakers in the assembly to lead the discussions. Mill's proposed commission of legislation is roughly analogous to the Athenian board of nomothetai, as I discuss next. This analogy illustrates the more general point that the Athenians, at the height of their democracy, recognized a distinction between the assembly's proper functions and the "skilled business" of government. The skilled business included the city's military and financial affairs, which the assembly typically entrusted to an elite by electing citizens with a reputation for competence to high offices, reserving the lot for the filling of less important offices. But it also included the framing of the laws, which the assembly entrusted to the nomothetai.

Skillful Drafting of a Code of Justice

Mill proposes that a small commission of experts, including, perhaps, judges, should be appointed by the chief executive for a fixed (renewable) term, to perform the skilled business of drafting and codifying all legislation (CW XIX: 428–32). The commission would draft laws on any subject and also make sure that the laws were consistent with one another and with traditional social customs and norms. The representative assembly would not be able to "tinker" with bills drafted by the commission. Nevertheless, the assembly would have exclusive authority to enact or reject the bills and thus would retain ultimate control over lawmaking. The assembly could also remove commissioners for personal misconduct or for refusing to draft legislation as demanded by the assembly. Because the commission is charged with ensuring beforehand that, if the assembly enacts any new bill into law, the whole body of laws will remain consistent and constitutional in the sense of being compatible with fundamental social norms, the courts apparently would not have authority to review and nullify legislation after its enactment. Rather, constitutional review would in effect be performed by the commission itself, prior to any enactment by the assembly.

Mill indicates that there are parallels between this commission and the board of nomothetai established by the Athenians when renovating their democratic institutions in 403–2, after the fall of the thirty tyrants. The Athenian board was a smaller body than the assembly, selected by lot as occasion demanded from a pool of eligible citizens, with exclusive authority to make or amend basic laws (*nomoi*) and a duty to make sure that all laws remained consistent with one another and with Athenian customs. The assembly retained authority to enact decrees (*psephisms*), but these were viewed as inferior to basic laws. The nomothetai did not actually draft laws – the drafting was presumably done by the leading orators, who proposed changes to existing laws and argued for them before the nomothetai, with help from advisors, including magistrates. Nevertheless, the nomothetai, not the assembly, did choose which drafts would survive as law after hearing arguments for and against any proposed change by competing orators.

The nomothetai can also be viewed as a kind of constitutional court that reviewed both proposed and existing laws, to determine which laws were most in accord with the permanent interests and customs of Athens. Moreover, the distinction that the Athenians drew between basic laws and inferior decrees gave rise to other types of judicial review in the popular courts proper. But I cannot pursue that point here.[13]

Electing Skilled Orators

Mill endorses Hare's single transferable vote (STV) electoral method, in part because it facilitates the election of at least some skilled orators into the assembly. Under STV, self-formed constituencies of a given size are given equal representation, and every elected legislator is the "personal representative" of everyone in his constituency. Virtually no citizens waste their votes on losing candidates. A highly educated class can, by voluntarily associating to form constituencies of the requisite size, be assured of electing candidates who possess the abilities to lead discussions, explain the pros and cons of bills drafted by the commission, and, perhaps, persuade a majority to enact laws that foster equal justice and the good of the community: "Modern democracy would have its occasional Pericles, and its habitual group of superior and guiding minds" (CW XIX: 460).

He also endorses STV as essential for a genuine representative democracy. The method has countermajoritarian properties: it acts as a check against exclusive representation of the popular majority in the assembly. As a result, it forestalls a "false democracy" in which majority decisions in

---

[13] For further discussion, see Hansen 1999, 161–75, 205–12.

the assembly represent only a minority (i.e., a majority of a majority) of the citizens. Moreover, it discourages legislative majorities from carelessly enacting oppressive laws merely because minority groups do not have any personal representatives to voice their claims in the assembly.[14]

An Electoral Check against Tyranny

Despite the virtues of Hare's method, Mill insists, plural voting remains useful as a check against oppressive legislation by ignorant and unjust majorities. Given his commitment to plural voting, he may seem to be committed to rule by an educated elite after all. His form of democracy would evidently collapse into such an oligarchy, for example, if plural voting were extended to decisions taken by the representative assembly.[15] But he confines plural voting to the election system, and argues that the allocation of votes must not permit the educated minority to elect a greater number of representatives than the number elected by the popular majority: "The plurality of votes must on no account be carried so far, that those who are privileged by it, or the class (if any) to which they mainly belong, shall outweigh by means of it all the rest of the community . . . [I]t must stop short of enabling [the educated elite] to practise class legislation on their own account" (CW XIX: 476). Under those conditions, plural voting is compatible with genuine democracy: each citizen can still cast a vote (although not an equal vote) that helps elect a personal representative who speaks for him in the assembly, and ultimate control can still rest with the popular majority because legislation cannot be enacted against the wishes of the majority or its representatives.

Plural voting is consistently combined with Hare's STV method in Mill's theory. Equal voting is not required for STV to provide equal representation for a variety of self-constituted constituencies. Moreover, plural voting does not upset STV's ability to give each citizen a personal representative for whom he or she has voted. True, individual citizens may not be equally represented if a highly educated citizen's plural votes are used to help elect multiple candidates. Yet even this inequality might be minimized by requiring any citizen's plural votes to be awarded in toto to a single candidate rather than permitting them to be split among multiple candidates. In any case, Mill is not committed to equal representation for individual voters.

---

[14] On the mechanics and properties of STV, see Riley 1990; Tideman 1995.

[15] Consider a simple example in which there are five deputies in the assembly, three of whom each have one vote, the remaining two each having two votes because of their superior educational qualifications. In that case, the educated minority has the power to enact legislation rejected by the numerical majority, as well as to block legislation favored by the majority and their constituents.

What plural voting is designed to do is to establish a balance of power between the representatives of the educated elite those of the less educated masses. Legislation can be enacted only if supported by the numerical majority of representatives, each of whom has an equal vote. But, now, the representatives of the elite are sufficient in number that, when united, they can block class legislation by the deputies of a popular majority faction, just as the deputies of the majority are sufficient in number to block class legislation by the educated elite. Thus, this balance of power within the assembly may help to encourage legislative majorities to pass legislation that promotes equal justice and the good of the community.

Unlike a representative democracy that extends the vote to all but gives greater weight to the votes of the educated elite, a representative oligarchy of the highly educated would restrict the franchise to the educated minority, giving no weight at all to the voices of the popular majority. Mill emphasizes how different these two forms of government are: "Entire exclusion from a voice in the common concerns, is one thing: the concession to others of a more potential voice, on the ground of greater capacity for the management of the joint interests, is another. The two things are not merely different, they are incommensurable" (CW XIX: 474). In the case of the oligarchy, the educated class has ultimate control of the government, and the voices of the rest count for nothing. A highly educated individual is effectively treated as a higher kind of being, whose voice is infinitely more valuable than that of his less educated compatriot. In the case of the democracy, every individual's voice counts for something, and the popular majority has ultimate control insofar as its elected representatives are sufficient in number to block any attempt to oppress the people. But the popular majority shares active sovereignty with the educated elite. Legislation cannot be enacted solely by the representatives of either group. The representatives of the elite, even if completely united, cannot pass any law unless they persuade at least some representatives of the masses to help form a legislative majority. The reverse is true as well.[16]

Despite what has been said, it may still seem that plural voting is a significant departure from the spirit of ancient Athenian democracy. After all, the

---

[16] An interesting case is presented by an oligarchy of the educated with a popular element akin to that of ancient Rome. In such a representative government, the franchise would be extended to all, but only members of the educated minority would be eligible to serve as representatives or to hold office in the bureaucracy. Such an oligarchy might reasonably be expected to experience periods of intense conflict between the elite and the masses and might also gradually become increasingly popular in form as long as it survived. The analogous trajectory of the Roman Republic has led some scholars to argue that the government had become a kind of democracy late in its career, until it was transformed into an absolute monarchy. See, for example, Millar 1998.

Athenians endorsed an equal opportunity for all citizens to speak and vote in the assembly. It is important to remember, however, that representative democracy cannot hope to match direct democracy when it comes to developing the capacities of the masses through participation in political decision making. To make up for this relative deficiency and the consequent danger that the popular majority will tend to favor less competent representatives like itself, the election system must be skewed such that enough members of the educated elite may be elected to serve as "a counterpoise" to the representatives of the masses. In short, the relative deficiency of representative democracy as an agent of national education arguably necessitates the device of plural voting to remedy the deficiency.

For Mill, then, a right to an equal vote is not among the basic rights that the best form of liberal democracy must secure for all citizens.[17] Rather, the franchise is grounded on a moral trust that can vary in degree across different persons, depending on the extent to which they have developed their capacities to identify and support enlightened and just representatives as well as policies.[18] Nevertheless, even he seems prepared to accept universal equal suffrage until the people can be persuaded to adopt plural voting, if they ever can be. Indeed, he admits that plural voting becomes increasingly unnecessary as the people develop into an ideal "society of equals." But he never abandons his view that plural voting tied to education is "best in principle" (CW XIX: 476).[19]

---

[17] Thus, except perhaps in the special case where all are equally educated, Mill would not accept the argument offered by Riley (1990) that utilitarianism reduces to democratic procedures when utility information is too poor to operate a utilitarian calculus. That purely formal argument presupposes the "one person, one vote" principle.

[18] Mill also draws an important distinction between voting in a political election, where he argues that the voter has a moral duty to vote in accord with "his best and most conscientious opinion of the public good," and voting in a club or private association, where the individual has no moral duty to consider the interests of others and should be free to vote as he pleases (CW XIX: 488–90). Open voting ought generally to be required in the political elections of civilized societies, he suggests, whereas the secret ballot is "unobjectionable" in the elections of private associations. His justification for saying this is worthy of further discussion but beyond the scope of this chapter.

[19] Some commentators insist that Mill regarded plural voting as nothing but a temporary expedient on the way to an egalitarian democracy and that he abandoned it in principle after 1865. Baum (2000, 240–5), for instance, cites Mill's parliamentary speech of 31 May 1866 (CW XXVIII: 83–5) as evidence for the temporary expedient view. But Baum is evidently confused. Mill is merely saying in that speech that plural voting is not needed as a check in the context of the proposed Reform Act. Given that the proposed act denied the franchise to men with less than £7 property as well as to all women, "it is ridiculous to suppose" that an ill-informed or prejudiced popular majority or its legislative representatives could abuse power to violate the rights of others – the majority is not even permitted to vote. Mill never deviates from his position that plural voting is desirable in the context of a universal franchise. But the need for plural voting as a check would only become apparent in the

Is a Better Representative Democracy Possible?

Mill shows that a liberal representative democracy in the Athenian spirit is possible. Unlike Finley, however, he does not think "new forms of popular participation" are involved. Rather, his prescribed system of institutions is designed to promote highly competent political decision making under popular sovereignty, taking for granted that both technical competence and moral competence can only be acquired by citizens on the basis of practice.

Thompson's claim that Mill's democratic theory falters in the face of intractable conflicts between the values of competent leadership and popular participation is not persuasive. For Mill, competence apparently takes priority over participation in cases of conflict, and participation is encouraged only to the extent that it does not conflict with competent decision making. Steps are taken to ensure that the "skilled business" is performed by a technically competent bureaucracy, for example, subject to suitable checks and balances, including legislative oversight and, ultimately, popular control. The ordinary citizen's participation is confined to voting for the overseers and expressing critical opinions, and even this limited amount of participation is justified as essential to prevent the bureaucracy from sliding into a pedantocracy. Similarly, steps are taken to ensure that political deliberations are guided as much as possible by an educated elite, without sacrificing a universal franchise or ultimate popular control. Again, ordinary citizens have few opportunities to participate beyond voting and expressing opinions. This limited participation is now justified as essential to prevent them from sliding into a kind of political torpor, in which they can no longer even begin to deliberate about equal justice and the good because their capacities to do so have wasted away from disuse.[20]

future, with the establishment of a universal franchise, whereas Hare's STV system could be usefully implemented right away, even without a universal franchise. Nevertheless, he does admit in his *Autobiography* that it will be difficult ever to persuade the people to accept plural voting. Moreover, he concedes that, although it may be best in principle, plural voting "would perhaps not be needed" after a national education system has been established (CW I; 262). In other words, equal voting would perhaps be tolerable once virtually all citizens had achieved some threshold level of education, even though highly educated elites were present in society. This is certainly not a ringing endorsement of equal voting in principle.

[20] There is clearly an epistemic element in Mill's democratic theory, calling to mind Condorcet's jury theorems as well as Rousseau's view of how the citizen must vote in a republic. Unlike Rousseau and Condorcet, however, he advocates broad freedom of discussion both inside and outside the assembly so that the educated elite might influence the rest. For further discussion of Rousseau and Condorcet, see Riley 2005b.

Perhaps better forms of liberal democracy than Mill's can be constructed for marshaling and developing citizens' competencies to achieve jointly their "permanent interests." This is a matter for further debate. But conventional forms of democracy, which reject Hare's method and plural voting as well as many of the other institutional arrangements prescribed by Mill, certainly have severe drawbacks. Indeed, by giving exclusive representation to popular majorities and encouraging assemblies to ignore highly instructed minorities who rarely even have a representative, conventional representative democracies, including modern Britain and the United States, may even be said to offend against human dignity as Mill understands the term.

Why does Mill bother at all with selfish and ill-informed citizens who are barely capable of rational persuasion and lack the sense of dignity that he thinks is acquired only in the course of developing a noble character? Why not opt for an oligarchy of the highly educated rather than a democracy? He seems to answer that a human being achieves genuine happiness only as a highly developed member of an ideal "society of equals." In short, a person of noble character cannot be fully happy unless his fellows are equally capable of framing and complying with a liberal democratic code of equal justice. This genuine happiness, the happiness of which his nature is capable allowing for different qualities of pleasure, is associated with a sense of dignity. With due caveats about what it takes to achieve this sense of dignity, Urbinati (2002) and Kateb (2003) are right to stress that Mill's firm commitment to liberal democracy is derived from a more fundamental commitment to human dignity.

10

John Stuart Mill on Education and Democracy

Wendy Donner

Introduction

In this chapter, I explore John Stuart Mill's philosophy of education and its connection and intersection with democracy, within the context of his distinctive form of utilitarianism and his egalitarian liberalism. Mill's writings are notably attentive to educational matters, and it is striking just how many of his works emphasize the themes of education and democracy. Mill's philosophy is frequently invoked in discussions of democratic theory, and his writings offer useful tools to contribute to thorny contemporary questions about appropriate democratic education, democracy and disagreement, and democratic deliberation. The historical position of Mill's liberal political philosophy amplifies its capacity to contribute to these debates. Mill is a watershed figure in the history of liberalism: although there is room to disagree over the precise nature of Mill's role in the history of liberalism, there is general agreement that Mill manages, on one hand, to continue the pedigree of his liberal forebears while, on the other hand, expanding and reconstructing some of liberalism's core notions and principles. The result is a form of liberalism that is very current and that moves beyond the liberalism of Jeremy Bentham and James Mill.

C. B. Macpherson adeptly pinpoints one of Mill's points of departure when he notes that Mill has greater hopes for the future of democracy than his father James Mill does because the younger Mill saw in democratic institutions and practices a means of promoting human development. Mill's theory of democracy has a "moral vision of the possibility of the improvement of mankind, and of a free and equal society not yet achieved. A democratic system is valued as a means to that improvement – a necessary though not a sufficient means; and a democratic society is seen as both a result of that improvement and a means to further improvement" (Macpherson

1977, 47). The purpose of democracy is not primarily protective, as earlier thinkers had maintained, but is much more expansive. Underlying these differences is another divide over the question of human nature and the capacities and potential of humans. The divide, in other words, is over the question of whether human nature is regarded as mostly fixed and static or as mutable and malleable, allowing room for development in the direction of progress and improvement. Mill criticized Bentham for what he viewed as his limited outlook: "Taking human beings as he finds them, he endeavours to supply such inducements as will constrain even persons of the dispositions the most at variance with the general happiness" (CW X: 9). But he fails to consider the larger questions of character formation and of "carrying forward the members of the community towards perfection" (CW X: 9). Mill believed that this limitation led Bentham and James Mill to hold to a model of protective democracy, in which the role of government is limited to the protection of individuals' interests. John Stuart Mill's model of developmental democracy has a much greater reach. One crucial function of democracy is to function as a means of improvement, in promoting self-development. Hence the change in models: "man is essentially not a consumer and appropriator . . . but an exerter and developer and enjoyer of his capacities. The good society is one which permits and encourages everyone to act as exerter, developer and enjoyer of the exertion and development, of his or her own capacities" (Macpherson 1977, 48).

The Millian Framework: Utilitarianism, Self-Development, and Virtue

Mill's formulation of the principle of utility in *Utilitarianism* is classic. Mill says that the principle of utility "holds that actions are right in proportion as they tend to promote happiness, wrong as they tend to promote the reverse of happiness" (CW X: 210). This utilitarian theory of morality is grounded in a "theory of life . . . namely, that pleasure, and freedom from pain, are the only things desirable as ends" (CW X: 210). The reference to the "theory of life" is clarified in Book VI of the *Logic,* where Mill carefully sets out the architecture of his moral and political philosophy and, in particular, the place of the moral arts and sciences within it. The principle of utility is a principle of the good. It governs and grounds morality, but it is not itself a moral principle. For it has a much wider jurisdiction as the governor of all of the practical arts and all of practical reasoning. Although Mill sets out the structure of his moral and political philosophy carefully, commentators often do not reciprocate this care; they commonly ignore the theoretical structure. As a result, misunderstandings of some of his central arguments frequently result.

One such misunderstanding involves virtue ethics and politics, which play a central but often overlooked role in Mill's philosophy and contribute to the distinctiveness of his democratic theory. His commitment to a view of human nature and the good that is unified around and oriented to development and self-development links his political theory to the tradition of virtue. His advocacy of the exercise of the intellectual and moral excellences as a lifelong pursuit is also reminiscent of virtue ethics and politics. Mill's extensive discussions of the educative processes of development and self-development can be viewed as laying down a program for the inculcation and cultivation and training in the mental and moral virtues. Mill's liberal egalitarianism channels these processes in a progressive direction, but he shares with the Greeks the goal of conceiving of a good human life as including essentially the training and habituation in these excellences.[1]

Mill's *Autobiography* begins with a chapter describing his early education, which featured the study of Greek at age three and a heavy emphasis on the classics. He pays tribute to the influence of classical writings on his philosophy and thought, and undeniably his moral and political thought is deeply imbued with these influences. Unsurprisingly, therefore, his moral and political thought is pervaded by and inspired by the classical thinkers he absorbed in his youthful education. It is salutary, then, that recent Mill scholarship recognizes this and undertakes to restore to its place of honor Mill's indebtedness to the classics.[2] It is also fortunate that this coincides with a resurgence of virtue ethics and the politics of virtue as an important part of the terrain of current moral and political philosophy in the latter half of the twentieth and the early part of the twenty-first centuries.

Roger Crisp and Michael Slote note that a "striking feature of virtue ethics is its focus on moral agents and their lives, rather than on discrete actions ... construed in isolation from the notion of character" (1997, 3). They go on to ask whether it is possible for utilitarians "to enlarge the focus of their own theories to incorporate agents' lives as a whole, their characters as well as ... their actions" (1997, 3). The answer is clearly affirmative in the case of Mill's utilitarianism. As he remarks in a comment near the end of the *Logic*, which may be taken as a summation of his perspective,

The character itself should be, to the individual, a paramount end, simply because the existence of this ideal nobleness of character ... in any abundance, would go further

---

[1] See Crisp and Slote 1997; Berkowitz 1998, 1999; Urbinati 2002.
[2] See Berkowitz 1998; Urbinati 2002.

than all things else towards making human life happy; both in the comparatively humble sense, of pleasure and freedom from pain, and in the higher meaning, of rendering life, not what it now is almost universally, puerile and insignificant – but such as human beings with highly developed faculties can care to have. (CW VIII: 952)

The recent reemergence of virtue ethics takes various forms and expressions. Kwame Anthony Appiah highlights the sea change noted by Crisp and Slote and the broadening focus it signals in moral philosophy, expanding its concerns beyond an excessive focus on moral obligations and rules of duty. As Appiah puts it, in moving outward from the focus on moral obligation to a scrutiny of ethical flourishing, "philosophical reflection among the moderns has returned to questions that absorbed the ancients: questions about what lives we should lead" (Appiah 2005, xiv). Mill would give heartfelt endorsement to this expansion of dialogue and reflection, although, as I will argue later, the actual schema that Appiah promotes is not one that Mill accepts.

Of course, his indebtedness to the ancients does not translate into a general agreement. In Mill's theory, moral foundations remain utilitarian, for the exercise of the virtues provides the best assurance for promoting the happiness of all. Virtues are characterized as admirable character traits that are productive of happiness and that have become habitual through association with pleasure (Berger 1984, 99–100). The culmination of the training happens when, through habituation, we have a confirmed character on which others and we can rely. Mill devotes extensive discussions to how the empiricist associationist psychology he holds to can be employed to cultivate virtuous habits. Mill says in the *Logic,*

A habit of willing is commonly called a purpose; and among the causes of our volitions, and of the actions which flow from them, must be reckoned not only likings and aversions, but also purposes. It is only when our purposes have become independent of the feelings of pain or pleasure from which they originally took their rise, that we are said to have a confirmed character. (CW VIII: 842–3)

In *Utilitarianism,* he explores the moral ramifications:

How can the will to be virtuous, where it does not exist in sufficient force, be implanted or awakened? Only by making the person *desire* virtue – by making him think of it in a pleasurable light, or of its absence in a painful one. It is by associating the doing right with pleasure, or the doing wrong with pain, or by eliciting and impressing and bringing home to the person's experience the pleasure naturally involved in the one or the pain in the other, that it is possible to call forth that will to be virtuous, which, when confirmed, acts without any thought of either pleasure or pain. Will is the child of desire, and passes out of the dominion of its parent only to come under that of habit. (CW X: 239)

Mill's characterization of human happiness is thus essentially interwoven with virtue. In his utilitarianism, happiness is the end that is realized and attained through the habitual exercise of the intellectual and moral virtues. His utilitarianism is more centered on character and ways of life than that of his predecessors and less excessively focused on moral obligation. Another key mark of an ethics and politics of virtue is the use of models and exemplars to be emulated by those training in the virtues. These models are often actual persons of noble character, the embodiment of the virtues, whom trainees or students learn to emulate and follow as examples in their own cultivation of these traits. Mill's writings are populated with examples of these models of the mental and moral virtues. Some of them are highly idealized and others are very down-to-earth and intimate. For example, near the end of the essay *Theism*, which is largely devoted to a scrutiny of some arguments for the existence of God, Mill's argument takes an interesting turn. He looks at the role of religion in promoting virtue, and the role of religious hope in enlarging feelings and lifting human aspirations. He argues that human hope and imagination have in the past been supported by religion, and is far from dismissive of the benefits of such hope. Religion in his view can be allied with the imagination. He says that this "most important exercise of imagination ... consists of the familiarity of the imagination with the conception of a morally perfect Being, and the habit of taking the approbation of such a Being as the *norma* or standard to which to refer and by which to regulate our own characters and lives. This idealization of our standard of excellence in a Person is quite possible, even when that Person is conceived as merely imaginary"(CW X: 485–6). In the same essay, Mill uses Christ as an actual historical figure furnishing an ideal of virtue to emulate. He remarks that "nor, even now, would it be easy, even for an unbeliever, to find a better translation of the rule of virtue from the abstract into the concrete, than to endeavour so to live that Christ would approve our life" (CW X: 488).

Mill's examples can be more personal, even intimate, such as his famous depiction in *On Liberty* of his wife Harriet Taylor Mill as his inspiration. She is "the friend and wife whose exalted sense of truth and right was my strongest incitement, and whose approbation was my chief reward" (CW XVIII: 216). In *On Liberty*, Mill offers copious examples from history of models of this sort, including both specific examples like Christ and Socrates and more general examples of persons with highly developed individuality and wisdom. Such persons of individuality set examples of enlightened conduct. He explains that

Many have let themselves be guided ... by the counsels and influence of a more highly gifted and instructed One or Few. The initiation of all wise or noble things, comes and must come from individuals.... The honour and glory of the average man is that he is capable of following that initiative; that he can respond internally to wise and noble things, and be led to them with his eyes open. (CW XVIII: 269)

Care is needed here to avoid a misunderstanding of Mill's point. Read in isolation, this quote might seem to support the elitist interpretation that is sometimes attributed to Mill. But this interpretation cannot withstand careful reading and analysis of Mill's work as a whole. Mill is quick to add a repudiation of elitism here. He clarifies that he is advocating emulation of models, not proposing "hero-worship" or imposition of values. "All he can claim is, freedom to point out the way. The power of compelling others into it, is not only inconsistent with the freedom and development of all the rest, but corrupting to the strong man himself" (CW XVIII: 269). Those Mill here deems wiser must teach by their example. Imposing their views rather than presenting them and demonstrating the skills of wise deliberation would be self-defeating. For the willingness to impose or use coercion rather than teach would reveal the corruption of a despot and so decisively defeat any claim to self-development and virtue. The moral virtues always operate in tandem with the mental virtues, and the failure to respect other members of the community who are less educated is clear evidence, in Mill's books, of the depravity of despots who desire power over others rather than their freedom (CW XXI: 338). The primacy of the goal of self-development of all cuts down the elitist interpretation at its very root.

If the principle of utility, which governs all of the practical arts including education, calls for the promotion of utility, much depends specifically on the conception of utility at its core. In Mill's view, utility is analyzed in terms of a conception of the good that is appropriate for human beings with a certain nature. The things that are valuable are satisfying or happy states of experience or consciousness. Mill argues that the quality or kind as well as the quantity are both correctly seen as the properties that determine the value of these satisfying states of consciousness. So promotion of the good for humans is inextricably linked to equipping people through education to be in a position to appreciate the more valuable kinds of satisfactions. Mill's philosophy of education lays out a method for educating children to develop their rational, emotional, and moral capacities. In adulthood, this process continues as self-development, and the person herself takes charge of the further training of the higher-order capacities of autonomy, individuality, compassion, and sociality. Mill follows the liberal program in treating the development of rationality as a fundamental aspect of education. He claims that intellectual training requires active exercise of the mind to develop habits of critical awareness. Intellectual powers can be trained in various ways, and Mill offers various suggestions that revolve around rejecting methods of rote learning and endorsing those that develop critical thinking and reflection. Mill's impassioned defense in *On Liberty* of the value of free and open debate for mental development is but one example (CW XVIII: 243). Unlike some other liberals, however, Mill places equal stress on the development of feelings, in part as a reaction against his own excessively rationalistic education. His "mental crisis" in early adulthood was a turning point in Mill's life. It led him to recognize that "internal culture" of the feelings or affective development is a necessary part of education (CW I: 147). In Mill's personal experience, encounters with writings of Romantic poets such as Wordsworth and Shelley helped to relieve his depression and revitalize his feelings. But in usual childhood development there are many tools used in the training of the emotions. The process of moral development, equally central in childhood education, teaches children to feel sympathetic connection with others and to take pleasure in their happiness. Cultivation of sympathy with others is the fount of moral development. Many of Mill's concerns are echoed in contemporary claims about the need for the capacity of empathy for moral agency.

This developmental part of the educative process normally occurs in childhood, when the students are largely under the authority of their teachers. In adulthood, the process transmutes into self-development, which continues throughout the rest of life under the authority of the agent herself. In this part of the process, the higher-order capacities of autonomy, individuality, sociability, and compassion are constructed on the groundwork of the generic capacities and cultivated by practice. Autonomy is the ability to reflect on, choose, and revise one's own conception of the good as well as the character, relationship, projects, and life plans that go with it. Individuality encourages the ability to explore the range of these goods most in harmony with one's own abilities; its close ally is authenticity. Although Mill does not accept that humans have one fixed and unchangeable essence, he maintains that they do have a (limited) range of potentials and a (limited) range of characters, lifestyles, and pursuits in harmony with their potential. The greatest happiness results from seeking out and discovering this range and then choosing and creating traits of character and commitments within it.

A number of options will accord with each individual's potential, and thus the process is partly one of discovery and partly one of creation (Gray 1983, 80). Moreover, Mill's individualism assumes social beings and not isolated individuals lacking deep social bonds.

[A]lready a person in whom the social feeling is at all developed, cannot bring himself to think of the rest of his fellow creatures as struggling rivals with him for the means of happiness, whom he must desire to see defeated in their object in order that he may succeed in his. The deeply-rooted conception which every individual even now has of himself as a social being, tends to make him feel it one of his natural wants that there should be harmony between his feelings and aims and those of his fellow creatures . . . few but those whose mind is a moral blank, could bear to lay out their course of life on the plan of paying no regard to others except so far as their own private interest compels. (CW X: 233)

Equally important in the mix are the higher-order social capacities, those that draw people into community and cooperative enterprises to work with others in the public domain for the common good. Mill says in *Utilitarianism,*

But there is this basis of powerful natural sentiment . . . This firm foundation is that of the social feelings of mankind; the desire to be in unity with our fellow creatures, which is already a powerful principle in human nature, and happily one of those which tend to become stronger, even without express inculcation, from the influences of advancing civilization. The social state is at once so natural, so necessary, and so habitual to man, that, except in some unusual circumstances or by an effort of voluntary abstraction, he never conceives himself otherwise than as a member of a body. (CW X: 231)

The moral and social faculties are elements of human nature that call for development in equal measure and in balance with intellectual and individualist capacities. Indeed, these clusters of capacities are interdependent. None must be allowed to take over a dominant role. Many liberal conceptions of personhood and agency create hierarchies among capacities, elevating the faculty of reason above that of emotion. Often the creation of hierarchies is accompanied by the construction of dualisms between reason and emotion and between individuality and sociality. Mill's refusal to create a hierarchy among these capacities and his insistence on a balance among them has important consequences for his conception of self-development, as well as for his liberal political theory. For one thing, it makes his theory harmonious with feminist theory, which has made the critique of the liberal patriarchal penchant for constructing hierarchies and dualisms a central focus of objection. On Mill's account, moral development is the appropriate accompaniment to mental development, and one without the other is a caricature of development. He says in *Utilitarianism*,

When people who are tolerably fortunate in their outward lot do not find in life sufficient enjoyment to make it valuable to them, the cause generally is, caring for nobody but themselves ... Next to selfishness, the principal cause which makes life unsatisfactory, is want of mental cultivation. . . . As little is there an inherent necessity that any human being should be a selfish egotist, devoid of every feeling or care but those which centre in his own miserable individuality. (CW X: 215–16)

Individuality requires that persons be in control of their own lives and not subject to domination by others. As bearers of value, they are entitled and accustomed to making and carrying through on their own choices, and their own ideas, commitments, relations, and life plans are an expression of their own particularity. They are self-governors and self-authors, but this self-authorship will include a healthy balance of sociability, of social bonds with others. The chapter in *On Liberty* on individuality is a sustained homage to its value to both individual and communal life. It is unmistakably part of the higher-order process of self-development, and it is proper for humans who have reached maturity to have full authority over this process. The tyranny of the majority and conformity to the customary are the adversaries, for to conform to something that is customary "does not educate or develope in him any of the qualities which are the distinctive endowment of a human being" (CW XVIII: 262). Those who let others choose their course of life sacrifice their distinctive human endowment. "He who chooses his plan for himself, employs all his faculties" and gains practice in "discerning or in desiring what is best ... The mental and moral, like the muscular powers, are improved only by being used" (CW XVIII: 262).

From this brief overview of the processes of development and self-development, some significant implications for Mill's egalitarian liberalism emerge. The education he argues children are morally entitled to receive already includes that form of education that develops in them the human capacities of personhood and moral agency. Thus to deny someone the opportunity of development and self-development is to deny them the status of moral agency. Although much goes into the socialization and educational experience of self-development, almost everybody, in Mill's view, has the potential to attain such status, and it is usually their social circumstances that determine whether their potential unfolds. Thus Mill's ideals require that all adult members of society have the opportunity and social resources to achieve self-development. Furthermore, Mill's utilitarianism, with its fundamental commitment to the nurturing of self-developed competent moral agents, inclines his moral and political theory toward radical egalitarianism. According to the fundamental tenets of Mill's moral and political philosophy, people have a right to liberty of self-development, and their rights are violated if their social circumstances do not provide adequate resources for them to attain and exercise self-development.[3]

Democratic Education

Mill's philosophy of education is best understood by placing it in the context of his design for the moral arts and sciences as laid out in the *Logic*. Mill claims that education is one of the primary moral arts. In his system, a moral or practical art defines the ends that promote utility and ought to be aimed at within each sphere or domain. Each moral art is coupled with its corresponding moral science whose role is to study the "course of nature" so as to devise effective means to promote the ends defined by the art. Mill explains:

The art proposes to itself an end to be attained, defines the end, and hands it over to the science. The science receives it, considers it as a phenomenon to be studied, and having investigated its causes and conditions, sends it back to art with a theorem of the combinations of circumstances by which it could be produced. (CW VII: 944).

The moral science is charged with furnishing the means to promote the end, but the choice and definition of the ends remains firmly within the jurisdiction of art (CW VIII: 949). The principle of utility is called in to decide questions of precedence or conflicts among ends, when we need the services of the general principle of teleology (CW VIII: 950). He explains further, "there must be some standard by which to determine the goodness or badness, absolute and comparative, of ends. . . . And whatever that standard is, there can be but one"(CW VIII: 951). This standard is, of course, the promotion of happiness, which is the fundamental principle of teleology (CW VIII: 951).

In Mill's schema in the *Logic*, education is one of the more important particular moral arts. The most important and foundational, to which all other arts are subordinate, is the "Art of Life, in its three departments, Morality, Prudence or Policy, and Aesthetics; the Right, the Expedient, and the Beautiful or Noble, in human conduct and works"(CW VIII: 949). Ethology, or the moral science of character formation, is coupled with the moral art of education in the larger sense that includes the formation of individual, collective,

---

[3] I have developed these ideas in greater depth in Donner 1991, especially 91–159.

and national character (CW VIII: 869). Education is thus conceived of in very broad terms as the art of character formation, and the science of ethology also is conceived of broadly, as having the mandate to furnish the tools to promote the ends of appropriate character formation. The goals are to promote the development and self-development of agents who embody the appropriate balance of rational, emotional, and moral development and of autonomy and individuality with compassion, sympathy and ability to cooperative for the common good.

As Stefan Collini puts it,

Mill's conception of society is an exceptionally and pervasively educative one . . . he makes their effect on the shaping of character the ultimate test of all institutions and policies, and one could without strain regard his whole notion of political activity itself as an extended and strenuous adult-education course. (CW XXI: xlviii)

Collini's perspicacious comment on Mill's philosophy of education furnishes an apt insight into the very heart of Mill's democratic and political theory. Mill's views on the moral art of education crystallize around his extensive reflections on how social and political institutions, including the family, can all be employed as educational sites to promote human well-being and happiness. The most striking feature of his philosophy of education is his championing of a unified and systematic project of developmental activity across all of these domains. As Collini puts it, "for Mill, everything can be education" (CW XXI: xlviii). Indeed, although Mill is often accused of not having a unified theory, this accusation is belied by the palpable interconnectedness of his educational goals, whatever the domain or institutional setting in which these processes occur. What comes through most compellingly is the single-mindedness with which Mill promotes his educational agenda across all of these domains. Schools and universities, the family, and other political and economic institutions are all treated equally in their prospects for advancing his developmental principles. Schools, families, workplaces, and political institutions may be disparate in their institutional goals, but Mill's underlying educational agenda is consistent and virtually identical in all of these settings. His concern with cultivation of virtues unifies and pervades all of his reflections on education. In what follows, I draw attention to the depth and richness of his systematic application of his theory in these manifold settings.

Although education in the sense examined in the *Logic* is not at all restricted to schooling, Mill does have definite views on children's education and on university education. Mill had the ideal opportunity to propound his views on university education when he lectured on the subject in his *Inaugural Address Delivered to the University of St. Andrews* after being elected rector. In his public lecture, Mill distinguishes two senses of education, one broad and one narrower. The first, broad sense of education is that expounded in the *Logic*. Mill says that

Not only does it include whatever we do for ourselves, and whatever is done for us by others, for the express purpose of bringing us somewhat nearer to the perfection of our nature; it does more: in its largest acceptation, it comprehends even the indirect effects produced on character and on the human faculties, by things of which the direct purposes are quite different; by laws, by forms of government, by the industrial arts, by modes of social life. (CW, XXI: 217)

This first larger sense of education is the one that preoccupies him and to which he devotes many writings. The notion that educative processes are not restricted to schools and universities but occur in an astonishing variety of domains of everyday life makes Mill's philosophy of education stand out. He proclaims that "whatever helps to shape the human being; to make the individual what he is, or to hinder him from being what he is not – is part of his education" (CW XXI: 217). The narrower sense of education that occurs in schools and universities is defined as "the culture which each generation purposely gives to those who are to be its successors, in order to qualify them for at least keeping up, and if possible for raising, the level of improvement which has been attained" (CW XXI: 218).

Neither does Mill overlook the crucial importance of children's education, even though most of his reflections are directed toward the wider sense of education, or the lifelong processes of self-development. In many ways, he was far ahead of his time in his social and political vision, and he devoted himself to a number of significant activist causes. Indeed, he was as committed to his activist causes as to his philosophical writings, and he distinguished himself by fighting not only for women's suffrage but also for the universal right to schooling in the era before these rights to education were widely accepted. In *On Liberty*, for example, Mill argues that the process of development of the human capacities requires that the groundwork be laid in childhood education. Hence his argument that children have a right to an education. He says

Is it not almost a self-evident axiom, that the State should require and compel the education, up to a certain standard, of every human being who is born its citizen? . . . It still remains unrecognised, that to bring a child into existence without a fair prospect of being able, not only to provide food for its body, but instruction and training for its mind, is a moral crime, both against the unfortunate offspring and against society. (CW XVIII: 301–302)

Mill argues that the state ought to enforce this right where parents do not carry out this responsibility, and so believes that there is a duty to enforce universal education (CW XVIII: 302).

Mill does express his views on schooling forcefully, though it is the broader notion of education as a lifelong pursuit that occupies center stage in his thought. Mill's promotion of public and political institutions as educative sites is familiar. The radically democratic orientation of his theory prevails over the elitist elements that are also undoubtedly present in his theory. His philosophy of education has powerful implications for his political philosophy, because Mill sees active participation in the political and social life of the community as one of the main arenas for the exercise of these mental and moral excellences.

Mill's philosophy of education must be understood by examining the entire spectrum of his writings on social, public, and political institutions, and not just those whose announced purpose is to educate. In *Representative Government,* for example, he proclaims that democratic political institutions are agents of "national education." One key criterion of a good government is "the degree in which it tends to increase the sum of good qualities in the governed, collectively and individually" (CW XIX: 390). In his later writings on economics, Mill argues for participatory democratic workplace partnerships and associations and hopes that this will result in "the conversion of each human being's daily occupation into a school of the social sympathies and the practical intelligence" (CW III: 792). In *The Subjection of Women,* Mill propounds a classic feminist argument for gender equality in relations and power between women and men. He argues that the moral principle governing gender relations within the family should be "a principle of perfect equality, admitting no power or privilege on one side" (CW XXI: 261). The family should be "a school of sympathy in equality, of living together in love, without power on one side or obedience on the other" (CW XXI: 295).

The road map Mill draws leads decisively to the end of human happiness as the grounding of all of the subsidiary ends of public, social, and political institutions. Human happiness is ineluctably entwined with the process of self-development and the exercise of the virtues. All institutions are charged with this educational purpose, and this responsibility is discharged through offering opportunities for active, effective participation. They are the everyday forums for the practice that habituates students in intellectual and moral virtue.

Mill elaborates on the moral benefits of active political participation with great clarity. It is a theme to which he returns incessantly. Democratic political institutions require the active participation, not the passive acquiescence of the people. Mill's democratic theory promotes active characters rather than passive servile ones, and these are produced by political participation. The moral instruction gained by taking on public duties leads citizens to raise their sights above their narrow private self-interests and partialities to focus on the common good and the community.

> He is made to feel himself one of the public, and whatever is for their benefit to be for his benefit. Where this school of public spirit does not exist, scarcely any sense is entertained that private persons . . . owe any duties to society, except to obey the laws . . . the man never thinks of any collective interests, of any objects to be pursued jointly with others, but only in competition with them, and in some measure at their expense. (CW XIX: 412)

In this negative scenario, absent the opportunities for active political participation, neighbors are merely competitive rivals and are not thought of as colleagues or associates. This self-interested perspective, if not counterbalanced by education, undermines private morality, and can even extinguish public morality.

Mill also strongly voices his concerns about the dangers of despotism allied with elitism. He resoundingly repudiates any policy of cultivating the mental and moral virtues of only an elite select few, and he combines this repudiation with an endorsement of the benefits of inculcating a spirit of cooperation in all members of society. "A people among whom there is no habit of spontaneous action for a collective interest . . . have their faculties only half developed; their education is defective in one of its most important branches" (CW III: 943). He says,

> There cannot be a combination of circumstances more dangerous to human welfare, than that in which intelligence and talent are maintained at a high standard within a governing corporation, but starved and discouraged outside the pale. Such a system, more completely than any other, embodies the idea of despotism, by arming with intellectual superiority as an additional weapon, those who have already the legal power. (CW III: 943)

This sentiment is repeated in *Representative Government* where he also replies to defenders of elitism that placing power in the hands of even an eminent select group "leave[s] out of the idea of good government its principal element, the improvement of the people themselves"(CW XIX: 403).

Mill's concern over despotism and its effects on individual character extends also into his economic writings, where his goal is much more radical than the representative democracy he supports in the political arena. In his later writings on economics, Mill pursues the implications of his own moral and political principles to their conclusion and sets out his expectation and his hope that an economic system of associations and worker cooperatives will eventually replace the capitalist system of ownership, whose limitations and injustices he sees with a clear eye. The progression to a more just economic system, he believes, will be due to the natural improvement that is to be expected and hoped for if workplaces are treated as sites of schooling in the intellectual and moral virtues. The advance of the economic cooperative movement, if widespread, would lead to a "moral revolution" and a "transformation of human life" and "the conversion of each human being's daily occupation into a school of the social sympathies and the practical intelligence" (CW III: 792). The class conflicts would dissipate, and, if gender equality were included in the transformation, "the most beneficial ordering of industrial affairs for the universal good, which it is possible at present to foresee" would be the result (CW III: 794).

Mill values worker-run collective enterprises in large part because he expects them to provide the training in the virtues that he so values. To be effective educationally, the participation in economic associations must be genuine and authentic, not ersatz. Genuine participation occurs when there is control over work and effective decision-making power. Absent these, the participation is ersatz.[4]

Associations...by the very process of their success, are a course of education in those moral and active qualities by which alone success can be either deserved or attained. As associations multiplied, they would tend more and more to absorb all work-people, except those who have too little understanding, or too little virtue, to be capable of learning to act on any other system than that of narrow selfishness. (CW III: 793)

In this process, capitalism will gradually and almost spontaneously evolve into the superior system of associations and cooperatives. Relations of inequality and dependence give way to equality and independence.

Mill's essay *The Subjection of Women* also follows these themes and plot lines, but with a new twist. Mill was in a long-term intimate relationship and marriage to Harriet Taylor Mill, a relationship that was unconventional in his time but not at all unusual in ours. Their collaboration in personal life and in work was extensive and enduring. While there is much controversy over the extent of their work collaboration, Harriet Taylor Mill's influence is unmistakably present in Mill's sensitivity to the pain of gender inequality. As a result, Mill was acutely aware of the debilitating effects of domination, inequality and dependence in gender relations and especially in marital and parent-child relations. Since so much early socialization and training in the

---

4 Pateman, 1970, 28–66.

development of the human capacities happens during childhood, the family is a particularly potent site for education in the wider sense: in the virtues or, deplorably, in the vices. Mill's keen perception of the brutality of domestic violence and its crippling effect on the development and self-development of women and men alike gives a depth to his analysis that is compelling and so far in advance of his era that it can still be directly applied without any alteration to diagnose the problems of gender oppression and domestic violence today.

The essay begins with a clear statement of the main argument of the work:

> That the principle which regulates the existing social relations between the two sexes – the legal subordination of one sex to the other – is wrong in itself, and now one of the chief hindrances to human improvement; and that it ought to be replaced by a principle of perfect equality, admitting no power or privilege on the one side, nor disability on the other. (CW XXI: 261)

Mill's argument for gender equality in the essay rests on a more general defense of the principle of equality. Mill argues that progress in human affairs has reached the point at which justice will become a primary virtue, that it will be based on "sympathetic association," that it will be grounded not in self-protection but instead in "cultivated sympathy." The circle of equality will be extended with "no one being now left out, but an equal measure being extended to all" (CW XXI: 294). One major line of argument dovetails interestingly with the theme of *On Liberty,* for in both works Mill stresses that liberty and individuality are essential components of human happiness. Indeed, the summation at the end of *The Subjection of Women* could be straight out of *On Liberty.* He states that "every restraint on the freedom of conduct of any of their human fellow creatures, (otherwise than by making them responsible for any evil actually caused by it), dries up *pro tanto* the principal fountain of human happiness, and leaves the species less rich, to an inappreciable degree, in all that makes life valuable to the individual human being" (CW XXI: 340).

In his writings on representative government and economic democracy, Mill does display much insight into the debasing effects of repression, poverty, and class and economic inequality on human self-development. And in his analysis of political and economic inequality, he does exhibit an awareness of the corrupting effects of power on despots, in addition to the great harms inflicted on the vulnerable members of oppressed and exploited groups. These insights, however, really come alive in his dissection of the grim harms of gender oppression and inequality on women and of the brutalizing and corrupting effects on those men who take advantage of their positions as oppressors to repress the autonomy and individuality of their intimates. Violence is the extreme form used in this repression, but despotic power is often exercised in more insidious forms of coercion. Liberals, including Mill, are sometimes accused of a lack of awareness of the harms of oppressions and of misunderstanding the relation between freedom and power. The objection is that liberal freedoms are supposedly linked with the desire for (private) power over others. That this accusation does not apply to Mill is evident when he gets to the core of things:

> The love of power and the love of liberty are in eternal antagonism ... The desire of power over others can only cease to be a depraving agency among mankind, when each of them individually is able to do without it: which can only be where respect for liberty in the personal concerns of each is an established principle. (CW XXI: 338)

Families can be schools for training in the virtues if children are taught that "the true virtue of human beings is fitness to live together as equals" (CW XXI: 294). Families should function as schools for the virtues of freedom and of living together lovingly. They ought to operate on and promulgate principles of mutuality, sympathy, and loving respect. The model of marriage is one of friendship, cooperation, and equality. Instead, Mill argues, the family by and large functions as a school for despots, and the intimacy of the relationship often results in a despotism that is corrosive to fundamental self-respect and self-development. Families in which parents practice the moral virtues of gender equality and treat each other lovingly, respecting equal freedom and individuality provide "a model to the children of the feelings and conduct which their temporary training ... is designed to render habitual, and therefore natural to them" (CW XXI: 295). The training in the virtues or in the vices that children are habituated to in their families has the power to influence their orientation toward liberty or toward despotism, and it can and does function as an educative site for parents in their marital and parental relations.[5] Although the family is sometimes treated as a private domain in liberal theory, it has notable social and political roles within Mill's liberalism.

Objections: Virtue Versus Individuality

Mill's philosophy of education is complex, and his goals involve his lifelong commitment to encourage development of the human virtues and excellences while protecting a secure place for human liberty and individuality.

---

[5] For excellent discussions of Mill's views on the family, gender equality, and marriage, see Robson and Robson 1994; Morales 1996, 2005; Shanley 1998; and Urbinati 2002, pp. 180–9.

Of course, in Mill's view, individuality and autonomy are essentially bound up with the human good and are prime conditions for and elements of his conception of happiness. Yet there are objections to Mill's theory based on perceived tensions among liberty, individuality, and the cultivation of virtue. The general theme of these objections is that Mill's philosophy of education may be intolerant of forms of character, such as those based on traditional, religious, or ethnic identities, which do not conform to Mill's ideal. If Mill's philosophy of education is concerned with promoting and developing specific character types that are taken to be ideal or desirable, then he is faced with the problem of reconciling the favored ideal character types with the ideals and values of individualism and autonomy. And the reconciliation problem, posed in these terms, would be substantial, for individuality and autonomy inevitably go against the grain of expecting or wanting any particular result from the educative development process. Anthony Appiah identifies "one strain of Mill's liberalism with the view that I should be permitted (in particular, by the state) to make whatever life flows from my choices, provided that I give you what I owe you and do you no harm. But, of course, the fact that each of us has a life to make can at least raise the possibility that others, the state among them, ought to act to help us in that prospect. And at least some of these possibilities entail some sort of involvement in our *ethical* selves" (Appiah 2005, 163). The problem with Appiah's point is that the distinction between the moral and the ethical is not found in Mill's theory, and, as I argue subsequently, importing it creates distortion and confusion for Mill's theory.

What, then, are we to make of the objection that Mill's encouragement of virtue might interfere with his defense of individuality? I claim that simply setting out the objection clearly, against the backdrop of my previous analysis of Mill's theory of education, shows that this way of formulating the question is seriously misconceived. The objection is misdirected on several fronts. For one thing, Mill does not maintain the sort of ideal of character that the objection assumes, and so the objection fails to get off the ground. Mill recognizes the dangers of promoting more specific forms of character, because such promotion is fundamentally at odds with his commitment to human liberty and individuality. The famous third chapter of *On Liberty*, "Of Individuality, as One of the Elements of Well-Being," is the clearest statement of his thoughts on this question. Here he strongly repudiates the position that there can be specific ideals of character that should be promoted or forms that should not be tolerated. My analysis of Mill's philosophy of education and its connections to virtue operates at a much higher level of abstraction, so as to avoid even the appearance of promoting a specific form of character, or even many specific forms, because this would inevitably run afoul of Mill's own clear commitments. The accurate view of Mill's philosophy of education is of one that encourages the educative processes of development and self-development. These educative processes cultivate and develop and then exercise certain human capacities and faculties, such as reason, emotion, sympathy, autonomy, individuality, compassion, sociality, and so on. Mill is always at pains to emphasize that these capacities must be balanced against each other and that they can manifest in myriad combinations and forms. He recognizes the dangers of promoting more specific forms of character. His analysis, in *On Liberty* and elsewhere, is that any such attempted imposition of forms of character, ideal or otherwise, is a kind of despotism and does immeasurable damage to human well-being. It would short circuit the entire process of self-development and self-authorship and thus would be self-defeating. He rejects this route in the strongest possible terms, and he states with crystal clarity that the conditions that promote improvement and development are "remarkable diversity of character" (CW XVIII: 274). He reiterates over and over again (to the extent that he is sometimes interpreted as valuing idiosyncrasy unduly) that it is necessary for development "to render people unlike one another" (CW XVIII: 274). These arguments are a resounding rejection of any form of character as an ideal. The process of development is set out in terms of cultivation of capacities that can take as many forms as there are people.

The argument that Mill's promotion of the human excellences and virtues could lead to such coercion, imposition, and intolerance arise from serious misreadings of his theory. To get to the root of these mistakes, I must delve into the source of an even more fundamental misunderstanding of the basic structure of his moral philosophy.[6]

The claim that Mill's commitment to the development of the virtues could lead to intolerance of some forms of character flagrantly clashes with his argument in *On Liberty* that there are limits to "the power which can be legitimately exercised by society over the individual" (CW XVIII 217). His Liberty Principle expresses the boundaries of society's legitimate use of compulsion and coercion over individuals. It is worth quoting at length from his reflections to illustrate how categorically he rules out coercion and control over forms of character. He argues:

the only purpose for which power can be rightfully exercised over any member of a civilized community, against his will, is to prevent harm to others. His own good, either physical or moral, is not a sufficient warrant. He cannot rightfully be

---

[6] I have examined the structure of Mill's theory in more depth than I can explore here in Donner 1998, 278–91, and 1991, especially 118–87.

compelled to do or forbear because it will be better for him to do so, because it will make him happier, because, in the opinion of others, to do so would be wise, or even right. These are good reasons for remonstrating with him, or reasoning with him, or persuading him, or entreating him, but not for compelling him, or visiting him with any evil in case he do otherwise. (CW XVIII: 223–4)

A number of lines of argument in Mill's moral philosophy all converge on this central salient point. Because his theory is amenable to a range of plausible interpretations on many issues, it is worth highlighting that on this point his meaning is clear and his key claim is incontrovertible. The root of the problem lies in misunderstanding the difference between Morality and Virtue (two of the three components of the Art of Life) in Mill's theory. This bedrock element of Mill's moral philosophy is almost universally ignored in explorations of his thought, even though his reliance on it affects almost everything he writes about in these areas. A brief excursion into the framework of Mill's moral philosophy clarifies why this commitment is so fundamental to his thought. Indeed, it is because scholars routinely overlook the backbone schema of his moral and political philosophy that their discussions on specific aspects of his theory, like his views on individuality and character, go awry. Mill's Liberty Principle is a principle of justice within this structure. The chapter in *Utilitarianism* "On the Connexion between Justice and Utility" pins down the place of the Liberty Principle and the implications of its occupation of this place within the theoretical structure.

To reiterate: the principle of utility is a principle of the good. As such it furnishes the grounding for all of the numerous practical arts, including morality. In the chapter on justice and utility in *Utilitarianism*, Mill's exploration of the structure of his theory first carves out the place of the category of morality within the widest and all-inclusive category of "expediency" or the general promotion of good. He says,

We do not call anything wrong, unless we mean to imply that a person ought to be punished in some way or other for doing it. . . . This seems to be the real turning point of the distinction between morality and simple expediency. It is a part of the notion of Duty in every one of its forms, that a person may rightfully be compelled to fulfill it. . . . There are other things . . . which we wish that people should do, which we like or admire them for doing, perhaps dislike or despise them for not doing, but yet admit that they are not bound to do it; it is not a case of moral obligation . . . we say that it would be right to do so and so, or merely that it would be desirable or laudable, according as we would wish to see the person whom it concerns, compelled, or only persuaded and exhorted, to act in that manner. (CW X: 246)

The domain of morality has jurisdiction over rules of duty or obligation, whose violation calls for coercive moral sanctions. *This means that not all acts that fail to promote the good are wrong.* The vast majority of actions, in fact, are outside of this domain. Morally wrong acts are those that, by definition, are liable to punishment and coercion.[7] Thus punishment, coercive sanctions, and moral duty are conceptually linked. Moral duties form but a small part of the numerous practical arts, all of which are grounded in the principle of utility. Most of the practical arts therefore pertain to actions and behavior that are free from the threat of sanctions and coercion. Misunderstanding of this distinction between expediency and morality leads to the false and untenable position that morality swallows up large tracts of practical reasoning, whereas in Mill's clearly stated view, it occupies only a small portion of it.

Mill next demarcates a further subclass within the class of moral duties, namely, the rules of justice that protect rights. His definition of a right is as follows:

> When we call anything a person's right, we mean that he has a valid claim on society to protect him in the possession of it, either by the force of law, or by that of education and opinion. If he has what we consider a sufficient claim, on whatever account, to have something guaranteed to him by society, we say that he has a right to it. (CW X: 250)

Rules of justice protect rights, and rights are designed to protect the most vital human interests, those that are most crucial to well-being. He says that "justice is a name for certain classes of moral rules, which concern the essentials of human well-being more nearly, and are therefore of more absolute obligation, than any other rules for the guidance of life" (CW X: 255). The Liberty Principle is a prime example of such a principle of justice. Coercion, punishment and harm, under Mill's structure, are only called for when a moral duty (including a right) is violated. People cannot, in his design, be coerced in the pursuit of their liberty and individuality, unless these pursuits violate moral duties, including rights. In other words, coercion and interference are only permitted if the pursuit of liberty harms others. In Mill's theory, such harm only occurs when agents break moral rules of duty or justice.

Arguments claiming that Mill's theory might allow intolerance of or coercive interference with agents' forms of character implicitly and illicitly assume that in Mill's theory agents have moral duties *to themselves,* because it is only the apparatus of Duty that calls for coercion. Many moral theories do in fact assign a place for moral duties to self. This route fails in Mill's theory, however. Mill specifically and resoundingly repudiates the

---

[7] For a further examination of these points, see Lyons 1994, especially 47–65.

idea of duties to oneself. And in rejecting the very idea that humans can have duties to themselves, Mill cuts off at the source any avenue for claiming that people can be coerced or sanctioned or treated intolerantly for choosing certain forms of character. In *On Liberty,* he contrasts breaches of moral duties with "the self-regarding faults...which are not properly immoralities, and to whatever pitch they may be carried, do not constitute wickedness. They may be proofs of any amount of folly, or want of personal dignity and self-respect; but they are only a subject of moral reprobation when they involve a breach of duty to others.... What are called duties to ourselves are not socially obligatory, unless circumstances render them at the same time duties to others. The term duty to oneself, when it means anything more than prudence, means self-respect or self-development; and for none of these is any one accountable to his fellow creatures" (CW XVIII: 279).

It is a contradiction to maintain, on one hand, that we have individuality, or the right to liberty to choose our own life plans, forms of character, and other commitments and, on the other hand, that we are appropriately subject to coercion, sanctions, or interference if we make certain choices about these that others judge to be irrational or unworthy. Mill does not hold this contradictory position, because he repudiates the use of coercion and interference with life choices of this nature. The contradiction occurs within the position he explicitly rejects. The contradiction is maintained by commentators and critics who misconstrue Mill on these fundamentals.

Confusion also arises from neglecting Mill's careful exposition of the difference between self-regarding *duties,* which he rejects, and self-regarding *virtues,* which he embraces. Although his examination of these notions is prominently featured in *Utilitarianism,* this discussion is widely overlooked, even though it is a salient component of his case for promoting the development of the virtues while protecting the right to liberty and individuality. Mill's theory calls for extensive positive encouragement and engagement with others as part of the process of development of virtue. Self-regarding virtues correspond to the sphere of beauty and nobility in the Art of Life (the other two spheres being morality and prudence). He says,

Human beings owe to each other help to distinguish the better from the worse, and encouragement to choose the former and avoid the latter. They should be forever stimulating each other to increased exercise of their higher faculties.... But neither one person, nor any number of persons, is warranted in saying to another human creature of ripe years, that he shall not do with his life for his own benefit what he chooses to do with it.... In this department, therefore, of human affairs, Individuality has its proper field of action.... Considerations to aid his judgment, exhortations to strengthen his will, may be offered to him . . . but he himself is the final judge. All errors which he is likely to commit against advice and warning, are far outweighed by the evil of allowing others to constrain him to what they deem his good. (CW XVIII: 277)

Although Mill's theory discourages lack of engagement with others, the rules governing the permissible encouragement of virtue and development are firmly delineated to prevent abuse of the boundaries protecting liberty. Encouragement of the development of virtue to increase opportunities for people to lead the best possible lives cannot, within Mill's theory, be turned into a moral duty or a requirement to lead a better life, with the baggage of coercion and intolerance this brings. Mutual encouragement and engagement, using persuasion and models for emulation and habituation, are permissible, whereas coercion, control, and intolerance are definitively ruled out.

Anthony Appiah neglects Mill's carefully drawn distinction between self-regarding duties and self-regarding virtues at a critical juncture of his argument about soul-making and identities. Appiah regards Mill as his traveling companion, and in some ways he insightfully and accurately uses Mill's company to advance his own arguments. But at a critical moment Appiah departs from Mill's theory, and although Appiah's subsequent discussion holds up well on its own terms, it does not do justice to Mill. Appiah draws on and quotes from Mill's discussion of the self-regarding virtues in which he makes the point that people should engage with others to promote their mutual good. "They should be for ever stimulating each other to increased exercise of their higher faculties," says Mill (CW XVIII: 277). Rather than correctly identifying Mill's comment as located in his discussion of self-regarding *virtue*, Appiah erroneously categorizes this encouragement as an "*obligation*" (Appiah, 32). Appiah leaves out the portion of the paragraph of *On Liberty*, from which the quote is taken, in which Mill specifies that he is talking about self-regarding virtues, *not* obligations. Mill here says,

I am the last person to undervalue the self-regarding virtues; they are only second in importance, if even second, to the social. It is equally the business of education to cultivate both. But even education works by conviction and persuasion as well as by compulsion, and it is by the former only that, when the period of education[8] is past, the self-regarding virtues should be inculcated. (CW XVIII: 277)

Appiah illicitly concludes that in Mill's framework, the encouragement of virtue involves obligations. It does not.

---

[8] Meaning here childhood education.

The error is complicated by Appiah's use of an entirely different distinction between *moral* obligation and *ethical* obligation. In much of his exploration of the ethics of identity, Appiah's invocation and application of the Millian framework is accurate, and Mill is indeed an authentic fellow traveler. But at a critical junction, Appiah turns to a different philosophical tradition that relies on the schema of moral obligation and ethical obligation. This distinction is alien to Mill, and the result is that Appiah creates confusion concerning Mill's argument and philosophy. Appiah says, "associative duties can be categorized as *ethical* rather than moral. They involve duties to yourself (in Dworkin's terms), insofar as they reflect your commitment to living a certain kind of life" (Appiah 2005, 232). The plan and pattern of Appiah's distinction between ethical and moral obligations is not my concern here and is beyond the scope of my discussion. However, Appiah's reading back onto Mill of a set of concepts that are alien to Mill's philosophy and that, at this key point, are fundamentally at odds with it, is central to my point. It constitutes an illuminating example of how neglect of the basic structure of Mill's philosophy, a structure he sets out in two of his most widely read essays (as well as in many other writings), can lead to serious misunderstanding of his philosophy. And it can lead to red herring objections that are not directed at arguments he actually makes. Here Appiah's confusion leads to attributing erroneously to Mill the claim that the self-regarding virtues involve obligations, which bring with them, in Mill's framework, the baggage of coercion. In Mill's view, coercion has no place in the territory of the virtues.

Conclusion

Mill's emancipatory vision of education for freedom and democracy is still unattained. Many of his hopes for creating social and political conditions that will sustain authentic human excellences have not yet been realized. Although lip service is often paid to Millian ideals, theorists of democracy and liberalism still confront the dilemmas and problems of systems that have not lived up to these ideals, even though the material resources are available to bring them about or at least bring them closer to fruition. Mill's vision of a social and political life that encourages human flourishing and fosters human self-development continues to hold out the promise of a revitalized communal and political life. Mill's project of education for freedom and democracy continues to be played in out twenty-first-century arenas, and his philosophy also continues to inspire and guide contemporary dialogue.

If one test of the adequacy of a theory is how well it works out in application, Mill's own life provides proof of the soundness of the theory. Mill's writings set out theoretical approaches that he penned to serve as guiding principles for activist struggles. His own activism was tireless, and in these campaigns he was guided by the principles he articulated in his writings. The efficacy of his activism in extending the suffrage, fighting for women's rights and equality, working for universal schooling, and numerous other struggles are in themselves ample evidence of the vitality of his moral and political philosophy. Although his vision is still in progress, his moral and political philosophy furnishes a framework and accompanying ideals to fuel our continuing endeavors.

PART THREE

BEYOND NATIONAL BORDERS

11

Cosmopolitan Patriotism in J. S. Mill's Political Thought and Activism

Georgios Varouxakis

No one disapproves more, or is in the habit of expressing his disapprobation more strongly than I do of the narrow, exclusive patriotism of former ages which made the good of the whole human race a subordinate consideration to the good, or worse still, to the mere power & external importance, of the country of one's birth. I believe that the good of no country can be obtained by any means but such as tend to that of all countries, nor ought to be sought otherwise, even if obtainable.

J. S. Mill, "Letter to Maurice Wakeman," 25 October 1865, CWXVII: 1108–9

Mill's reputation is as a thinker; but we shall never fully understand his thought if we fail to recognize that he was always politically engaged and had a strong sense of himself as a shrewd strategist.

William Stafford, 1998b, 108

Like many other aspects of John Stuart Mill's thought, his attitude towards nationhood, nationalism, and related issues has been subjected to all sorts of misinterpretations and partial readings. In a vast body of literature (from at least as early as the publication of John [later Lord] Acton's essay 'Nationality' (1862) to the beginning of the twenty-first century), Mill has been seen as representing – and often incarnating – some of the most extreme – and, at the same time, mutually contradictory – positions vis-à-vis nationality and related phenomena.[1]

I have already argued elsewhere that despite a common misunderstanding, Mill was far from being an uncritical and naïve supporter of 'nationalism' or 'nationality'. Rather, his position was closest to what I call 'cosmopolitan patriotism'. In this chapter, I develop this argument as follows. Mill as a philosopher subscribed to what contemporary political theorists and philosophers would call 'moral cosmopolitanism', to a cosmopolitan viewpoint as far as one's ultimate moral commitment or allegiance was

---

[1] For a short (and by no means exhaustive) list of all sorts of different positions attributed to Mill, see Varouxakis 2002a, 3–7.

concerned. Utilitarianism is a fundamentally cosmopolitan tradition; and the 'Religion of Humanity' that Mill advocated demanded of individuals fellow-feeling with the whole of mankind. However, being, at the same time, a political activist, journalist, politician, and a 'public moralist' – to use Stefan Collini's felicitous term – who had to take account of people *as they were* rather than *as they ought to be,* and work strategically to raise them from where they were to where they could get, Mill adopted a strategy which he followed throughout his mature life. Being aware that, for the foreseeable future, the vast majority of people were not going to be converted to his 'Religion of Humanity' with its cosmopolitan commitments overnight (although he hoped they might gradually one day), he chose to promote the kind of particularistic attachment, the kind of patriotism, which was most consistent with his cosmopolitan ultimate commitment. If most people at his time needed to feel that they belonged to a community smaller than mankind as a whole, felt attached to it, and were likely to take pride or feel shame on its behalf, then he would work hard to convince his fellow countrymen (and, if possible, the French as well, and whomever else would listen) to take pride in the right things and feel shame when their country was doing the wrong things – right or wrong from the point of view of the welfare, 'civilization' and 'improvement' of mankind as a whole of course. Thus, he fought militantly and ferociously against what he saw as the flag-waving kind of patriotism (such as that practiced by James Fitzjames Stephen at the time) – patriotism that took pride in military prowess and conquest. Instead, he wished people to want to be proud of their country for what it was doing for the welfare of humanity and 'civilization' and to feel shame if their government either was acting against the interests of mankind at large or even if it refrained from rendering mankind services simply because no 'British interests' were concerned. This is one sense in which his brand of patriotism was 'cosmopolitan'. Another (far from unrelated) sense is the kind of language he wanted used and the kind of arguments he thought should be part of the deliberations of the nation. To an extent that has to be appreciated given the levels of ethnocentric smugness of the time and place, Mill tried seriously to convince his Victorian compatriots to consider the point of view of other nations when they were discussing international affairs.

I

To go into more detail now, first of all, I need to face the preconceived notions of many people who have read in the literature that Mill was favourable to 'nationality', or was a 'nationalist' or a 'liberal nationalist' and the like. Most accounts of Mill's position in these issues are based on his treatment of 'nationality' in the famous chapter XVI of his *Considerations on Representative Government* (1861). In the first place, then, I argue that this text, although it is routinely adduced as proof that Mill promoted 'nationality', does nothing of the kind, if perused fully and carefully. What Mill said in that chapter did not endorse or celebrate 'nationality'. Mill did indeed write: 'Where the sentiment of nationality exists in any force, there is a *primâ facie* case for uniting all the members of the nationality under the same government, and a government to themselves apart.' (CW XIX: 547). However, as Alfred Cobban has cogently remarked, referring to this very passage: 'With his supreme capacity for digging deeper than his own principles, and sometimes, it is true, undermining them, Mill proceeds after this to introduce qualifications which completely alter the complexion of his views on nationality'; but, as Cobban continues, 'as is usually the case, the general statement is remembered and the all-important modifications are forgotten' (Cobban 1969, 131). Thus, even if we were to read that chapter in isolation from the rest of Mill's writings (which is far from what I am proposing to do), Mill does not emerge from it having advocated the active promotion of 'nationality'. All Mill said was that nationality was a fact of life and that, if people felt so strongly about their nationality that they could not live with people of different nationalities or be ruled by rulers who were not co-nationals (which he regretted), they should be allowed to form their own state, in the cases where this latter option was feasible. His rationale for this recommendation was that representative government was not likely to work in a state composed of mutually hostile groups of people (nationalities) that put their 'sentiment of nationality' above 'the love of liberty' – which he very strongly regretted, as he made clear both in chapter XVI of *Considerations on Representative Government* and in the earlier essay 'Vindication of the French Revolution of February 1848', published in 1849. Here is what he had to say in that earlier essay of 1849:

It is far from our intention to defend or apologise for the feelings which make men reckless of, or at least indifferent to, the rights and interests of any portion of the human species, save that which is called by the same name and speaks the same language as themselves. *These feelings are characteristic of barbarians; in proportion as a nation is nearer to barbarism it has them in a greater degree:* and no one has seen with deeper regret, not to say disgust, than ourselves, the evidence which recent events have afforded, that in the backward parts of Europe, and even (where better things might have been expected) in Germany, the sentiment of nationality so far outweighs the love of liberty, that the people are willing to abet their rulers in crushing the liberty and independence of any people not of their own race and language. (CW XX: 347, emphasis added)

However, Mill's own wishes and tastes were one thing, and the realities of the world another. So he hastened to add: 'But grievous as are these things, yet so long as they exist, the question of nationality is practically of the very first importance.' Thus, 'When portions of mankind, living under the same government, cherish these barbarous feelings – when they feel towards each other as enemies, or as strangers, indifferent to each other – they are scarcely capable of merging into one and the same free people.' They did not have 'the fellow-feeling which would enable them to unite in maintaining their liberties, or in forming a paramount public opinion'. Even the separation of feeling which mere difference of language created, was 'already a serious hindrance to the establishment of a common freedom'. Moreover: 'When to this are added national or provincial antipathies, the obstacle becomes insuperable. The Government, being the only real link of union, is able, by playing off one race and people against another, to suppress the liberties of all.' Thus, how could a free constitution establish itself in the Austrian Empire, asked Mill, 'when Bohemians are ready to join in putting down the liberties of the Viennese – when Croats and Serbs are eager to crush Hungarians – and all unite in retaining Italy in slavery to their common despot?' This is why he concluded: 'Nationality is desirable, *as a means to the attainment of liberty*;[2] and this is reason enough for sympathizing in the attempts of Italians to re-constitute an Italy, and in those of the people of Posen to become a Poland.' He clarified:

So long, indeed, as a people are incapable of self-government, it is often better for them to be under the despotism of foreigners than of natives, when those foreigners are more advanced in civilization and cultivation than themselves. But when their hour of freedom . . . has struck, without their having become merged and blended in the nationality of their conquerors, the re-conquest of their own is often an indispensable condition either to obtaining free institutions, or to the possibility, were they even obtained, of working them in the spirit of freedom.' (CW XX: 347–8)

This hardly sounds like the enthusiastic celebration of 'the sentiment of nationality' that Mill has been time and again presented as having offered.[3] National self-determination was at best accepted instrumentally, as a means to the better working of free representative government. But the nationalist 'sentiments' involved, even if they had to be pragmatically accommodated, were 'characteristic of barbarians'.

---

[2] Emphasis added.

[3] See, for some examples, Gray 1995, 99–100; Miller 1995, 10 and passim; Vincent 1997, 279; Lichtenberg 1999, 167. For a fuller (but by no means exhaustive) list, see Varouxakis 2002a, 3–7.

II

But this is only the beginning. In the second place, to an extent that has gone unnoticed so far, Mill came in his later years to be explicitly wary of the associations of the term 'nationality', or at any rate of 'nationality in the vulgar sense of the term'. In a passage more often quoted or referred to than properly analysed,[4] which occurs both in his essay 'Coleridge' (1840) and in his *System of Logic* (first published in 1843 – bk. VI, chap. 10) Mill effected some changes from the earlier to the later editions that deserve much more attention than they have received. Although I concluded my book *Mill on Nationality* by drawing attention to these changes (Varouxakis 2002a, 126–7), I did not stress their significance explicitly enough there but rather left the reader to draw what I thought was the obvious conclusion. It is fitting for the purposes of this chapter to look closer to this question and, this time, analyse the changes more closely.

To start with, whereas in the earliest version (1840) Mill specified as one of the three conditions of stability in political society '*a strong and active principle of nationality*', in later editions of the text he changed this into: '*a strong and active principle of cohesion among the members of the same community or state*' (CW X: 134–5, emphases added). (Needless to say, the authors who assert that Mill advocated the importance of nationality quote the former formulation and ignore the fact that Mill substituted the latter later.) What is more, in the lines immediately following what I have just quoted, Mill also changed the original text from 'We need scarcely say that we do not mean a senseless antipathy to foreigners' to 'We need scarcely say *that we do not mean nationality in the vulgar sense of the term; a senseless antipathy to foreigners*'.[5] Moreover, in the later editions, he also added, immediately following this, that he did *not* mean 'an indifference to the general welfare of the human race, or an unjust preference of the supposed interest of our own country' (CW X: 135). Although it has escaped attention for too long, the implication seems to me to be crystal clear: whereas in the early 1840s Mill was proposing '*a strong and active principle of nationality*' as one of the sine qua non of stability in political society, in *later* editions (1859 and 1867), he did not name what he said was needed 'nationality' but rather 'a strong and active principle of cohesion among the members of the same community or state'. And, *even more revealingly*, he then described all the deplorable manifestations of nationalist feeling that he went on to

---

[4] See, e.g., Gray 1995, 174, n. 3; Viroli 1995, epigraph.
[5] Emphasis added.

enumerate, as '*nationality in the vulgar sense of the term*'. To all intents and purposes, Mill not only substituted 'a strong and active principle of cohesion among the members of the same community or state' for 'nationality' as the principle which he was proposing, but he also went on to include all the deplorable manifestations of what is today called 'tribalism' or 'chauvinism' under the heading of 'nationality in the vulgar sense'. The importance of the text is such that it is well worth quoting. Here is how he concluded the text in the later version: 'We need scarcely say that we do not mean nationality in the vulgar sense of the term; a senseless antipathy to foreigners; an indifference to the general welfare of the human race, or an unjust preference of the supposed interests of our own country; a cherishing of bad peculiarities because they are national or a refusal to adopt what has been found good by other countries'. Instead, he went on to explain what he *did* mean by 'a strong and active principle of cohesion among the members of the same community or state':

We mean a principle of sympathy, not of hostility; of union, not of separation. We mean a feeling of common interest among those who live under the same government, and are contained within the same natural or historical boundaries. We mean, that one part of the community shall not consider themselves as foreigners with regard to another part; that they shall cherish the tie which holds them together; shall feel that they are one people, that their lot is cast together, that evil to any of their fellow-countrymen is evil to themselves, and that they cannot selfishly free themselves from their share of any common inconvenience by severing the connexion. (CW VIII: 923)[6]

In other words, Mill was advocating a kind of 'patriotism', *which he defined carefully so as not to identify it with 'nationality'.* What is striking about these characteristics of 'nationality in the vulgar sense' which he rejected emphatically is that they all refer to a community's relation with 'foreigners', with 'the general welfare of the human race', or to whether one should adopt 'what has been found good by other countries'. Mill was explicit, that is, that the 'principle' he was proposing had to be compatible with 'the general welfare of the human race', should not be turned against 'foreigners', and should not lead to the rejection of 'what has been found good by other countries' and a 'cherishing of absurd peculiarities because they are national'. Preserving a nation's 'authenticity' and 'national' culture were far from being his concerns. On the contrary, adopting what had been found good by other countries was not only acceptable but highly – and militantly – recommended by him (see Varouxakis 2002b, chaps. 1 and 2).

---

[6] See also Mill's 1840 essay 'Coleridge', for the earlier version CW X: 135–6.

But this did not make of him an advocate of 'rootless' cosmopolitanism either. The way he described the 'principle of cohesion' means that he was setting great value in solidarity among the members of a political community. Thus, if we try to read this in the context of debates in contemporary political theory, in that passage Mill proposed that members of a political community need to share 'a feeling of common interest' and mutual solidarity but did not promote 'nationality' as a means to that end, as David Miller would have one believe (Miller 1995, 10; cf. Miller 2000, 36), and would by no means invest 'nationality' with intrinsic ethical value, as Miller does (cf. Benner 1997; Vincent 1997).

III

In the third place, Mill spoke favourably innumerable times of 'patriotism' or 'enlightened patriotism'. From a very early age, he had articulated a distinction between different kinds of 'patriotism', making clear that he emphatically rejected one of them. At this point, I have to take issue with some of the assertions made recently by Julia Stapleton, in some important and well-researched works where she drew attention to the national-patriotic dimension of the writings of self-appointed defenders and definers of real 'liberalism' such as J. F. Stephen, R. H. Hutton, A. V. Dicey, and others (Stapleton 1998; Stapleton 2001, 26–7). Stapleton is right in maintaining that people like Stephen and Hutton developed their patriotic discourse in direct and explicit opposition to the utterances of people like J. S. Mill (and Matthew Arnold, I would add). However, it does not follow that they were right in attributing lack of patriotism to Mill (or Arnold). We need here to draw a distinction between at least two concepts of patriotism. Stapleton has argued that 'Above all, the growth of English national consciousness after 1850 took place in reaction to the perceived *absence* of patriotism *of any description*[7] among the forces of British radicalism.' Stapleton went on to claim that 'This perception was not entirely groundless. The English/British *patria* appeared in much radical discourse on citizenship only as an object of abuse.' After citing Richard Cobden and John Bright in this connection, she goes on to include Mill among the radicals who were justly seen as unpatriotic (Stapleton 1998; Stapleton 2001, 24–5). I regard the comments she adduced by way of evidence as by no means proving lack of patriotism in Mill. One could find much more striking texts than those Stapleton quotes, in which he tried to shame his compatriots into improving themselves. This,

---

[7] The former emphasis ('*absence*') is in the original; the latter ('of any description') is mine.

however, does not reflect lack of patriotism, unless one means by 'patriotism' the 'my country right or wrong' attitude. Now, apparently this is what J. F. Stephen had in mind when he was identifying 'the chief shortcoming of his master turned adversary [Mill] as a lamentable want of patriotism'.[8] James Fitzjames's brother, Leslie Stephen, in his volume on J. S. Mill (and apparently including Bentham and James Mill in the observation), also opined: 'Patriotism, indeed, was scarcely held to be a virtue by the Utilitarians. It meant for them the state of mind of the country squire or his hanger-on the parson; and is generally mentioned as giving a sufficient explanation of unreasoning prejudice' (L. Stephen 1900, 12–13).

However, Mill did not simply reject 'patriotism' tout court – as Stapleton repeated in her recent book, adding that 'Mill was noticeably antipathetic to all things English' (Stapleton 2001, 26). What is true is that Mill – as well as Matthew Arnold, John Morley, T. H. Green, Herbert Spencer, Frederic Harrison, and several other Victorian liberals (see Varouxakis 2006) – would have no truck with *a certain conception of patriotism,* which saw patriotism as consisting of – as Mill put it – 'a cherishing of bad peculiarities because they are national or a refusal to adopt what has been found good by other countries'. This he called 'nationality in the vulgar sense of the term'. When contemporaries accused Mill or Arnold of anti-patriotism or un-English sentiments, it was because Mill and Arnold were vociferously hostile to, and contemptuous of, all manifestations of feelings and attitudes arising from such a conception of 'patriotism'.

Some examples may elucidate the difference. J. F. Stephen wrote in *Liberty, Equality, Fraternity*: 'I do not envy the Englishman whose heart does not beat high as he looks at the scarred and shattered walls of Delhi or at the union jack flying from the fort at Lahore' (Stapleton 1998, 251). Stapleton notes, furthermore, that despite his dislike of popular literature, Stephen made an exception to praise Macaulay, because, as his brother Leslie had put it, 'he strongly sympathised with the patriotism represented by Macaulay' (Stapleton 1998, 244). Among the things James Fitzjames Stephen found worthy of praise in his article on Macaulay was that '[h]e was . . . full of patriotic feelings. . . . He was an enthusiastic Englishman' (Stephen 1866b, 208). It is characteristic that, on the other hand, Mill, while in the process of reading the first two volumes of Macaulay's *History of England*, wrote to Harriet Taylor that he perceived 'no very bad tendency in it as yet, except

---

[8] Stapleton 2000, 249. Cf. the remark of his brother, Leslie Stephen, that what J. F. Stephen desiderated in Mill's theory of liberty was 'the great patriotic passions which are the main-springs of history'; see Stapleton 1998, 247.

that it in some degree ministers to English conceit' (CW XIX: 6). Very simply, ministering to English conceit, or giving encouragement to 'the already ample self-conceit of John Bull', was not a patriotic thing to do in Mill's eyes. The person who loved his or her country should offer fellow countrymen what they most needed; and, in the context of complacent, smug, ethnocentric post-1815 Britain, this did not mean reinforcing their self-conceit.

Already at the age of twenty, in 1826, Mill asserted, in a review article on 'Modern French Historical Works', that he was 'far from being unconscious' of how much his compatriots had 'really to be proud of, and in how many respects they might be taken as models by all the nations of the world.' He clarified that if he 'saw them in any danger of forgetting their own merits', he too 'might preach them a sermon on that hacknied text'. But it was not 'their failing to underrate themselves, or to overrate other nations'. They were 'more in need of monitors than adulators'. And, further on in the same article (talking of the reactions in France of those who were attacking historian J. P. Dulaure for his exposure of what he saw as French vices), Mill went on, in the same spirit. What he said is worth quoting, because it illustrates his clear understanding and articulation of at least two distinct conceptions, two sorts of 'patriotism':

We own that we are in general predisposed in favour of a man whom we hear accused by a certain class of politicians of being an enemy to his country. We at once conclude, that he has either actually rendered, or shown himself disposed to render, some signal service to his country. We conclude, either that he has had discernment to see, and courage to point out, something in his own that stands in need of amendment, or something in another country which it would be for the advantage of his own to imitate; *or that he loved his country well enough to wish it free from that greatest of misfortunes, the misfortune of being successful in an unjust cause;*[9] ... Whoever is guilty of any of these crimes in this country, is a fortunate man if he escapes being accused of un-English feelings. This is the epithet which we observe to be appropriated to those, whose wish is that their country should deserve to be thought well of. The man of English feelings is the man whose wish is, that his country should be thought well of; and, above all, should think well of itself, peculiarly in those points wherein it deserves the least. The modern English version of the maxim *Spartam nactus es, hanc exorna,* may be given thus – England is your country, be sure to praise it lustily. *This sort of patriotism* is, it would appear, no less in request with certain persons in France.[10]

---

[9] Emphasis added.

[10] CW XX: 17, 21–2, emphasis added. Cf. what Mill wrote to Macvey Napier on 20 October 1845: CW XIII: 683. Cf. what Mill was to write in the same vein in a letter to an American correspondent, during the last decade of his life, in the quotation on the epigraph of this article (CW XVI: 1108–9 – letter to Maurice Wakeman, 25 October 1865).

I have argued so far that (a) Mill had no wish to promote 'nationality', although he recognized that nationalist feelings were part of life and had to be reckoned with; (b) he argued that a political society needed a strong sense of cohesion and solidarity among its members in order for it to be stable, but that this should by no means take the form of 'nationality in the vulgar sense'(I would call this formulation of the principle of cohesion 'enlightened patriotism'); and (c) he thought that there were different kinds of 'patriotism' and some were more commendable than others. I now endeavour to establish that among the different conceptions of 'patriotism' one could think of, Mill tried to promote a particular kind of patriotism or 'principle of cohesion' that was not only compatible with, but moreover conducive to, cosmopolitan commitment to humanity at large. I call this type of patriotism 'cosmopolitan patriotism'.

IV

The assertion that Mill promoted 'cosmopolitan patriotism' may sound like a contradiction in terms. Obviously, a lot depends on what one means by 'cosmopolitan'. In the last few years, there has been an explosion of writing on 'cosmopolitanism', 'cosmopolitan citizenship', 'global citizenship', 'global justice', and related concepts in political theory. But what does 'cosmopolitanism' or 'cosmopolitan' mean? Many conceptions have been identified.[11] If one looks at conceptions and definitions of 'cosmopolitanism' historically, in the long run, there is a lot of truth in the remark that 'the form which cosmopolitanism assumes is in general conditioned by the particular social entity or group ideal from which it represents a reaction' (Boehm 1931, 458). In accordance with this tendency, much of the recent discussion of cosmopolitanism is related to a reaction to the Rawlsian conception of the appropriate field of justice as being within each nation-state rather than directly applying to individuals at a global level (global justice). Critics have tried to apply Rawls's principles of justice to the global level to which he himself did not apply them and have offered various arguments in favour of large-scale redistribution of resources on the basis of Rawls's own premises – for example, Thomas Pogge, Charles Beitz, or Brian Barry (see Jones 1999, 2; see also Nussbaum 2005).

---

[11] See, e.g., Heater 1996, 2002; Nussbaum 1996; Cheah and Robbins 1998; Hutchings and Dannreuther 1999, 3–32; Jones 1999; Scheffler 1999; Lu 2000; Waldron 2000; Anderson-Gold 2001, 10–43; Brennan 2001, 76–8; Carter 2001; Held 2002, 63–8; Kymlicka 2002, 268–70, 312–15; Vertovec and Cohen 2002; Vincent 2002, 191–224.

But cosmopolitan thinking does not refer only to debates about justice. No less than a full-length book is needed to begin to offer an account of the different meanings of cosmopolitanism. However, a useful brief road map has been contributed by David Held, who has identified 'three broad accounts of cosmopolitanism which ... contribute to its contemporary meaning'. The first account was that of the Stoics, whose main point was the idea 'that they were, in the first instance, human beings living in a world of human beings and only incidentally members of polities'. The upshot of this idea is that '[t]he individual belongs to the wider world of humanity; moral worth cannot be specified by the yardstick of a single political community' (Held 2002, 64). The second account of cosmopolitanism was that introduced in the eighteenth century 'when the term [W]eltbürger (world citizen) became one of the key terms of the Enlightenment'. The central figure was Immanuel Kant who 'linked the idea of cosmopolitanism to an innovative conception of "the public use of reason" and explored the ways in which this conception of reason can generate a critical vantage point from which to scrutinize civil society'.[12] Finally, the third conception of cosmopolitanism is a contemporary one and expounded in the work of Beitz, Pogge, and Barry, among others. As Held has maintained, 'In certain respects, this work seems to explicate, and offer a compelling elucidation of the classical conception of belonging to the human community first and foremost, and the Kantian conception of subjecting all beliefs, relations and practices to the test of whether or not they allow open-ended interaction, uncoerced agreement and impartial judgment' (Held 2002, 64).

But most of the recent literature does not attain this degree of conceptual clarity and historical contextualization. Most of the debates involve quite partial accounts of what 'cosmopolitanism' is supposed to mean. Strawman arguments abound in the writings of cosmopolitanism's many critics. Also frequent are autobiographical accounts on the part of supporters of 'cosmopolitanism' (e.g., Waldron 1995) or attributions, on the part of critics of cosmopolitanism, of autobiographical shortcomings to the supporters of cosmopolitanism – or, to be more blunt, it is a standard argument among their critics that cosmopolitan theorists are blinded to the realities of the world because they are ivory-tower academics who spend too much time with people like themselves and fly all the time to international conferences

---

[12] In accordance with that conception, '[i]ndividuals can step out of their entrenched positions in civil society and enter a sphere of reason free of "dictatorial authority"... and can, from this vantage point, examine the one-sidedness, partiality and limits of everyday knowledge, understanding and regulations' (Held 2002, 64). For some important comments on the significance of Kant, see Waldron 2000; see also Carter 2001, 33–50).

and the like (see, e.g., Scheffler 1996).[13] Thus, it is no surprise that 'cosmopolitanism' has come to be referred to as 'that tainted term' (Cheah and Robins 1998, vii).

A very common conception of cosmopolitanism is the following: 'Understood as a fundamental devotion to the interests of humanity as a whole, cosmopolitanism has often seemed to claim universality *by virtue of its independence, its detachment from the bonds, commitments, and affiliations that constrain ordinary nation-bound lives. It has seemed to be a luxuriously free-floating view from above*' (Cheah and Robins 1998, 1, emphasis added).

A similar meaning was given to 'cosmopolitanism' by a theorist who accepted and advocated it, Jeremy Waldron, in the early 1990s ('Minority cultures and the cosmopolitan alternative', Waldron 1995). As he summarized it himself in a later article:

I spoke of someone who did not associate his identity with any secure sense of place, someone who did not take his cultural identity to be defined by any bounded subset of the cultural resources available in the world. He did not take his identity as anything definitive, as anything homogenous that might be muddied or compromised when he studied Greek, ate Chinese, wore clothes made in Korea, worshipped with the Book of Common Prayer, listened to arias by Verdi sung by a Maori diva on Japanese equipment, gave lectures in Buenos Aires, followed Israeli politics, or practiced Buddhist meditation techniques. I spoke of this person as a creature of modernity, conscious, even proud, of living in a mixed-up world having a mixed-up self. (Waldron 2000, 228)

This is the conception of cosmopolitanism as consisting in an individual experience characterized by 'a bit of this and a bit of that', as Salman Rushdie has put it.[14]

Yet does 'cosmopolitanism' have to involve this detached attitude, do cosmopolitans need to be 'rootless', 'elitist', and even 'parasitic' (according to conservative British philosopher Roger Scruton), or at the very least mixed up, as they have been portrayed by many commentators? (See Carter 2001, 8–13.) My point is that this is only one of the many conceptualisations of 'cosmopolitanism' and far from the one I wish to explore here.

It is exactly the combination of cosmopolitan moral commitment with commitment to a particular political community (patriotism) that Mill propagated that makes him interesting in this context. Mill, like Bentham before him, adopted a cosmopolitan viewpoint when it came to the group

---

[13] Cf. Brennan 2001, 77: 'cosmopolitanism springs from a comfortable culture of middle-class travelers, intellectuals and businessmen'.

[14] Salman Rushdie, *Imaginary Homelands: Essays and Criticism 1981–1991*, London: Granta Books, 1991, 394; quoted in Waldron 1995, 93).

that should command people's supreme and ultimate allegiance.[15] It may be worth quoting what he had to say on the issue of the proper focus of one's allegiance during his mature years, in the 1850s. In 'Utility of Religion', Mill declared that it would be wrong to assume that 'only the more eminent of our species, in mind and heart', were 'capable of identifying their feelings with the entire life of the human race'. There was no gainsaying that '[t]his noble capability implies indeed a certain cultivation', but this cultivation was 'not superior to that which might be, and certainly will be if human improvement continues, the lot of all' (CW X: 420–1). He adduced the degree of selfless dedication and allegiance inspired by patriotism, love of one's country, as proof of the capacity of human beings, once properly cultivated and educated, to attain to disinterested devotion to the good of the entire humanity: 'When we consider how ardent a sentiment, in favourable circumstances of education, *the love of country* has become, we cannot judge it impossible that *the love of that larger country, the world*, may be nursed into similar strength, both *as a source of elevated emotion* and *as a principle of duty*' (CW X: 421, emphases added). If, then, people could be trained to regard the good of their country as the supreme object, 'so also may they be made to feel the same absolute obligation towards the universal good.' What was needed was a morality 'grounded on large and wise views of the good of the whole', which would neither sacrifice the individual to the aggregate nor the aggregate to the individual, but would give to 'duty' on the one hand, and to 'freedom and spontaneity', on the other, 'their proper province'. Crucially, for the purposes of my argument, he goes on to say that such a morality would 'derive its power in the superior natures from sympathy and benevolence and the passion for ideal excellence: in the inferior, from the same feelings cultivated up to the measure of their capacity, *with the superadded force of shame*' (CW X: 421, emphasis added).[16] Mill based this

---

[15] On Bentham and cosmopolitanism, see Ellis 1992, 164. Cf. Conway 1990, 231: 'Bentham declared himself "an Englishman by birth" but "a citizen of the world by naturalization"'. Cf. Hayes 1931, 128. On J. S. Mill's comment on the 'cosmopolitan character' of Bentham's writings, see CW XVII: 1812. For a more general assessment, Charles Jones also argues that 'Utilitarianism is a clear case of a cosmopolitan theory'. This is his definition of 'cosmopolitanism': 'Cosmopolitanism is a moral perspective with several basic components. The cosmopolitan standpoint is impartial, universal, individualist, and egalitarian. The fundamental idea is that each person affected by an institutional arrangement should be given equal consideration. Individuals are the basic units of moral concern, and the interests of individuals should be taken into account by the adoption of an impartial standpoint for evaluation' (Jones 1999, 15).

[16] According to Mill, 'to call these sentiments by the name of morality . . . is claiming too little for them'. Rather, they were 'a real religion'. For the essence of religion was 'the strong and earnest direction of the emotions and desires towards an ideal object, recognized as

assertion on the belief that (as he had put it earlier on in the same text) '[t]he power of education is almost boundless: there is not one natural inclination which it is not strong enough to coerce, and, if needful, to destroy by disuse' ('Utility of Religion', CW X: 409).

The notion that the historical success of attempts to instil strong attachment to one's country (patriotism) can be used as a proof of the possibility of cosmopolitan 'ideal devotion to a greater country, the world' may strike some people as paradoxical. Most people – today at least – tend to see patriotism and cosmopolitanism as antagonistic to each other. Most (though by no means all) of today's 'cosmopolitans' tend to assume that if only it were not for nationalism/patriotism and the particularistic barriers created by attachment to the nation-state, people would naturally identify with the whole of humanity. Needless to say, this assumption is historically ill-informed and politically naïve. Whatever else they might have done, the nation-building projects of nation-states have tended to enlarge people's circle of fellow-feelings from the smaller units of family, tribe, village, or region to the much broader one of a whole nation.[17]

This latter understanding of the role of 'patriotism' was quite widespread among Victorian liberals. For many Victorian liberal political thinkers, 'patriotism' (which they defined in various ways, of course) was seen as a stepping stone towards universalist commitment to the whole of 'humanity', rather than as antithetical to the latter (see Jones 2000, 49; Varouxakis 2006). Thus, it was clearly 'as a step away from the particular and toward the universal' (Jones 2000, 49) that Victorian liberals, including Mill, approved of attachment to the nation, provided it manifested itself in the 'enlightened patriotism' that people like Mill had in mind. Mill saw patriotism as commendable only to the extent that it conduced to the interests of the whole of humanity. This is why he distinguished among different kinds of 'patriotism' and tried to promote a certain version of what he called 'enlightened patriotism'.[18]

But this is only one of the possible objections I need to deal with. For if one wished to be the devil's advocate one would say that, although the move

---

of the highest excellence, and as rightfully paramount over all selfish objects of desire'. This condition was fulfilled by what he was proposing, 'the Religion of Humanity'. He was convinced 'that the sense of unity with mankind, and a deep feeling for the general good, may be cultivated into a sentiment and a principle capable of fulfilling every important function of religion and itself justly entitled to the name' (CW X: 420–3).

[17] Cf. Kymlicka 2002, 270.

[18] For one of the many instances in which Mill used the term enlightened patriotism in French (*patriotisme éclairé*), see CW XVII: 1769.

from local to national patriotism/sympathy makes psychological sense, it is difficult to imagine a corresponding move from national to global patriotism/sympathy. In a sense, substituting national for local or regional identifications and allegiances may be said to be just substituting one 'us–them' divide for another with another. But how can people identify with the whole of humanity? Or at least work in its best interests even while identifying with smaller portions of it? Thus, not only is there the well-known objection bound to be raised by those who would say, like Adam Ferguson had done in the eighteenth century, that patriotism and solidarity within a group had to be built on hostility towards some other group. But even if one does not regard hostility towards an 'other' as necessary for building patriotic allegiances, one may still think that identification with the whole of mankind is either a chimera or too loose and weak (too 'thin', in contemporary parlance) to sustain and mobilize solidarity. For instance, Mill's contemporary Alexis de Tocqueville was convinced that 'the interests of the human race are better served by giving every man a particular fatherland than by trying to inflame his passions for the whole of humanity.' Tocqueville, like Rousseau before him, feared that cosmopolitan citizens 'will perceive only from a viewpoint that is distant, aloof, uncertain, and cold' (Neidleman 2001, 156). According to Tocqueville, 'Man has been created by God (I do not know why) in such a way that the larger the object of his love the less directly attached he is to it. His heart needs particular passions; he needs limited objects for his affections to keep these firm and enduring. There are but few who will burn with ardent love for the entire human species' (quoted in: Neidleman 2001, 169).

Mill was far from unaware of this problem. But he had an answer, I think. Here is what he wrote in 'Nature' (one of the 'Three Essays on Religion'):

Of the social virtues it is almost superfluous to speak; so completely is it the verdict of all experience that selfishness is natural. By this I do not mean in any wise mean to deny that sympathy is natural also; I believe on the contrary that on that important fact rests the possibility of any cultivation of goodness and nobleness, and the hope of their ultimate entire ascendancy. But sympathetic characters, left uncultivated, and given up to their sympathetic instincts, are as selfish as others. The difference is in the *kind* of selfishness: theirs is not solitary but sympathetic selfishness; *l'egoïsme à deux, à trois*, or *à quatre*; and they may be very amiable and delightful to those with whom they sympathize, and grossly unjust and unfeeling to the rest of the world. (CW X: 394)

But Mill was not resigned to reconciling himself with what were the 'natural' inclinations of human beings. The whole point of the essay 'Nature' was to assert the opposite. He summarized his conclusions himself:

The word Nature has two principal meanings: it either denotes the entire system of things, with the aggregate of all their properties, or it denotes things as they would be, apart from human intervention. . . . In the [second] sense of the term, the doctrine that man ought to follow nature, or in other words, ought to make the spontaneous course of things the model of his voluntary actions, is equally irrational and immoral. Irrational, because all human action whatever, consists in altering, and all useful action in improving, the spontaneous course of nature: Immoral, because the course of natural phenomena being replete with everything which when committed by human beings is most worthy of abhorrence, any one who endeavoured in his actions to imitate the natural course of things would be universally seen and acknowledged to be the wickedest of men. The scheme of Nature regarded in its whole extent, cannot have had, for its sole or even principal object, the good of human or other sentient beings. What good it brings to them, is mostly the result of their own exertions. Whatsoever, in nature, gives indication of beneficent design, proves this beneficence to be armed only with limited power; *and the duty of man is to co-operate with the beneficent powers, not by imitating but by perpetually striving to amend the course of nature – and bringing that part of it over which we can exercise control, more nearly into conformity with a high standard of justice and goodness.* (CW X: 401–2, emphasis added)

It seems to me that – in the light of what I have said so far – if we collate them, the two preceding quotes from 'Nature' can offer a clear clue to what Mill was up to regarding the patriotism – cosmopolitanism continuum. What he called 'sympathetic selfishness', or *'l'egoïsme à deux, à trois*, or *à quatre'*, was in 'the spontaneous course of things' and it was an example of beneficence 'armed only with limited power'. Its power for good was limited because the same people who 'may be very amiable and delightful to those with whom they sympathize' could simultaneously be 'grossly unjust and unfeeling to the rest of the world'. Now, if 'the duty of man is to co-operate with the beneficent powers, not by imitating but by perpetually striving to amend the course of nature – and bringing that part of it over which we can exercise control, more nearly into conformity with a high standard of justice and goodness', then the course Mill chose is rather clear: He thought we should strive (and he as a 'public moralist' strove) 'to amend the course of nature' and '[bring] the part of it over which we can exercise control, *more nearly into conformity with* a high standard of justice and goodness'.[19] The standard of justice and goodness was universal benevolence towards all human beings. This was clearly *not* the natural course of things. At best, in nature, 'beneficence' was 'armed only with limited power', in this case, in the form of 'sympathetic selfishness' which leads people to treat well those with whom they sympathize. Mill was recommending a strategy

[19] Emphasis added.

designed to make use of this limited benevolence in order to bring it '*more nearly into conformity with* a high standard of justice and goodness', to help approximate that standard as much as possible by artificial (non-'natural') means. He was fully aware that most people (at least the 'inferior' natures) would probably go on having fellow-feelings only with particular groups ('sympathetic selfishness'). He would therefore use 'the superadded force of shame' to lead them to behave decently and generously towards the rest of humanity out of selfish regard for the reputation of their own group.[20] This is how national/group pride or shame would be used in service of cosmopolitan/universalist ends.

When all is said and done, what was at the heart of Mill's philosophy was the desire, through education and the cultivation of character, intellect and feelings, to overcome selfishness. Ultimately Mill wanted human beings to develop fellow-feelings with the whole of humanity, those living, those dead, and those yet to be born. However, acknowledging, at the same time, that not all humans were of as lofty, generous, and high-minded natures as he (and people like himself), he conceded that, as a step towards the desired expansion of the circle of fellow-feelings toward the whole of humanity, extending them to include a whole nation (or better, the inhabitants of a 'community or state' (CW X: 135) was a step of progress in the right direction – as long as the way in which they were expanded was not through 'nationality in the vulgar sense'. But the content of the motivational material, the kind of patriotism involved, was crucial. So he tried assiduously to promote a certain conception of love of country which was in his eyes not just compatible with but moreover conducive to the welfare of mankind at large. For him this meant trying to make his own country the country most worth loving, the country which pursued its interests in ways that promoted the interests of mankind as a whole, and this is the idea of England/Britain he consistently tried to inspire in the consciences of his fellow-countrymen.

In this respect, idealized Britain as he described it – *while prescribing it –* in the first part of his article 'A Few Words on Non-Intervention' (1859) was the quintessential cosmopolitan nation. One of his several aims there was to caution British statesmen against using a discourse (justification of acts or failures to act purely on grounds of national interest) which gave rise to foreign perceptions about English selfishness and perfidy. It would be 'foolish attempting to despise all this': 'Nations, like individuals, ought to suspect some fault in themselves when they find they are generally worse thought of than they think they deserve; and they may well know that they

---

[20] CW X: 421.

are somehow in fault when almost everybody but themselves thinks them crafty and hypocritical' (CW XXI: 112).

Mill wanted people to divert their feelings of pride to what their country was doing for humanity and 'civilization' and to feel shame if their government either was acting against the interests of mankind at large or even refrained from rendering mankind services simply because no 'British interests' were concerned. Moreover, he wanted his fellow-countrymen to be able to defend their country's international behaviour with arguments that would be acceptable to foreign nations. The kind of language he wanted used and the kind of arguments he thought should be part of the deliberations of the nation had to be, in that sense, cosmopolitan. Mill tried seriously to convince his compatriots to consider the point of view of other nations when they were discussing international affairs.[21]

In this respect, by trying to elevate the opinion of foreigners as one of the major concerns of the British nation and its governments, Mill was at one with a man with otherwise quite different views, language, and temperament, Matthew Arnold. Instead of ignoring what the rest of 'Europe' and the world thought of Britain, as other Victorian thinkers did (and some, like J. F. Stephen [1866a], explicitly recommended), to say nothing of the British public a large (as Nassau Senior [1842]had explained), Arnold and Mill believed that it was part of being a good patriot to strive to improve the way one's country was perceived abroad, to make its voice heard and respected, and all this for the right reasons, for commendable achievements, distinctions, and contributions to the welfare of mankind and the common fund of 'civilization', which other nations would recognise as well. More important, they believed that by making the British public aware of, and sensitive to, the judgments of an international 'tribunal of public opinion', they would inculcate in them the right kind of patriotism, the patriotism that feeds on appropriate and commendable feelings and aspires to the right sort of collective-national distinction and 'greatness'.[22]

---

[21] An analogy one can think of is Mill's rationale for his rejection of the secret ballot. He wanted people to vote openly in order for them to feel constrained to make electoral choices which they would be able to justify publicly in front of their fellow-constituents, choices therefore for which they could invoke reasons based on common interests and shared principles. If one applies this idea to the international arena, nations would have to 'prove' their greatness by invoking what they were contributing to the common fund of humanity, to civilization, and what they were excelling in according to commonly accepted criteria.

[22] Arnold, like Mill, had his own views as to what is healthy and defensible patriotism and what is sheer prejudice. Commenting on one of the many attacks he had received on account of his essay 'My Countrymen', he wrote to his mother: 'I should be sorry to be a

Although I do not wish to exaggerate the case, and I would not argue that Mill or Arnold had a fully developed or refined and satisfactory account of what is today called 'impartial reasoning', it is arguable that, to an extent not sufficiently appreciated, they groped towards an attempt at establishing the need for what we call impartial reasoning in the relations between different states and peoples, and particularly with regard to their country's dealings with other countries[23] – although they confined this in practice to what they would call 'civilized' nations. Albeit limited by the Euro-centrism that characterised the thought of the time, the position they adopted was, in principle, 'cosmopolitan' in terms of their demand for impartiality in the language and arguments used.

Thus, what I have argued here is that Mill promoted a position that I call 'cosmopolitan patriotism'. It is 'patriotism' (as opposed to 'nationalism') to the extent that Mill was very wary of the implications of nationalist sentiment and the tribalism that it could entail and preferred to promote 'a strong and active principle of cohesion among the members of the same community or state'.[24] Now, this patriotism is 'cosmopolitan' in that he consistently defined it in such a way as to equate it with an outward-looking noble emulation among different human communities ('nations' or other) of achievements that would promote the welfare and civilization of the whole of mankind. Moreover, the criteria through which such achievements would be judged, the language that would be used, the arguments that would be appealed to, would have to be impartial and, to that extent, cosmopolitan.

What makes Mill's 'cosmopolitan patriotism' more interesting and more down-to-earth than other attempts to promote cosmopolitanism is that it

Frenchman, a German, or American, or anything but an Englishman; but I know that this native instinct which other nations, too, have, does not *prove* one's superiority, but that one has to achieve this by undeniable, excellent performance' (Arnold 1996–2002, vol. 3, 17–18, emphasis added). Note the word 'prove'. Obviously, Arnold had in mind some sort of international tribunal of public opinion, in front of which it would not be enough for Englishmen, Frenchmen, Americans, and so on to boast that they were great and superior following their 'native instinct', but rather they would have to 'prove' their superiority and greatness 'by undeniable, excellent performance', presumably in identifiable, commonly accepted domains of excellence.

23 An oft-quoted formulation of the impartiality thesis is the following: 'All the impartiality thesis says is that, if and when one raises questions regarding fundamental moral standards, the court of appeal that on addresses is a court in which no particular individual, group, or country has special standing. Before the court, declaring "I like it", "it serves my country", and the like, is not decisive; principles must be defensible to anyone looking at the matter apart from his or her special attachments, from a larger, human perspective' (quoted in Held 2002, 66).

24 Of course there are difficulties with the distinction between 'nationalism' and 'patriotism'; see Varouxakis 2001.

does not shun more particularistic attachments such as nations or father-lands, love of country, and the feelings of pride or shame most people feel on behalf of their respective countries in their relations with other countries. Instead, Mill tried to utilize those feelings of pride or shame and the mobilizing power they generated in the service of cosmopolitan ultimate goals. Instead of preaching cosmopolitanism applied to individual identities (which could rightly be accused of being rootless and free-floating, 'from above', and parasitic), Mill was consistently trying to turn *the whole nation* towards a cosmopolitan orientation, to make it part of the national project and aspirations to excel in 'doing good' for humanity at large.

Thus, although some might object that Mill's ideal of cosmopolitan patriotism is implausible psychologically, there is evidence to suggest otherwise. The closest real-world examples in the contemporary world of national identities being – at least partly – built on relatively cosmopolitan ideals of 'doing good' for the world (being generous donors of international aid, participating in UN peace-keeping missions, serving as honest brokers in international disputes, etc.) seem to be Canada and Norway.[25] Will Kymlicka, commenting on this issue in the case of Canada, has argued recently that in many cases 'the most effective way to get people to take seriously their international obligations is to present them as a matter of national honour and national identity: i.e., that is the "Canadian" thing to do, and that it would cast shame on Canada's reputation internationally if Canadians were seen as selfish or indifferent' (Kymlicka 2003, 358, n. 2). This is exactly what Mill was doing, very consciously, deliberately and consistently. This was one of his most important aims in the first part of 'A Few Words on Non-Intervention', where he was prescribing what he saw as the right, cosmopolitan, foreign policy by presenting it as the 'British/English' thing to do. There are many examples of this strategy in Mill's journalism in particular (see Varouxakis 2002b, passim).

Let me conclude by going back to where I started. As the quote from William Stafford's introduction to Mill cited in the epigraph of this article suggests, besides being a philosopher and a thinker, Mill was a public intellectual, an activist deeply engaged in political causes and aiming at changing the world as much as he could. He himself said no less in describing what he was up to in his *Autobiography*. It is not accidental that the 'theorist' and the 'practical man' appear together at the end of chapter 3. Mill clearly saw his role as being 'either as theorist or as practical man, to effect the

---

[25] For details of what this means in the case of Canada (and some references to Norway), see Kymlicka 2003, 358–61.

greatest amount of good compatible with his opportunities' (CW I: 87). Now, it is not accidental either that he wrote no treatise on 'patriotism' or on 'cosmopolitan patriotism' and that the latter term ('cosmopolitan patriotism') never appeared in his works. What I have tried to describe is *a strategy*, first and foremost. If asked where he stood as a philosopher on patriotism/nationalism/cosmopolitanism, he would have replied that he was subscribing to what is today called moral cosmopolitanism. His utilitarianism and his 'Religion of Humanity' point to that direction inexorably. Meanwhile, however, he worked hard and consistently to use and divert the patriotic feelings that people were displaying in the direction of serving the ultimate cosmopolitan goals of the improvement of mankind. At the very least, the 'inferior natures' needed this, and he would use 'the superadded force of shame' in that direction (CW X: 421). That is why 'cosmopolitan patriotism' is the best way to describe where he stood and what he was up to.

12

Mill and the Imperial Predicament

Karuna Mantena

I

In the late pamphlet titled "England and Ireland" (1868), J. S. Mill perceptively noted the tenuous grounds underlying even the most confident presumptions of liberal imperialism in nineteenth-century Britain. Written during a period of intense Fenian activity in Britain and Ireland – when popular perceptions of Irish political resistance were less than sympathetic – the pamphlet contained pointed reflections on the root causes of the deteriorating political situation in Ireland as well as Mill's most searching analysis of the fraught dynamics of imperial power and ideology. Of English attitudes towards its civilizing project in Ireland, he wrote,

> we, or our ruling classes, thought, that there could be no boon to any country equal to that of imparting these [English] institutions to her, and as none of their benefits were any longer withheld from Ireland, Ireland, it seemed, could have nothing more to desire. What was not too bad for us, must be good enough for Ireland, or if not, Ireland or the nature of things was alone in fault. (CW VI, 511)

In marking the ways in which the project of imperial liberal reform when faced with resistance or disappointment shifted the burden of responsibility for this failure onto colonized societies themselves, Mill's critical portrait exposed a fragility at the heart of the liberal imperial project. In its disavowal, in locating responsibility solely with "Ireland or the nature of things," liberal imperialism revealed at once the limits to its own discourse of ethical rule and its persistent blindness to these limits.

Mill himself was not immune to accusations of blindness, and, despite his occasional misgivings on aspects of British imperial policy, Mill consistently defended the empire and the prestige it conferred to be "a great advantage to mankind" (CW XVII: 767). Indeed, Mill's defense of empire, one that remained remarkably consistent throughout his writings and political career, has been seen as the apotheosis of "liberal imperialism" itself. Mill's account represented an important and articulate justification of liberal imperialism but it also, in its internal tensions and elaboration, contained some key and characteristic vulnerabilities of the discourse of liberal empire, vulnerabilities that would become increasingly apparent in the changing political and intellectual climate of Victorian Britain.

One of the most important features of late Victorian debates about empire is the degree to which the vision of liberal empire enunciated by Mill (and his predecessors) had ceased to carry the political weight it had previously enjoyed. In the wake of a series of imperial crises, the most important of which were the Indian Mutiny (1857–9) and the Morant Bay rebellion (1865), the liberal discourse of empire became subject to mounting suspicion. Liberal imperialism, as a distinctive theory of imperial legitimacy, was founded on a specific link between a project of liberal reform or improvement and the ends of empire. This idiom of improvement (or civilizing project), which had formed the ethical horizon of liberal imperialism, became precisely the main target of criticism. In questioning both the practical and theoretical possibility of a genuine project of improvement and modernization, late Victorian critics of liberal imperialism provoked a broad-ranging transition in imperial ideology. From a "universalist" stance in which imperial rule was seen as necessarily imbued with a transformative dimension, a new emphasis on ingrained cultural and racial differences became ever more decisive in imperial debates. Moreover, this profound shift in attitudes was enabled, in part, by an opening up of the fissures of liberal imperialism itself, exposing the internal tensions in the theoretical claims of liberal imperialism and the tenuous grounds of liberal imperial confidence, both of which were increasingly exploited by liberal empire's sharpest critics.

Although this chapter focuses specifically on the vulnerabilities of liberal imperialism in nineteenth-century Britain, I hope to also highlight a more general dynamic common perhaps to all forms of universalist defenses of empire. At the peak of imperial confidence in nineteenth-century Britain, when the project of liberal reform encountered resistance, its universalism easily gave way to harsh attitudes about the intractable differences between people, the inscrutability of other ways of life, and the ever-present potential for racial and cultural conflict. When the moral vision of civilization was challenged, when it produced consequences that do not fit neatly into its singular vision of progress, the error was understood to lie less with structure of imperial power than in the nature of colonized societies themselves. Resistance, especially political resistance, when refracted through the imperial lens, was interpreted as a deep-seated cultural intransigence to universal norms of civilization. The ways in which liberal confidence and capaciousness could slide into moral disavowal, disillusionment, and an unforgiving stance towards others, I would argue, reveals an instability internal to the structure of imperial ideology. And the oscillation between universalist justifications and culturalist alibis, between viewing colonized societies as either amenable or resistant to transformation, may prove to be a necessary and general feature of the political logic of empire.

Mill's views on empire, especially in recent times, have attracted a great deal of scholarly attention (Sullivan 1983; Zastoupil 1994; P. Mehta 1996; Habibi 1999; U. Mehta 1999; Pitts 2005; Schultz and Varouxakis 2005). Two conundrums continue to animate interpretations of Mill's justification of empire. The first pertains to a more general concern with how Mill's liberalism, his defense of liberty and representative government, can be reconciled with his arguments for the necessity of imperial rule over non-European peoples, especially with respect to British rule in India. Rather than seeing these positions as anomalous, commentators instead have emphasized the ways in which Mill's views of empire were fundamentally consistent with his larger moral, philosophical, and theoretical commitments. Mill's conceptualization of and investment in hierarchical conceptions of civilization and progress, in particular, have been singled out as the theoretical terrain upon which Mill simultaneously enunciated his ideals of liberal democracy at home as well as justified forms of imperial despotism abroad. If the justification of empire was in large part compatible with the theoretical core of Mill's liberalism, this consistency raises a number of important and pressing questions about the nature and potential limits of liberal political theory (Parekh 1994; Mehta 1999; Pitts 2005).

The second related conundrum focuses more narrowly on how to make sense of the totality of Mill's political positions on different facets of imperial policy. Evaluations of Mill's views of empire can be remarkably different depending on whether one lays emphasis on his positions on slavery and abolition, the situation in Ireland, and the Eyre controversy in Jamaica or on his views of non-European societies and his defense of East India Company rule in India (Miller 2005; Varouxakis 2005). Concentrating on the former often reveals a more principled, progressive Mill, more in line with the received view of his overall politics and political theory. By contrast, focusing on Mill's work as a Company servant and his vision of world divided between civilized and barbarian peoples produce an altogether more parochial Mill. Both aspects of Mill's work, however, were tied together by a set of core ideas about the purpose of imperial rule and ethics of empire. This is not to downplay the differences between Mill's view on India and Ireland. Rather, what rendered Mill's positions on Eyre and Ireland admirable is the way in which they stood out against a changing political climate that was increasingly turning against such ethical discourses. And to make sense of these "two Mills" requires an attention to the nature of that shift as one that can be understood from within the theoretical fissures of the liberal project itself. In others words, Mill's articulation of a liberal defense of empire was in a sense both the apotheosis and denouement of the project of liberal imperialism. As the political critique of liberal imperialism gained ground, what became clear was that the theoretical tensions and instabilities internal to Mill's formulation itself could be usefully exploited to undermine and eclipse the ethical core of his arguments. In this regard, Mill stands as a crucial transitional figure in the transformation of imperial ideology from a "universalist" to a "culturalist" stance by the end of the nineteenth century.

In this sense, whereas many interpreters and critics of Mill have importantly investigated the relationship between Mill's liberalism and his defense of empire, I am here more interested in the instabilities inherent in his account of legitimate imperial rule itself. Mill's account of the grounds of liberal empire attempted to conjoin an ethical discourse of improvement towards self-government and with a philosophy of history which, at the same time, revealed the precarious and slow nature of progress towards civilization. The distance between these two aspects, that is, the gap between the theoretical commitment to improvement and the practical account of the limitations to progress in barbarous societies, would be exploited by critics of liberal empire to both sever the link between empire and duty of reform as well as to insist on the radical difference between civilized and barbarian societies as the permanent ground of imperial rule. In this way, Mill's particular characterization of civilized and barbarian societies which undergirded his justification of empire was itself complicit in shifting the burden of imperial legitimation (and responsibility) onto colonized societies themselves. Thus, the ambiguity I hope to highlight is less about an inherent tension within liberalism per se but rather something more specific about the kinds of theoretical and political conundrums that transformative, universalist discourses of empire necessarily encounter.

II

Mill's most famous formulation of his justification of empire appeared in the introduction to *On Liberty* (to be repeated in similar terms in *Considerations on Representative Government* two years later): "[d]espotism is a legitimate mode of government in dealing with barbarians, provided the end be their improvement, and the means justified by actually effecting that end" (*On Liberty*, CW XVIII, 224).[1] In emphasizing "improvement" as the legitimate goal of imperial rule, Mill's account rendered the foundations of empire ethical in a specific sense. Since the assumption of British rule in India, there existed amongst leading commentators such as Edmund Burke and James Mill a common attempt to frame these debates in ethical terms, specifically in terms of a higher moral standard of duty and responsibility concomitant to the status of the ruling power as a free, civilized people. Similarly, for the younger Mill, however difficult it was to attain such an ideal,

> unless some approach to it is, the rulers are guilty of a dereliction of the highest moral trust which can devolve upon a nation: and if they do not even aim at it, they are selfish usurpers, on par in criminality with any of those whose ambition and rapacity have sported from age to age with the destiny of masses of mankind. (*Considerations on Representative Government*, CW XIX, 567–8)

Building on the work of an earlier generation of liberal imperial reformers, including that of his father, Mill understood the ethical horizon of empire to be bounded specifically by a liberal educative or reform project, a civilizing mission in which subject societies would be reshaped along modern (English) models, which included incremental training towards self-government. Not only would arguments for imperial rule in terms of augmenting domestic prestige or wealth be, in principle, unjust, in orienting the project of empire towards the future telos of civilization and eventual self-government, liberal imperialism was also premised on the disavowal of conquest and force as legitimate sources of imperial authority. In the arguments of Burke, James Mill, and Charles Grant, for example, this link between the morality of empire and the critique of conquest was elaborated most often in critical portrayals of early Company rule as resting on a nexus of criminal acts. Indeed, many argued for a liberal framework of imperial rule precisely as a way to compensate and atone for the original injustice and resultant burdens of imperial conquest. For many early reformers, what was needed to overcome these precarious and illegitimate beginnings was "good government," that is, the creation of a form of rule that would work towards the improvement of the subject race, thereby intertwining the moral defense of empire with a platform of liberal reform.

---

[1] In *Considerations,* Mill writes, "This mode of government is as legitimate as any other if it is the one which in the existing state of civilization of the subject people most facilitates their transition to a higher stage of improvement," 415 (CW XIX: 567).

Although the centrality of the idiom of improvement importantly tied Mill's views to the ethical horizon of an older discourse of empire, there were, however, important modifications in Mill's own articulation that distanced his position from these earlier variants. Indeed, the idea of improvement, or progress, was an even more fundamental feature of Mill's political philosophy and one that profoundly shaped his theories of liberty and representative government. For Mill, utility as a principle of evaluation must be understood in "the largest sense, grounded on the permanent interests of man as progressive being" (*On Liberty*, CW XVIII: 224). Likewise, a good government worked to improve the character of its subjects, that is, to create the proper conditions to support progressive improvement. This theory of government entailed a intensely reciprocal relationship between political institutions and the character of a people: not only is the institutional competence of a government dependent on the right character of its subjects – their virtues and intelligence – but, more important, the institutions themselves had to be so modified as to suit the specific demands that peoples in various "states of society" and "stages of civilization" required for progressive improvement (*Considerations*, CW XIX, chaps. 1–3).

Mill's account of his theoretical advance over Bentham's theory of motivation also emphasized his more detailed attention to ways in which government served as the one of the great means of forming national character, "of carrying forward the members of a community towards perfection or preserving them from degeneracy" ("Remarks on Bentham's Philosophy," CW X: 10). One of Bentham's blind spots, according to Mill, was that

it never seems to have occurred to him to regard political institutions in a higher light, as the principle means of the social education of a people. Had he done so, he would have seen that the same institutions will no more suit two nations in different stages of civilization, than the same lessons will suit two children of different ages. (CW X: 10)

Thus, the central error of Bentham's theory of government was its austere universalism, its tendency to assume "that mankind are alike in all times and all places," (CW X: 10) an error that Mill thought was common to the political theories "of the last age . . . in which it was customary to claim representative democracy for England and France by arguments which would equally have proved it the only fit form of government for Bedouins or Malays." For Mill, what marked "the main point of superiority in the political theories of the present" was the recognition of an important and fundamental truth, that governing "institutions need to be radically different, according to the stage of advancement already reached" (*Considerations*, CW XIX: 393–4).

Mill's insistence that governing practices and institutions demanded radical alterations depending on the virtues and intelligence of its people, or in his terms the "state of society" or "stage of civilization," was of paramount importance to his defense of imperial despotism.[2] Indeed, in Mill's framework, the specific contrast between civilized and "backward states of society" was crucial in justifying the exclusion of savage, barbarous, and semi-barbarous peoples from the norms of liberty and self-government. For Mill, liberty was not an unqualified benefit in all times and for all peoples and specifically did not apply to "any state of things anterior to the time when mankind have become capable of being improved by free and equal discussion" (*On Liberty*, CW XVIII: 224).

What, then, made despotism, rather than free institutions, more appropriate for savage or barbarous societies? Mill's accounts of the various historical stages of civilization, and the sociological and psychological portraits attached to them, were never carefully elaborated. Although Mill's characterizations were at times loosely reminiscent of the four-stage theory formulated by the Scottish theorists of the previous century, his portraits not only lacked their precision but also were motivated by very different concerns. Unlike his predecessors, Mill rarely linked the terms of "savage" and "barbarian" with specific social structures, property relations, or modes of subsistence (Haakonsen 1996; Pitts 2005). Rather, the portraits themselves were more psychologically or behaviorally oriented, which, when taken in sequence, yielded a precarious, developmental logic that swung between the twin poles of excessive liberty and extreme slavery. Thus savage/barbarian societies were construed as too independent, lacking the ability to obey, whereas barbarian/stationary societies (and formers slaves) were seen as suffering from dependence on custom and therefore lacking the instincts for self-government and spontaneity.

In an early essay titled "Civilization," Mill distinguished most straightforwardly the central features of savage/barbarian society, and thus obliquely

---

[2] It was also one of the central lessons he had learnt from James Mill's *History of British India* in which the elder Mill argued, "[n]o scheme of government can happily conduce to the end of government, unless it is adapted to the state of the people for whose use it is intended.... If the mistake in regard to Hindu society, committed by the British nation, and the British government, be very great, if they have conceived the Hindus to be a people of high civilization, while they in reality made but a few of the earliest steps in the progress to civilization, it is impossible that in many of the measures pursued for the government of that people, the mark aimed at should not have been wrong." In James Mill, *The History of British India* (New Delhi: 1990), I, 456.

delineated the substantive preconditions for the exercise of liberty. Mill outlined the main features of civilized life as the "direct converse or contrary of rudeness or barbarism." He wrote,

a savage tribe consists of a handful of individuals, wandering or thinly scattered over a vast tract of country: a dense population, therefore, dwelling in fixed habitations, and largely collected in towns and villages, we term civilized. In savage life there is no commerce, no manufactures, no agriculture: a country rich in the fruits of agriculture: commerce, and manufactures, we call civilized. . . . Wherever, therefore, we find human beings acting together for common purposes in large bodies, and enjoying the pleasures of social intercourse, we term them civilized. (CW XVIII: 120)

In moving from the sociological to the psychological traits of both forms of social life, Mill deduced what he saw as the fundamental feature of civilized life, namely, the power of co-operation. For Mill, what makes the life of the savage materially poor and fragile is his inability to compromise, to sacrifice "some portion of individual will, for a common purpose" (CW VIII: 122). The savage was pure ego, a selfish will that did not know how to calculate beyond *immediate* impulses. This portrait would reappear in later writings as one of the principle reasons for why barbarous societies fall outside the community of nations and norms of international law. As Mill wrote,

the rules of ordinary international morality imply reciprocity. But barbarians will not reciprocate. They cannot be depended on for observing any rules. Their minds are not capable of so great an effort, nor their will sufficiently under the influence of distant motives. ("A Few Words on Non-Intervention," CW XXI: 119)

Thus a savage or barbarous society, unable to either suppress immediate instincts or conceptualize long-term interests were thus fundamentally incapable of the organization and discipline necessary for the development of the division of labor, for commerce and manufacture, and for military achievement – in short, for civilization. In such a state, according to Mill, a "vigorous despotism" would be the form of government ideally suited to teach the lesson of obedience (*Considerations*, CW XIX: 394, 567). Moreover, discipline, or "perfect co-operation" – the central attribute of civilized society – was also deemed something that could only be learnt incrementally through practice and thus this training in obedience required a vast length of time, perhaps even centuries, to render discipline an unconscious habit.

Although the lesson of obedience was the first and necessary condition for government, and the indispensable step towards future improvement and civilization, for Mill, it was also only a partial advance and one that could easily solidify into an unwieldy form of societal stagnation. Even previously progressive societies, such as the civilizations of Egypt, India, and China fell prey to this kind of immobility, where "the springs of spontaneity" and individuality are emasculated in the vast "despotism of Custom" (*On Liberty*, CW XVIII: 272; *Considerations*, CW XIX: 567). In this case, however, the governmental form most appropriate to break the bonds of unquestioned obedience was less clear. An ordinary, native despotism would only teach a lesson "only too completely learnt" (*Considerations*, CW XIX: 567) and thus the solution must be sought in either the extraordinary appearance of a good despot, in "an Akbar or a Charlemagne, if they are so fortunate to find one" (*On Liberty*, CW XVIII: 224) or under the tutelary despotism of an advanced people, who through guidance rather than force can "superinduce from without" the improvement a stationary or slavish people cannot muster themselves (*Considerations*, CW XIX: 395). Moreover, in the age of empire, Mill noted, it was becoming "the universal condition of the more backward populations to be held in direct subjection by the more advanced" (CW XIX: 568). Fortunately, an advanced, civilized people, was able, in principle, to provide a constant supply of good despots and could thus counteract the potential evils of imperial subjection. For an advanced people, having already treaded the path of civilization, had the knowledge and foresight to provide a form of government conducive to "future permanent improvement" (CW XIX: 568).

Mill never specified in great detail what kinds of policies would educate a subject population towards greater individuality. Even in his defense of the East India Company and the superiority of rule through an apolitical and expert bureaucracy, Mill rather offered a predominately institutionalist account of the appropriate mechanisms of imperial governance (CW XIX: 568–77). Mill then compounded his somewhat indistinct prescriptions for improvement in societies yoked to the sway of custom by insisting that the threat of stagnation and appeal of custom affected even the most advanced societies. In *On Liberty*, Mill describes the precarious dynamic between custom and individuality, between the love of liberty and tendency towards (mental) slavery, which had hitherto shaped human history, as a permanent condition of even the most progressive states of societies. In doing so, Mill's analysis raises the theoretical question of why the expansion of the sphere of liberty, the promotion of free institutions, and the relaxation of governmental authority as mechanisms of improvement – that is, liberal institutions – were not considered equally applicable to both advanced and stationary societies.

III

Mill's reliance on the historical contrast between barbarism and civilization as the central pivot of his defense of imperial despotism, coupled with the ambiguities in his specific characterization of the stages and dynamics of civilization, exposed a number of internal tensions in Mill's theoretical project, tensions which provided critics the resources for questioning the viability of the project of liberal imperialism itself. In Mill's theoretical framework, the temporal contrast between the civilized and the barbarian functioned to exclude the latter from the benefits of liberty and self-government as well as an equal status in the community of nations. As Mill writes in the introduction to *On Liberty,* the doctrine of liberty

> is meant to apply only to human beings in the maturity of their faculties. We are not speaking of children, or of young persons below the age at which the state may fix as that of manhood or womanhood. Those who are still in a state to require being taken care of by others, must be protected against their own actions as well as against external injury. For the same reason, we may leave out of consideration those backward states of society in which the race itself may be considered as in its nonage. (*On Liberty,* CW XVIII: 224)

Conceptually, Mill's recurrent analogy between the immaturity of children and the immaturity of barbarous societies reveals a characteristic vulnerability of liberal universalism. The political exclusion of children is a consistent and thorny issue for liberal political theory for it implies what Uday Mehta names a disjuncture or gap between the foundations and actualization of liberal universalism (Mehta 1999, 46–77). For Mehta, universalism in liberalism is derived from a minimalist philosophical anthropology, that is, from the articulation of a minimum set of characteristics and capacities taken to be common to all humans. In the liberal tradition, these common, universal, characteristics are often construed as natural freedom, moral equality, and the inbuilt capacity to reason. The political actualization of these universalist premises – for example, to be included in the political constituency of the Lockean social contract or to be capable of permanent improvement in the Millian sense – is nevertheless mediated by the real capacity of potential citizens to properly exercise their reason. This capacity, which Mill calls intellectual maturity, turns out to be empirically conditioned, and thus not-quite or not-yet universal. In this sense, the paradox of the child born free but not-yet-able to practice liberty is thus particularly revealing of how "behind the universal capacities ascribed [by liberalism] to all human beings exist a thicker set of social credentials that constitute the real bases of political inclusion" (Mehta 1999, 49). Mill projects the paradox of the child onto a scale of civilization and in so doing expands and heightens, in cultural and historical terms, the requirements for political inclusion.

In moving away from Bentham's strict universalism, Mill had already committed himself to a more diversified account of character, one more thoroughly conditioned by custom and society. By tightly binding the benefits of liberty and representative government to civilizational development, Mill further circumscribes the possibility of political liberty with the imperatives of culture and history. In limiting the applicability of liberalism in this manner, Mill's ethical justification of empire itself displaces the burden of legitimation onto to the terrain of empirical (cultural and historical) arguments about the nature of subject populations. If the question of how imperial rule ought to be structured is thus subordinated to a primary and prior question about colonized societies themselves, the responsibility for the imperial project becomes inextricably tied to questions about the empirical and theoretical possibility of progress in these societies.

Although Mill's theory of civilization in principle was premised on the inherent potential of all peoples to improve, in his substantive characterization of savage and barbarous states of society, Mill emphasized both the unpredictable, arduous development of civilization, everywhere threatened by potential degeneracy and stagnation, and the potentially limitless time-horizon needed for such advancement. Furthermore, Mill characterizes the process of civilization – this training that is the condition of possibility for progress – not only in terms of an incremental process of learning but also one that is collective in nature. In doing so, Mill exposed a deep theoretical tension between the commitment to liberal reform and improvement and the practical impediments for the realization of the progressive transformation of peoples. Thus, the sharp contrast between barbarism and civilization, when grounded in this particular philosophy of history, appeared more and more like a permanent barrier.

In his interest in character formation and improvement as the principle end of governance, Mill emphasizes the ways in individual character is dependent on and shaped by national character. Indeed, understanding the precise and formative interplay between individual and national character was to be the great theme of his proposed science of "ethology" (*Science of Logic,* CW VIII: 860–74). Although some consider Mill's concern with the diverse forms of national character and his reference to pyschologized portraits of the differences between, for example, Celtic, Anglo-Saxon, and Asiatic characters – and we could add, the savage and the barbarous mind – to be signs of an underlying racism, it is clear that Mill never thought of character as biological determined. Rather, Mill emphasizes the extraordinary variety of character within similar states of society and its malleability, impairment, and perfectibility over time. In his famous reply to Carlyle's racialized provocations, Mill was clear that any analytical investigation into "laws of the formation of character" would correct "the vulgar error of imputing every difference which he finds among human beings to an original difference of nature" ("The Negro Question," CW XXI: 93). At the same time, however, Mill also insisted that the improvement of character, especially "spontaneous" or internally generated improvement was "one of the rarest phenomena in history" and depended on an extraordinary concatenation of accidents and advantages.

But if Mill's concept of character was not a racial one, when conjoined with an emphasis on the group as the bearer of civilizational improvement, it functioned as an analogue of race as a principle of sociological and anthropological explanation. In other words, although Mill objected to racial theories of human diversity, his theory of character formation was meant in part to explain and account for these same, entrenched differences in collective terms. Furthermore, in Mill's reflections on the principle of nationality, collectivities – specifically, the nation – were endowed with a moral character. For Mill, the nation was not only the site for "the growth and development of a people," it was itself a form of cultural achievement, equivalent in normative status to civilization. Thus, barbarian societies were not true nations, indeed for them "nationality and independence are either a certain evil, or at best a questionable good ("Non-Intervention," CW XXI: 119). Nationality not only functioned as the means of justifying the exclusion of barbarous societies from norms of international law; more important, it revealed the extent to which, for Mill, civilization and barbarism were only ever features of collectivities.

With the focus on the collective nature of learning and cultivation, Mill's theory of civilization here (as well as Mill's proposed science of ethnology) anticipates the anthropological theory of culture, which also emphasizes the cultural and historical determination of behavior in the context of ongoing processes of social integration and collective learning. In Mill's characterization of civilization as both precarious and collective in nature, then, we begin to see the turn to culture as a mode of differentiation emerging from within the trajectory of liberal imperialism itself. Mill's ascription of collective characteristics to societies and peoples poses a number of specific challenges to the discourse of liberal empire. On one hand, it sharpens the contrast between civilization and barbarism in a such a way as to make the eventual transition from the one state to the other seem exceedingly difficult, if not impossible. Moreover, obstacles to improvement, or indeed failures in achieving this transformation, are effectively re-described as cultural impediments or cultural resistance to the norms and institutions of civilization. The emphasis on the group as the bearer of improvement thus also marks subject societies as the displaced site of imperial legitimation, as collectively responsible for the necessity of imperial rule.

A number of these tensions in Mill's portrait of civilization made the liberal project of empire vulnerable to critics who increasingly sought to emphasize the theoretical and practical obstacles to improvement. In Mill's work, the basic commitment to an idea of human nature as malleable and infinitely perfectible had seemingly lost its purchase when linked to a philosophy of history and a theory of character formation that at the same time emphasized the precarious and incremental development of progressive societies in human history. Critics would emphasize the latter aspect over the former, concluding either that models of perfectibility needed to be abandoned or that moral reform required a great deal more coercion than liberals could countenance. And as the modernizing transformation of native peoples was deemed suspect in this manner, which was increasingly the case in the late nineteenth century, empire quickly lost its most salient ethical justification.

IV

These criticisms revealingly came to the fore in the most prominent public debates on empire in late nineteenth century. In key imperial scandals – for example, the Indian Mutiny of 1857, the Governor Eyre controversy of 1865, and the Ilbert Bill crises of the 1883 – the theoretical fissures in the edifice of liberal justifications of empire would be effectively exploited by opponents to undermine liberal positions. Here, I begin with the Eyre controversy, not least because John Stuart Mill himself played a prominent role in this public debate. Moreover, the anxieties about race, colonial violence, and domestic unrest which infused the debate pointedly and dramatically exposed the tenuous nature of liberal confidence in its civilizing agenda.

The public controversy began in 1865 upon news from Jamaica of a "rebellion" in Morant Bay and its suppression by the then Governor of Jamaica, Edward John Eyre (Dutton 1967; Semmel 1976; Holt 1992; Hall 2002). As reports of the extent and brutal nature of the rebellion's suppression came to light, Mill (now a Liberal MP for Westminster) joined the Jamaica committee, which was formed initially to lobby the government for an official inquiry, and then (when it was clear that the government would do no more that dismiss Eyre from his post) to bring criminal charges against Eyre and his deputies. As the Jamaica committee's chair and leading spokesman, Mill made the case for Eyre's criminal prosecution on the grounds that Eyre's abuse of martial law, most egregiously in the military trial and execution of George William Gordon (a well-known mixed-race MP in the Jamaican assembly), was akin to state-sponsored murder. This amounted to a frontal assault on the rule of law itself, which for Mill was a principle that necessarily reached across the empire, for it was the duty of advanced, ruling countries to impart this "first necessity of human society" to subject races. If Eyre's actions were excused as the regrettable but understandable excesses of power endemic to the colonial situation (which was the basic gist of the Royal Inquiry into his actions), the liberal imperialist model of benevolent despotism that Mill thought was genuinely possible would be radically undermined. This possibility no doubt fueled Mill's vehement commitment to Eyre's prosecution, which after three years, came to nothing (Pitts 2005, 150–60).

Indeed, the vocal public campaign proved to be, in important respects, counterproductive. For the long campaign to publicize Eyre's abuses galvanized an even stronger opposition to the civilizing ideals of liberal imperialism. The widespread opposition to the prosecution of Eyre was, to say the least, multifaceted. As Stefan Collini writes, "this was one of those great moral earthquakes of Victorian public life whose fault lines are so revealing of the subterranean affinities and antipathies of the educated classes" (Collini 1984, xxvi). Prominent members of the Jamaica committee included Charles Darwin, Herbert Spencer, T. H. Huxley, Charles Lyell, and T. H. Green. On the other side, vocal supporters of Eyre included Thomas Carlyle, John Ruskin, A. L. Tennyson, Charles Dickens, and Matthew Arnold. On the one hand, the sharp polarization between the supporters and critics of Eyre intersected with and intimated the growing divide between the proponents and critics of liberal democracy. The Eyre controversy coincided with the public agitation and debate about the Reform Bill, and fear of unrest in the empire was necessarily intertwined with anxieties about the growth of popular government and mass democracy. The public support for Eyre revealed an increasingly unsympathetic view of subject peoples, for the Morant Bay rebellion, coming on the heals of the Indian Mutiny/Rebellion of 1857, signaled for many an ingratitude on the part of Jamaicans and Indians for the emancipatory and civilizing character of colonial rule. The fact of rebellion itself also seemed to call into question both the possibility and the practicality of an agenda of liberal reform in the colonies. The reform and improvement of native customs and morals seemed not only to be limited in effect but also potentially dangerous to the stability of empire. Thus, the reactions to the events of Morant Bay, like responses to the Indian Rebellion, were marked by hardening of racial attitudes and a distancing away from the universalist and assimilationist ideals of liberal imperialism.

Like the public debates unleashed by the Governor Eyre controversy, the Ilbert Bill crisis (1883) also exemplified and exposed important paradoxes in liberal justifications of empire. But whereas the Eyre controversy was instigated by the dramatic display of colonial violence which at times shaped the tenor of the debate, the Ilbert Bill crisis was peaked by a relatively minor piece of colonial legislation. In 1883, Courtney Ilbert, as Law Member of the Viceroy's Council, introduced a seemingly innocuous amendment to the Indian Criminal Procedure Code, extending the right to try cases involving Europeans to certain classes of native magistrates in rural districts (Hirschmann 1980; Dasgupta 1995; Sinha 1995). But in attempting to remove this minor "anomaly" to procedural universality, Ilbert unknowingly instigated widespread protest among the non-official British population in India and, thus, propelled the Government of India into a general crisis. For those British Indians, the bill's attempt to equalize the authority of British and native judges also implicitly advocated a philosophy of reform that sought to undermine any special rights, privileges, and protections that the British settlers now enjoyed. In doing so, the bill was clearly grounded in a basic commitment and belief in the equality between Indians and Britons, a principle that most British Indians of the time were loathe to admit. In the face of such widespread opposition, the bill in its original form could not pass the Legislative Council, and instead a watered down version of the bill was finally passed after two years of intense criticism.[3]

As criticism of the bill mounted in both Britain and India, it became increasingly clear that what was at stake was less the status of British Indians per se than the very grounds of a liberal philosophy of British rule in India. Lord Ripon, the Liberal Viceroy appointed by Gladstone and under whose watch the bill was introduced, articulated in the clearest of terms the "great question" that was now so openly debated. The question, according to Ripon, was not about the particular provisions supported by the bill,

but the principles upon which India is to be governed. Is she to be ruled for the benefit of the Indian people of all races, classes, and creeds, or in the sole interest of a small body of Europeans? Is it England's duty to try to elevate the Indian people,

---

[3] When it was clear that the bill in its original form would not pass, a compromise version was adopted in 1884. This bill allowed European settlers in the rural districts to appeal for jury trials (comprising Europeans) to compensate for their acceptance of the jurisdiction of native judges.

to raise them socially, to train them politically, to promote their progress in material prosperity, in education, and in morality; or is it to be the be all and end all of her rule to maintain a precarious power over what Mr. Branson[4] calls "a subject race with a profound hatred of their subjugators"? (Hirschmann 1980, 70)

Ripon thus articulated and defended the basic premises of a liberal justification of empire, one in which the purpose of imperial government must be the moral education and betterment of the subject people, rather than the benefit of the home country or some faction therein. In practical terms, the aim of the Government of India would be the timely introduction of and expansion of liberal principles in the central institutions of education, law, and government. For British and native supporters of the Ilbert Bill, the bill represented precisely the logical fruition of the liberal agenda, for it was due to the success of these policies that native judges qualified for promotion existed at all. The vehement contestation of the principle of legal equality that was at stake in the Ilbert Bill thus struck the very core of the transformative and educative project of liberal imperialism.

The most eminent spokesman for the opposition was James Fitzjames Stephen, who had also briefly served as Law Member of the Viceroy's Council under Lord Mayo. Stephen not only opposed the adoption of a similar bill under his tenure but, in the midst of the current crisis, published a provocative letter in the *Times* warning that the passage of such a bill would undermine the very foundations of British rule. As Stephen wrote,

[i]t has been observed that if the Government of India have decided on removing all anomalies from India, they ought to remove themselves and their countrymen. Whether or not that mode of expression can be fully justified, there can, I think, be no doubt that it is impossible to imagine any policy more fearfully dangerous and more certain in case of failure to lead to results to which the Mutiny would be child's play, than the policy of shifting the foundations on which the British government of India rests. It is essentially an absolute government, founded, not on consent, but on conquest. It does not represent the native principles of life or of government, and it can never do so until it represents heathenism and barbarism. It represents a belligerent civilization, and no anomaly can be so striking and so dangerous as its administration by men who, being at the head of a Government founded on conquest, implying at every point the superiority of the conquering race, of their ideas, their institutions, their opinions and their principles, and having no justification for its existence except that superiority, shrink from the open, uncompromising,

---

[4] Branson was one of most vocal opponents of the bill. In fact, his inflammatory speeches against the bill did much not only to fan the flames of settler rebellion but in polarizing the debate along racial lines, his speeches also instigated and emboldened a coordinated native opposition (one that eventually led to the creation of the Indian National Congress). See Hirschmann 1980.

straightforward assertion of it, seek to apologize for their own position, and refuse, from whatever cause, to uphold and support it. (Stephen 1883a, 8)

The corollary to the unabashed assertion of superiority, for Stephen, was unapologetic authoritarian rule in the colonies. For Stephen, liberal imperialists – and here his chief target was Mill – had confused good government with representative government and, in doing so, assumed that absolute or authoritarian government could only be justified "as a temporary expedient used for the purpose of superseding itself, and as a means of educating those whom it affects into a fitness for parliamentary institutions" (Stephen 1883b, 551). But, for Stephen, absolute government was not the same as arbitrary or despotic rule, and for the purpose of promoting the welfare of native subjects, it had "its own merits and conveniences."

Despite brashness of his rhetoric, Stephen was not merely a jingoistic defender of empire.[5] Stephen thought of himself as defending a more robust and consistent utilitarian liberalism, and indeed his argument for vigorous authoritarianism in India differed little from Mill's pronouncements on the need to inculcate habits of discipline in barbarous societies. Stephen's argument for absolute rule as form of legitimate and good government was premised on a theoretical account of the necessity of coercion as a mechanism for the improvement of native society. For Stephen, the most important mechanism, in this regard, was the implementation of a sound system of laws based on English principles that would induce peace and security and thereby effect a change in moral and religious practices. Without law and order, which was Britain's great export, India would dissolve into the chaos and anarchy in which it was found. For Stephen, coercion was a necessity for Britain's "great and characteristic task is that of imposing on India ways of life and modes of thought which the population regards, to say the least, without sympathy" (Stephen 1883b, 558).

This minimal commitment to substitute English civilization for Indian barbarism, however, was not conceived of as a moral duty, less still as a kind of atonement or apology for the sins of conquest. Rather, it was a sign of and the means by which to express England's virtue, honor, and superiority. As

---

[5] Whereas Eric Stokes considered Stephen's authoritarianism to be closed tied to the general trajectory of utilitarian thinking on India, I would argue that his justification of empire deviates quite sharply from the ethical horizon of the early utilitarian interest in and engagement with India. Two aspects of this ethical horizon which Stephen consciously distances himself from was (a) eventual self-government as the end of empire and (b) the critique of conquest. See Stokes 1959.

such it was in principle a permanent and not temporary enterprise (as Mill and the liberal imperialist camp proposed) and ought to be justified as such. Stephen straightforwardly criticized the view of empire as resting upon "a moral duty on the part of the English nation to try to educate the natives in such a way as to lead them to set up a democratic form government administered by representative institutions" (Stephen 1883b, 561). And it was here that Stephen veered away from Mill's imperial arguments, indeed he dramatically inverted them. By exploited Mill's tenuous distinction between civilized and barbarian societies, Stephen would argue that not only was self-government unfit for India, it was only a qualified benefit for England itself.

According to Stephen, it was his "Indian experience" which confirmed his belief in the dangers of "sentimental" liberalism of the Millian kind for both England and her empire. *Liberty, Fraternity, Equality,* Stephen's famous polemic against Mill, written furiously on his return voyage from India, was a wholesale attack on the philosophical basis and political and social consequences of Mill's moral commitment to the idea of liberty, as it was enunciated in *On Liberty*. For Stephen, Mill's proposition that self-protection could be the only grounds for coercion or compulsion was unsustainable and illustrative of a deeper set of commitments which Stephen found to be both philosophically untenable and practically objectionable. On one hand, Mill's attempt to delineate a sphere of free action, for Stephen, revealed Mill's illegitimate prioritizing of the principle of liberty over that of utility, revealing an absolute and independent commitment to the value of liberty. For Stephen, valuing liberty in this private, individual sense was as amoral as it was incoherent, for it undermined law as well as all systems of morality and religion. Indeed, for Stephen, what Mill claimed to be the practical effects of liberty in history – that is, the expansion of freedom of speech and discussion and the concomitant shift from compulsion to persuasion as the vehicle of moral improvement – was a misreading of the actual source of moral progress, namely, moral and legal coercion.

For Stephen, the benevolent despotism of imperial rule proved emphatically that liberty was not a necessity for the purpose of good government. For Stephen, man was not by nature a progressive being, but one who was at heart selfish and unruly and therefore needed to be continuously compelled to live peaceably and morally in society. Thus, Mill's tenuous distinction between civilized and barbarous societies could be reversed: what was deemed appropriate for barbarians was equally suitable for civilized society (or at least certain classes therein). Here is a characteristic passage of

Stephen's that turns on the inversion of Mill's distinction between barbarism and civilization;

[y]ou admit that children and human beings in "backward states of society" may be coerced for their own good. You would let Charlemagne coerce the Saxons, and Akbar the Hindoos. Why then may not educated men coerce the ignorant? What is there in the character of a very commonplace ignorant peasant or petty shopkeeper in these days which makes him a less fit subject for coercion on Mr. Mill's principle than the Hindoo nobles and princes who were coerced by Akbar? (Stephen [1873] 1991, 68–9)

Stephen pointedly questioned Mill's attribution of the status of civilization and barbarism only to societies and not to individuals therein. And if the collective nature of the classification of stages of civilization was undermined, for Stephen, the principles of imperial government, as a model of for moral and legal coercion, could no longer be held off at the water's edge; they could indeed be equally well suited for a rapidly democratizing Britain. As Stephen writes, "[i]t seems to me quite impossible to stop short of this principle if compulsion in the case of children and 'backward' races is admitted to be justifiable; for, after all, maturity and civilization are matters of degree" (Stephen 1991, 69).

Stephen's arguments exemplify the ways in which debates about empire often reflected and helped to consolidate a growing illiberal or anti-liberal consensus, specifically fueled by domestic anxieties about the growth of mass democracy. The divisions intimated in the Eyre controversy would peak with the debate on Irish Home Rule (1886), and the abandonment of the Liberal Party by its more conservative members. But although the conservative critique of mass democracy in the end did not stem the tide towards universal suffrage in Britain, this illiberal turn had distinct and enduring effects in the transformation of imperial policy.

V

Stephen's critique of the aims and premises of liberal imperialism served to retain the underlying model of despotic rule elaborated by Mill, now severed from its ethical horizons. No longer justified as a temporary mechanism for improvement towards eventual self-government, empire became a permanent enterprise. The collapse of liberal imperialism thus signaled the eclipse of ethical discourses of empire and the concomitant shift in the language of justification towards more straightforwardly realist and pragmatic claims for legitimacy. At the level of ideologies of rule – that is, in terms of imperial governing practices and policies on the ground – the transition itself, however, was deeper and with broad-ranging consequences. For it was in this sphere that the universalist premises of the liberal idiom of improvement gave way to culturalist arguments about the permanent and intractable differences between peoples (see Mantena, forthcoming).

In turning to the decline of liberal ideologies of imperial rule, the focus of inquiry inevitably turns to the history of British India. For British rule in India not only represented the longest instance of a dependency under continuous foreign rule, but India also proved to be a testing ground for models of rule which were to become, in the period of high empire, transportable in many key respects. In British India, the central crisis which precipitated the shift away from liberal models of rule was the so-called Indian Mutiny of 1857. In response to the rebellion, the Crown assumed direct responsibility over the East India Company's former Indian territories. And in its first official act, it explicitly put forth a doctrine of non-intervention as the directive principle of British rule:

[w]e declare it to be our royal will and pleasure that none be in anywise favoured, none molested or disquieted, by reason of their religious faith or observances, but that all shall alike enjoy the equal and impartial protection of the law; and we do strictly charge to enjoin all those who may be in authority under us that they abstain from all interference with the religious belief or worship of any of our subjects on pain of our highest displeasure. (Philips, et al. 1962, 11)

Moreover, it was determined "that generally, in framing and administration of law, due regard be paid to the ancient rights, usages and customs of India." For many contemporary observers, the outbreak of rebellion was a glaring sign of the failure of liberal reform to either transform native habits and customs or lend security to the imperial enterprise. The non-interference principle thus expressed both the difficulty of reforming the native and, indeed, the political danger that attempts at transformation could entail.

In one sense, political rebellion in Jamaica and India provoked harsher and more racialized attitudes towards native populations; Indians and the ex-slave population of Jamaica were construed as acting from "inscrutable" motivations. In India, this inscrutability was attributed to deep-seated cultural and religious sentiments that seemed to be resistant to change and reform. In this sense, and this was particularly the case for India, resistance was read as a sign of the rigidity of native customs, beliefs, and institutions. In this context, the anthropological theory of culture, which was only implicit in Mill's view of civilization, came to the fore as the dominant framework through which to understand the nature of native society, the mechanisms that ensured its stability, and the impact of colonial rule on these institutions.

In attributing to native society a new kind of stability and intransigence to reform, anthropological and sociological accounts of native society would buttress methods of rule that sought to harness and incorporate these native energies to ensure order and stability. Unlike liberal ruling strategies which construed "traditional" social structures and customs, such as those relating to caste and certain religious formations, as impediments to the project of improvement and thus good and moral governance, the new ideologies of rule stressed the need for reconciliation with native institutions and structures of authority. In India, what began as a principle of non-intervention into native societies in the wake of 1857 had, by the turn of the century, metamorphosed into an array of arguments for the protection and rehabilitation of native institutions, culminating in its elaborate articulation in the theory and practice of "indirect rule" in colonial Africa.

In contrast to liberal ideologies of rule, the emergent imperial strategies were founded in a deep skepticism about the possibility that native society could be rapidly and radically transformed. The appeal to non-intervention imagined the native as stubbornly tied to customs and beliefs and hence resistant to reform, conversion, education – in short, civilization. In this sense, the rethinking occurring in the wake of 1857 not only radically reversed the main tenets of the liberal, civilizing mission of the colonial state, conceived of as a wholesale project of transformation of native society, it also rendered the native a slave to custom. As modes of justification became more tentative in their moral and political aspirations, late imperial ideologies of rule were presented less in ideological than pragmatic terms, as practical responses to and accommodations of the nature of "native society." Under this cover, social, cultural, and racial theories entered through the backdoor, as it were, to explain and legitimate the existence of empire; they functioned less as justifications than as alibis for the fait accompli of empire.

13

Making Sense of Liberal Imperialism

Stephen Holmes

Can a militarily irresistible foreign power help establish a lastingly democratic form of government in a country with no history of democracy?[1] That a powerful military can more easily oust a dictator than erect a democracy has been demonstrated, if it needed demonstrating, by the U.S. invasion of Iraq. But one misbegotten experiment should not be allowed to disgrace and discredit the very possibility of democracy promotion in a previously undemocratic country by a foreign and therefore, by definition, undemocratic power. That is why it may be worthwhile to reinterrogate John Stuart Mill. Did the greatest nineteenth-century theorist of social improvement and liberal democracy believe that foreign rulers could foist this particular forward step on what he called "backward populations" (CW XIX: 568)? Why would foreign powers try? Is it rational for them to undertake such a project? Can there be *too much democracy* from their point of view? What are the principal reasons why foreign democratizers may fail?

In his general discussions of democratization, whether homegrown or imposed, Mill tried to occupy a middle position between voluntarism and fatalism. Liberal democracy has specific preconditions and cannot be established, at the crack of a whip, anywhere anytime. On the other hand, originally absent but essential preconditions of liberal democracy can themselves, at least occasionally, be conjured, intentionally as well as inadvertently, out of existing raw materials. This is why Mill repudiates determinism, concluding emphatically that "institutions and forms of government *are* a matter of choice" (CW XIX: 380). What is true of forms of government in general is also true of liberal democracy.

---

[1] I employ the word "democracy" throughout, in accord with current usage, as a synonym for "representative government" in Mill's sense.

A species of tree may be unknown in a given geographic area and may not materialize there spontaneously. Nevertheless, if implanted by a wandering arborist, a nonindigenous tree may survive, flourish, and reproduce. Analogously, a country that has long lived under autocracy and has not sprouted democratic government spontaneously may, if democracy is implanted by itinerant democratizers, become enduringly democratic. This is roughly Mill's position. Societies and cultures are complex and malleable enough to support a variety of political institutions different from those that currently exist. Production technology, such as the cotton gin, is easier to transplant than interaction technology, such as banking law. But even production technology has "cultural" preconditions. Workers must possess the skills needed to make the machinery function properly. With time and training, indigenous workers can familiarize themselves with novel technology, imported from abroad, and hone the skills necessary to operate it successfully. Something similar is true about legal and political institutions. Citizens of one country can learn to "work" institutions borrowed from another country. Legacies of a society's past, according to Mill, are far from negligible. They can hinder and even derail political reform. But they also underdetermine present and future behavior: "People are more easily induced to do, and do more easily, what they are already used to; but people also learn to do things new to them" (CW XIX: 379). Human beings chronically underestimate their own capacity to adapt successfully to change. Students of human behavior, instructed by hindsight, should not commit the same mistake.

I

The theory of democracy presupposes the theory of the state, for democracy exists only in organized and delineated communities. For the same reason, the theory of democratization presupposes the theory of state building. It is pointless to gain influence over lawmaking if properly enacted laws are never obeyed. And it is impossible to defer to the will of the majority until we know who is and who is not a member of the community. Habits of obedience and determinations of membership are predemocratic conditions of democracy. So when and why do they emerge? Mill's unsettling answer points not to morally enlightened despotism but to power-maximizing despotism alone. To understand why a foreign conqueror might encourage democratization in a subject nation, we need to look first at why, according to Mill, a domestic despot might aspire to do so.

Suffice it to say, at this point, that Mill accepts the priority of the theory of the state to the theory of democracy and of the theory of state building to the theory of democratization. He consistently argues that the pathway from the state of nature to representative government runs through an intermediary phase of nondemocratic, perhaps even harsh and oppressive, autocracy. Despotic government is valuable to the extent that it contributes to an initial "training of the people" (CW XIX: 393). Human beings need to be softened up for democracy just as wild horses need to be broken before being harnessed to carriages and loosed on city streets. Nineteenth-century political theory is superior to its antecedents, Mill remarks, because it is keyed into political evolution. It recognizes that the liberal democracy that suits England and France is not a "fit form of government for Bedouins or Malays" (CW XIX: 394). Different communities inhabit different states or stages of development and culture. At the low end, we find "a condition very little above the highest of the beasts" (CW XIX: 394). Mill's idealized transitology traces the move from this prehistoric condition first to an intermediary stage and then to the higher stages of development, culminating in representative government of the British sort. The transition is effected, he argues, by "a concourse of influences, among the principal of which is the government" (CW XIX: 394), to which the peoples in question are subject. Another important influence, alongside political power (relations of command and obedience), is religion – to be discussed later. Religion and government, including despotic government, make men what they are and prepare them to become what they can become.

To get to first base, it turns out, human beings need to be yoked and disciplined by an irresistibly superior power. In some "conditions of society," according to Mill, "a vigorous despotism is in itself the best mode of government for training the people in what is specifically wanting to render them capable of a higher civilization" (CW XIX: 567). Long before Leninism, in other words, liberalism conceived provisional or transitional dictatorship as a handmaiden of social progress, claiming that "unlimited monarchy overcomes obstacles to the progress of civilization" (CW XIX: 417). But what exactly does such a despotic power accomplish? According to Mill's stylized model of political development, early-stage despotism makes two essential contributions to the preconditions of collective self-rule. It instills habits of deference and passivity; and it forges collective identities.

Quite unlike Hobbes, Mill denounced with republican passion "the contemptuous trampling upon the mass of the people which pervaded the whole life of the monarchical countries" and "the disgusting individual tyranny which was of more than daily occurrence under the systems of plunder which they called fiscal arrangements, and in the secrecy of their frightful courts of justice" (CW XIX, 406). He condemns such cruel monarchs not from an ahistorical perspective, however, but only when they are out of sync with social development. Thus, in a perfectly Hobbesian spirit, he also argues that unchecked authority is indispensable for hoisting humankind out of the state of nature. A "rude people" may find civilized life appealing, in theory, but may nevertheless, if left to itself, be "unable to practise the forbearance which it demands" (CW XIX: 377). The problem is personal and psychological: "their passions may be too violent, or their personal pride too exacting, to forego private conflict, and leave to the laws the avenging of their real or supposed wrongs" (CW XIX: 377). To help them escape such an anarchical condition, the government that rules them will have to be "in a considerable degree despotic" (CW XIX: 377). Duelers will have to be summarily executed. Private castles will have to be torn down. In neither case will private preferences be taken into account. The government capable of disarming its subjects and monopolizing the legitimate use of violence will not be democratic. It will not be responsive to retrograde public opinion. Instead, it will operate independently of the consent and dissent of the governed. It will be a government "over which they [the governed] do not themselves exercise control, and which imposes a great amount of forcible restraint upon their actions" (CW XIX: 377).

The road from no-rule (anarchy) to self-rule (democracy) runs through undemocratic rule (despotism) because only undemocratic authority, "superinduced from without" (CW XIX: 395), can discipline human passions and thereby reconcile humankind to obedience. By offering only unappealing alternatives, the despot will "teach" his subjects to obey specific commands. (Only later will they learn to follow abstract rules.) Autonomy presupposes heteronomy. To drag humanity, kicking and screaming, out of the violent cauldron of private violence, government, during the transitional period, must be unrepresentative and unresponsive.

Only a political authority that is indifferent or hostile to its underlying society's caprices and ambitions can civilize its subjects and teach them the "lesson" of obedience: "a people in a state of savage independence, in which every one lives for himself, exempt, unless by fits, from any external control, is practically incapable of making any progress in civilisation until it has learnt to obey. The indispensable virtue, therefore, in a government which establishes itself over a people of this sort is, that it make itself obeyed. To enable it to do this, the constitution of the government must be nearly, or quite, despotic" (CW XIX: 385).

Mill's prestate anarchy, it needs stressing, is characterized not only by corrosive interpersonal distrust (as in the prisoners' dilemma) but also by raging private passions. These passions have to be squelched before liberal democracy can be made to function. Above all, individuals have to give up what they love most, namely, the chance to inflict excruciating pain or violent death on people they hate. Without this mental and emotional forbearance, representative institutions and government by discussion are unworkable. A representative assembly drawn from men habituated to violent self-help "would simply reflect their own turbulent insubordination" (CW XIX: 415). Mill describes the unappealing consequences in the following colorful passage: "How can a representative assembly work for good if its members can be bought, or if their excitability of temperament, uncorrected by public discipline or private self-control, makes them incapable of calm deliberation, and they resort to manual violence on the floor of the House, or shoot at one another with rifles?" (CW XIX: 389–90). In other words, the Hobbesian demand that subjects lay down their arms is just as much an indispensable precondition of late-developing representative government as of general peace and order.

Excitability of temperament, characteristic of "people in a state of savage independence" (CW XIX: 394), can be dialed down only by a ruthless nondemocratic government that, wielding despotic power, suffers no contradiction, severely penalizes private revenge, and makes offers that cannot be refused. Once again: "To enable it to do this, the constitution of the government must be nearly, or quite, despotic. A constitution in any degree popular, dependent on the voluntary surrender by the different members of the community of their individual freedom of action, would fail to enforce the first lesson which the pupils, in this stage of their progress, require" (CW XIX: 394). The "first lesson of civilization," it goes without saying, is "obedience" (CW XIX: 394).

II

The road from no-rule to self-rule runs through undemocratic rule for a second reason as well. Only despotism can, out of fissiparous clans and tribes, manufacture the enlarged "self" that engages in self-rule: "I am not aware that history furnishes any example in which a number of these political atoms or corpuscles have coalesced into a body, and learnt to feel themselves one people, except through previous subjection to a central authority common to all" (CW XIX: 417). A large group of people can "receive into their minds the conception of large interests, common to a considerable geographical extent" only "through the habit of deferring to that authority, entering into its plans and subserving its purposes" (CW XIX: 417). Solidarity in large societies, including eventually nation-states, originates in shared deference to a unifying despotic power.

Only an "unlimited monarchy" can successfully overcome the "inveterate spirit of locality" (CW XIX: 417) that characterizes mankind in its natural, that is, splintered, pluralistic, and tribal state. Only an unlimited monarchy can amalgamate clans and tribes into units capable of self-rule. It does this, once again, by coming down hard on the passions characteristic of clansmen and tribesmen, that is, by stripping away the "jealousies and antipathies that repel them from one another" (CW XIX: 417). In the state of nature, admittedly, *homo homini lupus.* But wolves are famous for hunting in packs. Human beings, too, hunt and gather in social units. And they also prey on each other as members of small hostile groupings, competing for survival in a stinting environment, not as atomized individuals. They feel no spontaneous sympathy or solidarity across clan lines, and they have "no habit or capacity of dealing with interests common to many such communities" (CW XIX: 417).

To help us appreciate the significance of this amalgamating function of despotic power, Mill recalls that despots frequently resort to strategies of divide-and-rule. Governing a community full of mutually distrustful subgroups, a despot may be "interested in keeping up and envenoming their antipathies that they may be prevented from coalescing, and it may be enabled to use some of them as tools for the enslavement of others" (CW XIX: 548). Instead of eliminating anarchy, a despot may want to preserve elements of it, because a divided population may be easier to govern and less able to rebel. The appeal of divide-and-rule is so great, in fact, that we must ask the following question: why would a despot ever abandon managed anarchy and assume the risks that accompany national solidarity, including the possible emergence of an effective opposition to his whims? The basic answer lies in *defensive consolidation.* Only a large kingdom with a powerful army and a substantial tax base can defend itself against rival kingdoms in a dangerous world.

The serious security concerns of formally unlimited monarchy in a threatening international environment supply the defect of better motives. Focused on defending his territory from foreign marauders, a despotic ruler will develop a strong interest in teaching his subject to consider themselves as members of a single community. Viewed as a stage in political development from no-rule to self-rule, the consolidation of a community through mutual identification creates an essential precondition for democracy, because it makes cooperative relations inside the wider collectivity "familiar to the general mind" (CW XIX: 417). Mill summarizes his argument at this point as follows: "it may be laid down as a political truth, that by irresponsible monarchy rather than by representative government can a multitude of insignificant political units be welded into a people, with *common feelings* of cohesion, power enough *to protect itself against conquest or foreign aggression,* and affairs sufficiently various and considerable of its own to occupy worthily and expand to fit proportions the social and political intelligence of the population" (CW XIX, 418: emphasis added).

From fear of foreign aggression, in sum, nondemocratic authority will sometimes yoke together previously hostile groupings, habituate them into cooperating for the common defense, and inculcate emotional solidarity and mutual identification. It will also, as we shall see, create economic, social, and political opportunities appealing enough to stimulate individuals into investing in their otherwise undeveloped skills and talents. It does this, when it does, chiefly to maintain an edge in a lethally competitive international system.

III

Mill sometimes writes as an idealist, alleging that "It is what men think that determines how they act" (CW XIX: 382). Because ideas and opinions shape behavior, men of ideas, including political reformers, have just as great a chance as men of action to effect and affect important political outcomes. Because opinion is "one of the greatest active social forces" (CW XIX: 381), opinion makers can be and have been shapers of history. This theme is not necessarily optimistic, of course, because opinion makers may be malicious and may successfully propagate hate-filled ideologies. But Mill fields it with an optimistic intent, using it to undermine determinism and argue for the basic realism of efforts at reform.

The problem with such optimism is that, according to Mill's own philosophy, it is not that easy to change what men think. His most pungent example of the recalcitrance of human belief to efforts at moral suasion concerns a proclivity to violence that notoriously survives the civilizing process, namely, the proclivity of adult males to domestic spousal and filial abuse. "It would be vain to attempt to persuade a man who beats his wife and ill-treats his children that he would be happier if he lived in love and kindness with them. He would be happier if he were the kind of person who could so live; but he is not, and it is probably too late for him to become, that kind of person. Being what he is, the gratification of his love of domineering, and the indulgence of his ferocious temper, are to his perceptions a greater good to himself than he would be capable of deriving from the pleasure and affection of those dependent on him. He has no pleasure in their pleasure, and does not care for their affection" (CW XIX: 444). You could point to his neighbor and say, look, he loves his wife, takes pleasure in her pleasure, and is therefore a happier man than you. But if you could convince him of this it would "only still further exasperate his malignity or his irritability" (CW XIX: 444). People who care for others, their family, their friends, their country, or humanity are happier than those who do not. But human beings do not automatically maximize their own happiness. They are often unable to escape from malicious habits of the heart. You cannot persuade them to care for other people. To try would be like "preaching to the worm who crawls on the ground how much better it would be for him if he were an eagle" (CW XIX: 444).

What people think and feel determines how they act. But what they think and feel cannot be modified by rational persuasion alone. If a man takes no pleasure in his wife's pleasure, it is useless to tell him the obvious truth, that he would be happier if he could. Truth will not improve his behavior, but worsen it. The same is true of a population habituated to resolving private disputes by private violence. Rational persuasion will not suffice to convince them to refer their private disputes to public authorities. They need to be dragged from anarchy to obedience by force majeure.

In this initial stage of social evolution, Mill adds, force can and probably must be seconded by fraud. To exit the state of nature, religion, too, is required. This is because religion, which grips the human mind at a pre-rational level, helps reduce a savage population to passive obedience. In Mill's words, "the religious feeling" has "generally existed in favour of the inactive character, as being more in harmony with the submission due to the divine will" (CW XIX: 407). In Europe, the biblical ethic was probably the strongest cultural force working to undermine and replace the old aristocratic-chivalric ethic, the wellspring of private violence that modern state builders strove mightily to repress. In savage society, remember, "personal pride" is "too exacting" (CW XIX: 377). Christianity helped reduce pride by damning *superbia* as a sin and elevating humility into a virtue. According to Christian morality, moreover, glory and vengeance belonged not to local noblemen, jousting on horseback, but to God alone. A transvaluation of values raised meekness above heroism and submission above domination. By making people worship a pathetically victimized and bloodied Christ rather than the "heroes" who inflict gory wounds and dance on their enemies' graves, biblical morality played into the society-pacifying project of centralizing monarchs.

That biblical morality also had its downsides was not lost on supporters of secular power. For Hobbes, the principal problem was the creation of an independent priesthood that could draw authority from Holy Scripture and use it to defy the king. Mill is no longer concerned with this problem. His issue is another. He blames religion for the same reason he blames despotic power. However useful at an early stage of development, both religion and despotism overshoot the mark. They help pull people out of bloody anarchy, but they do so by replacing savage independence with servile dependence, passivity, and inertness. They teach people to accept failure and injustice "as visitations of Nature" (CW XIX: 401). Slavery may be a step up from savagery; but it fatally blocks further progress. In particular, it obstructs the transition to democracy because it is impossible to make a dynamic whole out of such limp and unenterprising parts.

IV

Much of *Considerations* revolves around Mill's distinction between "two common types of character" (CW XIX: 406): namely, the active and the passive types, "that which struggles against evils, or that which endures them; that which bends to circumstances, or that which endeavours to make circumstances bend to itself" (CW XIX: 407). Simplifying grossly, political evolution, as Mill conceives it, involves two sequential steps: from no-rule to despotic rule and from despotic rule to self-rule. The problem for Mill is that the first step (from savagery to subjection) produces passive characters, and the second step (from subjection to democracy) requires active characters. Although despotism can teach obedience and forge collective identities, a people can also be "unfitted for representative government," he says, "by extreme passiveness, and ready submission to tyranny" (CW XIX: 416). Despotism is progressive to the extent that it teaches savages to obey; it is regressive to the extent that, by taming *savages*, it creates *slaves*, confirming them in their dependency and incapacity. So why does not history stop halfway? How can representative government ever emerge? How can despotism be a stepping stone toward democracy if the "passive type of character" is associated with "the government of one or a few," and "the active self-helping type" with "that of the Many" (CW XIX: 410)?

Despotism and religiosity, working together, discipline and quiet excitable passions by inducing passivity of character. But while removing one obstacle to democracy, such pacification creates another, seemingly insurmountable, obstacle. This is true because "there is a natural incompatibility" between "subjection to the will of others, and the virtues of self-help and self-government" (CW XIX: 410). It is next to impossible to democratize a population of slaves because it is next to impossible to create an active feeling in a population habituated to passivity. Authoritarianism, whereby one "man of superhuman mental activity" manages "the entire affairs of a mentally passive people," produces people incapable of self-rule" (CW XIX: 400). Exiting from anarchy seems to close the door to democracy. When this occurs, "the work of some one period has been so done as to bar the needful work of the ages following" (CW XIX: 418).

Most people personally prefer to be surrounded by acquiescent and submissive characters than by obstreperous and discontented ones. The reason is fairly obvious: "The passiveness of our neighbours increases our sense of security, and plays into the hands of our wilfulness" (CW XIX: 407). What is true of most people is even truer of despots. Their power is a hindrance to progress to the extent that their rule is cemented by the fatalism and resignation of their subjects. This is true because "nothing is more certain than that improvement in human affairs is wholly the work of the uncontented characters" (CW XIX: 407).

Mill's explanation of the "second" step in social evolution, from subjection to democracy, focuses on the way power wielders, needing allies to fend off competitors, begin to prefer active to passive subjects. Peoples have emerged from "extreme passiveness and ready submission to tyranny," he says, not by their own bootstrapping efforts, but only "by the aid of a central authority" (CW XIX: 416). This central authority, for its part, comes to appreciate discontented and striving characters when the latter weaken the central authority's principal rivals. The ruling power that prefers active to passive characters is the one "whose position has made it the rival, and has ended by making it the master, of the local despots" (CW XIX: 416). Centralizing monarchs, to weaken the power of noblemen, have typically enfranchised the townspeople within their domains. Their motives were not eleemosynary. They were forced by circumstances to side with the cause of freedom. Although despotic "in principle," their rule became "restricted in practice" (CW XIX: 416) because they obtained the social cooperation they needed only by imposing constraints on themselves. In Mill's words, "the monarch was long *compelled by necessities of position* to exert his authority as *the ally rather than the master* of the classes whom he has aided in effecting their liberation" (CW XIX: 416, emphasis added).

The driving logic here is easy to grasp. Although power wielders have a palpable interest in the submissiveness of their subjects, they also have a palpable interest in the nonsubmissiveness of their enemy's subjects. "The king's interest lay in encouraging all partial attempts on the part of the serfs to emancipate themselves from their masters" (CW XIX: 416). He gave people "refuge and protection" from their "immediate oppressors" (CW XIX: 416). His "progress to ascendancy was slow" but "sure," resulting from his "taking advantage of opportunities" as they presented themselves. As the king's power grew, "it abated, in the oppressed portion of the community, the habit of submitting to oppression" (CW XIX: 416).

Mill's contemporary, Abraham Lincoln, issued the Emancipation Proclamation (1863) under the authority of the laws of war, which declared it lawful for a belligerent to improve its relative position by depriving its enemy of an important source of labor. The dynamic is parallel to the one Mill describes. Conflict between rival centers of power creates the conditions under which power wielders begin to appreciate the practical benefits of freedom.

Despotism will be "instrumental in carrying the people through a necessary stage of improvement" (CW XIX: 416) and even prepare the way for democracy when despots, trying to consolidate or increase their power, begin encouraging active virtues as well as passive ones among their subjects. When this occurs, despotism can smooth the path to democracy. Mill hints at this idea when he says that "Passive characters, if we do not happen to need their activity, seem an obstruction the less in our own path" (CW XIX: 407). The key thought here lies hidden in the dependent clause "if we do not happen to need their activity" (CW XIX: 407). This implies, if flipped around, that if despots *do* happen to need the active cooperation of people in achieving their purposes, they will prefer that their subjects have active rather than passive characters.

Mill repeatedly says that people are also "unfitted for representative government" not just by unruliness but also by "extreme passiveness, and ready submission to tyranny" (CW XIX: 416). But to clarify the logic of his argument, we need to approach the question from the opposite direction, from the top down or from the viewpoint of the ruler. To understand the political evolution that results in democracy, we have to see why power-maximizing rulers can take an interest in the active and entrepreneurial behavior of their subjects.

The underlying point is this: no despot is powerful enough to rule without cooperation. As their power grows, rulers need more independent-minded and resourceful allies. Fawning sycophants pleasure the king's vanity but do not help him foresee, analyze, and solve difficult problems. Passive compliance is psychologically comforting, but active and voluntary cooperation is practically useful. A "mentally passive people" (CW XIX: 400) will submit to the despot's will, but a mentally *active* people, if the incentives are right, will help the despot solve his most difficult problems. That is why despots can be lead, in pursuit of their own power, to activate and empower a previously servile population. Such liberalization will not necessarily disorganize political society because "it is much easier for an active mind to acquire the virtues of patience than for a passive one to assume those of energy" (CW XIX: 407). This, in a nutshell, is how Mill explained the emergence of liberalizing autocracy.

V

The primary reason despots, even though they have a good reason to repress private vendettas and private armies, cannot be satisfied with a totally passive population, is that they need soldiers to fend off foreign invaders and seize adjacent lands. As a result, they cannot bleed all aggression out of their subjects. At the very least, the armed wing of the state bureaucracy (especially the army and navy) must be able to recruit young men capable of aggressive behavior. Physically violent and aggressive subjects create a security problem for political rulers, but they are also a security asset. The problem can be minimized if these subjects can be "professionalized" in a specialized fighting body, although recruitment requires that the surrounding society, too, honor physical courage in battle and willingness to wade to victory through enemy blood. Thus, the biblical ethic, however useful as a brake on glory seeking and revenge, cannot be allowed simply to eradicate and replace the martial ethic.

Conflict among rival centers of power, such as neighboring monarchies, gives the powerful an interest in cultivating active rather than passive virtues, at least in one part of the community. If the *libido dominandi* of young men can be channeled away from private self-aggrandizement and into national defense and foreign annexationism, it will subserve the interests of a centralizing ruler. This channeling involves a paradoxical combination of domination and subjugation or unleashing and inhibition. It also works through a kind of magical spell: "the private soldier in an army" is willing "to abdicate his personal freedom of action into the hands of his general, provided the army is triumphant and victorious, and he is able to flatter himself that he is one of a conquering host, although the notion that he has himself any share in the domination exercised over the conquered is an illusion" (CW XIX: 420). Human behavior is extraordinarily plastic because it is driven by self-interest, that is, by a totally amorphous motive that can be radically redirected when the imagined "self" expands or shrinks, varying with sympathies and identifications, and by a completely undefined goal that can induce almost any behavior, depending on what the individual finds interesting at the moment. For instance, the soldier who takes vicarious satisfaction in his army's conquests can understand his voluntary servitude as both morally obligatory and socially honorable.

Soldiers are probably the most important allies that a despot bent on maximizing power must have on his side. But such despots also need other partners to rule effectively. An important example, stressed by Mill, involves information. The problem with the category "the good despot," he says, is that no despot can govern well if he is not "all-seeing" (CW XIX: 399). But omniscience is a problem, because no individual has the capacity to gather, let alone process, the daunting quantity of information needed to govern a large country. "He must be at all times informed correctly, in considerable detail, of the conduct and working of every branch of administration, in every district of the country, and must be able, in the twenty-four hours per day which are all that is granted to a king as to the humblest labourer, to give an effective share of attention and superintendence to all parts of this vast field" (CW XIX: 399). True, the ruler can create a bureaucracy to help him superintend his domains, but this does not eliminate the despot's information problem for "he must at least be capable of discerning and choosing out, from among the mass of his subjects, not only a large abundance of honest and able men, fit to conduct every branch of public administration under supervision and control, but also the small number of men of eminent virtues and talents who can be trusted not only to do without that supervision, but to exercise it themselves over others" (CW XIX: 399).[2] But the second problem can at least be solved to some extent. A professional bureaucracy can be established and trained. Training, however, does not insure loyalty. The despot may treat ordinary citizens arbitrarily and abusively. But to instill the necessary loyalty into his administration, his principal information-gathering organ and the main instrument of his rule, he must treat it with some degree of respect, decency, fairness, and predictability. This is another reason why the behavior of a power-maximizing despot, although unlimited in principle, will often be restricted in practice.

The despot's need for voluntary cooperation extends beyond soldiers and bureaucrats to ordinary subjects as well. It takes less raw power to govern a cooperative than an uncooperative population. Coercion is a scarce resource, and a despot mindful of opportunity costs will not want his subjects to view

---

[2] He concludes this passage, interestingly enough, on a Platonic note: "So extraordinary are the faculties and energies required for performing this task in any supportable manner, that the good despot whom we are supposing can hardly be imagined as consenting to undertake it, unless as a refuge from intolerable evils, and a transitional preparation for something beyond" (CW XIX: 399–400).

public authorities simply as predators and enemies. He will prefer subjects who are "willing to give active assistance" in the enforcement of law and "co-operate actively with the law and the public authorities in the repression of evil-doers" (CW XIX: 377).

Trust of the police, far from being a natural development, is a historical achievement. It also provides an indispensable precondition for eventual democratization. Hardened distrust of the police, in fact, is characteristic of people who are still unfit for freedom: "A people who are more disposed to shelter a criminal than to apprehend him; who, like the Hindoos, will perjure themselves to screen the man who has robbed them, rather than take trouble or expose themselves to vindictiveness by giving evidence against him; who, like some nations of Europe down to a recent date, if a man poniards another in the public street, pass by on the other side, because it is the business of the police to look to the matter," such a cowardly and uncooperative people "require that the public authorities should be armed with much sterner powers of repression than elsewhere, since the first indispensable requisites of civilised life have nothing else to rest on" (CW XIX: 377). The dynamic Mill describes here is familiar enough and, once again, involves the detailed, real-time information any ruler needs to govern effectively. The police are often more brutal in pursuing victimless crimes, such as drug possession and use, because they are not helped by the social informants who naturally step forth after crimes with victims such as physical assault and theft.

So what can a power-maximizing despot do to unlock from his subjects the information he needs to govern them efficiently? He must, first of all, protect potential informants from the vindictiveness of those on whom they inform. But he must also limit and restrict the arbitrarily abusive behavior of the police. When a population feels that its rights are routinely traduced, its members will "regard the law as made for other ends than their good" (CW XIX: 377–8). Viewing law as a stick with which the powerful beat the weak, they may passively comply but they will not cooperate actively with its enforcement. This is costly for the ruler because "a people so disposed cannot be governed with as little power exercised over them as a people whose sympathies are on the side of the law" (CW XIX: 378). A people whose rights are respected can be governed with a lighter touch, allowing the ruler to apply his scarce coercive resources to other more immediately useful ends.

The classical example of channeling primitive passions into civilized formats is criminal law. Instead of abolishing the avenging of wrongs or counting on Christianity's turn-the-other-cheek morality to extinguish the revenge instinct, criminal law encourages men to "leave to the laws the avenging of their real or supposed wrongs" (CW XIX: 377). It rides the tiger of vengeance instead of trying vainly to kill it. Because fantasy runs unchecked in the realm of wrongs, criminal law *disciplines* revenge, winnowing fact from rumor ("supposed wrongs"). It also disciplines vengeance in a second sense, encouraging the injured to abandon collective punishment and accept individualized findings of guilt, thereby cauterizing tit-for-tat spirals of retaliation. The replacement of private revenge by criminal law was not spontaneous. It was a purposive innovation, introduced to strengthen societies against external enemies who were happy to take advantage of a neighboring community's internal conflicts and bloodletting.

Mill takes this logic a step further, arguing that effective policing and physical security increase the resources available to the ruler by fomenting both individual creativity and community solidarity: "The release of the individual from the cares and anxieties of a state of imperfect protection, sets his faculties free to be employed in any new effort for improving his own state and that of others: while the same cause, by attaching him to social existence, and making him no longer see present or prospective enemies in his fellow creatures, fosters all those feelings of kindness and fellowship towards others, and interest in the general well-being of the community, which are such important parts of social improvement" (CW XIX: 386).

Political development, in its most general sense, requires "the preservation of peace by the cessation of private violence" (CW XIX: 385). Political development takes a liberal turn when despotic authority starts restricting itself, reliably and predictably, to maximize its power. To escape the state of nature, individuals must acquire "the habit of referring the decision of their disputes and the redress of their injuries to the public authorities" (CW XIX: 385). But this habit, once established, is not self-sustaining. It must be constantly reinforced. To keep it up, the power-maximizing despot must make available tribunals that punish wrongs and resolve conflicts with some degree of fairness. According to Mill, in other words, "the impartiality belonging to a judicial hearing" (CW XIX: 528) is just as important, for pacifying society, as nonabusive policing. It is not enough for people to "refer" their private quarrels to public authorities, the latter must resolve them competently, intelligently, justly, and impartially. In other words, fairness plays a role in persuading individuals to renounce self-help. Because it is in the interest of the rational despot to convince private individuals to recoil from private justice and private warfare, it is also in the interest of the rational despot to provide impartial justice. Fairness is cost-effective and, Mill suggests, would never have emerged and been stabilized historically if it were not.

VI

The first step toward civilization, according to Mill's scheme, involves the teaching of obedience or the transformation of savages into slaves. The second step involves a dramatic and difficult change in the style of obedience, from obedience to specific commands to obedience to general rules. According to Mill, the minds of slaves are not sufficiently under the influence of distant motives for them to keep their promises and play by the rules. But only those who have learned to abide by rules can learn to give rules even to themselves. So when and why does the transition from slavery to self-government occur? It usually occurs, Mill implicitly argues, when it serves the palpable interest of the ruling authority to maximize its power.

Most of those who, in civilized nations, now participate in ruling themselves were originally enslaved. Some were able to escape from slavery because they were "energetic by nature" (CW XIX: 395) and therefore not reduced to passivity by their miserable condition. For such exceptional individuals, legal manumission was sufficient to end personal servility. This was also true for former slaves who were lucky enough to find themselves in the same community with "an industrious class who [were] neither slaves nor slave-owners (as was the case in Greece)." Such free neighbors and companions could presumably teach former slaves the habits of disciplined freedom, allowing the latter to be "admitted at once to the full rights of citizenship," as in Rome (CW XIX: 395).

But this spontaneous process is not generally the way slavery ends. The transition to freedom is so difficult because the slave has abandoned the savage instinct for violent self-help (i.e., private revenge) but "has not learnt to help himself" (CW XIX: 395) in a civilized sense. Formulated differently, the slave has learned the lesson of obedience only in its most primitive form: "He has learnt to obey. But what he obeys is only a direct command. It is the characteristic of born slaves to be incapable of conforming their conduct to a rule, or law" (CW XIX: 395). This proclivity to follow commands is quite useful, in the short run, to those who issue the commands. But it is not optimal, for it requires constant vigilance and time-consuming micromanaging by the ruling powers. Slaves "can only do what they are ordered, and only when they are ordered to do it. If a man whom they fear is standing over them and threatening them with punishment, they obey; but when his back is turned, the work remains undone" (CW XIX: 395).

The principal reason masters would want their slaves to learn to obey general rules rather than specific commands is self-evident. The rich and powerful want obedience from the poor and weak, but they do not want to stand over their shoulders. That takes too many evenings. To be released from the annoying burden of giving specific commands, the powerful have to inculcate in their dependents the habit of following general rules. For this revolutionary transformation of domination to occur, rulers must appeal to the long-term "interests" of their subjects, not only to "their instincts," namely, "immediate hope or immediate terror" (CW XIX: 395). The capacity to act according to self-interest is no more natural or spontaneous than the capacity to follow general rules. It is a social achievement, a product of training.

The transition from savagery to slavery prepares the way to democracy, but only when the slaves begin to learn how to obey rules rather than commands. But how and why does this change occur? Recruitment into rule-governed civilian or military bureaucracies obviously plays a role for a portion of the population. But Mill's general answer involves "parental despotism" (CW XIX: 395) or government of "leading-strings" (CW XIX: 396). This concept is notoriously obscure, but it definitely refers to a style of rule that is self-limiting for political rather than moral reasons. Parental despotism possesses force but seldom uses it. Instead, it helps former slaves learn to walk on their own. Mill's examples seem eccentric: the Incas of Peru and the Jesuits of Paraguay. But he was also thinking of British rule in India. The style of government he has in mind, in any case, "leaves and induces individuals to do much of themselves" (CW XIX: 396). But why exactly would a despot curb his own power and encourage the independence of underlings?

At one point in *Considerations,* Mill argues that "It was not by any change in the distribution of material interests, but by the spread of moral convictions, that negro slavery has been put an end to in the British Empire and elsewhere" (CW XIX: 382). But the deeper logic of his argument points in a less idealistic direction. Power willingly sheds power not because of a conversion from base to honorable moral convictions, but because power is a liability and a burden, not only an asset and a benefit. Mill is thinking especially of "the impossibility of descending to regulate all the minutiae of industry and life" (CW XIX: 396). The powerful give up minute-by-minute control of their subordinates because time is scarce and they have better things to do. They willingly abandon the particular superintendence characteristic of slave societies for the "general superintendence over all the operations of society" (CW XIX: 396) possible in a hierarchical order where the subordinated classes possess some active virtues and have learned to obey general rules not merely specific commands.

VII

The Marxist theory of liberalizing autocracy stresses the way police power is used to repress wages and steer social wealth into the pockets of the middle classes that then provide a solid constituency, or partisan friend, of the governing power. Mill's account is more liberal, though not necessarily incompatible with such an account. Its premise is that "the general prosperity attains a great height, and is more widely diffused, in proportion to the amount and variety of personal energies enlisted in promoting it" (CW XIX: 404). A power-maximizing despot, however much he may fear rebellion, also wants to expand his tax base. He therefore has a palpable interest in the general prosperity. To achieve it, he will have to abandon the use of insecurity as an instrument of rule (keeping potential troublemakers off balance) and commit himself, instead, to some degree of legal certainty and reliable enforcement of property rights. By opening up commercial opportunities, the power-maximizing ruler can transform a mentally passive people into a mentally active people. Mentally active people are valued first of all, by resource-hungry despots, as contributors to taxable economic growth.

Despotism is "stunting" and therefore self-impoverishing when it offers no opportunity or prospect of using natural talents or acquired skills. "Endeavour is even more effectually restrained by the certainty of its impotence than by any positive discouragement" (CW XIX: 410). By contrast, "The only sufficient incitement to mental exertion, in any but a few minds in a generation, is the prospect of some practical use to be made of its results" (CW XIX: 400). Economic endeavor, in particular, is encouraged by the reliability of property rights. Police protection "enables everyone to feel his person and property secure" (CW XIX: 386). A sense of security encourages people to invest in improvements, both of their property and of themselves. "The greater security of property," which is an achievement of "the common institution of a police," is "one of the main conditions and causes of greater production, which is Progress in its most familiar and vulgarest aspect" (CW XIX: 386). To increase the wealth of his tax base, therefore, the rational despot will tie his own hands and abstain from arbitrary confiscations.

The path to democracy is prepared when power-maximizing and revenue-seeking rulers promote active rather than passive virtues not only in their civilian and military bureaucracies but in the citizen body as a whole. The deliberate fostering of private commercial activity, for its indirect public benefits, involved both a channeling and taming of passions. Commerce, first of all, provides a nonviolent outlet for aggressive, competitive, prideful, and acquisitive passions. It also channels envy, turning the destructive and impoverishing envy of the evil eye into the creative and enriching envy of competitive emulation.

Viewing failure and injustice as visitations of nature, fatalists are naturally envious. "In proportion as success in life is seen or believed to be the fruit of fatality or accident, and not of exertion, in that same ratio does envy develop itself as a point of national character" (CW XIX: 408). Envy, in turn, is a powerful retardant to economic development. The "envious man," according to Mill, "is the terror of all who possess anything desirable, be it a palace, a handsome child, or even good health and spirits: the supposed effect of his mere look constitutes the all-pervading superstition of the evil eye" (CW XIX: 408). To escape the evil eye, people will hide their wealth. But a society that hides its wealth will not strive energetically to increase its wealth. Hence, virulent envy helps keep premodern economies mired in stagnation.

To transform a stagnant economy into a dynamic economy, political elites cannot be satisfied with passive, and that means inherently envious, characters: "those who, while desiring what others possess, put no energy into striving for it, are either incessantly grumbling that fortune does not do for them what they do not attempt to do for themselves, or overflowing with envy and ill-will towards those who possess what they would like to have" (CW XIX: 408). To weaken growth-stifling envy, and thereby increase his tax base, a ruler must contrive a way to help his subjects escape their deadening fatalism. The most direct strategy for a ruler to overcome popular fatalism is to open up opportunities for his subjects' self-improvement. That is why a power-maximizing autocrat, if thinking strategically, will become a liberalizing autocrat, according to Mill.

VIII

How useful is Mill's stylized account of liberalizing autocracy for analyzing liberal imperialism and, in particular, for helping us understand efforts by a dominant power to export democracy abroad? Victorious in World War II, the United States had a strong interest in helping West Germany develop a working democracy. But this commitment to democracy promotion was highly context-dependent. In other parts of the world, the United States had no trouble, after World War II, cooperating intimately with authoritarian governments to pursue ostensibly shared goals. Latin America and the Far East provide plentiful and sorrowful examples. But the United States could not have partnered with authoritarianism in Germany after 1945, having just mopped up a bloody war against the old authoritarian elite of that country. It needed to replace the old despised and in any case decimated ruling group with another, and a democratically elected governing class was probably the best option. Moreover, the United States ended up needing the voluntary cooperation of the West Germans in the drawn-out Cold War against the USSR, and giving ordinary citizens political freedom, along with economic prosperity, was an effective way to cement loyalty and mobilize cooperation. For understanding post–World War II democracy promotion, therefore, Mill's ideas about liberal imperialism remain illuminating. In postwar West Germany, liberty emerged exactly as Mill would have anticipated, as a by-product of lethal enmity between rival centers of power.

But what about the current American proposal to democratize the Arab Middle East, starting with Iraq? What would Mill have made of the ambition, expressed in President George W. Bush's Second Inaugural Address, that "it is the policy of the United States to seek and support the growth of democratic movements and institutions in every nation and culture, with the ultimate goal of ending tyranny in our world"?[3]

Having conquered Iraq militarily, the United States wields undemocratic authority there, operating independently of the consent of the governed. Mill would not have been particularly scandalized by this, even though he wished his own countrymen would resist the parochial-narcissistic impulse "to force English ideas down the throats of the natives" (CW XIX: 570). He believed that government by foreigners was "as legitimate as any other," but only on one condition – namely, if in "the existing state of civilisation of the subject people," government by foreigners "facilitates their transition to a higher stage of improvement" (CW XIX: 567). Undemocratic rule, including undemocratic rule by foreigners, is justifiable if, after teaching the lesson of obedience, it goes on to promote the emergence of self-government. More-over, foreign rule may be the best form of undemocratic rule, at least when the foreign ruler happens to be as civilized as the United Kingdom. In a backward country, local rulers are likely to suffer from so many vices that governing will often be done best by foreigners who belong "to a superior people or a more advanced state of society" (CW XIX: 418). Mill elab-orates on this theme as follows: "subjection to a foreign government of this description, notwithstanding its inevitable evils, is often of the great-est advantage to a people, carrying them rapidly through several stages of progress, and clearing away obstacles to improvement which might have

[3] George W. Bush, Second Inaugural, January 20, 2005.

lasted indefinitely if the subject population had been left unassisted to its native tendencies and chances" (CW XIX: 419).

So Mill would not have objected in principle to democratization by militarily dominant foreigners of Iraq and other states of the Arab Middle East. But his analysis, as we have seen, is immensely complex and nuanced. It can also help us, as it turns out, to understand the daunting problems and catastrophic failures that have afflicted the foreign attempt to democratize Iraq. Difficulties have arisen on both the foreign and Iraqi sides.

The first problem, from Mill's perspective, concerns the confusing welter of motives behind the operation in Iraq. Mill's account implies that a power-maximizing ruling authority will be serious about liberalization and democratization only if liberalization and democratization are aligned with its interests, including its interest in maximizing its own power. What does this principle suggest about the American attempt to democratize Iraq?

To answer this question we need to ask what happens, according to Mill's theory, if the ruling power's interests are ambiguous or conflicting. What if the ruling power has strong interests in both democracy and its opposite, in both nation-building and nation-dismantling? If the ruling power's motives are mixed and even self-contradictory, then we would expect its democracy-promotion efforts to be erratic, stop-and-go, confused, and eventually self-defeating. Conversely, when we observe halfhearted and incoherent efforts at democracy promotion, we can surmise, following Mill's analysis, that the democratizer's motives are miscellaneous and incoherent.

Let us assume, for the sake of argument, that U.S. forces in Iraq are among those who, in Mill's words, "honestly attempt to govern well a country in which they are foreigners" (CW XIX: 569). Even if the occupying power is perfectly well-intentioned, according to Mill, it will still have a serious problem in guiding the transition to democracy because of its abysmal lack of knowledge. The "good despot," recall, cannot govern well unless he is "all-seeing" (CW XIX: 399). This is why Mill believes that it "is always under great difficulties, and very imperfectly, that a country can be governed by foreigners" (CW XIX: 568). Native politicians know things by instinct that foreign administrators learn only imperfectly and by protracted study. The basic problem is that "Foreigners do not feel with the people. They cannot judge, by the light in which a thing appears to their own minds, or the manner in which it affects their feelings, how it will affect the feelings or appear to the minds of the subject population" (CW XIX: 568). It turns out that for "most of their detailed knowledge they must depend on the information of natives." This is unfortunate because "it is difficult for them to know whom to trust." Even worse, "they are prone to think that the servilely submissive are the trustworthy" (CW XIX: 569).

Culturally obtuse and linguistically challenged foreign officials, Mill says, will lead the occupier to be "feared, suspected, [and] probably disliked by the population" (CW XIX: 569). These tensions are exacerbated by profiteers. Mill warns especially against "the individuals of the ruling people who resort to the foreign country to make their fortunes" (CW XIX: 571). They are serious troublemakers. Public officials, military and civilian, feel at least some sense of responsibility toward subject peoples. But private booty seekers, "filled with the scornful overbearingness of the conquering nation" (CW XIX: 571), exhibit no such tendency to self-restraint. Mill is thinking, in this passage, mostly of settlers and "private adventurers" (CW XIX: 571), but he explicitly extends his observations to some of Britain's civilian and military officers posted in India: "they think the people of the country mere dirt under their feet: it seems to them monstrous that any rights of the natives should stand in the way of their smallest pretensions" (CW XIX: 571). Because the people of the country will perceive that they are being treated like human waste, they will not be warmly cooperative and therefore will not be governable with a light touch.

Although the conquerors run the risk of despising those they conquered, Mill continues, the subdued population runs the risk of "disbelieving that anything the strangers do can be intended for their good" (CW XIX: 569). Such corrosive distrust will derail any reform proposals issuing from the occupying authority. But Mill is even more concerned about a second problem, namely, the unfitness for democracy of any people that did not fight to achieve it: "the evil is, that if they have not sufficient love of liberty to be able to wrest it from merely domestic oppressors, the liberty which is bestowed on them by other hands than their own, will have nothing real, nothing permanent. No people ever was and remained free, but because it was determined to be so" (CW XXI: 122). That is to say, the only people that can benefit from the toppling of a tyrant is a people that participates actively in the toppling. This is a powerful thought, although not necessarily a true one, as the example of post–World War II West Germany suggests. More persuasive and more relevant to Iraq may be Mill's underlying suggestion that political and legal institutions, although a matter of choice, can be more easily imported than exported.

For those seeking to understand the impasse often faced by foreign promoters of democracy, Mill's theory teaches an even more pertinent lesson. I am referring to Mill's famous and perhaps debatable claim that "Free institutions are next to impossible in a country made up of different nationalities"

(CW XIX: 547). The key to self-government is public opinion, he argues, and public opinion is likely to be incoherent and inoperative in a multiethnic or multisectarian state.

> Among a people without fellow-feeling, especially if they read and speak different languages, the united public opinion, necessary to the working of representative government, cannot exist. The influences which form opinions and decide political acts are different in the different sections of the country. An altogether different set of leaders have the confidence of one part of the country and of another. The same books, newspapers, pamphlets, speeches, do not reach them. One section does not know what opinions, or what instigations, are circulating in another. The same incidents, the same acts, the same system of government, affect them in different ways; and each fears more injury to itself from the other nationalities than from the common arbiter, the state. Their mutual antipathies are generally much stronger than jealousy of the government. That any one of them feels aggrieved by the policy of the common ruler is sufficient to determine another to support that policy. Even if all are aggrieved, none feel that they can rely on the others for fidelity in a joint resistance. (CW XIX: 547)

The principal obstacle to democratization that Mill isolates in this fascinating passage is not culture, obviously, but rather the structure of organized interests. In a highly pluralistic society, especially a society "divided within itself by strong antipathies of race, language, or nationality" (CW XIX: 446–7), government cannot be simultaneously coherent and representative. The relevance of this analysis to Iraq is obvious.

IX

The Baath regime was coherent because it was unrepresentative, being monopolized essentially by a Tikriti clan. Saddam's government, to speak euphemistically, operated "under the influence of interests not identical with the general welfare of the community" (CW XIX: 358). Mill's understanding of such state capture by a violent minority is an essential element in his theory of democratization. One of the principal objections to the idea that political institutions are susceptible to choice is the determinist theory that the most powerful force in society will automatically rule. Political power, according to this quasi-Marxist theory, simply reflects social power, "and a change in the political constitution cannot be durable unless preceded or accompanied by an altered distribution of power in society itself" (CW XIX: 380). As a consequence, this theory concludes, nations cannot choose their forms of government.

Mill believes that this determinist line of thought is hopelessly confused. It is impossible, by looking into the way power is distributed in society, to discover the *cause,* at any given time, of the allocation of political power. A relationship between x and y presupposes a distinction between x and y. Society and politics are too thoroughly blurred together to allow us to draw causal arrows between the two. Formulated differently, political arrangements are *constitutive* of social power, and the former cannot, therefore, be *caused* by the latter. It is not wrong to say that the strongest power in society will always be the strongest power in government. It is merely tautological.

Social power is not the product of sheer numbers, "otherwise pure democracy would be the only form of polity that could exist" (CW XIX: 381). Nor is social power the expression solely of knowledge and wealth. Historically, in fact, small minorities have ruled large majorities even when the ruling group has less knowledge and wealth than the ruled: "Not only is a greater number often kept down by a less, but the greater number may have a preponderance in property, and individually in intelligence, and may yet be held in subjection, forcibly or otherwise, by a minority in both respects inferior to it" (CW XIX: 381). How is this possible?

It is possible because the greatest source of social power is the capacity to organize, "and the advantage in organisation is necessarily with those who are in possession of the government" (CW XIX, 381). A small group inferior in numbers and intelligence and wealth, if well-disciplined and skillfully commanded, can prevail over a large majority that is poorly organized and incapable of coordinated action. It can do this by seizing control of the machinery of state. If it manages – by force, fraud, timing, and craft – to seize the reins of power, it will also rule society.

State capture by a compact minority is not historically unusual. It is essentially the story, to stick with our example, of Saddam's Iraq. Saddam used a tribally homogeneous security apparatus (army, police, and secret service) to dominate a multiethnic and multidenominational society. Although ordinary Iraqis may have acquired some sort of shared national identity during the eighty-five years since the country was created by Great Britain, the Iraqi security apparatus, built up under Saddam, viewed itself as a people apart. It did not identify emotionally with Iraqi Kurds and Shiites. Mill would have traced the terrible cruelty of the Baath regime to this source: "Soldiers to whose feelings half or three-fourths of the subjects of the same government are foreigners will have no more scruple in mowing them down, and no more desire to ask the reason why, than they would have in doing the same thing against declared enemies" (CW XIX: 548).

A small minority can rule a large majority, Mill says, by controlling the levers of power, including the organized agencies capable of applying lethal force. Most of the power in existence is quiescent or dormant. What matters politically, according to Mill, is not potential power but "power actually exerted; that is to say, a very small portion of all the power in existence" (CW XIX: 381). Unorganized power is latent or inert. Organized power can be deployed to keep it that way. This is why the few have never had much trouble ruling the many. The gap between quiescent power and active power helps explain why social power will not automatically determine the form of government. What Mill is talking about, in essence, are increasing returns to political power. Whatever group, by skill or luck, first gets the instruments of government in its hands, can weaken and paralyze rival centers of power. It can use fear to atomize society, making coordinated resistance and challenges to its power difficult or impossible.

This is why a "much weaker party in all other elements of power may greatly preponderate when the powers of government are thrown into the scale; and may long retain its predominance through this alone" (CW XIX: 381). Of course, this arrangement is vulnerable to outside interference because "a government so situated is in the condition called in mechanics unstable equilibrium, like a thing balanced on its smaller end, which, if once disturbed, tends more and more to depart from, instead of reverting to, its previous state" (CW XIX: 381). Thus, to return to the example of Iraq, when a superior foreign army appeared in the country, it was able quickly to knock over the entire house of cards by simply plucking the relatively homogeneous security apparatus out of the relatively heterogeneous society. The result was a sudden reversion from despotic rule to no-rule, from cruel tyranny to cruel assassinations, kidnapping, insurgency and sectarian strife. The Iraqi calamity, it should be said, fully confirms Mill's principle that physical security and police protection constitute the bedrock of an economically and culturally dynamic society.

The American project in Iraq seems incoherent, from a Millian perspective, because it is driven by contradictory impulses. The U.S. endeavor to democratize Iraq is a futile attempt (in a society honeycombed with ethnic, sectarian, and tribal divisions) to create a government that is *simultaneously representative and coherent*. Mill would have diagnosed such a project as doomed to fail. Iraq might have been capable of self-government if the Iraqi "demos" had survived the fall of Saddam emotionally unified. It would have then qualified as a "nationality" in precisely Mill's sense: "A portion of mankind may be said to constitute a Nationality if they are united among themselves by common sympathies which do not exist between them and any others – which make them co-operate with each other more willingly than with other people, desire to be under the same government, and desire that it should be government by themselves or a portion of themselves exclusively" (CW XIX: 546). Unless it is emotionally and morally bound together in these ways, no "portion of mankind" will be capable of self-rule. According to Mill, a common religion, a common language, and a shared history do not suffice to create these common sympathies. After three years of bloody anarchy, in any case, the "corpuscles" of the Iraqi population have not coalesced into the kind of deeply felt national coherence that, for Mill, was an indispensable precondition for democratic self-government.

Mill thought that "subjection to a central authority common to all" would help the subordinated overcome the "inveterate spirit of locality" and "feel themselves one people." They would first defer to the superintendent authority, entering into its plans and subserving its purposes, and would then "receive into their minds the conception of large interests, common to a considerable geographical extent" (CW XIX: 417). This is exactly the opposite of what happened in Iraq. Far from being rinsed away, the "jealousies and antipathies that repel" Iraqi factions "from one another" (CW XIX: 417) have been further inflamed with time. Perhaps this is because the occupying forces did not act, from the start, with sufficient vigor. But it may have occurred because the conquering power was drawn, from the outset, into exploiting and magnifying, rather than healing, the country's internal divisions.

Here again, Mill helps us analyze the prospects: "When the nationality which succeeds in overpowering the other is both the most numerous and the most improved; and especially if the subdued nationality is small, and has no hope of reasserting its independence; then, if it is governed with any tolerable justice, and if the members of the more powerful nationality are not made odious by being invested with exclusive privileges, the smaller nationality is gradually reconciled to its position, and becomes amalgamated with the larger" (CW XIX: 550).

What does Mill's analysis here tell us about Iraq? First of all, Iraqi Shiites are the most numerous group in the country, if not the most "improved." But the Sunni minority is not yet subdued. Nor has it abandoned all hopes of reasserting itself. It has refused to submit or reconcile itself to its reduced position, perhaps because some of its leaders do not expect that the Sunnis will be "governed with any tolerable justice" (CW XIX: 550) in a Shiite-controlled Iraqi democracy. They presumably expect that the Shiites, once they control the machinery of organized violence, will invest themselves with what Mill called "exclusive privileges," reserving for the Sunnis the worthless right to be outvoted in periodic elections. The Sunnis may be reluctant to play along, in other words because they anticipate increasing returns to Shiite power. By gaining control of the levers of authority, especially the security apparatus, the Shiites may, over time, reduce the Sunnis to helpless subjection. At least the Sunnis have no reason to believe that they will refrain from doing so. Instead of subordinating group anger to public justice, the Shiites are likely to make public justice a tool of sectarian revenge. They are very unlikely to create a government in which, to cite Mill, "the benefits of freedom . . . are extended impartially to all" (CW XIX: 406). The Sunnis, in sum, are perfectly aware that "Every kind and degree of evil of which mankind are susceptible may be inflicted on them by their government" (CW XIX: 383). Given the country's recent history, the Sunnis can easily imagine the kinds and degrees of evil which the Shiites have in store for them. This is one reason why some Sunnis, at least, have chosen to fight now rather than later, when they will be even weaker than they currently are.

Conclusion

Liberal democracy, in Mill's conception, is distinct from majority rule. It is different because it is constitutional. To say that liberal democracy is constitutional is to say that it places formal and informal limits on increasing returns to power. If incumbents use their incumbency to weaken or destroy their competitors permanently, then free-wheeling public debate will be squelched and rotation in office will end. Liberal democracy, as Mill understands it, requires all social factions to renounce their natural impulse to seek monopoly power. At one point, Mill describes a representative assembly as "the nation's Committee of Grievances, and its Congress of Opinions" where "every party or opinion in the country can muster its strength, and be cured of any illusion concerning the number or power of its adherents" (CW XIX: 432). He ascribes the same function to periodic multiparty elections: "It is useful that there should be a periodical general muster of opposing forces, to gauge the state of the national mind, and ascertain, beyond dispute, the relative strength of different parties and opinions" (CW XIX: 502).

On election day, in a liberal democracy, the citizenry paints a collective portrait of itself, informing itself by this method of the *relative strength* of different factions and parties. Mill's assumption here is that such a collectively observed joint self-portrait will inject a *spirit of moderation* into public opinion, because no party will believe or contend that it deserves to prevail 100 percent of the time. This logic of moderation, needless to say, does not apply especially well to multiethnic and multidenominational societies, especially when majoritarian elections produce winner-take-all outcomes. In such a society, a collective self-portrait, painted on election day, may fill one segment of the community with an arrogant feeling that it deserves to rule alone and unobstructed. By signaling to the outvoted minority community that losing power means losing everything, democratic elections are unlikely to pacify a multiethnic or multidenominational society or reconcile its various factions to peaceful coexistence. That is exactly what Mill's still-pertinent theory of the obstacles to democracy would lead us to expect.

14

Mill's "A Few Words on Non-Intervention"

A Commentary

Michael Walzer

Mill's "few words" actually make up a longish essay, which I shall reduce to a few paragraphs, for the purposes of commentary. I want to isolate the key arguments and consider whether they still make sense. They made a lot of sense in the 1960s, when Americans were arguing about the Vietnam War and when many liberal and leftist intellectuals first started thinking and writing about the question of military intervention. The Millian claim that Vietnamese freedom depended on the Vietnamese themselves – on how much they valued freedom and on what sacrifices they were prepared to make for its sake – was repeated by just about every American political and military leader, but it was the opponents of the war who took it most seriously. Mill's essay was a favorite text of the antiwar movement. But there was never a simple right–left disagreement on intervention. Depending on the local circumstances, each side has been ready to send troops into someone else's country, and each side has criticized the government that sent (or didn't send) them in. The right wanted to roll back Soviet tyranny in Europe; many leftists would probably have supported a military intervention to end apartheid in South Africa. Neither right nor left has been entirely consistent, and both have divided in unpredictable ways. Perhaps another look at Mill's categories and criteria might help us all maintain a steady course.

For Mill, the central issue was despotism, and in one way or another that still seemed true in the 1960s, in the Vietnam years, and it still seems true today (2005) when the United States is engaged in coercive "regime change" in Iraq. But we also have to consider, against all our hopes and expectations, the most frightening consequence of some (but not all) depotisms: mass murder. This is the major difference between the cases that preoccupied us 40 years ago and the cases that worry us today. The despots have certainly not gone away, but the threat they always posed to liberty has now been overwhelmed by the threat they pose to life. The latter threat, of course, was always there: Nazi genocide and the Soviet Gulag were also the work of despotic regimes. Somehow, in the years after World War II, we convinced ourselves that the slogan "Never again!" would actually shape our common future. It obviously hasn't. The twenty-first century looks to be a continuation of the twentieth and not a return to Mill's nineteenth, whose politics looks, well, not bloodless but almost innocent. Still, whenever we need to argue about whether it is right or wrong, just or unjust, to send an army across a border, it is useful to return to Mill's "few words."

Textual commentary is not a common genre in political theory these days. Authoritative religious texts like the Bible and legal texts like the U.S. Constitution are often quoted and commented on – sometimes criticized, more often revised through interpretation. It is customary in such commentaries to claim that one is seeking the true meaning, the deepest meaning, of the text. I make no such claim with regard to Mill's essay, which has neither religious nor constitutional authority. Nor do I want to claim that I am carrying on a conversation with Mill, since he is incapable of responding. As with any engagement with a long dead but still influential author, my commentary is an act of homage but also an act of appropriation and use.

The excerpts (in italics) on which I comment follow the development of Mill's argument. They are all from the second part of the essay; the first part deals more narrowly with British foreign policy and is not of interest here.

We have heard something lately about being willing to go to war for an idea. To go to war for an idea, if the war is aggressive, not defensive, is as criminal as to go to war for territory or revenue; for it is as little justifiable to force our ideas on other people, as to compel them to submit to our will in any other respect. But there assuredly are cases in which it is allowable to go to war, without having been ourselves attacked, or threatened with attack; and it is very important that nations should make up their minds in time, as to what these cases are. There are few questions which more require to be taken in hand by ethical and political philosophers, with a view to establish some rule or criterion whereby the justifiableness of intervening in the affairs of other countries, and (what is sometimes fully as questionable) the justifiableness of refraining from intervention, may be brought to a definite and rational test. (CW XXI: 118)

I think that the "idea" in question was liberty, as it is democracy today, and Mill's assertion that we cannot force such ideas on other people is as true today as it was in 1859. But the hard question, not dealt with in this opening paragraph, is how we respond to the radical deprivation of liberty and democracy, that is, to slavery and despotism. Do these two ever justify the resort to war? This is a question that still needs to be "taken in hand." Note that Mill is looking for a moral argument here – from "ethical and political philosophers." But for more than a century after he wrote, the study of international politics was dominated by "realists," who thought such arguments otiose. Mill looked old-fashioned to them. He is our contemporary. Indeed, I argue that he speaks directly to current U.S. debates about foreign policy and international society.

> *There is a great difference . . . between the case in which the nations concerned are of the same, or something like the same, degree of civilization, and that in which one of the parties to the situation is of a high, and the other of a very low, grade of social improvement. To suppose that the same international customs, and the same rules of international morality, can obtain between one civilized nation and another, and between civilized nations and barbarians, is a grave error, and one which no statesman can fall into. . . . Among many reasons why the same rules cannot be applicable to situations so different, the two following are among the most important. In the first place, the rules of ordinary international morality imply reciprocity. But barbarians will not reciprocate. They cannot be depended on for observing any rules. Their minds are not capable of so great an effort, nor their will sufficiently under the influence of distant motives. In the next place, nations which are still barbarous have not got beyond the period during which it is likely to be for their benefit that they should be conquered and held in subjection by foreigners.* (CW XXI: 118)

This doesn't sound at all contemporary; indeed, it is politically incorrect in the strongest possible sense. And in this case, unlike many others, that description seems entirely justified. Surely it is astonishing that Mill should tell us that the people of India – the most relevant case, which he knew well – could not understand the idea of reciprocity or that Hindus and Muslims were incapable of "observing any rules" (it might have been a more legitimate criticism to say that they observed too many rules). But the last sentence of this excerpt requires more prolonged discussion. Even Karl Marx believed that it was in the interest of the Indians to be ruled by the British, although his account of "social improvement" was more dialectical and more violent than Mill's. And it is probably true that many leaders of the Congress Party, India's national liberation movement, believed that it had once been in the interests of Indians to be ruled by the British, however critical they were of many aspects of British rule. Still, I doubt that things like the (temporary) unification of the country, or the abolition of *sati*, or the establishment of a parliamentary system could actually justify the "conquest and subjection" of a country like India. And what about the destruction of the Indian cloth industry, the reinforcement of the caste system, and the establishment of separate electoral lists for Hindus and Muslims? It would require a very complicated counterfactual analysis to figure out whether the sum of British actions was "to the benefit" of the Indians. And no other argument will do: for good reasons, we no longer believe that a theory of historical development or a belief in progress ("social improvement") is sufficient to the task.

If we give up any such theory, then we are forced to recognize the possible coexistence in time and space of civilization and barbarism – which opens the way for a more balanced argument about foreign intervention. Certain forms of barbarism can indeed justify a version of "conquest and subjection," and these forms can and do appear at very different levels of what Mill calls social improvement; they certainly appear in "advanced" European societies as well as in "backward" African and Asian societies (where Mill expected to find them). When a government begins a massacre of its own people or of some subset of its own people, or when it launches a program of "ethnic cleansing," or when it imposes a slave system, then it is greatly to the benefit of the victims and potential victims that their country be invaded and their government overthrown by foreign troops. We call this "humanitarian intervention," and it is widely defended these days, although not widely or reliably practiced. How to deal with governmental brutality short of massacre, ethnic cleansing, and enslavement – with ordinary authoritarianism – is, however, a question that still needs to be "taken in hand."

But among civilized peoples, members of an equal community of nations, like Christian Europe, the question assumes another aspect, and must be decided on totally different principles.

The principles are, in fact, the same across the community of nations, whether or not its members or, better, the governments of its members, are moral equals. It is precisely because governments are not equally just or benevolent or responsive to the needs of their people, in "Christian Europe" as well as in the rest of the world, that we need a theory of military intervention. But we also need, what no one has yet produced, a theoretical account of the full range of coercive responses to injustice, from diplomatic pressure to economic sanctions to the use of force short of war.

The disputed question is that of interfering in the regulation of another country's internal concerns; the question whether a nation is justified in taking part, on either side, in the civil wars or party contests of another; and chiefly, whether it may justifiably aid the people of another country in struggling for liberty; or may impose on a country any particular government or institutions, either as being best for the country itself, or as necessary for the security of its neighbors. (CW XXI: 121)

This is Mill's subject. If he doesn't acknowledge the possibility of barbarism in Christian Europe, he does acknowledge the possibility of despotism. Can a foreign state and army come to the aid of people struggling to overthrow a despot? Can they simply intervene and overthrow the despot themselves, whether or not there is a popular struggle? The primary issue here is the "benefit" of the invaded country. But Mill also raises the question of preventive war, which he doesn't discuss in any sufficient way in this essay. Suppose that there is a tyrannical regime with a record of aggression against its neighbors or a regime (thought to be) prone to aggression – can its neighbors intervene to change the regime, in their own interests, for their own benefit? Preventive war is very hard to justify because the threat is speculative in nature, possibly also distant in time, and there are other things to do: military preparations and diplomatic alliances may well serve to deter any attack. On the other hand, the security of neighboring states seems a very good reason for regime change *after* the military defeat of an aggressor state, as in Germany after World War II. Before 1939, forceful measures short of war would probably have prevented the war and possibly also led to the downfall of the Nazi regime – Mill, as we will see, is not prepared to contemplate anything more. After 1945, he would have thought the allies right to "impose" a new (and democratic) government on the German people.

Assistance to the government of a country in keeping down the people, unhappily by far the most frequent case of foreign intervention, no one writing in a free country needs take the trouble of stigmatizing. A government which needs foreign support to enforce obedience from its own citizens, is one which ought not to exist; and the assistance given to it by foreigners is hardly ever anything but the sympathy of one despotism with another. A case requiring consideration is that of a protracted civil war, in which the contending parties are so equally balanced that there is no probability of a speedy issue; or if there is, the victorious side cannot hope to keep down the vanquished but by severities repugnant to humanity, and injurious to the permanent welfare of the country. In this exceptional case it seems now to be an admitted doctrine, that the neighboring nations, or one powerful neighbor with the acquiescence of the rest, are warranted in demanding that the contest shall cease, and a reconciliation take place on equitable terms of compromise. (CW XXI: 121)

Mill isn't thinking here of political and economic support for despotism, for then he would have to acknowledge that liberal and democratic governments have sometimes (often?) found it in their interest to ally themselves with despots. That is usually a bad policy, but it isn't what concerns him here. He also thinks it unnecessary "in a free country" to condemn military intervention on behalf of despotism. But what about intervention in a "protracted civil war," possibly between the forces of freedom and unfreedom? Mill claims that foreign powers should impose a compromise (rather than assist one side in the war); they should aim simply to stop the fighting, when the fighting itself has become the chief source of injury or when the victory of either side, given the division of the country, would lead to brutal repression of the other. He takes this to be uncontroversial, although it is hard to imagine a case where the question of who would actually impose the compromise and on what terms wouldn't be contested in the international community. Mill never asks how such contests are best resolved. The standard answer today would be to turn to the United Nations (UN), and certainly it would be worthwhile to aim at creating a UN capable of formulating and enforcing "equitable terms." But no such UN exists today. We haven't gotten much further than Mill's description of the available agents: "the neighboring nations or one powerful neighbor with [or, in practice, without: MW] the acquiescence of the rest."

With respect to the question, whether one country is justified in helping the people of another in a struggle against their government for free institutions, the answer will be different, according as the yoke which the people are attempting to throw off is that of a purely native government, or of foreigners; considering as one of foreigners, every government which maintains itself by foreign support. When the contest is only with native rulers, and with such native strength as those rulers can enlist in their defense, the answer I should give to the question of the legitimacy of intervention is, as a general rule, No. The reason is, that there can seldom be anything approaching to assurance that intervention, even if successful, would be for the good of the people themselves. The only test possessing any real value, of a people's having become fit for popular institutions, is that they, or a sufficient portion of them to prevail in the contest, are willing to brave labor and danger for their liberation. (CW XXI: 122)

Foreign states and armies can come to the aid of a national liberation struggle against foreign rule, but they cannot come to the aid of a revolutionary struggle against domestic despotism – this is Mill's argument. French assistance to the American war for independence would be justified by his rule, and this was probably one of the cases in his mind, although his primary focus was on the failure of Britain to help the Hungarians in 1848. Presumably it is only when the liberation forces are losing the war (or perhaps only when they are sure to be overwhelmed, as the Hungarians were) that a military invasion would be justified. Mill's rule would not have justified a Japanese invasion of India in 1940, even if its announced purpose had been to install a Congress government. It is because such invasions so often have a different purpose that the justification is always problematic – also because third-party invasions may open the way to a wider war. Mill acknowledges this latter difficulty, and I return to it later.

Revolutions, by contrast, must be won or lost by the local forces that initiate them. This is Mill's hardest argument and, leaving aside his views about civilization and barbarism, it is by far his most controversial argument. People have a right (this is our language, not Mill's) to be rescued from foreign rule, but not from domestic despotism – because domestic despotism is taken to be reflective of their own history and culture. Revolution is always a *kulturkampf*, and the transformation of a political culture can only be the work of the people whose culture it is. Consider the Jacobin claim that Louis XVI was not really a Frenchman and therefore not a traitor, as the Girondins claimed, but an "enemy of the people." In the Jacobin mind, Europe was ruled by an international aristocracy, a continental (and familial) alliance of kings and feudal nobles, whose members were citizens and patriots nowhere, with no loyalty except to one another. If we imagine a Europe of that sort, then aristocratic rule could justly be opposed by an international alliance of democrats. The military intervention of any democratic nation (had there been any) in support of the French revolutionaries would have been justified. But if, more plausibly, we think of Louis as a Frenchman, even as an embodiment of Frenchness, then he has to be dealt with, and a new embodiment realized (or not), by the French themselves. Only they can do that because it is only in the course of doing it that they will create the new political culture necessary to support a free state.

Mill writes as if his argument is about desert: the revolutionaries must prove by "braving labor and danger" that they are worthy of freedom. But he also knows that the worthiness of some may not be sufficient. He is willing to let the revolutionaries lose, even if their cause is just, even if each of them is very brave, so long as they are unable to mobilize a sufficient number of their fellows. And the reason for this has less to do with desert than, more practically, as we shall see, with the preconditions of stable democratic rule.

But the evil is, that if they have not sufficient love of liberty to be able to wrest it from merely domestic oppressors, the liberty which is bestowed on them by other hands than their own, will have nothing real, nothing permanent. No people ever was and remained free, but because it was determined to be so. (CW XXI: 122)

Here is Mill's argument against what is now called, and what I have already been calling, "regime change." It doesn't work. Free institutions require free men and (Mill may be the first political theorist for whom this addition is necessary) free women. That doesn't mean "free" in the minimalist sense of "not slaves." What is required to sustain a free politics is much more than that: a body of men and women, fellow citizens, who value their freedom, who act freely in the political arena, and who are prepared to defend their right to act freely. And citizens like that are themselves created in the course of creating the politics that makes them free. This is a very attractive argument, especially so, perhaps, to political activists. But it has an obvious problem. It accounts only for the freedom of the first generation. The next generation doesn't have to "brave labor and danger" to be free – which may be why Thomas Jefferson, a Millian before Mill, wrote to a friend after Shays's Rebellion: "God forbid we should be 20 years without such a rebellion, . . . What country can preserve its liberties if their rulers are not warned from time to time that their people preserve the spirit of resistance?" And then, more famously, "The tree of liberty must be refreshed from time to time with the blood of patriots and tyrants. It is its natural manure." That is almost certainly Mill's argument as well, although he was too sober a writer to put it so bluntly. The political culture of freedom is sustained not only by vigilance but also by active participation. Mill has a very stern view of citizenship: if it is especially hard for the first generation of citizens, it is never easy. The claim of foreigners to bring the gift of liberty must always be rejected. This is a poisonous gift, for the people who accept it and then think themselves free will not be able to sustain their freedom. They will find their masters, or their masters will find them.

So, again, when a nation, in her own defense, has gone to war with a despot, and has had the rare good fortune not only to succeed in her own resistance, but to hold the conditions of peace in her own hands, she is entitled to say that she will make no treaty, unless with some other ruler than the one whose existence as such may be a perpetual menace to her safety and freedom. (CW XXI: 123)

Mill may have an example in mind, but for us the most obvious case is that of World War II, which I have already described. The allies were, rightly, not prepared to sign a peace treaty with Hitler or with any representative of the Nazi regime. But note that Mill does not explicitly endorse military occupation and political reconstruction by the victors. He would presumably have preferred that the people of the defeated nation themselves produce "some other ruler" than the despot who began the war. But given the character of modern totalitarian regimes and the destructiveness of modern warfare, this may not be possible. Instead, it may be necessary for the victors to rebuild not only the economy but also the government of the people they have defeated. If this is so, then we need an account, which Mill does not provide, of the regulative conditions of this work – a theory of *jus post bellum* (Mill seems interested only in the more standard questions of *jus ad bellum*). Perhaps it should be a feature of any such theory that the singular "nation" that is the subject of Mill's argument has to be joined in the work by other nations or by some regional or international organization that can set limits on the self-interested behavior that commonly accompanies singularity.

But the case of a people struggling against a foreign yoke, or against a native tyranny upheld by foreign arms, illustrates the reasons for non-intervention in an opposite way; for in this case the reasons themselves do not exist. A people the most attached to freedom, the most capable of defending and of making a good use of free institutions, may be unable to contend successfully for them against the military strength of another nation much more powerful. To assist a people thus kept down, is not to disturb the balance of forces on which the permanent maintenance of freedom in a country depends, but to redress that balance when it is already unfairly and violently disturbed. . . . Intervention to enforce non-intervention is always rightful, always moral, if not always prudent. (CW XXI: 123)

Here is a classic example of the exception that proves the rule. Non-intervention in the politics of another people is the rule, but sometimes intervention is the only way to make the rule good, and then, and only then, can it be right to intervene, that is, to send an army across a political frontier. We are barred from trying to shape political conditions in another country, but we are permitted, perhaps required, to prevent anyone else from doing that. Even here, we are only to intervene if local resistance is about to be overwhelmed. If a nation is able to defend its own freedom or to win its own freedom, even at high cost, Mill would not intervene simply to reduce the cost. The difficulty here is that when a people is about to be overwhelmed by superior force, the same superior force may make any intervention on their behalf dangerous – not only to the intervening state but to many other states as well. The obvious case is Hungary again: a little over a century after the British declined to intervene in 1848, the United States declined to intervene in 1956 – in both cases against the Russian army. Contemporary Tibet is another example: no one will risk a full-scale war with China for the sake of Tibetan freedom. As Mill says, intervention is such cases is justified but "not always prudent." Still, one might think here of measures short of war, which, if they were imposed internationally, with a disciplined refusal of "business as usual," might be effective.

The first nation which, being powerful enough to make its voice effectual, has the spirit and courage to say that not a gun shall be fired in Europe by soldiers of one Power against the revolted subjects of another, will be the idol of the friends of freedom. . . . The declaration alone will ensure the almost immediate emancipation of every people which desires liberty sufficiently to be capable of maintaining it; and the nation which gives the word will soon find itself at the head of an alliance of free peoples. . . . The prize is too glorious not be snatched sooner or later by some free country, and the time may not be distant when England, if she does not take this heroic part because of its heroism, will be compelled to take it from consideration of her own safety. (CW XXI: 124)

Mill's ambition for his country is very grand (although I come in a moment to its important limits): he wants Britain to be not only a beacon of freedom but an active political and, if necessary, military agent. He predicts that if it acts with sufficient courage, it will find itself "at the head of an alliance of free peoples." But what he is advocating, at the first moment, is unilateral action. All this has a familiar ring in these latter days. It is important to note, therefore, that Mill's mandate for Britain extends only to Europe – if only because the barbarism (in his eyes) of the rest of the world does not invite a politics of freedom. The moral prerequisites of freedom must exist before foreign powers can open the way for the achievement of freedom. This is an argument that one might make even without Mill's theory of "social improvement." But his ambition is limited in another sense: all he wants Britain to do is to open the way. The actual achievement must still be the work of people who "desire liberty sufficiently to be able to maintain it." Looking at the despotic regimes of Europe, Mill hopes for regime change, but he does not pin his hopes on the British Royal Navy (the nineteenth-century equivalent of the U.S. Air Force) but on the energy and commitment of ordinary people in the countries the despots rule.

Mill would be heartened, I think, by the development of an international civil society in which nongovernmental, and hence nonmilitary, organizations support a politics of freedom in other people's countries without undermining the necessary self-help of those same people. Groups such as Human Rights Watch and Amnesty International, although they cannot describe their projects in this way, work effectively for regime change. But they don't enlist the military power of any nation in their pursuit of the "glorious" prize of liberty; they don't impose a new regime, and the success of their work depends ultimately on local energy and commitment. We might think of the support they provide for the forces of freedom and democracy as a contemporary version of what the old left called "solidarity." It is an intervention of hearts and minds, but not of armies, and it falls well within the Millian program.

Bibliography

Althusser, Louis. 1972. *Politics and History: Montesquieu, Hegel and Marx*. Trans. Ben Brewster. London: NLB.

Anderson, Elizabeth. 1991. "John Stuart Mill and Experiments in Living." *Ethics* 102: 4–26.

Anderson, Perry. 2000. "Renewals." *New Left Review*, new series, no. 1 (January/February): 5–24.

Anderson-Gold, Sharon. 2001. *Cosmopolitanism and Human Rights*. Cardiff: University of Wales Press.

Andrews, Stuart. 1967. *Enlightened Despotism*. London: Longmans.

Annas, Julia. 1977. "Mill and *The Subjection of Women*." *Philosophy* 52: 179–94.

Appiah, Kwame Anthony. 2005. *The Ethics of Identity*. Princeton: Princeton University Press.

Aristotle. 1995. *The Politics*. Translated by Ernest Backer. Oxford: Oxford University Press.

Arkes, Hadley. 1981. *The Philosopher in the City: The Moral Dimensions of Urban Politics*. Princeton: Princeton University Press.

Arneson, Richard J. 1979. "Mill's Doubts about Freedom under Socialism." In *New Essays on John Stuart Mill and Utilitarianism*. Edited by Wesley E. Cooper, Kai Nielson, and Steven C. Patton. Guelph, Ontario: Canadian Association for Publishing in Philosophy.

———. 1982. "Democracy and Liberty in Mill's Theory of Government." *Journal of the History of Philosophy* XX (January): 43–64.

Arnold, Matthew. 1996–2002. *The Letters of Matthew Arnold*. Edited by Cecil Y. Lang. 6 vols., Charlottesville and London: University Press of Virginia.

Ashcraft, Richard. 1989. "Class Conflict and Constitutionalism in J.S. Mill's Thought." *Liberalism and the Moral Life*. Ed Nancy Rosenblum. Cambridge: Cambridge University Press.

———. 1998. "John Stuart Mill and the Theoretical Foundations of Democratic Socialism." In *Mill and the Moral Character of Liberalism*. Edited by Eldon J. Eisenach. University Park: The Pennsylvania University Press.

Bailey, Alison. 1998. *Journal of Social Philosophy* (Winter): 104–19.

Bain, A. 1882. *John Stuart Mill: A Criticism With Personal Recollections*. London: Longmans, Green.

Barrell, J. 1972. "Introduction" to Samuel Taylor Coleridge, *On the Constitution of the Church and State*. London: J. M. Dent.

Barry, Brian. 1997 [1982]. "Humanity and Justice in Global Perspective." In *Contemporary Political Philosophy: An Anthology*. Edited by Robert E. Goodin and Philip Pettit. Oxford: Blackwell.

Bartky, Sandra Lee. 1990. *Femininity and Domination: Studies in the Phenomenology of Oppression*. New York and London: Routledge.

Bartley, Paula. 2000. *Prostitution: Prevention and Reform in England, 1860–1914*. London: Routledge.

Baum, Bruce. 2000. *Rereading Power and Freedom in J. S. Mill*. Toronto: University of Toronto Press.

———. 2003. "Millian Radical Democracy: Education for Freedom and Dilemmas of Liberal Equality." *Political Studies* 51, no. 2 (Summer): 404–428.

Bauman, Zygmunt. 1988. *Freedom*. Minneapolis: University of Minnesota Press.

Beitz, Charles. 1979. *Political Theory and International Relations*. Princeton: Princeton University Press.

———. 1994. "Cosmopolitan Liberalism and the States System." In *Political Restructuring in Europe: Ethical Perspectives*. Edited by Chris Brown. London: Routledge.

Benditt, Theodore M. 1979. "Compromising Interests and Principles." In *Compromise in Ethics, Law and Politics*. Edited by J. Roland Pennock and John W. Chapman. New York: New York University Press.

Benjamin, Martin. 1990. *Splitting the Difference: Compromise and Integrity in Ethics and Politics*. Lawrence: University Press of Kansas.

Benner, Erica. 1997. "Nationality without Nationalism." *Journal of Political Ideologies* 2, no. 2: 189–206.

Bentham, J. 1838–43. *The Works of Jeremy Bentham*. Edited by J. Bowring. 11 vols. Edinburgh: W. Tait; London: Simpkin, Marshall.

———. 1931. *Principles of the Civil Code in his book, The Theory of Legislation*. Edited by C. K. Ogden. London: Kegan Paul, Trench, Trubner.

———. 1962a. *The Works of Jeremy Bentham*. Edited by John Bowring. 10 vols. New York: Russell and Russell.

———. 1962b [1793]. "Essay on the Influence of Time and Place in Matters of Legislation." In *The Works of Jeremy Bentham Published Under the Superintendence of His Executor, John Bowring*. Vol. I: 169–94. New York: Russell & Russell.

———. 1962c [1793]. Emancipate your Colonies! In *The Works of Jeremy Bentham Published Under the Superintendence of His Executor, John Bowring*. Vol. IV. New York: Russell & Russell.

———. 1970. *The Collected Works of Jeremy Bentham: An Introduction to the Principles of Morals and Legislation*. Edited by J. H. Burns and H. L. A. Hart. London: Athlone Press.

———. 1983 [1830]. *Constitutional Code, Volume I*. Edited by F. Rosen and J. H. Burns [*Collected Works of Jeremy Bentham*]. Oxford: Clarendon Press.

———. 1996 [1789]). *An Introduction to the Principles of Morals and Legislation*. Edited by J. H. Burns and H. L. A. Hart, with a new introduction by F. Rosen [*Collected Works of Jeremy Bentham*]. Oxford: Clarendon Press.

Berger, Fred R. 1984. *Happiness, Justice, and Freedom: The Moral and Political Philosophy of John Stuart Mill*. Berkeley: University of California Press.

Berkowitz, Peter. 1998. "Mill: Liberty, Virtue, and the Discipline of Individuality." In *Mill and the Moral Character of Liberalism.* Edited by E. J. Eisenach. University Park: Pennsylvania State University Press.

————. 1999. *Virtue and the Making of Modern Liberalism.* Princeton: Princeton University press.

Berlin, Isaiah. 1969 [1959]. "John Stuart Mill and the Ends of Life." *Four Essays on Liberty.* New York: Oxford University Press.

————. 1992 [1958]. "Two Concepts of Liberty." In *Four Essays on Liberty.* Oxford: Oxford University Press.

————. 1997 [1959]. "John Stuart Mill and the Ends of Life." In *Mill.* Edited by Alan Ryan. New York: Norton.

Bernstein, Eduard. 1993 [1899]. *The Preconditions of Socialism.* Edited by Henry Tudor. Cambridge: Cambridge University Press.

Biagini, E. 1996. "John Stuart Mill and the Model of Ancient Athens." In *Citizenship and Community.* Edited by E. Biagini. Cambridge: Cambridge University Press.

Blackburn, Robin. 1991. "Fin de Siecle: Socialism after the Crash." In *After the Fall: The Failure of Socialism and the Future of Socialism.* Edited by R. Blackburn. London: Verso.

Bluche, François. 1968. *Le Despotisme éclaire.* Paris: Fayard.

Bobbio, Norberto. 1987. *Which Socialism? Marxism, Socialism and Democracy.* Translated by Roger Griffin. Edited by Richard Bellamy. Cambridge, England: Polity Press.

Boehm, Max. 1931. "Cosmopolitanism." In *The Encyclopedia of the Social Sciences.* Vol. IV. New York: Macmillan, 457–61.

Boralevi, Lea Campos. 1984. *Bentham and the Oppressed.* European University Institute Series C. Berlin and New York: de Gruyter.

Brennan, Timothy. 2001. "Cosmopolitanism and Internationalism." *New Left Review,* second series, 7 (January–February): 75–84.

Brink, David O. 1992. "Mill's Deliberative Utilitarianism." *Philosophy & Public Affairs* 21, no. 1 (Winter): 67–103.

Bristow, Edward. 1978. *Vice and Vigilance: Purity Movements in Britain since 1700.* Dublin: Rowman and Littlefield.

Brogran, Hugh. 1973. *Tocqueville.* London: Collins/Fontana.

Bromwich, David, and George Kateb, editors. 2002. *On Liberty.* New Haven: Yale University Press.

Brown, D. G. 1972. "Mill on Liberty and Morality." *Philosophical Review* 81: 133–58.

Buber, Martin. 1970. *I and Thou.* New York and London: Simon & Schuster.

Bulwer, E. 1833. *England and the English.* 2 vols. London: R. Bentley.

Burgess-Jackson, Keith. 1995. "John Stuart Mill, Radical Feminist." *Social Theory and Practice* 21: 369–96.

Burns, J. H. 1968 [1957]. "J.S. Mill and Democracy, 1829–61." In *Mill, A Collection of Critical Essays.* Edited by J. B. Schneewind. Garden City: Anchor Books.

Butler, Brian E. 2001. "There Are Peoples and There Are Peoples: A Critique of Rawls's 'The Law of Peoples.'" *Florida Philosophical Review* 1 (Winter): 6–24.

Caine, Barbara. 1992. *Victorian Feminists.* Oxford: Oxford University Press.

Capaldi, N. 2004. *John Stuart Mill: A Biography.* Cambridge: Cambridge University Press.

Carens, Joseph. 1987. "Aliens and Citizens: The Case for Open Borders." *Review of Politics* 49, no. 3: 251–73.

Carter, April. 2001. *The Political Theory of Global Citizenship.* London and New York: Routledge.

Chambers, Simone. 1996. *Reasonable Democracy: Jürgen Habermas and The Politics of Discourse.* Ithaca: Cornell University Press.

Cheah, Pheng, and Bruce Robbins, editors. 1998. *Cosmopolitics: Thinking and Feeling beyond the Nation.* Minneapolis: University of Minnesota Press.

Claeys, Gregory. 1987. "Justice, Independence, and Industrial Democracy: The Development of John Stuart Mill's Views on Socialism." *Journal of Politics* 49 (February): 122–147.

Cobban, Alfred. 1969. *The Nation State and National Self-Determination.* London: Collins (the Fontana Library).

Cohen, G. A. 1992. "The Future of a Disillusion." *Queen's Quarterly* 99, no. 2 (Summer): 280–96.

———. 2000. *If You're an Egalitarian, How Come You're So Rich?* Cambridge, MA: Harvard University Press.

Cole, David. 2003. "Their Liberties, Our Security." *Boston Review,* December 2002–January 2003. http://www.bostonreview.net/BR27.6/cole.html#1.

Cole, G. D. H. 1964 [1920]. "Guild Socialism Restated." In *Socialist Thought: A Documentary History.* Edited by Albert Fried and Ronald Sanders. Garden City, NY: Anchor Books.

Coleridge, S. T. 1972 [1830]. *On the Constitution of the Church and State.* Edited by J. Barrell. London: J. M. Dent.

Collini, Stefan. 1984. "Introduction" to J. S. Mill, *Essays on Equality, Law, and Education: Collected Works XXI.* Toronto: University of Toronto Press.

———. 1991. *Public Moralists: Political Thought and Intellectual Life in Britain, 1850–1930.* Oxford: Clarendon Press.

Colmer, J. 1976. "Editor's Introduction" to S. T. Coleridge, *On the Constitution of the Church and State [The Collected Works of Samuel Taylor Coleridge,* vol. X]. Princeton: Princeton University Press; London: Routledge and Kegan Paul.

Condorcet, Marie Jean Antoine Nicolas Caritat, Marquis de. 1970 [1793]. *Esquisse d'un tableau historique des progrès de l'ésprit humain.* Yvon Belaval, ed. Paris: Librairie Philosophique Vrin.

Constant, Benjamin. 1988 [1814]. *The Spirit of Conquest and Usurpation and Their Relation to European Civilization.* In *Political Writings.* Edited by Biancamaria Fontana. Cambridge: Cambridge University Press.

Conway, Stephen. 1989. "Bentham on Peace and War." *Utilitas* 1, no. 1: 82–101.

———. 1990. "Bentham, the Benthamites, and the Nineteenth-Century British Peace Movement." *Utilitas* 2, no. 2: 221–43.

Coser, Lewis, and Irving Howe. 1966. "Images of Socialism." In *The Radical Papers.* Edited by Irving Howe. Garden City, NY: Anchor Books.

Cott, Nancy F. 1987. *The Grounding of Modern Feminism.* New Haven: Yale University Press.

Crisp, Roger. 1997. *Mill on Utilitarianism.* London: Routledge.

Crisp, Roger, and Michael Slote. 1997. *Virtue Ethics.* Oxford: Oxford University Press.

Crosland, C. A. R. 1964 [1956]. "The Future of Socialism." In *Socialist Thought: A Documentary History.* Edited by Albert Fried and Ronald Sanders. Garden City, NY: Anchor Books.

Dahl, R. A. 1989. *Democracy and Its Critics*. New Haven: Yale University Press.

———. 2001. *How Democratic Is the American Constitution?* New Haven: Yale University Press.

Dasgupta, Uma. 1995. "The Ilbert Bill Agitation, 1883." In *We Fought Together for Freedom: Chapters from the Indian Nationalist Movement*. Edited by Ravi Dayal. New Delhi: Oxford University Press.

Department of Justice. Criminal Victimization 2002. Washington, DC: U.S. Government Printing Office. Publication No. 199994.

Dewey, John. 1991 [1927]. *Liberalism and Social Action*. Amherst, NY: Prometheus Books.

———. 1958 [1935]. "Liberty and Social Control." In *Philosophy of Education*. Totawa, NJ: Littlefield, Adams.

di Stefano, Christine. 1991. "John Stuart Mill: The Heart of Liberalism." In *Configurations of Masculinity: A Feminist Perspective on Modern Political Theory*. Edited by C. di Stefano. Ithaca: Cornell University Press.

Donner, Wendy. 1991. *The Liberal Self: John Stuart Mill's Moral and Political Philosophy*. Ithaca: Cornell University Press.

———. 1993. "John Stuart Mill's Liberal Feminism." *Philosophical Studies* 69: 155–66.

———. 1998. "Mill's Utilitarianism." *The Cambridge Companion to Mill* Edited by John Skorupski. Cambridge: Cambridge University Press.

———. 1999. "A Millian Perspective on the Relations between Persons and Their Bodies." In *Persons and Their Bodies: Rights, Responsibilities, Relationships*. Edited by Mark J. Cherry and Thomas J. Bole III. Dordrecht: Kluwer Academic Publishers.

———. 2005. "Mill's Theory of Value." *The Blackwell Guide to Mill's "Utilitarianism."* Edited by Henry West. Oxford: Blackwell.

Duncan, Graeme. 1973. *Marx and Mill: Two Views of Social Conflict and Social Harmony*. Cambridge: Cambridge University Press.

Dutton, Geoffrey. 1967. *The Hero as Murderer: The Life of Edward John Eyre, Australian Explorer and Governor of Jamaica, 1815–1901*. Melbourne: Cheshire.

Dworkin, Gerald. 1997a. *Mill's "On Liberty": Critical Essays*. New York: Rowman and Littlefield.

———. 1997b [1972]. "Paternalism." In *Mill's "On Liberty": Critical Essays*. Edited by Gerald Dworkin. London, New York, Oxford: Rowman & Littlefield.

Dworkin, Ronald. 1978. "Liberalism." In *Public and Private Morality*. Edited by Stuart Hampshire. Cambridge: Cambridge University Press.

———. 1996a. "Do Liberty and Equality Conflict?" In *Living as Equals*. Edited by Paul Barker. Oxford: Oxford University Press.

———. 1996b. "Foundations of Liberal Equality." In *Equal Freedom: Selected Tanner Lectures on Human Values*. Edited by Stephen Darwall. Ann Arbor: University of Michigan Press.

———. 2000. *Sovereign Virtue: The Theory and Practice of Equality*. Cambridge: Harvard University Press.

———. 2002. "The Threat to Patriotism." *New York Review of Books*, February 28: 44–49.

Eisenach, Eldon J., editor. 1998. *Mill and the Moral Character of Liberalism*. University Park: Pennsylvania State University Press.

Eisenstein, Zillah. 1981. *The Radical Future of Liberal Feminism*. New York: Longman.

Ellis, Anthony. 1992. "Utilitarianism and International Ethics." *Traditions of International Ethics.* Edited by Terry Nardin and David R. Mapel. Cambridge: Cambridge University Press.

Elster, Jon, and Karl Ove Moene. 1989. "Introduction." In *Alternatives to Capitalism.* Edited by Jon Elster and Karl Ove Moene. Cambridge: Cambridge University Press.

Fabre, Cécile, and David Miller. 2003. "Justice and Culture: Rawls, Sen, Nussbaum and O'Neill." *Political Studies Review* 1: 4–17.

Feinberg, Joel. 1980. *Rights, Justice and the Bounds of Liberty: Essays in Social Philosophy.* Princeton: Princeton University Press.

Finley, M. I. 1985 [1973]. *Democracy Ancient and Modern.* New Brunswick, NJ: Rutgers University Press.

Friedman, Milton. 1962. *Capitalism and Freedom.* Chicago: University of Chicago Press.

Friedman, Richard B. 1966. "A New Exploration of Mill's Essay *On Liberty.*" *Political Studies* 14 (October): 281–304.

Gibbons, John. 1990. "J. S. Mill, Liberalism, and Progress." In *Victorian Liberalism: Nineteenth Century Political Thought and Practice.* Edited by Richard Bellamy. London: Routledge.

Gray, John. 1983. *Mill on Liberty: A Defense.* London: Routledge.

———. 1989. "Indirect Liberty and Fundamental Rights." In *Liberalisms: Essays in Political Philosophy.* London: Routledge.

———. 1989. *Liberalisms: Essays in Political Philosophy.* London and New York: Routledge.

———. 1995. "Harnessing the Market." *New Left Review*, no. 210 (March/April): 147–52.

Grosrichard, Alain. 1979. *Structure du sérial: La fiction du despotisme asiatique dans l'Occident classique.* Paris: Éditions du Seuil.

Grote, George. 1906 [1846–56]. *A History of Greece.* 12 vols. London: J. M. Dent; New York: E. P. Dutton.

———. 2000 [1846–56]. *A History of Greece.* 12 vols. Bristol: Thoemmes. (Reprint of 4th ed., 1872, in 10 vols.)

Gutmann, Amy. 1987. *Democratic Education.* Princeton: Princeton University Press.

———. *Liberal Equality.* Cambridge: Cambridge University Press, 1980.

———, and Dennis, Thompson. 1996. *Democracy and Disagreement.* Cambridge: Harvard University Press.

Haakonsen, Knud. 1996. *Natural Law and Moral Philosophy.* Cambridge: Cambridge University Press.

Habermas, Jürgen. 1996 [1992]. *Between Facts and Norms: Contribution to a Discourse Theory of Law and Democracy.* Translated by William Rehg. Cambridge, MA and London: MIT Press.

———, and Adam Michnik. 1994. "More Humility, Fewer Illusions." *New York Review of Books* 41 (March 24): 24–29.

Habibi, Don A. 1999. "The Moral Dimensions of J. S. Mill's Colonialism." *Journal of Social Philosophy* 30(1): 125–146.

Hall, Catherine. 2002. *Civilizing Subjects: Metropole and Colony in the English Imagination, 1830–1867.* Oxford: Polity.

Hamburger, Joseph. 1965. *Intellectuals in Politics.* New Haven: Yale University Press.

Hansen, H. 2005. " 'The Great Business of Life': Mill and Argumentation." Unpublished paper presented at the International Society for Utilitarian Studies Conference, Dartmouth College, USA, August.

Hansen, M. H. 1996. "The Ancient Athenian and the Modern Liberal View of Liberty as a Democratic Ideal." In *Demokratia: A Conversation on Democracies, Ancient and Modern*. Edited by J. Ober and C. Hedrick. Princeton: Princeton University Press.

_____. 1999. *The Athenian Democracy in the Age of Demosthenes* [1991]. Translated by J. A. Crook. Norman: University of Oklahoma Press (Oxford: Blackwell).

Harris, Abram L. 1956. "John Stuart Mill's Theory of Progress." *Ethics* 66: 157–75.

_____. 1964. "John Stuart Mill: Servant of the East India Company." *Canadian Journal of Economics and Political Science* 30: 185–202.

Harris, Ian. 2004. "Edmund Burke." *The Stanford Encyclopedia of Philosophy*. Edited by Edward N. Zalta. Spring Edition. http://plato.stanford.edu/archives/spr2004/entries/burke/.

Haslanger, Sally. 1995. "Ontology and Social Construction." *Philosophical Topics* 23:2 (Fall): 95–125.

_____. 2002a. "On Being Objective and Being Objectified." In *A Mind of One's Own: Feminist Essays on Reason and Objectivity*. Edited by L. M. Antony and C. E. Witt. Boulder, CO: Westview Press.

_____. 2002b. "Social Construction: The Debunking Project." In *Socializing Metaphysics*. Edited by F. Schmitt. Lanham, MD: Rowman & Littlefield.

_____. 2002c. "Ontology and Social Construction." *Philosophical Topics* 23(2): 95–125.

Hayes, Carlton J. H. 1931. *The Historical Evolution of Modern Nationalism*. New York: R. R. Smith.

Heater, Derek. 1996. *World Citizenship and Government: Cosmopolitan Ideas in the History of Western Political Thought*. Basingstoke: Macmillan.

_____. 2002. *World Citizenship: Cosmopolitan Thinking and Its Opponents*. London and New York: Cotinuum.

Heckman, Susan. 1992. "John Stuart Mill's *The Subjection of Women*: The Foundations of Liberal Feminism." *History of European Ideas* 15: 681–6.

Held, David. 1995. *Democracy and the Global Order: From the Modern State to Cosmopolitan Governance*. Cambridge: Polity Press.

_____. 2002. "Globalization, Corporate Practice and Cosmopolitan Social Standards." *Contemporary Political Theory* 1: 59–78.

Himmelfarb, Gertrude. 1963. "Introduction." *Essays on Politics and Culture*. J. S. Mill. Edited by Gertrude Himmelfarb. New York: Doubleday.

_____. 1974. *On Liberty and Liberalism: The Case of John Stuart Mill*. New York: Alfred Knopf.

Hirschmann, Edwin. 1980. *'White Mutiny:' The Ilbert Bill Crisis and the Genesis of the Indian National Congress*. New Delhi: Heritage.

Hoag, Robert W. 1986. "Happiness and Freedom: Recent Work on John Stuart Mill." *Philosophy & Public Affairs* 15(2): 188–99.

Hobhouse, Leonard T. 1980 [1911]. *Liberalism*. Westport, CT: Greenwood Press.

Holcolme, Lee. 1983. *Wives and Property: Reform of the Married Women's Property Law in Nineteenth-Century England*. Toronto: University of Toronto Press.

Hollander, Samuel. 1985. *The Economics of John Stuart Mill.* Vol. 2. Toronto: University of Toronto Press.

Holmes, Stephen, and Cass R. Sunstein. 1999. *The Cost of Rights: Why Liberty Depends on Taxes.* New York and London: Norton.

Holt, Thomas. 1992. *The Problem of Freedom: Race, Labor, and Politics in Jamaica and Britain, 1832–1938.* Baltimore: Johns Hopkins University Press.

Howe, Irving. 1966. "Introduction: The Radical Perspectiver." The Radical Papers, ed. Irving Howe. Garden City, NY: Doubleday.

Howes, John. 1986. "Mill on Women and Human Development." *Australasian Journal of Philosophy* 64 (supplement): 66–74.

Hutchings, Kimberly and Roland Dannreuther, eds. 1999. *Cosmopolitan Citizenship.* Houndmills, Basingstoke, Hampshire: Macmillan Press; NewYork: St. Martin's Press.

Jaggar, Alison. 1983. *Feminist Politics and Human Nature.* Totowa, NJ: Rowman & Allanheld.

Jardin, André. 1988. *Tocqueville: A Biography.* Translated by Lydia Davis with Robert Hemenway. New York: Farrar, Straus & Giroux.

Johnston, David. 1994. *The Idea of a Liberal Theory: A Critique and Reconstruction.* Princeton: Princeton University Press.

Jones, Charles. 1999. *Global Justice: Defending Cosmopolitanism.* Oxford: Oxford University Press.

Jones, Deiniol. 2003. "The origins of the global city: ethics and morality in contemporary cosmopolitanism." *British Journal of Politics and International Relations* 5(1): 50–73.

Jones, H. S. 2000. *Victorian Political Thought.* Basingstoke: Macmillan.

Kalsem, Kristin Brandser. 2004. "Looking for law in all the 'wrong' places: Outlaw texts and early women's advocacy." *Southern California Review of Law and Women's Studies* 13: 273–325.

Kant, Immanuel. 1991. *The Metaphysics of Morals.* Edited by Mary Gregor. Cambridge: Cambridge University Press.

Kateb, G. 2003. "A Reading of *On Liberty.*" In *On Liberty: John Stuart Mill.* Edited by D. Bromwich and G. Kateb. New Haven and London: Yale University Press.

Katznelson, Ira. 2003. *Desolation and Enlightenment: Political Knowledge After Total War, Totalitarianism, and the Holocaust.* New York : Columbia University Press.

Kilpatrick, D. G., Edmunds, C. N., and Seymour, A. K. 1992. *Rape in America: A Report to the Nation.* Arlington, VA: National Victim Center and Medical University of North Carolina.

Kinzer, Bruce L. 1978. "J. S. Mill and the Secret Ballot." *Historical Reflections* 5 (Summer): 19–39. Reprinted in G. W. Smith, ed. *J.S. Mill's Social and Political Thought: Critical Assessments.* London: Routledge, 1997.

———. 1984. "Mill and the Cattle Plague." *The Mill News Letter* 19: 2–12.

———. 1997. "J. S. Mill and the Problem of Party." In *John Stuart Mill's Social and Political Thought: Critical Assessments.* Edited by G. W. Smith. London: Routledge.

———, Ann P. Robson, and John M. Robson. 1992. *A Moralist in and out of Parliament: John Stuart Mill at Westminster, 1865–1868.* Toronto: University of Toronto Press.

Koebner, R. 1951. "Despot and Despotism: Vicissitudes of a Political Term." *Journal of the Warburg and Courtauld Institutes* 14: 292–302.

Kojève, Alexandre. 2000 [1950]. "Tyranny and Wisdom." In Leo Strauss, *On Tyranny: Including the Strauss-Kojève Correspondence*. Edited by Victor Gourevitch and Michael S. Roth. Chicago and London: University of Chicago Press.

Krieger, Leonard. 1975. *An Essay on the Theory of Enlightened Despotism*. Chicago and London: University of Chicago Press.

Krouse, Richard W. 1982. "Patriarchal Liberalism and Beyond: From John Stuart Mill to Harriet Taylor." In *The Family in Political Thought*. Edited by J. B. Elshtain. Amherst: University of Massachusetts Press.

Krug, E. G., Dahlberg, L. L., Mercy, J. A., Zwi, A. B., and Lozano, R., editors. 2004. *World Report on Violence and Health*. Geneva: World Health Organization.

Kuflik, Arthur. 1979. "Morality and Compromise." In *Compromise in Ethics, Law and Politics*. Edited by J. Roland Pennock and John W. Chapman. New York: New York University Press.

Kurtfirst, Robert. 1996. "J. S. Mill on Oriental Despotism, Including Its British variant." *Utilitas* 8(1): 73–87.

Kuttner, Robert. 1992. "Liberalism, Socialism, and Democracy." *The American Prospect* 9 (Spring): 7–12.

Kymlicka, Will. 2001. *Politics in the Vernacular: Nationalism, Multiculturalism, and Citizenship*. Oxford: Oxford University Press.

_____. 2002. *Contemporary Political Philosophy: An Introduction*. 2d ed. Oxford: Oxford University Press.

_____. 2003. "Being Canadian." *Government and Opposition* 38(3): 357–85.

Laine, Michael, ed. 1991. *A Cultivated Mind: Essays on J.S. Mill Presented to John Robson*. Toronto: University of Toronto Press.

Laski, Harold. 1924. "Introduction." In John Stuart Mill, *Autobiography*. Oxford: Oxford University Press.

Leavis, F. R. 1980[1950]. 'Introduction' to *Mill on Bentham and Coleridge*. Cambridge: Cambridge University Press.

Leliepvre-Botton, Sylvie. 1996. *Droit du sol, droit du sang: Patriotisme et sentiment national chez Rousseau*. Paris: Ellipses.

Levin, Michael. 2003. "John Stuart Mill: A Liberal Looks at Utopian Socialism in the Years of Revolution." *Utopian Studies* 14(2): 68–82.

Lichtenberg, Judith. 1999. "How Liberal can Nationalism Be?" In *Theorizing Nationalism*. Edited by Ronald Biener. Albany: State University of New York Press.

Lichtheim, George. 1975. *A Short History of Socialism*. London: Fontana.

Lindsay, Peter. 2000. "Overcoming False Dichotomies: Mill, Marx, and the Welfare State." *History of Political Thought* 21(4): 657–81.

Lock, F. P. 1998. *Edmund Burke*. Vol. I. Oxford: Clarendon Press.

Locke, John. 1988 [c. 1681]. *Two Treatises of Government*. Edited by Peter Laslett. Cambridge: Cambridge University Press.

_____. 1993 [c. 1681]. *The Second Treatise of Government: An Essay Concerning the True Original, Extent, and the End of Civil Government*. In *Political Writings of John Locke*. Edited by David Wootton. New York: Mentor.

_____. 1997 [1669]. "The Fundamental Constitutions of Carolina." In *Locke: Political Essays*. Edited by Mark Goldie. Cambridge: Cambridge University Press.

Lu, Catherine. 2000. "The One and Many Faces of Cosmopolitanism." *Journal of Political Philosophy* 8(2): 244–67.

Lyons, David. 1979. "Mill on Liberty and Harm to Others." *Canadian Journal of Philosophy* 5 (supplementary volume): 1–19.

———. 1994. *Rights, Welfare, and Mill's Moral Theory.* Oxford: Clarendon Press.

———, editor. 1997. *Mill's Utilitarianism: Critical Essays.* Lanham, MD: Rowman & Littlefield.

Macaulay, Thomas Babington. 1875. "Government of India. A Speech delivered in the House of Commons on the 10th of July, 1833. In *Speeches of Lord Macaulay corrected by Himself.* London: Longmans, Green.

MacIntosh, Peggy. 1991. "White Privilege and Male Privilege: A Personal Account of Coming to See Their Correspondence through Work in Women Studies." In *Race, Class, and Gender: An Anthology.* Edited by M. L. Andersen and P. H. Collins. New York: Wadsworth.

Macpherson, C. B. 1962. *The Political Theory of Possessive Individualism.* Oxford: Oxford University Press.

———. 1977. *The Life and Times of Liberal Democracy.* Oxford: Oxford University Press.

Majeed, Javed. 1992. *Ungoverned Imaginings: James Mill's The History of British India and Orientalism.* Oxford: Clarendon Press.

Manent, Pierre. 1994. *An Intellectual History of Liberalism.* Translated by Rebecca Balinski. Princeton, NJ: Princeton University Press.

Mantena, Karuna. *Alibis of Empire: Henry Maine and the Transformation of Imperial Ideology.* Princeton: Princeton University Press (forthcoming).

Marcuse, Herbert. 1991 [1964]. *One-Dimensional Man: Studies in the Ideology of Advanced Industrial Society.* Boston: Beacon Press.

Markovits, Daniel. 2005. "Quarantines and Distributive Justice." *Journal of Law, Medicine and Ethics* 33: 323–38.

Marx, Karl. 1983 [1871]. "The Civil War in France." In *The Portable Karl Marx.* Edited by Eugene Kamenka. Harmondsworth, England: Penguin Books.

———. 1983 [1875]. "Marginal Notes to the Programme of the German Workers' Party [Critique of the Gotha Programme]." In *The Portable Karl Marx.* Edited by Eugene Kamenka. Harmondsworth, England: Penguin Books.

——— and Friedrich Engels. 1983 [1848]. "Manifesto of the Communist Party." In *The Portable Karl Marx.* Harmondsworth, England: Penguin Books.

Mazlish, Bruce. 1975. *James and John Stuart Mill: Father and Son in the Nineteenth Century.* New York: Basic Books.

McCallum, Gerald C. 1973. "Negative and Positive Freedom." In *Concepts in Social and Political Philosophy.* Edited by Richard Flathman. New York: Macmillan.

McElroy, Wendy. 2000. "The Contagious Disease Acts." *Freedom Daily,* March 2000. http://www.zetetics.com/-mac/articles/contagious.html.

McHugh, Paul. 1980. *Prostitution and Victorian Social Reform.* New York: St. Martin's Press.

McKinnon, Catharine. 1987. *Feminism Unmodified: Discourses on Life and Law.* Cambridge, MA: Harvard University Press.

———. 1989. *Toward a Feminist Theory of the State.* Cambridge, MA: Harvard University Press.

Medearis, John. 2005. "Labor, Democracy, Utility, and Mill's Critique of Private Property." *American Journal of Political Science* 49 (January): 135–49.

Mehta, Pratap Bhanu. 1996. "Liberalism, Nation and Empire: The Case of J. S. Mill," Paper Presented at the Annual Meeting of the American Political Science Association.

Mehta, Uday. 1999. *Liberalism and Empire: A Study in Nineteenth-Century British Liberal Thought.* Chicago: University of Chicago Press.

Mill, James. 1967 [1829]. *An Analysis of the Phenomena of the Human Mind.* 2 vols. London: Longmans, Green & Dyer (reprint New York: Augustus M. Kelly).

_____. 1858 [1817]. *The History of British India.* 5th ed. with Notes and Continuation by H. H. Wilson. 10 vol. London: James Madden, Piper, Stephenson, and Spence.

_____. 1990 [1817]. *The History of British India.* New Delhi: Atlantic.

_____. 1978. "Essay on Government." In *Utilitarian Logic and Politics.* Edited by Jack Lively and John Rees. Oxford: Oxford University Press.

Mill, John Stuart. 1870a. "Letter to Williams Malleson," 18 January, 1870. In *The Letters of John Stuart Mill.* Edited by Hugh S. R. Elliot. Vol. III. London: Longmans Green.

_____. 1870b, "Letter to Professor J. Nichol, of Glasgow." 29 December, 1870. In *The Letters of John Stuart Mill.* Edited by Hugh S. R. Elliot. Vol. III. London: Longmans Green.

_____. 1963–91. *The Collected Works of John Stuart Mill.* Edited by John M. *Robson.* 33 vols. Toronto: University of Toronto Press.

Millar, F. 1998. *The Crowd in Rome in the Late Republic.* Ann Arbor: University of Michigan Press.

Miller, Dale. 2000. "John Stuart Mill's Civil Liberalism." *History of Political Thought* XXI, no. 1 (Spring): 88–113.

_____. 2003. "Mill's 'Socialism.'" *Politics, Philosophy and Economics* 2, no. 2: 213–38.

Miller, David. 1995. *On Nationality.* Oxford: Clarendon Press.

_____. 2000. *Citizenship and National Identity.* Cambridge: Polity Press.

Moody, Kim. 1997. *Workers in a Lean World: Unions in the International Economy.* London: Verso.

Morales, Maria H. 1996. *Perfect Equality: John Stuart Mill on Well-Constituted Communities.* Lanham, MD: Rowman & Littlefield.

Morrow, J. 1990. *Coleridge's Political Thought, Property, Morality, and the Limits of Traditional Discourse.* Basingstoke: Macmillan.

Morton, James. 1987. "AIDS and the Contagious Diseases Acts." *New Law Journal* 137: 764–6.

Mouffe, Chantal. 1993. "Towards a Liberal Socialism." In *The Return of the Political.* London: Verso.

Murray, Janet Horowitz. 1982. *Strong-Minded Women and Other Lost Voices from Nineteenth-Century England.* New York: Pantheon Books.

Nagel, Thomas. 2003. "Rawls and Liberalism." In *The Cambridge Companion to Rawls.* Edited by Samuel Freeman. Cambridge: Cambridge University Press.

Neidleman, Jason Andrew. 2001. *The General Will Is Citizenship: Inquiries into French Political Thought.* Lanham, MD: Rowman & Littlefield.

New Left Review. 1960. "Introducing NLR." *New Left Review,* no. 1 (January/February): 1–3.

Nove, Alex. 1987. "Socialism." In *The New Palgrave: A Dictionary of Economics,* Vol. 4. Edited by John Eatwell et al. London: Macmillan Press.

Nussbaum, Martha C. 1999. *Sex and Social Justice.* Oxford: Oxford University Press.

———. 2005. *Frontiers of Justice: Disability, Nationality, Species Membership.* Cambridge, MA: Harvard University Press.

———. 1994. "Patriotism and Cosmopolitanism." *The Boston Review* 19: 5 (October/November): 3–34.

Oakeshott, Michael. 1991 [1962]. *Rationalism in Politics and other Essays,* expanded edition. Edited by Timothy Fuller. Indianapolis: Liberty Press.

Ober, J. 1989. *Mass and Elite in Democratic Athens.* Princeton: Princeton University Press.

———. 1996. *The Athenian Revolution.* Princeton: Princeton University Press.

———. 1998. *Political Dissent in Democratic Athens.* Princeton: Princeton University Press.

Okin, Susan Moller. 1973. "John Stuart Mill's Feminism: The Subjection of Women and The Improvement of Mankind." *New Zealand Journal of History* 7: 105–27.

———. 1979. "John Stuart Mill, Liberal Feminist." In *Women in Western Political Thought.* Princeton: Princeton University Press.

O'Rourke, K. 2001. *John Stuart Mill and Freedom of Expression, The Genesis of a Theory.* London: Routledge.

Parekh, Bhikhu. 1994. "The Narrowness of Liberalism from Mill to Rawls." *Times Literary Supplement* (25 February): 11–13.

———. 1995. "Liberalism and Colonialism: A Critique of Locke and Mill." In *The Decolonization of Imagination: Culture, Knowledge, and Power.* Edited by Jan Nederveen Pieterse and Bhikhu Parekh. London: Zed Books.

———. 2000. *Rethinking Multiculturalism: Cultural diversity and Political Theory.* London: Macmillan.

Parry, G. 1967. "Enlightened Government and Its Critics in Germany." In *Enlightened Despotism.* Edited by Stuart Andrews. London: Longmans.

Pateman, Carole. 1970. *Participation and Democratic Theory.* Cambridge: Cambridge University Press.

———. 1988. *The Sexual Contract.* Stanford: Stanford University Press.

Pearson, Michael. 1972. *The Age of Consent: Victorian Prostitution and Its Enemies.* Newton Abbot: David and Charles.

Peers, Douglas M. 1999. "Imperial Epitaph: John Stuart Mill's Defense of the East India Company." In *J.S. Mill's Encounter with India,* edited Martin I. Moir, Douglas M. Peers, and Lynn Zastoupil. Toronto: University of Toronto Press.

Petrie, Glen. 1971. *A Singular Iniquity: The Campaigns of Josephine Butler.* London: Macmillan.

Pettit, Philip. 2001. *A Theory of Freedom: From the Psychology to the Politics of Agency.* Oxford: Oxford University Press.

Philips, C. H., H. L. Singh, and B. N. Pandey, editors. 1962. *The Evolution of India and Pakistan, 1858 to 1947: Select Documents.* London: Oxford University Press.

Pitts, Jennifer. 2005. *A Turn to Empire: The Rise of Imperial Liberalism in Britain and France.* Princeton: Princeton University Press.

Pogge, Thomas W. 2002. "Moral Universalism and Global Economic Justice." *Politics, Philosophy and Economics* 1(1): 29–58.

Pyle, Andrew, ed. 1994. *The Subjection of Women: Contemporary Responses to John Stuart Mill.* Bristol: Thoemmes Press.

Radcliff, Peter. 1966. *Limits of Liberty: Studies of Mill's On Liberty.* Belmont, CA: Wadsworth.

Rawls, John. 1971. *A Theory of Justice.* Cambridge, MA: Belknap Press of Harvard University Press.

———. 1985. "Justice as Fairness: Political Not Metaphysical." *Philosophy and Public Affairs* 14: 223–52.

———. 1988. "The Priority of Right and Ideas of the Good." *Philosophy and Public Affairs* 17: 251–76.

———. 1993. *Political Liberalism.* New York: Columbia University Press.

———. 1999. *A Theory of Justice.* Revised edition. Cambridge, MA: Belknap Press of Harvard University Press.

———. 2001. *Justice as Fairness: A Restatement.* Edited by Erin Kelly. Cambridge, MA: Belknap Press of Harvard University Press.

Raz, Joseph. 1988. *The Morality of Freedom.* Oxford: Oxford University Press.

Rees, J. C. 1960. "A Re-reading of Mill on Liberty" *Political Studies* 8: 113–29.

———. 1985. *John Stuart Mill's "On Liberty."* Edited by G. L. Williams. Oxford: Clarendon Press.

"Report of the Jamaica Royal Commission." *British Parliamentary Papers*, 1866, vol. XXX: 518–28.

Richter, Melvin. 1977. *The Political Theory of Montesquieu.* Cambridge: Cambridge University Press.

Riley, J. 1988. *Liberal Utilitarianism.* Cambridge: Cambridge University Press.

———. 1990. "Utilitarian Ethics and Democratic Government." *Ethics* 100: 335–48.

———. 1994. "Introduction." In John Stuart Mill, *Principles of Political Economy and Chapters on Socialism.* Edited by Jonathan Riley. Oxford: Oxford University Press.

———. 1996a. "J. S. Mill's Liberal Utilitarian Assessment of Capitalism Versus Socialism." *Utilitas* 8: 39–72.

———. 1996b. "*On Liberty* and the Periclean Ideal." *Qwerty* 6: 241–9.

———. 1998a. *Mill on Liberty.* London: Routledge.

———. 1998b. "Mill's Political Economy: Ricardian Science and Liberal Utilitarian Art." In *The Cambridge Companion to Mill.* Edited by John Skorupski. Cambridge: Cambridge University Press.

———. 2005a. "Mill's Doctrine of Freedom of Expression." *Utilitas* 17: 147–79.

———. 2005b. "Rousseau: *The Social Contract.*" In *Central Works of Philosophy.* 5 vols. Edited by J. Shand, II. Chesham: Acumen.

———. 2006a. *Mill's Radical Liberalism.* London: Routledge.

———. 2006b. "Justice as a Higher Pleasure." Keynote lecture delivered at the Mill Bicentennial Conference, University College London, 5–7 April 2006.

Ring, Jennifer. 1985. "Mill's *The Subjection of Women*: The Methodological Limits of Liberal Feminism." *Review of Politics* 47: 27–44.

Robbins, Lionel. 1952. *The Theory of Economic Policy in Classical Political Economy.* London: Macmillan.

Roberts, J. T. 1982. *Accountability in Athenian Government.* Madison: University of Wisconsin Press.

———. 1994. *Athens on Trial.* Princeton: Princeton University Press.

Robson, Ann P., and John M. Robson, editors. 1994. *Sexual Equality: Writings by John Stuart Mill, Harriet Taylor Mill, and Helen Taylor.* Toronto: University of Toronto Press.

Robson, John M. 1968. *The Improvement of Mankind: The Social and Political Thought of John Stuart Mill.* Toronto: University of Toronto Press.

———. 1998. "Civilization and Culture as Moral Concepts." In *The Cambridge Companion to Mill.* Edited by John Skorupski. Cambridge: Cambridge University Press.

Rosen, F. 1983. *Jeremy Bentham and Representative Democracy, A Study of the Constitutional Code.* Oxford: Clarendon Press.

———. 2003. *Classical Utilitarianism from Hume to Mill.* London: Routledge.

———. 2007. "From Jeremy Bentham's Radical Philosophy to J. S. Mill's Philosophic Radicalism." In *Cambridge History of Nineteenth Century Political Thought.* Edited by G. Stedman Jones and G. Claeys. Cambridge: Cambridge University Press.

Rosenblum, Nancy. 1987. *Another Liberalism: Romanticism and the Reconstruction of Liberal Thought.* Cambridge, MA: Harvard University Press.

Rosselli, Carlo. 1994 [1929]. *Liberal Socialism.* Translated by William McCuaig. Edited by Nadia Urbanati. Princeton: Princeton University Press.

Russett, Cynthia. 1989. *Sexual Science: The Victorian Construction of Womanhood.* Cambridge, MA: Harvard University Press.

Ryan, Alan. 1972. "Utilitarianism and Bureaucracy: The Views of J.S. Mill." In *Studies in the Growth of Nineteenth-Century Government.* Edited by Gillian Sutherland. London: Routledge and Kegan Paul.

———. 1974. *J.S. Mill.* London: Routledge and Kegan Paul.

———. 1983. "Property, Liberty, and *On Liberty.*" In *Of Liberty.* Edited by A. Phillips Griffiths. Cambridge: Cambridge University Press.

———. 1990 [1970]. *The Philosophy of John Stuart Mill.* 2d ed. Atlantic Highlands, NJ: Humanities Press International.

Sarvasy, Wendy. 1984. "J.S. Mill's Theory of Democracy for a Period of Transition Between Capitalism and Socialism." *Polity* 16 (Summer): 567–87.

———. 1985. "A Reconsideration of the Development and Structure of John Stuart Mill's Socialism." *Western Political Quarterly* 38 (June): 312–333.

Sassoon, Donald. 1996. *One Hundred Years of Socialism: The West European Left in the Twentieth Century.* London: I.B. Tauris.

Scalia, Antonin. 1997. *A Matter of Interpretation: Federal Courts and the Law.* Princeton: Princeton University Press.

Schackleton, Robert. 1961. *Montesquieu: A Critical Biography.* Oxford: Oxford University Press.

Scheffler, Samuel. 1996. "Family and Friends First?" (review article on Martha C. Nussbaum, *For Love of Country: Debating the Limits of Patriotism,* edited by Joshua Cohen, Boston: Beacon, 1996), *Times Literary Supplement* (27 December 1996): 8–9.

———. 1999. "Conceptions of Cosmopolitanism." *Utilitas* 11, no. 3: 255–76.

Schmitt, Carl. 1988 [1923]. *The Crisis of Parliamentary Democracy.* Translated by Ellen Kennedy. Cambridge, MA: The MIT Press.

Schultz, Bart, and Georgios Varouxakis, editors. 2005. *Utilitarianism and Empire.* Lanham, MD: Lexington Books.

Schwartz, Pedro. 1968. "John Stuart Mill and Socialism." *The Mill News Letter* 4 (Fall): 3–7.

———. 1972. *The New Political Economy of J. S. Mill.* English translation. Durham: Duke University Press.

Semmel, Bernard. 1976. *Jamaican Blood and Victorian Conscience: The Governor Eyre Controversy.* Westport, CT: Greenwood.

———. 1984. *John Stuart Mill and the Pursuit of Virtue.* New Haven: Yale University Press.

Senior, Nassau W. 1842. "France, America, and Britain." *Edingurgh Review* 75: 1–48.

Shanley, Mary Lyndon. 1981. "Marital Slavery and Friendship: John Stuart Mill's *The Subjection of Women.*" *Political Theory* 9: 229–47.

———. 1989. *Feminism, Marriage, and the Law in Victorian England, 1850–1895.* Princeton: Princeton University Press.

———. 1998. "The Subjection of Women." In *The Cambridge Companion to Mill.* Edited by J. Skorupski. Cambridge: Cambridge University Press.

——— and Carole Pateman, editors. 1991. *Feminist Interpretations and Political Theory.* University Park: Pennsylvania State University Press.

Shields, Johanna Nicol. 1985. *The Line of Duty: Maverick Congressmen and the Development of American Political Culture, 1836–1860.* Westport CT: Greenwood.

Sinha, Mrinalini. 1995. *Colonial Masculinity: The 'Manly' Englishman and the 'Effeminate' Bengali.* New York: St. Martin's Press.

Skinner, Quentin. 1988. "Meaning and Understanding in the History of Ideas." In *Meaning and Context: Quentin Skinner and his Critics.* Edited by James Tully. Princeton: Princeton University Press.

Skorupski, John. 1989. *John Stuart Mill.* London: Routledge.

———, editor. 1998. *The Cambridge Companion to Mill.* Cambridge: Cambridge University Press.

Smith, F. B. 1971. "Ethics and Disease in the Later Nineteenth Century: The Contagious Diseases Acts." *Historical Studies* 15: 118–39.

Smith, G. W. 1984. "J. S. Mill on Freedom." In *Conceptions of Liberty in Political Philosophy.* Edited by Zbigniew Pelczynski and John Gray. New York: St. Martin's Press.

Smout, T. C. 1993. Review of *The Magdalenes: Prostitution in the Nineteenth Century* by Linda Mahood. *English Historical Review* 108: 1048–9.

Snyder, A. D. 1929. *Coleridge on Logic and Learning with Selections from the Unpublished Manuscripts.* New Haven: Yale University Press.

Spitz, Jean-Fabian. 1995. *La liberté politique: Essai de généalogie conceptuelle.* Paris: Presses Universitaires de France.

Stafford, William. 1998a. "How Can a Pragmatic Liberal Call Himself a Socialist? The Case of John Stuart Mill." *Journal of Political Ideologies* 3 (October): 325–45.

———. 1998b. *John Stuart Mill.* New York: St. Martin's Press.

Stapleton, Julia. 1998. "James Fitzjames Stephen: Liberalism, Patriotism, and English Liberty." *Victorian Studies* 41: 243–63.

———. 2001. *Political Intellectuals and Public Identities in Britain since 1850.* Manchester: Manchester University Press.

Starr, Paul. 1991. "Liberalism after Socialism." *The American Prospect* 7 (Fall): 70–80.

Stephen, James Fitzjames. 1866a. "Mr. Arnold and the Middle Classes." *Saturday Review* 21 (10 February): 161–3.

———. 1866b. "Lord Macaulay's Works." *Saturday Review* 22 (18 August): 207–9.

———. 1883a. "Criminal Procedure in India." *The Times.* March 1.

————. 1883b. "Foundations of the Government of India." *The Nineteenth Century* LXXX (October): 541–568.

————. 1991 [1873]. *Liberty, Equality, Fraternity.* Chicago: University of Chicago Press.

————. 1993 [1873]. *Liberty, Equality, Fraternity.* Edited by Stuart D. Warner. Indianapolis: Liberty Classics.

Stephen, Leslie. 1900. *The English Utilitarians.* Vol. III. London: Duckworth.

Stetson, Dorothy. 1982. *A Woman's Issue: The Politics of Family Reform in England.* London: Greenwood.

Stokes, Eric. 1959. *The English Utilitarians and India.* Oxford: Clarendon.

St. John-Packe, Michael. 1954. *The Life of John Stuart Mill.* London: Secker and Warburg.

Strachey, Lytton. 1988 [1918]. "Florence Nightingale." In *Eminent Victorians: The Illustrated Edition.* New York: Weidenfeld and Nicholson.

Sullivan, Eileen P. 1983. "Liberalism and Imperialism: J. S. Mill's Defense of the British Empire." *Journal of the History of Ideas* 44: 599–617.

Sumner, L. W. 1979. "The Good and the Right." In *New Essays on John Stuart Mill and Utilitarianism.* Edited by Wesley E. Cooper, Kai Nielsen, and Steven C. Patten. *Canadian Journal of Philosophy*, 5 (supplementary volume): 99–114.

————. 1992. "Welfare, Happiness, and Pleasure." *Utilitas* 4(2): 199–206.

————. 1997. *The Moral Foundation of Rights.* Oxford: Clarendon Press.

Ten, C. L. 1980. *Mill on Liberty.* Oxford: Oxford University Press.

————. 1998. "Democracy, Socialism, and the Working Classes." In *The Cambridge Companion to Mill.* Edited by John Skorupski. Cambridge: Cambridge University Press.

Thomas, Keith. 1959. "The Double Standard." *Journal of the History of Ideas* 20: 199–216.

Thomas, W. 1979. *The Philosophic Radicals: Nine Studies in Theory and Practice, 1817–41.* Oxford: Clarendon.

Thompson, Dennis. 1976. *John Stuart Mill and Representative Government.* Princeton: Princeton University Press.

————. 1987. *Political Ethics and Public Office.* Cambridge, MA, and London: Harvard University Press.

Thucydides. 1991. *The Peloponnesian War.* Indianapolis: Hackett.

Tideman, N. 1995. "The Single Transferable Vote." *Journal of Economic Perspectives* 9: 27–38.

Tjaden, P., and N. Thoennes. 2000. *Full Report on the Prevalence, Incidence, and Consequences of Violence against Women: Findings from the National Violence against Women Survey.* Washington, DC: National Institute of Justice. Report NCJ 183781.

Tulloch, Gail. 1989. *Mill and Sexual Equality.* Hertfordshire: Harvester Wheatsheaf.

Turk, C. 1988. *Coleridge and Mill: A Study of Influence.* Aldershot: Gower.

Urbinati, Nadia. 1991. "John Stuart Mill on Androgyny and Ideal Marriage." *Political Theory* 19: 626–48.

————. 1994. "Introduction: Another Socialism." In *Liberal Socialism* by Carlo Roselli. Translated by William McCuaig. Edited by Nadia Urbanati. Princeton: Princeton University Press.

————. 2002. *Mill on Democracy: From the Athenian Polis to Representative Government.* Chicago: University of Chicago Press.

————. 2004. "The Importance of Norberto Bobbio." *Dissent* 51 (Spring): 78–80.

Varouxakis, Georgios. 1997. "John Stuart Mill on Intervention and Non-Intervention." *Millennium: Journal of International Studies* 26(1): 57–76.

———. 2001. "Patriotism," in *Encyclopaedia of Nationalism*. Edited by Athena S. Leoussi. Brunwick and London: Transaction.

———. 2002a. *Mill on Nationality*. London and New York: Routledge.

———. 2002b. *Victorian Political Thought on France and the French*. Basingstoke and New York: Palgrave.

———. 2005. "Empire, Race, Euro-centrism: John Stuart Mill and His Critics." In *Utilitarianism and Empire*. Edited by Bart Schultz and Georgios Varouxakis. Lanham, MD: Lexington Books.

———. 2006. " 'Patriotism,' 'Cosmopolitanism' and 'Humanity' in Victorian Political Thought." *European Journal of Political Theory* 5(1): 100–18.

Venturi, Franco. 1960. "Dispotismo orientale." *Rivista storica italiana* (March): 119–43.

Vertovec, Steven, and Robin Cohen, editors. 2002. *Conceiving Cosmopolitanism: Theory, Context, and Practice*. Oxford: Oxford University Press.

Villa, Dana. 2001. *Socratic Citizenship*. Princeton: Princeton University Press.

Vincent, Andrew. 1997. "Liberal Nationalism: An Irresponsible Compound?" *Political Studies* 45(2): 275–95.

———. (2002): *Nationalism and Particularity*. Cambridge: Cambridge University Press.

Vincent, John. 1966. *The Formation of the Liberal Party, 1857–1868*. London: Constable.

Viroli, Maurizio. 1995. *For Love of Country: An Essay on Patriotism and Nationalism*. Oxford: Clarendon Press.

Waldron, Jeremy. 1987. "Mill and the Value of Moral Distress." *Political Studies* 35: 410–23. Reprinted in Waldron 1993.

———. 1991. "Homelessness and the Issue of Freedom." *UCLA Law Review*, 39: 295–324. Reprinted in Waldron 1993.

———. 1993. *Liberal Rights: Collected Papers 1981–1991*. Cambridge: Cambridge University Press.

———. 1995 [1992]. "Minority Cultures and the Cosmopolitan Alternative." In *The Rights of Minority Cultures*. Edited by Will Kymlicka. Oxford: Oxford University Press.

———. 2000. "What Is Cosmopolitan?" *Journal of Political Philosophy* 8(2): 227–43.

———. 2002a. *God, Locke, and Equality: Christian Foundations of in Locke's Political Thought*. Cambridge: Cambridge University Press.

———. 2002b. "Mill as a Critic of Culture and Society." In J. S. Mill, *On Liberty*. Edited by Bromwich and Kateb. New Haven: Yale University Press.

———. 2003. "Security and Liberty: The Image of Balance." *Journal of Political Philosophy* 11: 191–210.

Walkowitz, Judith R. 1980. *Prostitution and Victorian Society: Women, Class and the State*. Cambridge: Cambridge University Press.

Weber, Max. 1958. *From Max Weber: Essays in Sociology*. Edited by H. H. Gerth and C. Wright Mills. New York: Oxford University Press.

Welchman, Jennifer. 1995. "Locke on Slavery and Inalienable Rights." *Canadian Journal of Philosophy* 25: 67–81.

West, Henry. 2004. *An Introduction to Mill's Utilitarian Ethics*. Cambridge: Cambridge University Press.

Williams, Geraint. 1989. "J. S. Mill and Political Violence." *Utilitas* 1: 102–11.

Williams, R. 1958. *Culture and Society 1780–1950.* New York: Columbia University Press.

Wittfogel, Karl A. 1957. *Oriental Despotism: A Comparative Study of Total Power.* New Haven: Yale University Press.

Wollheim, Richard. 1973. "John Stuart Mill and the Limits of State Action." *Social Research* 40: 1–30.

Zastoupil, Lynn. 1994. *John Stuart Mill and India.* Stanford: Stanford University Press.

———. 1999. "India, J. S. Mill, and 'Western' Culture." In *J.S. Mill's Encounter with India.* Edited by Martin I. Moir, Douglas M. Peers, and Lynn Zastoupil. Toronto: University of Toronto Press.

Index